THEOCRACY IN MASSACHUSETTS

*Reformation and Separation in Early
Puritan New England*

Avihu Zakai

Mellen University Press
Lewiston/Queenston/Lampeter

Library of Congress Cataloging-in-Publication Data

Zakai, Avihu.
    Theocracy in Massachusetts : reformation and separation in early
Puritan New England / Avihu Zakai.
        p.   cm.
    Includes bibliographical references and index.
    ISBN 0-7734-9970-9
    1. Puritans--New England--History--17th century. 2. Eschatology-
-History of doctrines--17th century. 3. New England--Church
history--17th century. I. Title.
BX9355.N35Z36   1993
285'.9'0974--dc20   93-37010
                                                                               CIP

The Edwin Mellen Press   The Edwin Mellen Press
            Box 450   Box 67
    Lewiston, New York   Queenston, Ontario
    USA 14092-0450   CANADA L0S 1L0

The Edwin Mellen Press, Ltd.
Lampeter, Dyfed, Wales
UNITED KINGDOM SA48 7DY

Printed in the United States of America

TABLE OF CONTENTS

INTRODUCTION 1

CHAPTER ONE:
THE PURSUIT OF REFORMATION THE ORIGINS OF THE GREAT
PURITAN MIGRATION 15
I   Covenant and the Puritan Migration 16
II   The Role of the Laity in the Puritan Movement 25
III Covenant and Social Reformation 30
IV   Migration and Separation 34
V   Migration and the Rhetoric of Persecution 40
VI   Migration as an Act of Social and Religious
     Reformation 48

CHAPTER TWO:
THE ESCHATOLOGY AND APOCALYPSE OF THE PURITAN
MIGRATION 59
I   The Eschatology of the Puritan Migration 61
II   Prophecy, Apocalypse and History 69
III Thomas Brightman and the Millennium at Hand 79
IV   The Church and the Wilderness 102

CHAPTER THREE:
REFORMATION AND SEPARATION: MASSACHUSETTS'
RELATIONSHIP WITH ENGLAND DURING THE 1630s 117
I   Two Concepts of Liberty 119
II   Religion and the Colonization of New England 122
III Reformation and Separation 133
IV   The "Call" to New England 141
V   The Struggle Over the Charter 153
VI   Covenant and Revolt 172

CHAPTER FOUR:
THEOCRACY IN THE WILDERNESS THE PURITAN HOLY
EXPERIMENT IN NEW ENGLAND 183
I   The Politics of Covenant 187
II   Covenant and Theocracy 190
III Magistrates and the Pursuit of Religious Unity and Conformity . 199
IV   The Struggle Against Heresy: The Antinomian Controversy 204
V   In Defense of Theocracy 209
VI   The Ministers' View of Church and State 215

VII Theocracy and English Rights 219
VIII Theocracy, Monarchy, Aristocracy and Democracy 224
IX Magistrates as "Nursing Fathers and Mothers to the Church" 229
X Theocracy in England and New England 235
XI Theocracy and the Millennium 241

CHAPTER FIVE:
MASSACHUSETTS AND THE LONG PARLIAMENT DURING
THE 1640s 253

I "New England's Tears for Old England's Feares" 257
II Massachusetts' Commission to the Long Parliament 262
III Massachusetts and Religious Reformation in England 271
IV Crisis in the "City Upon the Hill" 279
V Transfer of the Civil War to America 287
VI "New England's Sence of Old Englands and Irelands Sorrowes . . 293
VII Social and Political Agitation in Massachusetts 295
VIII Massachusetts and the Long Parliament 303

CHAPTER SIX:
RELIGIOUS TOLERATION AND ITS ENEMIES: ORTHODOXY IN
OLD AND NEW ENGLAND 319
I Reformation, Revolution and Order 322
II Puritan Debates - Reformation, Separation and the Millennium . 326
III Puritan Rage for Order: "The Fast Sermons to Parliament" 338
IV Religious Toleration and Its Enemies 347
  1. Puritans and Toleration 347
  2. Puritan Independent Divines and the Issue of Toleration . . . 349
  3. Independents and Presbyterians in the Westminster Assembly 354
  4. Independents, Presbyterians, and Religious Toleration 357
  5. Independents, Sectarians and Toleration 360
  6. Orthodoxy in England 364
V Orthodoxy in England and New England 368
VI The Essence of Puritan Orthodoxy 378

BIBLIOGRAPHY 395

INDEX 427

FOREWORD

Dr. Avihu Zakai of the Hebrew University of Jerusalem completed this important work as a doctoral dissertation at The Johns Hopkins University in the early 1980s. The first scholar to show the crucial role of the works of the English Puritan thinker, Thomas Brightman, in the intellectual construction of Puritan New England, Dr. Zakai, in this work, helped to reshape understanding of the nature of the Puritan experiment in America. In contrast to previous scholars, he showed how the reliance of American Puritan leaders, both secular and clerical, upon the religious ideas of Brightman turned their experiment in a millenial direction. Few earlier scholars had recognized, and none had stressed, this significant dimension of the Puritan experiment. Although other scholars, including Dr. Zakai in other works, have explored some of these themes during the decade since the dissertation was written, this work, retitled *Theocracy in Massachusetts: Reformation and Separation in Early Puritan New England* remains an extremely valuable, if controversial, work that challenges existing historiographical conventions and contributes significantly to the reassessment of the Puritans' errand into the American wilderness. To put his work in the context of more recent historiography, Dr. Zakai has added a new introduction that is itself an important commentary on Puritan studies over the past decade.

Jack P. Greene
The Johns Hopkins University

FOREWORD

In *Theocracy in Massachusetts*, Avihu Zakai makes a daring and essential contribution to Puritan studies in England and America. He restores to us the radicalism that the seventeenth century saw - and often resented mightily - in those God-obsessed men and women. He retrieves for us the very rage for purity that earned them their unmistakably pejorative name. And in so doing, he stands against the best of an older scholarship and most of his own contemporaries in the field.

In defining orthodoxy in Massachusetts, Perry Miller established an orthodoxy of his own, an interpretive orthodoxy that declared the American Puritans people of the center, people who insisted upon the presence of evil but did not seek to separate themselves from evil, people neither complacent nor fanatic, people who sought to hold to the middle ground against extremists of every sort. Miller's notion of the Puritans as non-separating congregationalists has held essential sway ever since.

Avihu Zakai rejects Miller's domestication of the Puritans' intransigent zealotry on several significant scores. He insists that the American Puritans were separatists, not non-separatists. So far from seeking to live in the world and come to some accommodation with its sinfulness, they sought to dissociate themselves from all that defiled God's grand plan and they migrated to the New World exactly in order to do so. He maintains unflinchingly that the American Puritans were apocalyptic and millennial, not moderate and "sensible." So far from living in the psychic world we do, they expected the end of days imminently, and they expected to play the central role in that divine drama.

Where Miller wrote in an era when the Puritans stood in strong disrepute and sought to make them more palatable to American audiences, Zakai writes in the wake of Miller's immense influence and can be more candid. He can acknowledge, as Miller was loath to do, their unabashed theocratic ambitions and their avowedly revolutionary project. Indeed, no one has elaborated the abounding radicalism of the American Puritan mission in the wilderness as imaginatively and expansively as Zakai has.

If the exposition of that strand of Puritan thought is his triumph, it is also his failing. He sets himself against Miller's conservative exposition, but he never really reckons with the materials that Miller drew upon to warrant such conservatism. He admires but disagrees with other leading interpretations, but he never quite explains why their emphases on the past rather than on the millennial future, on England rather than on America, and on politics rather than on eschatology can be discounted as he does. He acknowledges the importance of the massive outpouring of social histories of early New England, but he makes no effort to integrate his account with theirs.

Nonetheless, his account is invaluable. If he does not achieve the grander synthesis we might need, he makes clear that any such synthesis must be more encompassing than we have heretofore supposed. If he does not take Puritan orthodoxy sufficiently into the balance, he makes plain that others who have written about the American Puritans have not taken their fiercely militant radicalism into consideration either. Future scholars will have to wrestle with Zakai and with the challenge of the argument that he adduces here as he has wrestled, conscientiously and mightily, with the softer, more muffled and "reasonable" Puritanism of his predecessors.

Michael Zuckerman
Professor of History
University of Pennsylvania

ACKNOWLEDGEMENTS

I am particularly indebted to my advisor, Jack P. Greene, who has not only welcomed me most graciously into the stimulating intellectual milieu that characterizes the Department of History at Johns Hopkins University, but has also offered constant encouragement in support of my conviction that risk taking was essential to the success of this project. It will also be clear to any student of American colonial history that Professor Greene's understanding of America's relationship with the mother country has provided the necessary conceptual frame for my study. It has also been my great fortune to work closely with J.G.A. Pocock, whose subtle gifts as both teacher and writer have had an immense influence on my perception of the historian's task as interpreter of events in past time. Without his close yet gentle criticism, I am afraid that what follows would have been less readable than it is now. From the very beginning, Mack Walker has been generous with insights gleaned from his enormous knowledge of early modern history; Timothy L. Smith's expertise in American religious history has proven invaluable in my quest to decipher the often obscure world of New England Puritanism. I am also indebted to Professor Louis P. Galambos and a.J.R. Russell-Wood for their efforts to secure financial aid despite its scarcity. Professor Galambos, in particular, has come to my support in a time of great hardship. My mentor, Yehoshua Arieli, "The Father of American Studies" in Israel, has not only been a source of support and knowledge, but by his example, has been a constant reminder that the intellectual in modern times must not ignore his moral obligations. Needless to say, the members of Professor Greene's seminar in the history of Anglo-American colonization, though too often forced to endure lengthy chapters, were unfailing in their efforts to strengthen my arguments through sharp but constructive criticism. Finally my thanks to Marcia for her typing and considerable efforts to underwrite this work.

INTRODUCTION

Ever since Perry Miller wrote his brilliant and influential essay, "Errand into the Wilderness" (1952), historians have debated how best to describe the remarkable Puritan exodus to New England.[1] Very rarely indeed does history present us with examples to equal the Puritan migration to America; such bold determination and uncompromising zeal to depart from a home country, to cross a mighty ocean, and finally to establish a close-knit society in the wilderness of America. The remarkable Puritan achievement in creating such a highly organized Christian commonwealth in the New World stood in rigid contrast to the important historical events taking place in the Old World where the Thirty Years' War was raging over the whole continent of Europe, and great upheavals and transformations were unfolding in England and Scotland, first with the Bishops' Wars and later with the Puritan Revolution.

Yet, it is not only within these great historical occurrences that the extraordinary success of the Puritan migration ought to be understood. It should also be seen, and more importantly, in light of the entire course of the Puritan movement in England; its continuous unsuccessful effort to win over the soul of the English people, its traumatic failure to establish its premises during the Puritan Revolution, and its eventual total collapse with the Restoration of the house of Stuart. After almost a century of a fierce struggle over the faith of the English people, Puritanism as an important historical movement eventually broke down completely, leaving only a small, yet thriving and most successful stronghold upon the shore of New England.

Yet precisely what was the Puritans ultimate errand in the settlement of Massachusetts? This remains the most perennial question in Puritan

1

historiography.[2] Indeed, no other issue has created so much heat and controversy as that of the Puritan's ultimate mission in the Wilderness of America. The reason for this is clear enough. For in the answer to this issue lies indeed the whole meaning of the Puritan migration to, and the whole significance of the Puritan experience in, America.

Perry Miller's interpretation of the Puritan errand was based essentially upon the role he assigned to Puritanism in American history. Ultimately, as a cultural historian in the broadest sense, Miller was interested in the "narrative of the movement of European culture into the vacant wilderness of America." And believing that an interpretation of the American past ought to begin with explanation of those "traditions" that "have gone into the making of the American mind," Miller viewed the Puritans as the first principal transmitters and diffusers of European culture and ideas into America. Consequently, in his attempt to prove the establishment of "orthodoxy" - rather than radicalism - in Massachusetts, Miller was determined to refute any claim about the radicalism embodied in the Puritan errand to America. Yet, despite this reservation, every student of Puritanism in America would certainly concur that with the publication of "Errand into the Wilderness," Perry Miller inaugurated the most lively debated in Puritan historiography.

The impressive growth of social-history studies during the 1960s and 1970s has shifted attention from the debate over the Puritan errand into a wide-scale exploration of the various life-conditions that existed in the Puritan colonies in America. Yet the ability of social-history studies to illuminate the varieties of life experience in Puritan New England has rather raised again the pressing need to reformulate a unified ideological framework concerning the ultimate mission of the Puritan migration. For only within a well-defined and coherent ideological context can the rich findings of social history be meaningfully interpreted. And since the works of social historians never intended to provide the clue to the Puritan errand, this task once again was left in the hands of intellectual historians. consequently, the decade of the 1980s saw a return in Puritan historiography to

2

the debate over the Puritan errand, and some historians indeed have tended to dismiss it altogether.

With the important transformations taking place in Puritan studies in the last decades, however, Puritan historiography seems to have lost some of the wider historical context offered by Miller concerning the Puritan errand into New England. For despite the many revisions needed in Perry Miller's work, he nevertheless captured marvelously an essential dimension of the Puritan mission in the wilderness of America as a crucial revelatory, prophetic, and redemptive, event in the drama of human salvation, when he wrote that for the Puritans

> New England was the culmination of the Reformation, the climax of world history, the ultimate revelation through events of the objective toward which the whole human activity had been tending from the beginning of time.

This wider historical context of salvation history should not be overlooked, because without a full comprehension of the Puritan sense of time and view of history a crucial dimension of the Puritan migration to, and experience in, New England cannot be possibly understood.

Theocracy in Massachusetts argues that serious consideration of the apocalyptic, eschatological, and millennial dimension in the Puritan migration to New England would explain the Puritan holy experiment in America as a more radical and revolutionary social, political, and ecclesiastical system created by more radical Puritans than has been previously suggested. For when examined seriously, the eschatology and apocalypse of the Puritan migration was based upon the ultimate rejection of, and total separation from, corrupted history and degenerating human traditions in England and the old world in general. Ultimately, the presence of a powerful eschatological and millennial impulse in the Puritan migration obligates us to reconsider as a whole the Puritan errand into the wilderness of America. For theirs was a radical quest after a theocratic universe, ruled directly and immediately by God's divine Providence, in which every sphere of human life should be reconstructed upon the sacred word of God.

3

And in their advocacy of a theocratic government, Puritans sought nothing less than the transformation of the world into the Kingdom of God. Consequently, with the restoration of God to the center of a theocratic universe, Puritan apocalypse established a deep eschatological gulf separation the Old World from the New in the course of providential history, and their pursuit of the millennium acknowledged Christ, and only Christ, as a ruler over his saints in both church and state alike. Seen in this context, evidently, the Puritan mission was more radical and revolutionary in its character than has previously been argued. The Puritan errand in fact was nothing less than a daring attempt to realize in Massachusetts the most radical exercise in holiness - the reconstruction of every dimensions of human life upon a covenanted relationship with God.

The work of an historian is always based upon the achievements of past generations. This is especially true of Puritan studies in England and New England, where the important works of William Haller and Perry Miller obligate later historians to look seriously into the life of the mind of the Puritans in order to appreciate the meaning Puritans gave to their actions. For indeed there exists no other way fully to understand the Puritans and their role upon the stage of history than to take into serious consideration their ideological premises, their religious persuasions as well as their vision of time and sense of history. An initial premise of this study is, therefore, that serious examination of the ideological context and universe of thought is needed to understand men's action. For this reason, it is the historian's duty not only to ask what happened during the course of history, but also why, on the basis of what premises, people made choices.

The reader has already noted that I have intentionally chosen the title "Theocracy in Massachusetts" in order to point up my differences with Perry Miller's concept of "orthodoxy" in Massachusetts, and in order to illuminate more fully the radical thrust behind the Puritan migration and the revolutionary character of the holy experiment in Massachusetts. It is well known that Perry Miller explained the Puritan errand in terms of the transfer of "orthodox" Puritan

4

culture to America. It should be recognized, however, that the most prominent historian of Puritanism in American history was very suspicious of the presence, let alone the prominence, of eschatological visions and millennial expectations in the Puritan mind, and therefore attached little, if any, significance to the apocalyptic mode of historical thought in the foundation of New England. Yet, by ignoring the overwhelming evidence in Puritan writings that the pursuit of the millennium was an essential feature of the Puritan mind, and that discussion concerning prophecy about the Second Coming of Christ was widespread, Miller omitted a crucial dimension of the origins of the Puritan migration and the premises of the holy experiment in the wilderness. Perry Miller's interpretation of the Puritan errand, therefore, was based essentially upon a highly conservative view - the transfer of an "orthodox" Puritan culture to America by "orthodox" Puritans.

Recently, several excellent studies have appeared which have altered enormously our understanding of Puritanism in America. Theodore Bozeman's impressive work, To Live Ancient Lives: The Primitivist Dimension in Puritanism, is one of the most important studies of Puritanism to appear since Perry Miller's The New England Mind. Yet because Bozeman tends to emphasize the past in the Puritan sense of time, he underplays the role of millennial expectations in the Puritan mind. The millenarian impulse in Puritanism, however, sprang from roots reaching deep into the rise of Protestant historiography during the Reformation and the creation of a coherent apocalyptic tradition in England during the 16th century. My study attempts to show how central was the pursuit of the millennium in the Puritan migration and how crucially it informed the holy experiment in America.

Another fascinating study is Andrew Delbanco's The Puritan Ordeal. The reader will recognize, however, that I have not accepted Delbanco's thesis that England, and not New England, constituted the "wilderness" for the Puritans. For to accept Delbanco's thesis is to lose an essential dimension of the Puritan existential condition in America - the eschatologically oriented conception of the wilderness, and the Puritans' vivid sense of the Exile in the Wilderness of America. Finally, Stephen Foster's The Long Argument: English Puritanism and the Shaping of New England Culture, 1570-1700, is the most ambitious and successful attempt to place Puritan New England in the wider context of English Puritanism. The reader will clearly see in my work, however, that because I attach more importance to Puritan eschatology and millennialism, I consider the Puritan holy experiment in America as a more radical and a revolutionary system created by more radical Puritans than Foster would have us believe.

With all the great achievements of Puritan historiography in recent years, so far considerably less attention has been given to the ideological origins of the holy experiment in Massachusetts. Yet in order to understand the errand into the wilderness of America, several essential dimensions in the Puritan mind ought to be fully explored - the Puritan apocalyptic interpretation of history, eschatology, and the millennium. Puritan historiography traditionally describes the Puritan efforts to establish the true system of church-government, or Congregationalism, and only little attempt has been made to explore the extent to which those efforts were crucially informed by powerful eschatological visions and millennial expectations. But the Puritans apocalyptic mode of historical thought and pursuit of the millennium were both crucial animating forces in the Puritan migration to America and played a significant role in shaping the holy experiment in Massachusetts.

Puritans were ever confident about the ultimate significance of their migration to Massachusetts within the confines of the sacred history of the church upon earth, and they never relinquished their belief about the prophetic, redemptive, and revelatory significance of their presence in America within the unfolding drama of human salvation and redemption. Behind them lay the vast territory of the history of the church upon the stage of the world and the fate of God's chosen people within the vicissitudes of time. Hence, Puritans justified their migration to New England in the wider historical context of sacred, providential history. They based it upon "the role of Christ to his Apostles and Saints, and the practise

6

of Gods Saints in all ages...to fly into the Wilderness from the face of the Dragon." Such an apocalyptic imagination was inextricably intertwined in the Puritan mind with eschatological visions concerning New England's singular role within the boundaries of salvation history now reaching its final culmination. "How wonderful is the lorde in mercye," wrote one Puritan in England in 1629, "that hathe reysed this newe plantation" of Massachusetts Bay colony, "for so comfortable a refuge, for all suche whom he hathe exempted owte of the genreal devastation, which [England's] Synnes have so much deserved."

Apocalyptic and eschatological visions constituted in fact the ideological context of the Puritan migration to, and presence in, New England. Situated, as it were, in the middle of eschatological and apocalyptic occurrences, the Puritan migration was considered by its participants as a great prophetic, revelatory, and redemptive event in the all time drama of the history of salvation. Since Puritans defined their errand into the wilderness in such highly eschatological and apocalyptic terms, we may therefore rightly speak of the "eschatology" of the Puritan migration (or Puritan New England's singular role in the final stage of salvation history), and of the "apocalypse" of the Puritan migration (or the prophetic, redemptive, and revelatory significance of Puritan New England in the mystery of human salvation and redemption). A third important concept informed the Puritans' sense of their errand - the pursuit of the millennium, or the quest after the millennial rule of Christ and his saints upon earth. For Puritans were truly confident that "the downfall of Antichrist is at hand, and then the Kingdom[s] of the Earth shall become the Kingdome of our Lord Christ." Consequently, they further claimed, "we chose not the place for the Land, but for the government, that our Lord Christ might raigne over us, both in Churches and Common-wealth."

In the past millenniallism has posed a serious problem in Puritan historiography, especially in regard to "orthodox" Puritans in both England and New England. For it seemed hard to reconcile the activities and thought of the radical lunatic fringe of religious fanatics during the Puritan Revolution with those

7

of "orthodox" Puritans. Yet, when closely examined and properly understood, millennialism should not be associated exclusively with the radical and revolutionary plans of religious enthusiasts during the Puritan Revolution. After all, Puritans envisioned for many years the millennium as a feasible, earthly historical phenomenon taking place within time and history. The differences between "orthodox" and radical Puritans in both England and New England were not about the ultimate quest to realize this sacred prophetic revelation, which all agreed upon, but only upon the means to achieve it. For according to "orthodox" Puritans, millennialism meant "not that he [Christ] shall come personally to reigne upon Earth (as some vainly imagine) but his powerful Presence and Glorious brightness of his Gospell...shall not only spiritually cause the Churches of Christ to grow beyond number" all over the world, "but also the whole civil Government of people upon Earth shall become his, so that there shall not be any to move the hand, nor dog his tongue against his chosen."

This is the essence of the Puritan pursuit of the millennium, namely, the transformation of the world into the Kingdom of God through the millennial rule of Christ and his saints. In this context, indeed, as important dimension of the Puritan migration to New England was not only the quest to establish congregational churches of visible saints where Christ would rule directly over his saints, but also the creation of a unique system of social and political government, or theocracy as Puritans defined it, in which Christ would rule immediately over his people in the state.

The impressive growth of Puritan studies in recent years, however, should not hinder us from seeing as well that there are still several common assumptions regarding the Puritan migration to, and experience in, Massachusetts, which require revision and correction. These common assumptions concern the causes of the Puritan migration, the characterization of American Puritans as "non-separatist congregationalists," the nature of Puritan "orthodoxy" in Massachusetts, and most especially the meaning of the Puritan holy experiment, or theocracy, in the wilderness of America.

8

For many years the Puritan migration has been considered in the context of what may be called "the language of persecution and suffering," namely, that Puritans were terribly and unjustly persecuted by king and bishops in England and therefore forced to emigrate to the remote corner of the world. Less attention, however, however, was given to the Puritan experience in England in the late sixteenth century and early seventeenth century, and to the result of long-term trends in English society whereby Puritanism increasingly revealed itself not only as an ecclesiastical power but as a strong, and indeed revolutionary, social and political force able to disturb and divide communities by its radical and uncompromising plea to reconstruct every dimensions of human life upon the sacred word of God. The actual world, therefore, out of which the great Puritan migration to New England came was a world of conflict and strife in local communities, parishes, churches, villages, and towns, in which Puritans struggled for religious as well as social reform against fellow members of their own local societies.

Ultimately, what determined the migration of thousands of Puritans to America? It was the gradual diminishing of the prospects for reform at the local and national level, and the interaction between the godly and "ungodly" or "profane" people, as Puritans termed those who opposed their vision of godly life. Emigration emerged as a possible solution for those radical Puritans for whom the only alternative was life among the "profane." After all, Puritans carried with them not only theological doctrine but also and most importantly the framework for a godly Christian society. And when the attempt to create such a holy, godly society in England failed under Queen Elizabeth and the first Stuart kings, some of the radical, rather than orthodox, Puritans turned their eyes to New England, deeming it the ideal place to make their vision a reality.

Ever since Perry Miller coined the term "non-separatist congregationalism" and boldly advanced the notion that Massachusetts Puritans were not separatist, few historians have endeavoured to explore seriously this contention. Yet, as Puritans' actions and proclamations demonstrate, and as England authorities and

9

the majority of English Puritans came immediately to recognize, Bay Puritans zealously separated themselves from the Church of England. Not only did Bay Puritans refuse to use the traditional rites and ceremonies of the Church of England in the holy congregations in America, but they also radically transformed the old customs existing in the Church of England regarding the prerequisites for membership in the church by claiming that only "visible saints," or those persons who could prove the experiences of saving grace in their souls, should be admitted to the holy fellowship of the churches in New England. Evidently, this radical restriction of the gates of the "kingdom of Heaven," this revolutionary reconstruction of the holy fellowship of the church as based only on visible saints, had led not only the authorities in England, but most importantly the majority of English Puritans during the 1630s and 1640s strongly to denounce the Bay Puritans as a people who did explicitly separate from the Church of England.

American Puritans in fact made the stand of separation unmistakably explicit in their proclamations. For as regarding the concept of a national church, such as the Church of England, the implications of the establishment of congregational churches in Massachusetts were indeed revolutionary. For according to the premises of the Congregationalism as a system of church-government, each particular congregation - over which stood no ecclesiastical power - held the "Keys of the Kingdom of Heaven." As John Cotton declared, "in the Old Testament indeed we read of a national church...but we read of no such national church...in the New Testament." Or as Richard Mather wrote, "In the Old Testament the church of the Jewes was a national church, but in the New Test[ament] a nation or a country is not spoken of as one church, but there is mention of many churches in one nation or one country." Consequently, the whole Puritan migration to New England became, according to John Cotton's exegesis of the Book of Revelation, a deliverance "from this Monster...[and] from the remnant of the Image of this Beast, from all Diocesan and national Churches." Evidently, then, the establishment of Congregationalism in America staged a most radical ecclesiastical revolution.

10

It is equally safe to say that so far little attempt has been made to explore the nature and meaning of theocracy in Massachusetts. In their radical quest after a theocratic universe, the Puritans believed that they must keep their covenants with God in the ecclesiastical as well as the civil realm; this conviction required that only "visible saints," or those who proved their covenant relationship with God, become members of the congregational church, and that civil authority should be confined exclusively to the godly. Religious reformation, then, went hand in hand with social and political reformation in the Puritan colony in Massachusetts. And while the pursuit of the reformation led in the religious sphere to the policy of admitting only "visible saints' into the communion of the church, the very same radical drive for reformation led, in the social and political realm, to the establishment of theocratic government - a political system that entrusted authority only to those in the Puritan colony who belonged to the "gathered churches." Thus, political society, no less than the holy fellowship of the church, was confined in the Puritan commonwealth in America only to those capable of preserving the covenant. The exclusiveness of church fellowship led directly to the exclusiveness of the political system. This was indeed the essence of the Puritan holy experiment in the wilderness, or of theocracy in Massachusetts.

Yet one can only fully grasp the tremendous revolutionary, social, and political consequences of theocracy in Massachusetts in light of the Puritans radical pursuit of a theocratic universe in which every sphere of human life should be reconstructed upon the sacred word of God. For in their advocacy of a theocratic government which explicitly acknowledged Christ, and only Christ, as a ruler over his saints, the Bay Puritans were laying the foundation for a profound change in traditional English political and social obligations; no one, neither bishop nor king, could stand between God and his people. In this sense, theocracy indeed signified the republic of the saints, in which only God was the accepted ruler over his chosen people. Furthermore, theocratic government entailed not only a denial of the divine rights of king and bishops, but also a refusal to acknowledge that any right based on the privilege of property, heredity,

11

and wealth determined eligibility to participate in the political life of the holy experiment in Massachusetts. In as much as the political realm was held to be the exclusive domain of the saints by virtue of their covenanted relationship with God both in church and state, the sole prerequisites for membership in the body politic were sainthood, holiness, and saving grace. Religious obligations, thus, were transformed into political obligations, and the exclusiveness of the holy fellowship of the church led directly to the exclusiveness of the political system.

Theocracy in Massachusetts attempts to explore the eschatological and millennial dimension in the Puritan mind, and to show that out of a unique apocalyptic interpretation of history Puritans were not only able to justify their migration to America with sacred, providential history, but also able to define the meaning of their holy experiment in the course of salvation history. Only by acknowledging the essential radicalism embodied in the eschatology and apocalypse of the Puritan migration, can one grasp the ultimate goal and significance of the Puritan errand into the wilderness of America. For not only did Puritans believe in the imminence of the millennium; they also deemed themselves active actors in the providential drama of all time - the battle between Christ and Antichrist which would precede the transformation of the world into the Kingdom of God. As the Puritan emigrants themselves perceived it, their errand into the wilderness was not simply a utopian search after religious reformation, a flight from corrupted history and degenerating human traditions; it was rather a confrontation within time and history, an earthly stand against the power of Satan and Antichrist.

NOTES - INTRODUCTION

1. Perry Miller, "Errand into the Wilderness," Errand into the Wilderness (Cambridge MA, 1976), pp. 1-15.

2. Among the early accounts of the Puritan settlement of New England are, William Bradford, Of Plymouth Plantation, 1620-1647, ed. Samuel Eliot Morison (New York, 1967); Nathaniel Morton, New England's Memorial (Boston, 1826); William Hubbard, A General History of New England, 2nd ed. (Boston, 1848); Thomas Hutchinson, The History of the Colony and Province of Massachusetts Bay, ed. Lawrence Shaw Mayo, 3 vols. (Cambridge, 1936); Cotton Mather, Magnalia Christi Americana, or the Ecclesiastical History of New England, 1620-1698, 2 vols. (Hartford, 1820). The basic authorities on the settlement of New England remain Charles M. Andrews, The Colonial Period of American History (New Haven, 1934); James Truslow Adams, The Founding of New England (Boston, 1921); and Perry Miller, Orthodoxy in Massachusetts (Gloucester, 1965). Among more recent works, see David Crayson Allen, In English Ways: The Movement of Societies and the Transferal of English Local Law and Custom to Massachusetts Bay in the Seventeenth Century (Chapel Hill: 1981); Andrew Delbanco, The Puritan Ordeal (Cambridge, 1989); David Cressy, Coming Over: Migration and Communication between England and New England in the Seventeenth Century (Cambridge, 1987), Theodore D. Bozeman, To Live Ancient Lives: The Primitivist Dimension in Puritanism (Chapel Hill, 1988); and Stephen Foster, The Long Argument: English Puritanism and the Shaping of New England Culture, 1570-1700 (Chapel Hill, 1990).

CHAPTER ONE:
THE PURSUIT OF REFORMATION
THE ORIGINS OF THE GREAT PURITAN MIGRATION

We who today attempt to compare our civilisation with another and try in a sense to get behind the history of civilisation are continually learning the degree to which it was religion that shaped the mentality of our distant ancestors, deciding the "set" of their mind and governing the way in which they conceived the world of human happenings. The way of formulating to themselves their whole notion of the human drama emerges as the product of their religious outlook as a whole.

   --Herbert Butterfield[1]

To the Protestant...life seems a pilgrim's progress which, whether made solitarily or in company, proceeds through unpredictable contingencies and crises toward the destination beyond life and death where all the trumpets blow.... The Protestant memory of the past is not focused in one great event when the true human community was reconstituted by the Lord and when the church came into being as representative and guardian of that community. The great event was one of arrivals, departures, and promises of return; it has left behind in history not so much a visible, resurrected Body of Christ in the form of the church, as faith and hope and love, becoming incarnate now and again, but essentially as invisible as are all the movements of the spirit.

   --H. Richard Niebuhr[2]

> My Brethren all attend,
> And list to my relation:
> This the day, mark what I say,
> Tends to your renovation;
> Stay not among the Wicked,
> Lest that with them you perish,
> But let us to New England go
> And the Pagan People cherish....
>   --Anonymous[3]

15

I   Covenant and the Puritan Migration

Writing in his diary in 1587, Richard Rogers, a Puritan minister at Wethersfield, Essex, noted time and again his struggle to keep his covenant with God and lead a godly life in the world. Yet he was pleased that

> god hath been veary merciful to me in this time to awake me again when I have been declineine or growing weak or wearisome in well doeinge to offer me occasions many wayes of continuance by good company, as cul[verwel].

He and his friend, Ezekiel Culverwell, a famous Puritan divine and the author of a Treatise on Faith, 1623, consequently, made a covenant among themselves to lead a godly life and to watch over each other in that endeavor.

> Seinge the lord had graunted to us some sight of the coldnes and halfe service of his which is in the worlde, and our selves also much caryed away with it, that thus we woulde renue our covenaunt more firmely with the lorde, then we had done, to come neerer to the practize of godliness...and to indevour after a more continual watch from thing to thinge that as much as might be we might walk with the lord for the time of our abideinge here below. These and such lik we communed of togither...with great inflameing of our hartes farre above that which is common with us.

Later that year, other godly people joined the two convenanters, ministers and laymen alike, and so this godly group came to constitute a "covenant[ed] society" in Wethersfield. "Great hope we have by our private company among our neighbours to woorck as well more consc[ience] in their whole course as knowledge," wrote Rogers in his diary.[4] By mutual scrutiny and admonishment, the members of this godly company sought to support each other in their commitment to God.

Yet, Richard Rogers came to be prominent and famous among Puritans in the early seventeenth century not for his diary, but for his important book of 1603, Seven Treatises. By 1630 this book, which in over 600 pages prescribed daily routines of spiritual exercise for Christian readers, had passed through eight editions. In Seven Treatises, Rogers stressed above all else the importance of

16

godly company to a Christian life. In illustration he related much of his own hometown experience. There is, he wrote, "rule or dutie, directing us in companie," because men "who are ignorant and carelesse" should be "exhorted, stireed up, called upon and instructed," until they "might be edified and built up in our most holy faith." His aim was not to convert the sinners, but to edify the godly. "Scornefull, prophane and brutish persons" were not to be admitted into godly company. According to Rogers, godly company was but one company among many companies men entered into in their life and each of those companies should be made "sutable and correspondent to the other part of the Christian life."[5] For Rogers, godly company was thus only an extension of other social activities undertaken by men in this world.

Although he made it clear that godly company was not necessarily associated with the making of covenants, Rogers, towards the end of his book, gave "an example of a couvenant made by certain godly brethren" that, he hoped, would "help much to such as they are, to make better use of rules to direct them." Here, he cited at length from the covenant that his godly company had made in his town in 1588 and pointed out the blessings it had brought. The covenant, he wrote,

> did knit them in that love, the bond whereof could not be broken either on their part which now sleepe in the Lord, whiles they heere lived, nor in them which yet remaine, by any adversarie power unto this day.[6]

The contribution of Rogers' book was in its call for true "Christian fellowship" and corresponding condemnation of mere religion. In this effort, Rogers ventured forth on a path that Ernest Stoeffler has termed "Pietistic Puritanism": "indifference toward political issues and overriding concern for the religious welfare of individuals."[7] For Rogers, this path meant an increasing emphasis on the formation of godly companies "for our reprooving, exhorting, and comforting one another" and a concomitant de-emphasis on the Church of England as the focal religious institution in his life. With this new emphasis, he inaugurated an important trend, and indeed a revolutionary one, in the religious culture of England in that time. With many people, long-standing loyalties, both ecclesiastical and national, to the Church of England subsequently gave way to a new personal loyalty, religious and social in nature, to one's own covenanted society.[8]

John Winthrop's "Religious Experiencia," a diary in which he recorded his religious experiences from his early youth until his emigration to America in 1630, is in many ways quite similar to Rogers' diary, especially in its revelation of a restless striving for the godly life. Although there is evidence that during the late 1620s Winthrop slowly embraced what James C. Spalding has called "the Deuteronomic" interpretation of history by which God acted in and ruled through the events of ancient Israel's history, in his early years he was mainly guided by a pietistic yearning. Like Rogers, Winthrop found it hard always to keep his covenant with God, and he vowed many times in his diary "to stand to the Covenant of my baptisme, renued so often since." But once "the Sabbaothe came," noted Winthrop in 1616,

> I arose betymes, and read over the covenant of certaine Christians sett downe in Mr. Rogers booke, and therewith my heart beganne to breake, and my worldly delights which had heald my heart in suche slaverye before, beganne to be distastefull and of meane account with me, I concluded with prayer in teares; and so to my family exercise, and then to Churche, my heart beinge still somewhat humbled under Gods hand, yet could not gett at libertie from my vaine pleasures.[9]

Winthrop's pietistic search, however, led him, as was the case with Rogers, to see the crucial importance of godly company. In 1607, he wrote in his Religious Experiencia, "I with my companye," met with other godly people in a conference in which everyone promised "to be mindefull one of another in desiring God to grante the petitions that we were made to him that day, etc." Again, as with Rogers' religious experience, mutual surveillance and edification became foundations of covenant society or company. Family exercise also served in the keeping of one's covenant with God.

> I found at last that the conscionable and constant teachine of my

18

familye was a speciall businesse, wherein I might please God, and greatly further their and mine own salvation...and I perceived that my exercise therein did stirre up in me many considerations and muche life of affection, which otherwise I should not so often meet with.[10]

The Seven Treatises by Richard Rogers, wrote William Haller in his The Rise of Puritanism, "was the first important exposition of the code of behavior which expressed the English Calvinist, or, more broadly speaking, the Puritan, conception of the spiritual and moral life."[11] The book was widely read by Puritans in old and New England. Thomas Shepard, before he emigrated to the Bay colony, wrote that "Mr. Rogers' Seven Treatises...did first work upon my heart."[12] But Rogers' book was more than a book for reading only, it was a guide to the godly life in this world through the instrument of the covenant. The Rev. John Wilson, for example, before he came to Boston, Massachusetts, in 1630, was influenced by

that famous book of Mr. Rogers, called The Seven Treatises; which when he had read, he [was] so affected...and pursuant unto the advice which he had from Dr. Ames, he associated himself with a pious company in the university...who kept their meeting...for prayer, fasting, holy conference and the exercise of true devotion.[13]

Pietistic searching, then, led the way to social action, through which a godly company was formed with the intention of strengthening through mutual effort the resolve of individuals to keep their covenant with God. An understanding of the importance of this process of social covenanting is crucial to the comprehension of the nature of the Puritan emigration. Already by the early seventeenth century, some Puritans in England were sufficiently dissatisfied with the established Church of England as to cause them to withdraw into godly covenant societies formed to aid them in their efforts to lead a godly life.

The covenant that John White drew up in Dorchester, England, in the early seventeenth century, shows clearly how pietistic yearning could lead to social reformation. As minister in his town, White wrote the Ten Vows "for lifting up of ye weak hand and strengthening of ye feeble knees" so as "to bind orselves by

19

solemn Vow, and Covenant unto ye Ld our God." The vows sought to encourage "true and pure Worship of God according to his owne ordinance, opposing orselves to all wayes of Innovacion or Corruption." They entreated Christians "to labour for a growth in knowledge and understanding by attending to reading hearing and meditating Gods word," "to instruct O[u]r Children and families in the fear of ye Ld," "to watch O[u]r owne ways dayly," "to submit to brotherly admonicion and to perform that Christian duty towards others," and so on. Here, as employed by White, the covenant formed the basis for a close-knit spiritual society in which religious reformation entailed social reformation as well. Certainly, there were different circumstances surrounding Rogers' covenant and White's "Ten Vows," or covenant. The first bound together only a tiny minority of villagers in Wethersfield, while the Dorechester orders, designed for a town under Puritan discipline, were formed in order to embrance all but the ungoldy. But as Frances Rose-Troup shows, the importance of White's covenant in Dorchester was in fact that it served "as a touchstone to exclude the ungodly from the Sacrament." And others followed White in this effort. In 1633, Hugh Peters, to whom White sent his Ten Vows, closely emulated White's articles in the covenant he drew for his own congregation in Rotterdam.[14]

More evidence exists to show that many Puritans who emigrated to Massachusetts Bay during the 1630s engaged before their departure in forming godly covenanted societies in England. Francis Higginson, who had already come to Salem as a minister on behalf of the New England Company in 1629, lived before his emigration in Leicester, a town divided into two parties. "On the one side, a great multitude of Christians, then called Puritans," attended the worship of God not only within the framework of the Church of England but also in "their assemblies, and more secretly in their families, but also they frequently had their private meetings, for prayer (sometimes with fasting) and repeating of sermons, and maintaining of profitable conferences, at all which Mr. Higginson himself was often present." Against this godly party, "there was a profane party, filled with wolvish rage against the flock of the Lord Jesus."[15] Similarly, in John

20

Cotton's Boston, in Lincolnshire,

> there were some scores of pious people in the town, who more
> exactly formed themselves into an evangelical Church-State, by
> entering into purity of his worship.[16]

The details of the theological developments of the covenant theory need not
here detain us. In The New England Mind: The Seventeenth Century, Perry
Miller has dealt at length with "the covenant theory" and its many varieties,
including the covenant of grace, the federal theology, church covenants and social
covenants.[17] Apart from its theological implications, however, covenant theory
had important social and political implications for Puritans and non-Puritans in
Jacobean and Carolinean England. What is evident from the experience of
Rogers, Winthrop, Cotton, Wilson, and Higginson, is that godly people in
England during this period entered into covenants among themselves without
necessarily forming connections with the established church. "These covenants,"
wrote Collinson, "were not church covenants but belonged to the Puritan
experience of covenant grace, an area quite remote at this time from any overt
ecclesiastical reference."[18] They were, in this sense, social covenants and they
arose, as shown above, partly from the difficulties experienced by individuals in
keeping their private covenants with God. "God conveys his salvation by way of
covenant," wrote Thomas Cobbet, a minister in Lynn, Massachusetts,

> and he doth it to those onely that are in covenant.... This
> covenant must every soule enter into, every particular soule must
> enter into a particular covenant with God; out of this way there
> is no life.[19]

Godly society, or covenanting company, as Rogers recommended, was a
necessary device by which one could keep his covenant through actual
involvement with other members of one's company.

Thus, covenants were an essential part of the Puritan experience in early
seventeenth century England, and there is evidence that many Puritans, laymen
and clergy alike, engaged in the establishment of godly societies in order to shape
their life according to God's word. But covenants were also an essential part of

21

the Puritan migration to New England. The most famous civil covenant in regard to the Puritan migration is of course the Mayflower Compact of 1620, in which, as Bradford wrote, the pilgrims "solemnly and mutually, in the presence of God and one another, covenant and combine ourselves together into a Civil Body Politic, for our better ordering and preservation."[20] Another famous vision of the covenant idea in relation to the Puritan migration can be found in John Winthrop's lay sermon aboard the Arbella "A Model of Christian Charity" of 1630. In this lay sermon Winthrop made it clear towards what end the Puritan emigration was directed:

> The end is to improve our lives to do more service to the Lord the comforte and the encrease of the body of christe whereof we are members that our selves and posterity may be better preserved from the Common corrupcions of this evill world to serve the Lord and worke out our Salvacion under the power of purity of his holy Ordinances.

And the means for that aim? "For the meanes whereby this must bee effected, they are 2fold, A conformity with the worke and end wee aime at." Conformity and unity were, thus, according to Winthrop, necessary conditions for the success of the whole Puritan emigration. Hence, he forcefully invoked the idea of a sacred covenant which ought to regulate the saints' life in the wilderness of America:

> thus stands the cause betweene God and us, wee are entered into Covenant with him for this work, we have taken out a Commission, the Lord hath given us leave to drawe our owne Articles wee have professed to enterprise these Accion upon these and these ends, wee have hereupon besought his favour and blessing.[21]

These famous covenant expressions by American Puritans clearly were not church covenants. Likewise, as Lockridge has shown in A New England Town, before Dedham was a town and before it had a church, its settlers drew up a covenant in 1636, in which it was stated:

> that we shall by all means labor to keep off from us all such as are contrary minded, and receive only such unto us as may be probably of one heart with us.

22

The Dedham's covenant thus made it clear that only godly people could join the godly society of covenanters, and emphasized in explicit words the fact that ungodly and profane people should be excluded from it. Those who were within the company of covenanters had to work "for the edification of each other in the knowledge and faith of the Lord Jesus." [22] The earliest covenant in the Bay colony was of course that of Salem in 1629. There, on July 20, wrote the deacon in Salem church, Charles Gott, "a company of believers...joined together in covenant, to walk together in all the way of God." One month later, with the establishment of the church there, the members found it necessary to renew their previous covenant.

> We...members of the present Church of Christ in Salem, haveing found by sad experience how dangerous it is to sitt loose to the Covenant we make with out God.... Doe therefore...renewe that Church covenant we find this Church bound unto.... That we Covenant with the Lord and one with one another, and doe bynd our selves in the presence of God, to walk together in all his waies, according as he pleased to reveal him selfe unto us in his Blessed word of truth.

As a covenanted church, the members of the Salem church consequently declared that "we willingly doe nothing to the offence of the Church." [23] Yet, all the other articles of the covenant are similar to civil covenants cited above.

The Puritan emigrants who came to Massachusetts Bay, then, were engaged before and after their migration to America in an attempt to establish godly societies or companies based on social covenants. This kind of Puritan activity was necessarily related to and was indeed a precondition of the Puritan migration. For what these covenants reveal is a special engagement by Puritans to reconcile here on earth the law of nature and the law of grace. If the law of nature or the moral law was essential to -an as a rational being, the law of grace could be realized only by faith and by divine grace. "There is likewise," preached Winthrop aboard the Arbella in 1630, "a double lawe by which wee are regulated in our conversacion one towards another...the lawe of nature and the lawe of grace, or the morall lawe or the lawe of the gospel." Thus, while the law of

23

nature came to regulate civil society as such, the law of gospel or grace came to regulate Christian society, a godly society in which one's covenant with God corresponded to the covenant of society at large with God. By maintaining the law of grace or the law of gospel, which is the essence of the covenants described above, godly people fulfilled the conditions they took upon themselves in entering into covenant with God. At the same time, they could expect that God would fulfill the conditions he had taken upon himself concerning the covenant. "Now, if the Lord shall please to heare us...then hath hee ratified this Covenant and sealed our Commission [and] will expect a stricket performance of the Articles contained in it." And if the covenanters should succeed in their attempt, "the Lord will be our God and delight to dwell among us, as his owne people and will commaund blessing upon us in all our wayes."[24]

Above all else, Puritans of the covenant, in England and New England alike, sought to realize the law of grace in this world. In pursuit of this end, Puritans not only turned their backs on the established church but on society at large. Not surprisingly, then, it was on this point, the realization of the law of grace in one's life and society, that Puritans clashed with other groups in English society. In parish church, village, town, and city, Puritans arrayed against non-Puritans in what amounted to a battle for social reformation. The question at issue was how man was to live in society. Conflict over this basic social question, and not solely theological disagreement, thus provided the broad social context within which the Puritan migration movement first took root. Ultimately, Puritans would turn to America to attempt what they could not accomplish in England - the shaping of a Christian commonwealth on earth constructed according to God's word.

24

II The Role of the Laity in the Puritan Movement

The history of early Massachusetts is to a great extent the history of attempts to fulfill the articles of the covenants, to realize on the North American continent the law of grace. Yet, we must ask ourselves, why was it necessary to cross the Atlantic to put into practice the law of grace? What hindered these Puritans from realizing their covenanted society in England? And what most significantly obstructed the Puritan vision of a godly society and godly life? Our task here is to explore some dimensions of the real world from which the Puritan migration came. An examination of the laity's unique and decisive role in the Puritan movement, for example, is important within this context because it may, on the one hand, explain the broader social situation out of which emerged the Puritan movement, and on the other hand, clarify more fully the origins and causes of the Great Puritan migration.

In his well-known lay sermon aboard the Arbella, John Winthrop concluded by declaring by all who came with him that "wee must Consider that wee shall be as a Citty upon a Hill, the eies of all the people are upon us."[25] It is well known that Winthrop took this parable from Matthew V, 14: "Ye are the light of the world. A city that is set on a hill cannot be hid." What Jesus, according to Matthew, argued for, and what was probably also Winthrop's intention, is a demand for perfection.

> For I say unto you, That except your righteousness shall exceed
> the righteousness of the scribes and Pharisees, ye shall in no case
> enter into the kingdom of heaven. (Mat. V, 20)

The light of righteousness is therefore not mainly an exemplary model for the world. It is also a precondition for salvation. "Let your light so shine before men, that they may see your good works, and glorify your father which is in Heaven," (Mat. V, 16). What is not so well known, however, is that the vision of the "city upon the hill" had a long tradition in England among Protestants and Puritans. Henry Orinel, for example, who traveled to Colchester in 1555, wrote that

> this town for the earnest profession of the Gospel became like
> unto a Citie upon the hill as candle upon cnadlesticke gave great
> light to all those who for the comfort of their conscience came
> to confer there from divers places of the Realm.[26]

Orinel and Winthrop shared one important characteristic: both were laymen. Apart from studies of Puritan divines, recent studies of English Puritanism have stressed more and more the decisive role of the laity in the Puritan movement. These studies have thus shifted our attention from theological writings of ministers to the social and political foundations for this movement. In her investigation of English villagers in the sixteenth and seventeenth centuries, Margaret Spufford gives a vivid picture of Puritanism as a popular movement in the diocese of Ely. At one point she cites from an account of a Jesuit priest who had witnessed Puritan gatherings in the late 1580s or 1590s. "From the very beginning," she quotes the priest,

> a great number of Puritans gathered here. Some came from the
> outlying parts of the town, some from the villages round about,
> eager and vast crowds of them flocking to perform their practices
> - sermons, communions and fasts.... Each of them had his own
> Bible, and sedulously turned the pages and looked up the texts
> cited by the preachers, discussing the passages among themselves
> to see whether they had quoted them to the point, and accurately,
> and in harmony with their tenets. Also they would start arguing
> among themselves about the meaning of passages from the
> Scriptures - men, women, boys, girls, rustics, labourers and
> idiots...over a thousand of them sometimes assembled, their
> horses and pack animals burdened with a multitude of Bibles.

"There is then, proof, for the first time" in the late sixteenth century, notes Spufford, "that large numbers of the laity in the diocese...had been influenced by Puritan teachings, and were actively involved in doctrinal disputes." According to her, the picture of the Puritans described by the Jesuit priest "shows better than any other source the way the common people had been affected by the reformation and the growth of literacy."[27]

Many other studies of Puritanism in England confirm the importance of the laity in the Puritan movement. A. Tindal Hart has pointed out that "the mass of

26

the laity were much more protestant than their clergy, had little sympathy with the Laudian ideals, and greatly dreaded a re-introduction of popery."[28] In areas in which Puritanism was predominant, as R.C. Richardson shows, laymen "were sometimes even more insistent opponents of the sign of the cross than their ministers."[29] All this points to the fact that popular Puritanism was by no means guided and led by the clergy; the voice of the congregation or laity was important if not always decisive. Patrick Collinson describes the relationship between the clergy and laity thus:

> the popular protestant element in the Elizabethan society was not subordinate to the preachers, but possessed a mind and will of its own to which the conduct of the Puritan minister, including his own nonconformity, was partly a response.[30]

With regard to the Puritan migration to Massachusetts Bay, the role of the laity can hardly be exaggerated. One need only look at the Adventurers' list of both the New England Company and Massachusetts Bay Company, in which ministers made up only a tiny minority, to see how the laity initiated this migration. More important, the Company invariably initiated the movement to send ministers to the colony. "It was fully resolved, by God's assistance," wrote Matthew Cradock, governor of the New England Company and later first governor of the Bay Company, to John Endecott at Salem in February 1628/9, "to send over two ministers..." In another letter, dated the following April, Cradock assured Endecott:

> We have been careful to make plentiful provision of godly ministers.... And because their doctrine will hardly be esteemed whos persons are not reverenced, we desire that both by your own example, and by commanding all others to do the like, our ministers may receive due honor.[31]

The essential and decisive role of the laity in the Puritan migration to New England can be illustrated through a few examples. When Thomas Hooker departed for Holland in 1631, "Mr. Hookers' company," wrote Winthrop in his Journal in 1632, came to the Bay colony.[32] The godly people, the laity, did not follow their minister to Holland but journeyed to Massachusetts and there waited for him. Many parishioners of St. Stephen's, London, decided to emigrate to New England with Winthrop's fleet, so that their former vicar, John Davenport found himself preaching "before pews vacated by the great exodus to Massachusetts Bay."[33] Even before their ministers were willing and ready to emigrate, many laymen had chosen emigration.

Captain Roger Clap supplies us with first hand evidence as to the way godly people had been engaged in preparation for emigration. Upon leaving his parents' house, Clap writes, he went "to live with a worthy Gentleman, Mr. William Southcot," who lived near the city of Exon [Exter] in Devonshire. This gentleman "was careful to keep a Godly Family." Proceeding on in his search for good "preachers of the Word of God," Clap then traveled to Exter to Puritan gatherings where he met the Puritan minister John Warham. "I did desire to live near him: So I remove[d]...into the city." In Exter, Clap lived with "one Mr. Mossiour, as Famous a Family for Religion as I ever knew." In his house, a "conference" of godly people met each week. Clap does not tell us if this godly company was based on a covenant. But he does indicate that he himself "covenanted" with Mr. Mossiour. Later, now in the late 1620s, Clap describes how he came to emigrate to the Bay colony.

> I never so much as heard of New England, until I heard of many godly Persons that were going there, and that Mr. Warham was to go also.... These godly People resolved to live together; and therefore as they had made choice of these two Revd. Servants of God, Mr. John Warham and Mr. John Maverick to be their Ministers, so they kept a solemn Day of Fasting in the New Hospital in Plymouth in England, spending it in Preaching and Praying.[34]

What motivated these "godly people" to emigrate? Surprisingly, no clear answer to this question exists: historians of early Massachusetts have dealt almost exclusively with the emigration of clergymen not with that of the laity. Even in relation to John Winthrop, whose life has been the subject of many studies, we still do not know exactly his motivation for emigrating, because (surprisingly again) historians in many cases have tended to overlook his "Religious

Experiencia." Yet, if the argument about the decisive role of the laity in the development of Puritanism in England is correct, it seems that there is the place to look for explanations for the migration.

III Covenant and Social Reformation

From its beginnings, the Puritan movement in England did not operate in a
vacuum. Theological developments accompanied developments in social action
and behavior among Puritan; for this reason, Puritanism often drew the critical
attention of many sections of English society. religious reformation, as
contemporaries well knew, carried social implications. Illustrating this point are
the many satires penned against Puritans in the late and early seventeenth
centuries. In this genre many in England expressed their dislike of the Puritan
concept and practice of the godly life. For example, one W.M. wrote in 1609
in his satire about the social outcome of the Puritans' ideas:

> My calling is divine
> and I from God am sent,
> I will not chop-church be,
> nor pay my patron rent....

Satires against the Puritans' way of life were widespread, for to many the
religious and social manners of the Puritans and their devotion and pious behavior
caused irritation and outrage. Thus in Thyne's Emblemes and Epigrams (1600)
the author wrote of the Puritans that

> They sett upp churches twenties for their one.
> for everie private house spirituallie
> must be their church, for other will they none.

And the Puritans' militancy along with their pretense to exclusive possession of
the requisite knowledge of the true mode of salvation brought in 1614 one R.C.
in the Time Whistle to write:

> There is sort of purest seeming men,
> That aide this monster in her wrongfull cause,
> Those the world nameth - Puritanes I mean -
> Sent to supplant me from the very jawes
> Of hell, I think; by whose apparent shew
> Of sanctity doe greatest evils grow.

Most common were satires against Puritan insistence on the holiness of the
Sabbath. Those who preferred recreation and sport most often charged the
Puritans with hypocrisy: "Upon the Sabbath, they'l no Phisicke take, Lest it

should worke, and so the Sabbath breake." Or, in relation to Sunday, "Suppose his Cat on Sunday killed a Rat, She on Monday must be Hanged for that."[35] Although the term "Puritan" had not been sharply defined in the early seventeenth century, the satires evidence the fact that, among contemporaries, Puritanism had come to represent certain explicit manners and modes of behavior.

These satires of, and attacks upon, Puritans and their ways of life and belief clearly reflected the fears and anxieties they created in English society. Winthrop described this world in his "Religious Experiencia" in 1616, writing from the point of view of being Puritan and addressing God,

> Thou tellest me that in this way there is least companie, and that those which doe walke openly in this way shalbe despised, pointed at, hated of the world, made a byword, reviled, slandered, rebuked, made a gazing stocke, called puritans, nice fooles, hipocrites, hair brained fellows, rashes, indiscreet, vain glorious, and all that is naught is; all this is nothinge to that which many of thine exellent servants have been tried with, neither shall they lessen the glorie thou hast prepared for them.[36]

Richard Baxter gives a similarly vivid picture as to the making of a Puritan in his youth. He reports that in and near the village where he grew up in the 1620s many ministers lived

> scandalous lives and that only three or four constant competent preachers lived near us, and those (though conformable all save one) were the common marks of the people's obloquy and reproach and any that had but gone to hear them, when he had no preaching at home, was made the derision of the vulgar rabble under the odious name of a Puritan.

On Sundays "the reader read the Common Prayer briefly, and the rest of the day...was spent in dancing under a maypole and great tree...where all the town met together." With all this activity, Baxter continued,

> we could not read the Scripture in our family without the great disturbance of the tabor and pipe and noise in the street. Many times my mind was inclined to be among them, and sometimes I broke loose from conscience and joined with them; and the more I did the more I was inclined to it. But when I heard them call my father Puritan it did much to cure me and alienate me from them; for I considered my father's exercise of reading the

31

> Scripture was better than theirs...and I considered what it was
> for that he and others were thus derided.[37]

The picture presented by Winthrop and Baxter shows how the Puritans' way of life stood in clear contrast to that of other people and the extent to which their neighbors detested the Puritan vision of godly life. This world of "contrasting communities," as Margaret Spufford defines it, is the world of the great Puritan migration.

By entering into covenants to form godly societies and companies, Puritans not only took a step in determining their own way of life; they also commented adversely upon the way of life followed by those who continued to adhere to the old order of the established Church of England. When Puritan ministers refused to wear the surplice, or use the sign of the cross in baptism; when some of them opposed the practice of having godparents, or kneeling during the celebration of the sacrament; or when they opposed and preached against standing at the reading of the gospel or bowing in the name of Jesus - in all of these gestures of dissent Puritan ministers were not involving themselves in matters of narrow theological import. They were, in fact, challenging the appropriateness of ancient customs, rites and ceremonies, of the Church of England and thereby creating the potential for grave social conflict in parish, church, village, and town. For example, when in 1604 Peter White, vicar of Poulton in the field, failed to use the sign of the cross in Baptism, his manner "cause[d] many to be baptised out of the parish." And when the minister in Cheshire parish of Tarporley refused "to execute the holy orders of the church" of England regarding the use of the cross in Baptism, his action resulted in a child "be[ing] carried to another church" where he could be "baptised according to the lawful rites and ceremonies of the church of England."[38]

In these and other ways, Puritan ministers exercised their ministry to forward social reformation. They excluded "ungodly" parishoners from communion and church, insisted on godly discipline,and attempted to identify the visible saints with the Church. By such actions, they offended many of their parishioners and undermined the working framework of the religious settlement under which the parish church was designed to encompass all people in its jurisdiction. Thus in 1626 John Swan of Bunbury caused "sundry men that came prepare[d] to the communion to depart thence without any at all." The Puritan quest for reformation, social and ecclesiastical alike, carried with it severe penalties for those who were, as the Puritans defined them, "profane." What seemed to the Puritans as "reformation according to God's word" was to others obviously an attack on the ancient practices, "the lawful rites and ceremonies" of the Church of England.[39]

IV Migration and Separation

The conflicts between the "godly" and "profane" directly raised the issue of separation. The experience of John Cotton shows one of many ways Puritans could seek after true reformation within the Church of England, and how the parishioners reacted to it. As early as 1615, Cotton "with cautious firmness rather than enthusiastic zeal," as his biographer says, "set about distinguishing the lily from the thorns." The issue he confronted was how to maintain the ideal of the Church as a community of visible saints together with the notion of the established Church as inclusive of all the inhabitants of a given area. He did so "not by withdrawing from the parish church...but by identifying the elect and withdrawing into a tighter inner group with them." This chosen group consequently "entered into covenant with the Lord and with one another." Thus, what was formed by Cotton in his Lincolnshire parish was a godly company within the parish church. Such an arrangement amounted to what contemporaries referred to as semi-separation, which stopped short of total separation from the parish church and thereby from the Church of England as a whole. What Cotton formed was not a church but a godly company based on covenant, a company that - without leaving the church - could avoid "the offensive ceremonies" and "was truly qualified to receive the sacrament." The social implications of this act were immediately apparent. Those in the parish excluded from Cotton's godly group "were outraged at the action of the covenanters." They ran to the bishop's court in Lincoln, and the bishop suspended Cotton.[40]

But many Congregationalists in England did not stop where Cotton had stopped. In many cases during the 1640s and 1650s, as Geoffrey Nuttal shows in his book, Visible Saints, the godly group of the covenanters took over the parish church and made it after their own image.[41] Clearly, what could be done in the 1640s and 1650s, with the fall of the ecclesiastical order during the Puritan Revolution in England, could not have been so easily accomplished in the 1630s, namely, the identification of God's covenanted company with the Church and the exclusion from the Church of all those not belonging to the godly. It is true that most Puritans who demanded separation from the profane, including almost all of those who emigrated to Massachusetts, strongly denounced the stand of rigid separation which would unchurch the Church of England. Emigration as a legal and loyal withdrawal may therefore be seen as an acceptable alternative to separation, as John White, for example, wrote in his defense of the Puritan migration to Massachsuetts, The Planters Plea (1630). Evidence of the actual practices in the Massachusetts Bay churches indicates, however, explicit separation, as well as many instances in which the Bay Puritans accused the Church of England of being a false church. Emigration and the unlimited ecclesiastical freedom in Massachusetts thus radically transformed the Bay Puritans' attitidues towards separation from the Church of England. Full discussion of this important historical phenomenon would, however, lead well beyond the limits of the present study. In short, the option open to Puritans in the 1630s was the moderate course taken by Cotton in Lincolnshire whereby a congregation of godly people was assembled within the established Church.

From the point of view of the established Church, however, Cotton's moderate course carried the revolutionary threat of congregationalism. The nature of this threat was made explicit well before the Puritan Revolution by William Ames, the most prominent theologian of this form of church government. "A congregation or particular Church," proclaimed Ames in 1623, "is a society of believers joyned together by a special bond among themselves, for the constant exercise of the communion of Saints among themselves." In this proclamation, Ames made it clear both that the essential foundation of a particular church was the social covenant made among the godly people and that a necessary connection existed between the two.

> Believers doe not make a particular church, although peradventure many meete and live together in the same place, unlesse they be joyned by a special bond among themselves.... This bond is a covenant, either expresse or implicite, whereby believers doe particularly bind themselves to performe all those duties, both toward God and one toward another, which pertaine to the respect and edification of the Church.[42]

35

Ames thus enlarged the covenant's meaning, making it an indispensable feature of a true church. Ames had thus transformed Rogers' restricted notion of covenant - as a social covenant with an emphasis on mutual edification among Godly people - into nothing less than the essential core and the heart of the Church. Indeed, the godly company only became a Church by virtue of the covenant its members concluded among themselves.

The transformation defined by Ames was, in broad outline, the history of the early Massachusetts Bay colony. If godly people could not fulfill their religious goals in England, they had no other choice than to emigrate to America and seek those goals there. Already in 1630, the godly company to which Roger Clap belonged drew a covenant and formed a church in old Plymouth on the very eve of their migration. But such conduct was exceptional in the great Puritan migration. More common was the Dedham pattern in which emigration preceded the drawing up of a covenant and the forming a church. Cotton's attempt in old Boston was doomed to failure not only because the bishop objected to it, but because many parishioners vehemently objected to it as well. Yet, despite their uncomfortable predicament, Cotton and others of like mind were free to contemplate an enticing prospect. What if the godly simply left the parish churches in England and gathered in the Bay colony? There the way would be open to the proper execution of the premises of the true Church. Central to these was the belief that the Church should exclude all but visible saints. Precisely on this point Cotton and his associates in England had no hope. However, in New England prospects were entirely different. And so contemplation gave way to action. Emigration was far preferable to the forced inclusion of sinners in the church covenant. As Ames wrote, this was indeed the whole reason for the Puritan emigration to Massachusetts. Well informed in Holland concerning the migration, Ames, in 1630, in his book Conscience With the Power and Cases thereof, justified the Puritan migration to America on these grounds:

> Yet if Beleevers contending for their liberty cannot procure this
> right in that part, nor without most grievous discommodities

> depart to a more pure Church, and doe keep themselves from the
> approbation of sinne...they sine not.... [43]

Only by leaving sinners in England could the true reformation be fulfilled in New England.

The failure to achieve reform in their local societies, the impossibility of reconciling the principle of a Church based on visible saints with the established one, continuing attacks on the Puritan way of godliness - all these stood in the background of the Puritan migration to New England. For the emigrants demanded nothing less than the whole - the transformation of society and state according to God's word. This radical plea could not be fulfilled in England. It only raised the ire of other sections of society, so that the attempt to distinguish and separate godly from ungodly people was accompanied by social struggles within the community and within the parish church. Emigration therefore represented the possibility, not only of establishing a true Church, but also of achieving social reformation through social covenants. As Captain Edward Johnson who sailed with Winthrop's fleet wrote, "[In New England] the Lord will create a new Heaven and New Earth in, new Churches, and new Common-Wealth together."[44] For without a godly Christian commonwealth, godly people and their true churches could not be sustained.

Johnson, like Ames before him, revealed how much the social context in England caused and generated the migration.

> When England began to decline in Religion like lukewarme
> Laodicea, and instead of purging out Popery, a farther
> compliance was sought not only in vain Idolatrous Ceremonies,
> but also in prophaning the Sabbath, and by Proclamation through
> their Parish churches, exasperating lewd and prophane persons
> to celebrate a Sabbath like the Heathen to Venus, Baccus and
> Ceres; in so much that the multitude of irreligious lascivious and
> popish affected persons spred the whole land like Grashoppers.[45]

These "prophane persons" and that "multitude of irreligious lascivious persons had obstructed Puritans in England; they were a stumbling block to the Puritans' search for further reformation in social life and in the Church. The proclamation

37

Johnson mentioned was the Declaration concerning Sports, often called the Book of Sports. First issued in 1617 by James I, it was directed against the Puritans' attempt to apply the provision of the Mosaic Law to the English Sunday and to suppress the May games, morris dances, and other sports indulged in after service. "Such an attempt by the Lancashire magistrates, in 1617, caused James to issue a declaration that those who had already attended divine service might engage in certain lawful recreations afterward." One year later the application of this order was extended to all England, "and every minister was directed to read from the pulpit the declaration in favor of certain lawful sports, often called the Book of Sports." Later on, "a renewed Puritan attempt to suppress Sunday games - this time in Somersetshire - was responsible for the reissue of the Book of Sports" by Charles I in 1633, which was also ordered to be read in every parish church.[46]

To the Puritans' chagrin, this declaration allowed the populace to play games on Sunday after church service. Yet one needs to go beyond the royal proclamations, as in the case of Baxter above, to see in the interactions between the Puritans and the "prophane" how the highest interest of the Puritans - keeping the purity of the holy day - clashed with the multitude's interest in having recreation on the same day. Concerning the latter, wrote Johnson, "every corner of England was filled with the fury of malignant adversaries" of God and Godly people. So, when the Puritans emigrated to Massachusetts, they intentionally separated themselves not only from ceremonies, popery, and bishops, but also from this multitude of "malignant and prophane" people; for these people, in Puritan eyes, were the reason that further reformation was not attainable in England. It was, they believed, as a result of this struggle between godly and "malignant" people that "in this very time Christ the glorious King of his Churches" had raised "an Army out of our English Nation" and created "a New England to muster up the first of his Forces in."[47]

Evidently, only a small group among the Puritans in England shared with Johnson and other emigrants the urgent need to remove to New England during this period. "The church and common wealth heere at home," wrote the well known Suffolk antiquary, Robert Ryece, to Winthrop, "hath more neede of your beste abyllytie in these dangerous tymes." But many also shared with those who emigrated to New England the deep-seated pessimistic view concerning the state of England at that time,

> where every place mourneth for want of
> Justice, where the...synnes goe
> unponished, or unreproved, crueltye and
> bloodde is in our streetes, the lande
> abawndeth with murthers, slawghters,
> Adulteryes, Whoredome dronkennes,
> oppression and pride where well doinge is
> not mayntayned, or the godly
> cherished, but Idollatrye popery and what so
> ever is evyll is cowntenanced, even the
> leaste of these, is enowghe, and enowghe to
> make haste owte of Babylon, and to seeke to
> dye rather in the wylderness than styll to
> dwelle in Sodome Mescheck and in the tentes of Kedar.[48]

Puritan notions of the "godly ruler" in both England and New England become more comprehensible in the light of such sentiments. For society, Puritans believed, was always on the verge of becoming un-Godly and falling prey to Satan. To prevent such a terrifying development, both in the future newly Christian commonwealth of Massachusetts and in the renewed Christian commonwealth in England during the Puritan Revolution, government had to be in the hands of godly Christian magistrates. At the same time, the Puritans' eschatological and apocalyptic visions concerning England's gloomy fate in the course of providential history clearly show what the emigrants thought they were leaving behind and what they would try to create on the other side of the ocean.

V Migration and the Rhetoric of Persecution

So far the discussion has focused on the Puritan migration as an event arising out of the Puritan experience in England in the early seventeenth century. We may further look at this process in closer detail through some biographies of ministers emigrating to New England. First, it is necessary to voice caution about the nature of the accounts themselves. For as J. Sears McGee reminds us, we are entering the realm of "the rhetoric of suffering" and "persecutions." That is, suffering and persecutions were always the mark of the true faith and signs of progress to those who sought after the truth, the history of the "true church" having always been conceived of in such terms. As with other religious movements, including orthodox members of the Church of England, Puritans "firmly believed" suffering and persecution "to be integral part[s] of God's plan."[49]

The rhetoric of persecution employed by ministers to justify their emigration to America was filled with accounts of struggles within congregations, among clergymen, between clergymen and parishioners, and between churches and local authorities. Clergymen thus shared with laymen the same social experience of competing factions within localities. In many cases, their suspension from their ministry and silencing by bishops and ecclesiastical courts came because of their opponents' complaints against them. Although there is evidence that the issue of non-conformity was not so crucial for many ministers who wavered between conformity and non-conformity all during the 1630s, nevertheless non-conformity represented something more than mere disassociation from the religious rites and ceremonies of the established Church of England. It also involved disassociation from the traditional cultural consensus that prevailed in a given community. Finally, the ministers' lives show, as we have seen in relation to the laymen, that the appropriate context to examine their reasons for emigrating is in the small worlds of their individual communities. For it was in this immediate world of their everyday lives that they faced strong opposition to their visions of godly life

40

and that presented them with the dilemma of whether they should or should not continue to live among "prophane" people.

No single common pattern emerges from a comparison of emigrating ministers' lives in England. Each minister came to the colony in the wake of experiences peculiar to his situation. Many came because they had "a call" from a congregation, which they could hardly refuse. Sometimes this call came from Massachusetts from a congregation that had heard of a certain minister being suspended in England. Thus Richard Mather got a "call from New England" in 1635 after he had been suspended form his English ministry the year before, while Thomas Shepard "began to listen to the call to New England" in 1633 after he was forbidden to preach in 1630.[50] The call could come of course while the congregation was still in England, as Roger Clap's company had called John Warham and John Maverick to be their ministers on the very eve of their emigration. But "many of them," wrote David Hall on the emigrant ministers, "came straight from England without having suffered any interruption in their ministry."[51]

A fairly common characteristic of the ministerial emigration was that Massachusetts Bay was not the first choice for many who subsequently became prominent in the colony. After he was summoned to the High Commission, Thomas Hooker departed for Holland in the summer of 1631. Although he had talked with Roger Williams, John Cotton, and Winthrop concerning the plans of the Bay company in 1629 to establish a Puritan colony in the wilderness of America, Hooker decided against crossing the Atlantic, even though many of his parishioners chose to remove to the colony in 1632.[52] After they had tried in vain to persuade Laud to restore them to a ministry in England, Thomas Shepard and Thomas Weld thought "to go first unto Ireland and preach there, and to go by Scotland thither."[53] Before his emigration, Cotton first considered moving to Holland before he thought of "Barbados and New England as possible refuges to be considered."[54] Richard Mather's case suggests another possibility open to ministers after they had been suspended from their ministry in England; they

41

could retire to private life. "Mather had not left England," writes Robert Middlekauff, "so full of confidence. The two years preceding his departure in 1635 had been marked by uncertainty about his ministry."[55]

It is important to bear in mind the circumstances of the above-mentioned ministers, for those men soon came to the fore as defenders of the "New England way" against criticism of Puritans in England. Thus, when Thomas Shepard wrote the "Preface" to his and John Allin's book, A Defence of the Answers, in 1648, he urged Puritans in England "to consider and look back upon the season of this great enterprise" in Massachusetts and tried to convince them that divine necessity caused the emigration:

> For was it not a time when human Worship and innovations were growne to such intolerable height, that the consciences of Gods saints and servants inlightend in the truth could no longer bear them?[56]

But reasoning of this sort was not evidenced by Shepard when he lived in England prior to his emigration in 1635. At that time he had eagerly attempted to have Archbishop Laud restore him to his old ministry. Indeed, one need only look at the subdued tone of his Autobiography to appreciate how reluctant he was to emigrate to America after his suspension in 1630.[57]

Still others were less reluctant emigrants. John Wilson, who came with Winthrop in 1630 and served as minister in the church of Boston, had been ready since the late 1620s to emigrate to the colony. In those yeas his religious search led him to begin "in the worship of God, to omit some ceremonies, which he felt to be instituted in derogation from the kingly power of Christ in his Church." And not much later he made a solemn resolution before God "that if the Lord would grant him liberty of conscience, with purity of worship, he would be content, yea, thankful, though it were at the furthermost of the world."[58] In other words, Wilson was already prepared for the call from Massachusetts. But Wilson was not typical of the ministerial emigrants.

John Davenport, vicar of St. Stephen's, Coleman Street, London, presents another perspective. One of the few ministers who were members of the New

England Company, Davenport also took an active part in and was a member of the Massachusetts Bay Company, though his name was omitted in the royal charter for this company; he also took an active part in the discussion involving the transfer of the charter of the Massachusetts Bay Company to America. Additionally, many of his church's members left for the Bay colony with Winthrop in 1630. Though he was a staunch Puritan, conformity was not his ultimate problem in these years, as the following passage shows:

> About January 1631, a bitter quarrel between the vicar of St. Stephen's and his curate over the wearing of the surplice, the reading of the litany, the significance of the cross in baptism, the admission of strangers to communion, and the curate's refusal to live in the plague-in-fested parish was brought to the attention of Laud. At this time Davenport was not ready to refuse to conform, and excuse his actions on grounds other than doctrinal, but was far milder in his denial of non-conformity to the canons of the Church of England than he had been in 1624.

The struggle between the vicar and curate in St. Stephen's church highlights yet another dimension of the Puritan migration to New England. In 1633, Davenport followed Hooker to Holland where he remained until he removed to Massachusetts just in time to help the synod at Cambridge and the colony against the Antinomians. After taking part in this "blessed work," however, he and many others found themselves at odds with the Bay colony over the precise form the emerging Christian commonwealth should take. Accordingly, in 1638 they left for New Haven where they endeavored to set up "a yet stricter conformity to the word of God, in settling of all matters, both civil and sacred."[59] The Massachusetts' version of "reformation according to God's word" did not satisfy all Puritans, as the examples of Davenport, Hooker, Roger Williams and many more zealous Puritans make clear. While Puritans shared many premises concerning the formation of the true church, they divided over the issue of the nature of a Christian commonwealth and the social applications of theological premises.

Like Davenport, Ezekial Rogers wavered throughout the 1630s between conformity and non-conformity. When he was suspended for reading the Book of Sports to his parish, he was offered absolution on the condition that he would stop "from reading service except according to the Book of Common Prayer." When he was finally suspended from his ministry in 1636, he returned to private life. Not until 1638 did he decide to remove to the colony. Peter Saxton likewise got in trouble with his parishioners, who prevailed on the ecclesiastical court to order him "to rede divine service as it [was] set down by the book and to wear the surples as it apointed." In 1640 he came over to Massachusetts but spent only a year there before returning to England. We know surprisingly little about this kind of social dynamic in relation to the ministers' migration, though there are many examples to show the power of parishioners against their ministers. In the deanery of Doncaster, for example, parishioners so "troubled their Minister that he was silence."[60] As these cases show, we should not take the Puritan ministers' accounts of their "persecution" without critical examination. In the case of Saxton, for example, it was the members of the church, not the minister, who felt "persecuted." Above all, these examples suggest that ecclesiastical courts and bishops tried to silence Puritan ministers only after receiving complaints from their churches.

As a young vicar of St. Botolph's in Boston, Lincolnshire, John Cotton also found himself a center of controversy. He came to Boston in 1612 and immediately engaged in debates with the Arminian party there, arguing the Puritan tenets of election and predestination against the universal redemption of his Arminian opponents. In the process of discribing the controversy between the two parties, Cotton's biographer gives us a vivid picture of what happened: "In all the great feasts of the town, the chiefest discourse at the table, did ordinarily fall upon Arminian points, the great offence of godly ministers, both in Boston and neighbour towns." Being a young man and newly installed in the church, Cotton waited a while before he entered the controversy, but finally, "by the strength of Christ," he began "publickly to preach, and in private meetings to defend the doctrine of God's <u>eternal election</u>...and <u>redemption</u> (ex gratia) only of the elect." Eventually, Cotton's "godly party" in Boston won this battle. As in many other cases, however, victory had its costs. Complaints about Cotton from the parish reached the bishop and brought the Puritan minister into serious conflict with the ecclesiastical courts. Fortunately, only through the aid of influential laymen was Cotton able to continue his ministry. "It hence came to pass," his grandson wrote

> that our Lord Jesus Christ was now worshipped in Boston, without the use of the <u>liturgy</u>, or of...<u>vestments</u>...yea, the sign of the cross was laid aside, not only in <u>baptism</u>, but also in the <u>mayor's mace</u>...because it had been so much abuse unto idolatory...a great <u>reformation</u> [came to Boston] <u>profaneness</u> was extinguished, <u>superstition</u> was abandoned [and] the <u>Satanical party</u> was become insignificant.[61]

Cotton's actions in old Boston, as well as the actions of other Puritans in other villages and towns in England, show clearly that Laud and his High Church party held no monopoly on "innovation" in matters religious and ecclesiastical; Puritans likewise experimented with new religious and social formulations. This view partly contradicts the traditional assumption on the part of historians that the religious struggle in England from the mid-1620s on was caused by Laud and his bishops' Arminian innovations. Among the myths bound up with Puritanism in that period, writes William Lamont, "the fifty myth is that the ideological innovators were, not the Laudians, but their Puritan critics." And Nicholas Tyacke, in an important article, states that "in terms of English Protestant history the charge in 1640 that King Charles and Archbishop Laud were religious innovators is irrefutable.[62] Yet, this assumption clearly depends too much on the Puritan charges against Laud, without critically examining the social backdrop of those charges. This is not to claim, of course, that Laudians were not engaged in innovations on their own part, but to attempt to put their actions in perspective: not only Laud and the Arminian bishops but the Puritans themselves were to a great extent innovators in terms of religious ways and manners.

45

The history of Francis Higginson's ministry illustrates the social effects of Puritan ministerial efforts to implement their theological premises.

> Mr. Higginson, before he became non-conformist, professed this principle, the ignorant and scandalous persons are not to be admitted unto the Lord's Supper: and so far as he could, he practised what he professed.

Consequently, those who were not admitted by him to the sacrament "threatned what they would do against" him. One, turned away by Higginson from the sacrament, "went out full of...passion and poison against Mr. Higginson, and horror in his conscience." Another, "a very profane gentleman," outraged that his wife came to hear Higginson's sermons, "vowed that he would be revenged on Higginson; and accordingly he resolved upon a journey to London, there to exhibit complaint against this good man, at the High Commission court." Here, once again, is a case of parishioners initiating complaints, upon which ecclesiastical courts acted and Puritans were "persecuted." In his own home town, Leicester, Higginson found many aroused against his ministry. One Doctor of Divinity who lived there and served as chaplain to the Crown, "vowed, that he would certainly drive" Higginson "out of the town." In another case, Higginson, through his godly manners, even aroused the anger of local authorities, who failed to appreciate his admonishment of the mayor and alderman for being "shamefully and extremely drunk." The temperance lecture

> was variously resented; some of the people disliked it very much, and some of the aldermen were so disturbed and enraged at it that they breathed out threatnings till they were out of breath; but the better sort of people generally approved it.[63]

As the case of Higginson shows, the issue of conformity vs. non-conformity was not merely religious and ecclesiastical; it was also social. Samuel Whiting, for example, who came to the Bay colony in 1636, fell into trouble in his town, Skirbick, England,

> for his non-conformity to the vanities which men had received by tradition from their Popish fathers, and this through the complaint of some unhappy men...that he found he must go.

And the vicar of Braintree, England, must have felt relief when the "godly" left his parish church in 1632 and emigrated to Massachusetts. "These persons," the vicar complained in 1631/2, "have laboured to make his person and ministry contemptible and odious, because he would not hold correspondence with them."[64]

VI Migration as an Act of Social and Religious Reformation

An examination of the biographies of individual ministers and laymen reveals the real world out of which the great Puritan migration to New England came, a world of conflict in local communities, parishes, churches, villages, and towns, wherein Puritans struggled to achieve religious and social reformation alike. In this endeavor, Puritans ran afoul first and foremost of fellow members of their own local societies, who worked to defeat their social and ecclesiastical program. In this context, naturally, the rhetoric of "persecution" is not adequate for the historian, for it includes only the Puritan view of social reality, not the view of those who opposed them. Nevertheless, these divided communities and churches provided one of the primary sources of the Puritan migration. Those who emigrated to the colony did so because in England their ideals of godly life met with stern opposition from those who did not share their notion of social and religious reformation. Thus, Higginson, who faced unfavorable conditions in his church, was ready to emigrate in 1629, while Cotton, who for some further time enjoyed favorable conditions in Lincolnshire, did not decide to go until 1633. The very issue of non-conformity was thus a social problem at heart, a problem arising out of the process by which godly people alienated not only ecclesiastical authorities but, more importantly, their own local communities. Where a minister had a favorable response to his efforts in his community, as in the cases of Cotton and Mather, he could maintain his non-conformity for an extended period of time. When a minister met with heavy opposition among fellow townspeople and magistrates, as did Higginson, however, emigration appeared a desirable prospect once the New England Company or Massachusetts Bay Company offered the opportunity.

The present discussion has focused on the Puritan migration as an event arising out of the Puritan experience in England in the early seventeenth century. It is the thesis of this study that the appropriate context for examining the Puritans' reasons for emigrating is the small worlds of their individual

48

communities. It was in these immediate worlds of their everyday lives that the Puritans faced opposition to their vision of godly life and the dilemma of whether they should or should not continue to live among "prophane" people. This view partly contradicts the traditional assumption made by historians that the great Puritan migration was caused by a certain "crisis" in England in the late 1620s or early 1630s. The differences between these two points of departure are clear enough. The former calls our attention to the long-term trends in English society in which puritanism increasingly revealed itself not only as an ecclesiastical power but also as a strong social and political force able to distrub and divide communities by its uncompromising plea for full social and religious reformation. The latter explanation, or theory of "crisis," in attributing the origins of the Puritan migration to events occuring at the actual time of the migration, ignores some profound developments in English society that took place well before, and continued well after, the Puritans had sailed to the New World.

Undoubtedly, only further reasearch will fully reveal the whole story of the origins and causes of the Puritan migration. This chapter however, has attempted to explore some dimensions of the real and actual world out of which the great Puritan migration came, a world of conflict in local communities, parishes, churches, villages and towns, in which Puritans struggled for religious and social reformation against fellow members of their own local societies who worked to defeat their social and ecclesiastical program. These divided communities and churches provided one of the primary sources of the migration, and we should look more closely into the process by which godly people alienated not only ecclesiastical authorities but, more importantly, their own local communities. We know suprisingly little about this kind of social dynamic in relation to the Puritan movement in England as a whole, and in relation to the Puritan migration in particular, though there exists much evidence attesting to the profound social, political and ecclesiastical consequences of the rise of Puritanism on English society in the early seventeenth century.

49

In general, then, it seems that the lessening of the prospects for reform on the local level and the interactions there between godly and "prophane" people determined the causes and origins of the Puritan migration to New England. Emigration emerged as a possible solution for many for whom the only alternative was life among the "prophane." After all, Puritans carried with them not only theological tenets but also new visions of a godly, Christian society. And when the attempt to achieve and build a godly society in England failed, some of the Puritans turned their eyes to New England, deeming it the ideal place to make their vision a reality. Thomas Tillam, for example, describes this Puritan expectation upon his first sighting of New England in the summer of 1638:

> Hayle holy-land wherein our holy lord
> hath planted his most true and holy word
> hayle happye people who have dispossest
> yourselves of friends, and means, to find some rest
> for Jesus-sake....
> Posses this Country, free from all anoye
> heare I'le be with yow, heare yow shall Injoye
> my sabbaths, sacraments, my ministrye
> and ordinances in their purity.[65]

But the urgency of the need for emgiration is perhaps best revealed by the Rev. Thomas Welde in a message he wrote in 1633 in Massachusetts to his friends in England:

> Here are none of the men of Gibea the sonnes of Belial knocking
> at our doors disturbing our sweet peace or threatening violence.
> Here blessed by the Lord God for ever Our eares are not beaten
> nor the aire filled with Oaths. Swearers nor Railers, Nor our
> eyes and eares vexed with the unclea[n] Conversation of the
> wicked.[66]

Yet Puritan New England was still within the dimension of time and history so that the Christian drama would continue there:

> but yet beware of Satan wylye baites
> he lurkes among yow, Cunningly hee waites
> to Catch yow from me; live not then secure
> but fight 'gainst sinne, and let your lives be pure
> prepare to heare your sentence thus expressed
> Come yee my servants of my father Blessed.[67]

To Tillam, Welde and many other Puritan emigrants, Massachusetts Bay, as the next chapter will attempt to show, had a special place in history. Alongside social and ecclesiastical considerations, the Puritan emigration was conditioned by millennial expectations and eschatological visions, or by unique Puritan apocalyptic interpretations of history.

Notes

1. Herbert Butterfield, The Origins of History (New York, 1981), p. 15.

2. H. Richard Niebuhr, "The Protestant Movement and Democracy in the United States," in The Shaping of American Religion, eds. J.W. Smith and A.L. Jamison (Princeton, 1961), I, p. 23.

3. "The Zealous Puritan," in Builders of the Bay Colony, by Samuel E. Morison (Boston, 1930), p. 45.

4. Richard Rogers, "The Diary of Richard Rogers," in Two Elizabethan Puritan Diaries, ed. M.M. Knappen (Chicago, 1933), pp. 61, 63, 64. For the emergence of the Puritan movement as a distinguishable religious culture of English Protestantism, see A.G. Dickens, The English Reformation (New York, 1964); Keith Thomas, Religion and the Decline of Magic (London, 1971); William Haller, The Rise of Puritanism (New York, 1938); Patrick Collinson, The Elizabethan Puritan Movement (Berkeley, 1967); H.C. Porter, Puritanism in Tudor England (Columbia, 1971); M.M. Knappan, Tudor Puritanism: A Chapter in the History of Idealism (Chicago, 1965); Leonard J. Trinterud, ed., Elizabethan Puritanism (New York, 1971); Michael Walzer, The Revolution of the Saints: A Study in the Origins of Radical Politics (New York, 1969); Peter Lake, Moderate Puritans and the Elizabethan Church (Cambridge, 1982); R.L. Greaves, Society and Religion in Elizabethan England (Minneapolis, 1981); J.S. Coolidge, The Pauline Renaissance in England: Puritanism and the Bible (Oxford, 1970); P. Collinson, The Religion of the Protestants: The Church in English Society (Oxford, 1982), Godly People: Essays on English Protestantism and Puritanism (The Hambledon Press, London, 1983), English Puritanism (The Historical Association, London, 1983); Stephen Brachlow, The Communion of Saints: Radical Puritan and Separatist Ecclesiology, 1570-1620 (Oxford, 1988); John R. Knott, Jr., The Sword of the Spirit: Puritan Responses to the Bible (Chicago, 1980); Horton Davies, The Worship of English Puritans (Westminster, 1948); C.M. Dent, Protestant Reformers in Elizabethan Oxford (Oxford, 1983); J.W. Martin, Religious Radicals in Tudor England (London, 1989), and Nicholas Tyacke, "Popular Puritan Mentality in Late Elizabethan England," in The English Commonwealth, 1547-1640, eds. Peter Clark, et al., (New York, 1979), pp. 72-92. Any discussion, however, of Puritanism should take into account Michael G. Finlayson's important study, Historians, Puritanism, and the English Revolution: The Religious Factor in English Politics Before and After the Interregnum (Toronto, 1983). For the social and political context in which the Puritan movement developed in England during the sixteenth and seventeenth centuries, see Christopher Hill, Puritanism and Revolution (New York, 1964); Michael Walzer, The Revolution of the Saints (New York, 1973); Perez Zagorin, The Court and the Country: The Beginning of the English Reovlution (New York, 1971); Conard Russell, The Crisis of Parliaments, English History, 1509-1660 (Oxford, 1971), and Parliaments and English Politics, 1621-1629 (Oxford, 1979); Lawrence Stone, Social

Change and Revolution in England, 1540-1640 (New York, 1965), and The Causes of the English Revolution, 1529-1642 (New York, 1972).

5.   Richard Rogers, Seven Treatises, Containing Such Direction as is Gathe.ed out of the Holie Scriptures, Leading and Guiding to True Happines, Both in This Life, and in the life to come, and may be called the practise of Christianitie, 2nd ed. (London, 1605), pp. 381-382, 385, 389. In the following discussion of "covenant" and its important role in Puritan experience in the early seventeenth century, I owe much to Patrick Collinson's important article, "Toward a Broader Understanding of the Early Dissenting Tradition," in The Dissenting Tradition, eds. C. Robert Cole and Michael E. Moody (Athens, 1975), pp. 3-38. The quotation is from page 21.

6.   Rogers, Seven Treatises, pp. 389, 497-498.

7.   F. Ernest Stoeffler, The Rise of Evangelical Pietism (Leiden, 1965), p. 28. For the dynamic of Puritan piety in England and America, see the important studies of Charles E. Hambrick-Stowe, The Practice of Piety: Puritan Devotional Disciplines in Seventeenth-Century New England (Chapel Hill, 1982), and Charles L. Cohen, God's Caress: The Psychology of Puritan Experience (New York, 1986).

8.   Rogers, Seven Treatises, p. 387.

9.   James C. Spalding, "Sermons Before Parliament (1640-1660) As a Public Puritan Diary," Church History (March, 1967), p. 26; John Winthrop, "Religious Experiencia," in Winthrop Papers, ed. Allyn B. Forber, 5 vols (Boston, 1629-1647), I, pp. 194, 199, 169, 213. On the use of family exercise among Puritans during the period, see: Christopher Hill, "The Spiritualization of the Household," Society and Puritanism in Pre-Revolutionary England (London, 1966). On Puritanism and education, see John Morgan, Godly Learning: Puritan Attitudes Toward Reason, Learning and Education, 1560-1640 (Cambridge, 1986). Among the many studies of the life of John Winthrop are Edmund S. Morgan, The Puritan Dilemma (Boston, 1958); R.C. Winthrop, Life and Letters of John Winthrop (Boston, 1869) and Richard S. Dunn, Puritans and Yankees, the Winthrop Dynasty of New England 1630-1717 (Princeton, 1962).

10.   John Winthrop, "Religious Experiencia," Winthrop Papers, I, pp. 194, 199, 169, 213.

11.   William Haller, The Rise of Puritanism (Philadelphia, 1972), pp. 36-37.

12.   Thomas Shepard, "The Autobiography," in God's Plot: The Paradox of Puritan Piety, being the Autobiography & Journal of Thomas Shepard, ed. Michael McGiffert (Amherst, 1972), pp. 42-43.

13.   Cotton Mather, Magnalia Christi Americana, or the Ecclesiastical History of New England, 1620-1698, 2 vols. (Hartford, 1820), I, pp. 276-277. On books available in Massachusetts in the early seventeenth century, see: C.F. Robinson, "Three Early Massachusetts Libraries," Colonial Society of Massachusetts, Publications 28 (1930-33).

14.   John White, "The Ten Vows," in John White, by Frances Rose-Troup (New York, 1930), pp. 418-422.

15.   Mather, Magnalia, I, pp. 324, 238-239;16. Larzer Ziff, The Career of John Cotton (Princeton, 1962), pp. 43, 49.

17. Perry Miller, The New England Mind: the Seventeenth Century (New York, 1939), Book IV, "Sociology," pp. 365-462, and "Appendix B, the Federal School of Theology," pp. 502-505.

18. Collinson, "Toward a Broader Understanding of the Early Dissent Tradition," p. 21.

19. Thomas Cobbett, A Just Vindication of the Covenant (1648), cited by Miller, The New England Mind: The Seventeenth Century, p. 378. For theological developments of the covenant theory, see: Klaus Baltzer, The Covenant Formulary in Old Testament, Jewish, and Early Christian Writing (Philadelphia, 1971); Champlin Burrage, The Church Covenant Idea (Philadelphia, 1904); S.A. Burrell, "The Covenant Idea as a Revolutionary Symbol: Scotland, 1596-1637," Church History 27 (December, 1958), pp. 333-350; Jens G. Moller, "The Beginnings of Puritan Covenant Theology," The Journal of Ecclesiastical History 14 (April, 1963) pp. 48-67; Everett H. Emerson, "Calvin and Covenant Theology," Church History 25 (June, 1956) pp. 134-144; J. Wayne Baker, Heinrich Bullinger and the Covenant (Athens, 1980), David Zaret, The Heavenly Contract: Ideology and Organization in Pre-Revolutionary England (Chicago, 1985), and Margo Todd, Christian Humanism and the Puritan Social Order (Cambridge, 1987). For the relationship between the covenant idea and the emergence of Congregationalism, see Geoffrey Nuttall, Visible Saints: The Congregational Way, 1640-1660 (Oxford, 1957); Edmund Morgan, Visible Saints: The History of Puritan Idea (Ithaca, 1963); Robert G. Pope, The Half-Way Covenant: Church Membership in Puritan New England (Princeton, 1969); Norman Pettit, The Heart Prepared: Grace and Coversation in Puritan Spiritual Life (New Haven, 1966); Brooks E. Holifield, The Covenant Sealed: The Development of Puritan Sacramental Theology in Old and New England, 1570-1720 (New Haven, 1974), and William K.B. Stoever, "A Faire and Easie Way to Heaven": Covenant Theology and Antinomianism in Early Massachusetts (Middletown, Conn., 1978).

20. Edward Arber, ed., "The Mayflower Compact," in The Story of the Pilgrim Fathers, 1606-1623, As told by Themselves, their Friends, and their Enemies (London, 1897), p. 409.

21. John Winthrop, "A Model of Christian Charity," Winthrop Papers, II, pp. 283-284.

22. Kenneth A. Lockridge, A New England Town, the First Hundred Years (New York, 1970), p. 5.

23. Richard D. Pierce, ed., The Records of the First Church in Salem Massachusetts, 1629-1736 (Salem, 1974), xiii, pp. 3-4; and Mather, Magnalia, I, p. 66.

24. Winthrop, "A Model of Christian Charity," pp. 283, 294.

25. Winthrop, "A Model of Christian Charity," p. 295.

26. Henry Orinel, cited by Margaret Spufford, Contrasting Communities, English Villagers in the Sixteenth and Seventeenth Centuries (Cambridge, 1974), p. 246.

27. Spufford, Contrasting Communities, pp. 262-263. See also M. Spufford, "Puritanism and Social Control?", in Order and Disorder in Early Modern England, eds. A. Fletcher and J. Stevenson (Cambridge, 1985), pp. 41-57. On the issue of the laity and the church, see Claire Cross: Church and People, 1450-1660, the Triumph of the Laity in the English

Church (Wiltshire, 1976) and The Royal Supremacy in the Elizabethan Church (London, 1969); J.T. Cliffe, Puritans in Conflict: The Puritan Gentry During and After the Civil Wars (London, 1988), and The Puritan Gentry: The Great Puritan Families of Early Stuart England (London, 1984); and William Hunt, The Puritan Moment: The Coming of Revolution in an English County (Cambridge, Mass., 1983).

28.   Tindal Hart, The Country Clergy (London, 1958), p. 27.

29.   R.C. Richardson, Puritanism in North-West England (Manchester, 1972), p. 27.

30.   Patrick Collinson, "The Godly: Aspects of Popular Protestantism in Elizabethan England," cited by Richardson, Puritanism in North-West England, p. 74.

31.   Alexander Young, ed., Chronicles of the First Planters of the Colony of Massachusetts Bay, from 1623 to 1636 (Boston, 1846), pp. 234, 142, 144 (hereafter cited as Young, Chronicles).

32.   John Winthrop, The History of New England, from 1630 to 1649, ed. James Savage, 2 vols. (Boston, 1853), I, p. 74 (hereafter cited as Winthrop, History).

33.   Isabel M. Calder, The New Haven Colony (New Haven, 1934), p. 16.

34.   Roger Clap, Memoirs of Roger Clap (Boston, 1844), pp. 18, 39.

35.   William Holden, Anti-Puritan Satires, 1572-1642 (New Haven, 1954), pp. 77, 80, 57, 83. On the Puritan concept of the Sabbath, see: Richard L. Greaves, "The Origins of English Sabbatarian Thought," The Sixteenth Century Journal 12 (Fall, 1981) pp. 19-34; Keith L. Sprunger, "English and Dutch Sabbatarianism and the Development of Puritan Social Theology, 1600-1660," Church History 51 (March, 1982); Patrick Collinson, "The Beginnings of English Sabbatasianism," Studies in Church and History, eds. C.M. Dugmour and C. Duggan, 1 (1964), pp. 207-221; W.U. Solberg, Redeem the Time: The Puritan Sabbath in Early America (Cambridge, Mass., 1977).

36.   Winthrop, "Religious Experiencia," Winthrop Papers, I, p. 196.

37.   Richard Baxter, The Autobiography of Richard Baxter, eds. J.M. Lloyd Thomas and N.H. Keeble (London, 1974), pp. 4, 6.

38.   Richardson, Puritanism in North-West England, pp. 27-28.

39.   Ibid., pp. 27-28, 48.

40.   Ziff, The Career of John Cotton, p. 49.

41.   Geoffrey F. Nuttall, Visible Saints, The Congregational Way, 1640-1660 (Oxford, 1957), pp. 134-135.

42.   William Ames, The Marrow of Sacred Divinity (London, 1642 [1623]), pp. 140-141.

43.   William Ames, Conscience with the Power and Cases Thereof (London, 1641[1630]), p. 63. On the close relationship between Ames and the great Puritan migration from its

beginnings, see: K.L. Sprunger, "William Ames and the Settlement of Massachusetts Bay," NEQ 29 (1966), and The Learned Doctor William Ames: Dutch Backgrounds of English and American Puritanism (Urbana, 1972).

44. Edward Johnson, Wonder-Working Providence of Sion Saviour in New England, 1628-1651, ed. J. Franklin Jameson (New York, 1910), p. 25 (hereafter cited as Johnson, Wonder-Working).

45. Ibid., pp. 23-25.

46. Godfrey Davies, The Early Stuarts, 1603-1660, second edition (Oxford, 1976). p. 76.

47. Johnson, Wonder-Working, pp. 23-25.

48. Robert Ryece to John Winthrop (1629), Winthrop Papers, II, p. 105.

49. Sears McGee, The Godly Man in Stuart England, Anglicans, Puritans and the Two Tables, 1620-1670 (New Haven, 1976), p. 18.

50. Increase Mather, Life and Death of Richard Mather, eds. B. Franklin and W.K. Bottorff (Athens, 1966), p. 20; Robert Middlekauff, The Mathers, Three Generations of Puritan Intellectuals, 1596-1728 (New York, 1971), p. 17; B.R. Burg, Richard Mather of Dorchester (Kentucky, 1976), pp. 14-20; Ziff, The Career of John Cotton, p. 63-70; Shepard, "The Autobiography," pp. 49, 55; Sargent Bush, Jr., The Writing of Thomas Hooker, Spiritual Adventure in Two Worlds (Wisconsin, 1980), p. 74.

51. David Hall, The Faithful Shepherd (New York, 1972), p. 73.

52. Bush, The Writing of Thomas Hooker, p. 53.

53. Shepard, "The Autobiography," p. 50.

54. Ziff, The Career of John Cotton, pp. 63-70.

55. Middlekauff, The Mathers, p. 20.

56. Thomas Shepard and John Allin, A Defence of the Answer, 1648, "Preface," p. 3.

57. Shepard, "The Autobiography," p. 55. See there also the excellent "Introduction" to Shepard's life by M. McGiffert.

58. Mather, Magnalia, I, pp. 277-278.

59. Calder, The New Haven Colony, pp. 13-31, 48; Mather, Magnalia, I, p. 296.

60. Ronald A. Marchant, The Puritans and the Church Courts in the Diocese of York, 1560-1642 (London, 1960), pp. 111, 276, 23, n. 3 and n. 4.

61. Mather, Magnalia, I, pp. 236-239; Ziff, The Career of John Cotton, pp. 43, 49.

62. William Lamont and Sybil Oldfield, eds., Politics, Religion and Literature in the Seventeenth Century (London, 1975), xxii; Nicholas Tyacke, "Puritanism, Arminianism

and Counter-Revolution," in <u>The Origins of the English Civil War</u>, ed. Conard Russell (New York, 1973), p. 143. See also, Tyacke, <u>Anti-Calvinist: The Rise of English Arminianism, c. 1590-1660</u> (Oxford, 1987).

63.   Mather, <u>Magnalia</u>, I, pp. 324-326.

64.   Mather, <u>Magnalia</u>, I, p. 454; Mary Jeanne Anderson Jones, <u>Congregational Commonwealth, Connecticut, 1636-1662</u> (Middletown, 1968), p. 14.

65.   Thomas Tillam, "Uppon the First Sight of New England, June 29, 1638," in <u>Seventeenth Century American Poetry</u>, ed. Harrison T. Meserole (New York, 1968), pp. 397-398.

66.   Thomas Welde, "A letter of Master Wells from New England to Old England...1633," Massachusetts Colonial Society, <u>Transactions</u>, Vol. XIII (1910-11), pp. 130-131.

67.   Thomas Tillam, "Uppon the First Sight of New England," pp. 397-398.

CHAPTER TWO:
THE ESCHATOLOGY AND APOCALYPSE OF THE PURITAN MIGRATION

What bitter blasts, what smarting storms have been felt in
England during the space of certain years, till at last God's
pitiful grace sent us your Majesty to quench firebrands, to
assuage rage, to relieve innocents.
                            --John Foxe, 1563[1]

Christian Princes, that would be counted truly Religious...must
with all principally to see to this, that the integrity of doctrine,
and the purity of Gods worship may be preserved least the
Church...fly away from them.
                            --Thomas Brightman, 1609[2]

At first, our queen Elizabeth
ended her life and Reign;
To shew that all hope is a breath,
soon come, soon gone again;
Unless as children we depend
On God the surest stay
                            --John Wilson, 1604[3]

In the days of the voice of the seventh angel, when he shall
begin to sound, the mystery of God should be finished... And
the seventh angel sounded; and there were great voices in
heaven, saying, The kingdoms of this world are become the
kingdoms of our Lord, and of his Christ; and he shall reign for
ever and ever.
                            --The Revelation of St. John[4]

For now is the time begun when Christ shal raigne in all the
earth, having all his enemies round about subdued unto him and
broken in peeces.
                            --Thomas Brightman[5]

59

When you see Jerusalem compassed with armies, then flee to the mountains.

--Francis Higginson, 1629[6]

I   The Eschatology of the Puritan Migration

In the spring of 1629, leaders of the Puritan migration to America circulated in England among themselves and their friends a pamphlet entitled "General Observations for the Plantation of New England."[7] Both in the grievances it lists as justification for the pending migration and in the general picture it presents of one group of Puritans critically reviewing the state of England in the early seventeenth century, this revealing document offers an excellent summary of the arguments and justifications - economic, social, political, and religious - employed by the Puritans themselves to explain why they were emigrating to New England.

One searches these "observations" in vain for any reference to the recent "crisis" of the late 1620s and early 1630s so frequently associated with the Puritan migration by modern historians. The 1629 "crisis of Parliament," issues of conformity and non-conformity, ecclesiastical questions of separation versus non-separation, even the specter of Laud and his hostility toward the Puritans - none of these explanatory staples of modern scholarship appear. As far as the Puritan authors of the General Observations" were concerned, it would seem that these particular events and issues were not determinative in their decision to emigrate. More than an isolated series of recent political crises, we must then conclude, motivated the Puritan migrants of 1629-30.

This is not to deny that the Puritans of the "Observations" viewed England as reeling in the midst of an ominous crisis; they did. But the crisis they feared was neither political in nature nor of recent vintage; it was, instead, a general profound historical crisis which they traced back to England in the late sixteenth century. It was, moreover, a crisis discussable not in terms of a "crisis of Parliament," but in terms of the course of salvation history, the place of England in sacred, ecclesiastical history, and the future meaning of the Massachusetts Bay colony in providential history. These, indeed, are the prominent concerns of the "Observations."

61

Puritans, like English Protestants as a whole, thought of history in terms of Church History, or Ecclesiastical History, which constitutes a unique mode of historical thought. History was the story of the Church, its successes and failures, from the first coming of Christ until His Second Coming, the Last Judgment Day, and the final Conflagration. "Dothe not the history of the Church give us many examples" runs the common rhetorical refrain of the "Observations." "To carrye the Gospel into those partes of the world, and to rayse a bullwarke against the kingdom of Antichrist which the Jesuites labour to rear up in all places of the worlde," said the "Observations," would obviously be "a service to the Church of great Consequence." What gave this endeavor even greater importance, however, was its relationship to the long-developing crisis of the Protestant Churches in England and Europe. During the early seventeenth century, "All other Protestant Churches of Europe" had been "brought to desolation," and it seemed to the Puritan authors of the "Observations" that Judgment was "cominge upon us." "Who knows," they asked, "but that God Hathe provided this place [Massachusetts], to be a refuge for many, whom he meanes to save out of the general destruction."[8]

To understand the meaning of the "General Observations," it is obviously necessary to explore this Puritan sesne of impending divine judgment, or, ultimately, to analyze the Puritan apocalyptic interpretation of history. Like English Protestants as a whole, Puritan proponents of emigration in Summer 1629 thought of history almost exclusively in terms of the story of the Church as it had moved through the labyrinth of time and space experiencing both successes and failures in its efforts to transform this world into the Kingdom of God. Their ideology, or philosphy, of history was based upon Church history, or Ecclesiastical History, which constituted a unique mode or historical thought; history is salvation history (Heilsgeschichte), in which the church is the central agency in the history of the human drama of redemption and salvation. The changing fortunes of the Church, Puritans believed, were directly related to God's pleasure or displeasure with its efforts to keep His Word. Hence, if the Church

62

of England continued to "imytayte Sodom in her pride and intemperance,...Laodicea in her luckwarmness,...Ep[esus] Sardis etc. in the sins for which their Candlesticke was removed...the Sinagogue of Antichrist in her superstition," declared the "Observations" in reiterating a belief common to many Puritans in late sixteenth century England, it would evoke God's wrath and lose its status as the "true church." To prevent such a frightening development, Puritans believed, the Church of England had to reform itself immediately from within. For if they knew anything, they knew that Christ judges His church on earth according to its purity and faithfulness in maintaining His Word.[9]

Following the death of the Catholic Queen Mary, or Bloody Mary the great scourge of Protestantism, English Protestants looked forward with high hopes to the reign of Elizabeth, anticipating a "true" reformation of the Church of England. But towards the end of her reign and increasingly under James I and Charles I, such great expectations, dependent upon the reforming zeal of the godly monarch, faded rapidly. The Church of England, Puritans were forced to conclude, yet stood in a corrupted state. For this continuing failure, Puritans feared, the English nation soon would have to answer to God's wrath in the unfolding apocalyptic drama of redemption and salvation. Here was a crisis of terrifying proportions in terms of England's role in sacred, ecclesiastical history. Unless the Church of England could be brought in harmony with the ways of Christ, England, many feared, would be called to account for its apostasy, or for its abandonment of God's word.

In this Christian scenario, wherein England, its church corrupted, confronted the righteous ire of God, America occupied a prominent place. Long before the Puritans of the "Observations" contemplated planting Massachusetts Bay, even before the separatist band of pilgrims in Holland considered removing to Plymouth, George Herbert, a poet and clergyman later in the favor of Laud, composed his poem, "The Church Militant" (circa 1613). Impressed by the apparent success of the Virginia Company of London, chartered in 1605-06,

Herbert envisioned America as the place of refuge for the true church in flight from the corruption of England:

> Religion stands on tip-toe in our land
> Readie to pass to the American strand.
> When height of malice, and prodigious lusts,
> Impudent sinning, witchcrafts, and distrusts
> (The mark of future bane) shall fill our cup
> Unto the brimme, and make our measure up...
> Then shall Religion to America flee.[10]

The vision of the gospel fleeing England for America was common. Thus, in 1634, Dr. William Twisse, later an illustrious Presbyterian contributor to the Westminster Assembly of Divines of the 1640s, inquired of a correspondent, "what your opinion is of our English Plantation in the New World...not discovered till this old world of ours is almost at an end." "Why may not that be the place of New Jerusalem?" Twisse queried.[11]

As these two examples suggest, from the early seventeenth century on, America had begun to be associated in the visions of Englishmen with the reformation of the church. How widely held these visions were among Protestants and Puritans can only be established by further research. The point here, though, is that these visions existed, and that gradually some minds in England began to reconstruct the New World as a center of sacred space and sacred time within the confines of providential history. As far as some Englishmen were concerned, then, reform in the Church of England in England was a fading prospect. On this point, Herbert and the Puritans of the "Observations" agreed. Yet they disagreed on a more vital point. For Herbert viewed religious declension in England as remediable. Towards that end he remained in England and became a minister.

Matters stood otherwise for Puritans destined to emigrate to New England. Like Herbert, they decried the religious decline in England, but where Herbert hoped for remedial action and the return of true religion, the Puritans saw only the malic of Antichrist triumphant in England. Brought up on the Old Testament prophecies of Ezekiel and Daniel, and the Book of Revelation in the New

Testament, those Puritans believed that before the heavenly city could appear upon earth and before the apocalyptic drama of redemption would be resolved, the godly had to engage with Antichrist in a long and bloody battle. And so, to an important degree, they thought of their migration to New England in accordance with their apocalyptic interpretation of history as an army ready here and now to take its part in the fight against Antichrist. "Thus you have a touch of the time when this work began," noted Edward Johnson in relation to the origins of the Puritan migration,

> when England began to decline in Religion...in this very time
> Christ the glorious King of his Churches, raises an Army out of
> our English Nation, for freeing his people from their long
> servitude under usurping Prelacy; and...creates a New England
> to muster up the first of his Forces in.[12]

The Puritan migration, then, as the emigrants themselves perceived it, was not simply a utopian search after religious reformation, a flight from corrupt history and degenerated human traditions, as it were; it was rather a confrontation within time and history, an earthly stand against the powers of Satan and Antichrist. Before we can fully analyze this aspect of the Puritans' "errand into the wilderness," however, we must first unravel the patterns and modes of the Puritan apocalyptic interpretation of history as it had taken shape in England in the decades preceding the migration.

The most prominent historian of the seventeenth-century "New England mind" attached little importance to eschatological visions and millennial expectations in the Puritan movement in either Old or New England. "In Calvinist circles of 1630," asserts Perry Miller, "speculation about the end of the world - particularly as to whether the Second Coming of Christ was to precede or follow the millennium, had become highly suspect." As Calvin himself was very suspicious of any discussion concerning the time and coming of the Kingdom of God or the second coming of Christ on earth, this assertion would be true enough - if only the Puritans in England had been thoroughly Calvinistic. But English Puritans were Calvinists only to a degree, and to identify them entirely with Calvin or Calvinism is to overlook to a great extent the theological emendations made by Protestants in England on Calvin's theology following his death.[13] By ignoring the overwhelming evidence in English Puritan writings that the pursuit of the millennium was indeed an essential feature of the movement and that discussion concerning prophecy about the second coming of Christ was widespread, Miller thus excised from the origins of the Puritan migration the Book of Revelation, or the Apocalypse. In so doing, he distorted not only our understanding of the ideological origins of this Puritan migration but of the "New England mind" in the seventeenth century as well.

Confronted, for example, with Increase Mather's claim "that the doctrine of millennium was a teaching of 'the first and most famous Pastors in New-English Churches,'" Miller, perhaps out of his faith in the Calvinism of the early emigrants, assays to refute Mather's statement. "This is one of those half-truths of which he was so prolific," comments Miller. In this way, Miller depicted eschatolgoical visions and millennial expectations in seventeenth century New England mainly as family affairs, or more precisely, a family affair - the private domain of the Mathers. "There was something in him and his son," writes Miller of Increase and Cotton Mather, "that impelled them along the dangerous road of millennial thought." "The two Mathers were, in this respect at least," continued Miller, "peculiar in New England; possessed by the true apocalyptic spirit, they marched into the Age of Reason loudly crying that the end of the world was at hand." By limiting in this way millennial prophecy to the peculiar imaginings of one New England family, Miller freed himself to argue that the pursuit of the millennium was a product of the New England experience. Asserting that millennial pursuits were not essential to Puritanism in either England or in the early years of New England, Miller attributed this pattern of thought to the developing New England mind. In this approach, Miller made millennialism an important component of the American Puritan notion of "declension," of the rise of American patriotism, and of the American jeremiad. For both Mathers, writes Miller, the "discovering of the doctrine of millennium...arose out of their experience, and may be called the supreme symbol of their patriotism." For both Mathers, he writes elsewhere, "the preaching upon special providence was a strategic device for arousing the emotions of a sluggish generation."[14]

By leaving both millennial thought and the Book of Revelation out of Puritan cosmology and experience in Old and New England, Miller failed to depict a major dimension of the seventeenth-century Puritan outlook. When Miller argued that for the Puritan the past was "a drama, written, directed, produced and prompted by God" and for that reason had to "be as full of meanings at one time as at another," he was not speaking falsely. But neither was he telling the whole story.[15] Against the vast evidence in Puritan writings, in fact, he neglected the whole dimension of the future. For as the Puritan conceived it, the Christian drama of salvation and redemption concerned not only past and present; it related to future time as well. In themselves, past and present events, considered apart from any larger framework, signified little. As prefigurements, though, of the millennium to come, they signified everything. With this idea in mind, Puritans responded to day-to-day events with a set eye on the upcoming millennium. To ignore this orientation is to ignore much of Puritanism and, consequently, to misapprehend the Puritan migration movement. For not only did Puritans believe in the imminence of the millennium; they also deemed themselves actors at the center of the crucial events leading up to that second coming of Christ. For them, the main drama of the Church lay in the near future, when, in pursuit of the millennium, they would themselves take an essential part in the battle between Christ and Antichrist. Without considering the dimension of the future and the place of these millennial expectations and eschatological visions in Puritan thought one can thus hardly understand either the Puritan movement in England before and during the Puritan revolution or the Puritan migration to New England as a part of the Puritan movement in England.

At its source, Puritan millennial expectation in England rested on the Book of Revelation. From the sixteenth century on, commentators tried again and again to crack the secret of this book and thereby to gain foreknowledge of the future. Evidence of this preoccupation abounds in the writings of many New England Puritans. In the notes to the "General Observations," they cited the Book of Revelation repeatedly. In what follows, I will describe, first, the historical pattern defined in the Book of Revelation; second, the contribution of Revelation to the development of the Puritan apocalyptic philosophy of history as a unique mode of historical thought in the early seventeenth century; and, finally, the connection of that apocalyptic interpretation of history to the actual Puritan migration.[16]

II Prophecy, Apocalypse and History

Toward the end of the first century, A.D., someone, later identified as John of Patmos, experienced visions on the island of Patmos and set those visions down in the Book of Revelation, or the Apocalypse. In these visions John confronted the essential paradox faced by the early Christians of the pre-Constantine era: How was it that God's people, true in God's faith, were persecuted in a world created and directed by God and over which God had complete control? According to another John in the New Testament, "In the beginning was the Word, and the Word was with God, and the Word was God.... All things were made by him; and without him was not anything made that was made" (The Gospel of St. John 1:1. This St. John should not be identified with John of Patmos the writer of the Apocalypse). But while creating the world, God also created those who refused to acknowledge him and his omnipotence power. "He was in the world and the world made by him, and the world knew him not, He came into his own, and his own received him not" (The Gospel of St. John, 1:10, 11). And so history, or that dimension of time from the Fall of Adam to the final Conflagration, was the story of mankind declining to acknowledge God and refusing to set the world according to His divine word and will. In this context, the persecutions of God's people were indeed a central part in the divine drama of Ecclesiastical History, or in the progress of the Church upon earth in its pursuit to transform the world into the Kingdom of God.

The Book of Revelation, it is important to note, is not a story of past historical events; it is, rather, history of prophectic, revelatory, visions which will take place in the future. Contrary to other books of the New Testament, the Book of Revelation does not deal with the "golden age" of Christianity in the past, of those events surrounding the first coming of Christ, but with the "golden age" of Christianity to come, with the second coming of Christ and his reign on earth alongside his saints. In this sacred, providential scheme, the history of the Church is liberated from the secular dimension of time, wherein the Church suffers in a world denying God as its creator and is projected into the sacred dimension of time, into that time when God or his Son makes the profane world holy again, or into that time in which the world once again would reconcile with its Creator. In this way, the Book of Revelation directs attention away from the Christian drama of the past and the present toward the Christian drama of the future. In the process, past history, per se, is de-emphasized. It takes on significance only insofar as it relates to the unfolding apocalyptic and revelatory drama of the future. This is the radical solution offered by St. John in the Apocalypse to the paradox of God's people persecuted in God's world. In effect, St. John circumvents the entire problem posed by present persecutions; their meaning, obscure at the moment, will be made clear by events to come. History has meaning, but that meaning will be determined by the future, not by events of the present. And so, St. John can conclude, the persecution and suffering of this world are part of God's plan, yet unknown to man; they are not evidence of a grand paradox.

What St. John saw on the island of Patmos was "the Revelation of Jesus Christ, which God gave unto him, to shew unto his servants things which must shortly come to pass." The vision was delivered through an angel of Christ (Rev. 1:1). In his first vision, St. John receives a commission from the Lord:

> I was in the Spirit on the Lord's day, and heard behind me a great voice, as of a trumpet, saying, I am the Alpha and Omega, the first and the last; and, what thou seest, write in a book, and send it unto the seven churches which are in Asia; unto Ephesus, and unto Smyrna, and unto Pergamos, and unto Thyatira, and unto Sardis, and unto Philadelphia and unto Laodicea. (Rev. 1:10, 11)

From his heavenly place, Christ looks down upon earth and his seven churches in Asia Minor, judging each according to their keeping of his word; "and all the churches shall know that I am he which searcheth the reins and hearts; and I will give unto every one of you according to your works" (Rev. 1:16; 2:23). Out of the seven churches, God sharply admonishes six: the church of Ephesus because "thou hast left thy first love," the church of Smyrna because it was rich and part of "the synagogue of Satan," the church of Pergamos because God found it containing sinners, the church of Thyatira for it "sufferest that woman Jezebel, which calleth herself a prophetess, to teach and seduce my servants to commit fornications, and to eat things sacrificed unto idols." The church of Sardis he admonishes because "I have not found thy works perfect before God," and the church of Laodicea because "I know thy works, that thou art neither cold nor hot: I would thou wert cold or hot. So then because thou art lukewarm, and neither cold nor hot, I will spue thee out of my mouth" (Rev. 2:3, 9.14, 20; 3:2, 15-17).

Only one church Christ praises and exalts as his true and faithful church on earth.

> And to the angel of the church of Philadelphia write...I know thy works; behold, I have set before thee an open door, and no man can shut it: for thou hast a little strength, and hast kept my word, and hast not denied my name.... Because thou hast kept the word of my patience, I also will keep thee from the hour of temptation, which shall come upon all the world, to try them that dwell upon the earth. Behold, I come quickly: hold that fast which thou hast, that no man take thy crown. Him that overcometh will I make a pillar in the temple of my God, and he shall go no more out: and I will write upon him the name of my God, and the name of the city of my God, which is new Jerusalem, which cometh down out of heaven from my God: and I will write upon him my new name. (Rev. 3:7-12)

But there is more in this book than God's admonitions to his six churches and his exalting of Philadelphia. For in its main part, the Book of Revelation contains many apocalyptic visions and prophecies concerning the prophetic culminative process of the history of salvation and redemption; Christ's Second Coming and the role of the Church and the saints at this time. Apocalyptic thought, writes Paul Christianson, contains three characteristics: "a polarized view of the universe, a catastrophic explanation of events, and a firm concern with prophecy and its fulfillment." Another essential component of apocalyptic vision is the belief that a struggle between evil and good will occur in the world and that this struggle is only part of a dualistic cosmic struggle between evil and good in the universe as a whole. Apocalyptic visions, then, tend to find a point

71

in time, in the future, when the divided world of heaven and earth will cease to exist, or when the duality between St. Augustine's concept of civitas dei and civitas terrena will be abolished. For St. John, the final apocalyptic struggle would be that between Christ and Antichrist. In the resolution of that battle - with Christ victorious - the split between heaven and earth would cease to exist, and the millennium would be at hand.[17]

The Book of Revelation, then, provided a radical solution to the paradox of the persecutions of God's people in God's world, or within a theocratic universe ruled directly and immediately by God's divine providence. But above all the Apocalypse offered a revolutionary conception of the role of God's saints in this world. For when St. John came to describe the future drama of the Church, he presented it as an indispensable part of a cosmic drama of the Church within the confines of the imminent apocalyptic events surroundings the battle between Christ and Antichrist in the future; he located the meaning of present persecutions and sufferings in the future rather than the past and thereby associated the ongoing temporal struggles of the saints on earth with the cosmic struggle between Christ and Antichrist. No longer where Church and saints only passive witnesses in time and history. Rather, according to the holistic pattern of Revelation, they now assumed a decisive role and power in raising the Kingdom of God on earth. For Puritans, as we will see later, the most important part of Revelation was, then, its explanation of these imminent future apocalyptic events and of the role of the saints in them.

After St. John writes down his commission from the Lord for the seven churches in Asia, "a voice" tells him, "Come up hither, and I will shew thee things which must be hereafter" (Rev. 4:1) There in heaven, "in the midst of the throne and of the four beasts, and in the midst of the elders, stood a Lamb as it had been slain, having seven horns and seven eyes, which are the seven Spirits of God sent forth into all the earth." Near the heavenly throne St. John sees "a book written within and on the backsides, sealed with seven seals." No one of earth or heaven can open this book and read from it except the slain Lamb, for "thou wast slain, and hast redeemed us to God by thy blood out of every kindred, and tongue, and people and nation. And hast made us unto our God kings and priests: and we shall reign on the earth" (Rev. 5:6, 1, 9-10).

From this point on, the main prophetic discussion in the Apocalypse centers on how and when the saints with the Lord will come to rule over the world. The slain Lamb, a "type" or symbol for Christ, opens the seven seals one by one and each of them contains a divine prophetic revelation on how God will deal with those who refuse to acknowledge him as the sole sovereign within a theocratic universe. The first seal is a white horse whose rider comes to conquer the world. The second is a red horse whose rider comes to take the peace from earth. The third rider on the black horse carried with him a pair of balances in his hand. The fourth seal is a pale horse and the name of his rider is death, and with him he brings hell. The fifth seal is a vision of those slain for God and Christ's shake on earth. "And they cried with a loud voice, saying, How long, O Lord, holy and true, dost thou not judge and avenge our blood on them that dwell on earth?" (Rev. 6:1-10). With the opening of the sixth seal God begins to shake heaven and earth to show to the world that the great day of his wrath has come. But, in the middle of this Apocalyptic event, the four angels assigned to shake earth are stopped by a fifth angel, who tells them, "Hurt not the earth, neither the sea, nor the trees, till we have sealed the servants of our God in their foreheads." Then the elected people from all the nations are sealed and ascend into heaven, and there before the throne of God they "serve him day and night in his temple: and he that sitteth on the throne shall dwell among them." Only then is the seventh seal opened: seven angels with seven trumpets, each in turn sounding his trumpet and bringing plague to earth. At the end of this vision, a mighty angel comes down from heaven and proclaims: "But in the days of the voice of the seventh angel, when he shall begin to sound, the mystery of God should be finished, as he hath declared to his servants the prophets." Consequently, the angel "sware by him that liveth for ever and ever...that there should be time no longer." With the destruction of the sinful world prophane, secular history cease. "And the

73

seventh angel" sounds his trumpet, "and there were great voices in heaven, saying, The kingdoms of this world are become the kingdoms of our Lord, and of his Christ; and he shall reign for ever and ever" (Rev. 7:3, 15; 10:6-7; 11:15).

Of special interest in this vision is the resolution of he polar split between heaven and earth: the world is abolished - along with history - and the way is cleared for the proclamation about the Kingdom of God. From the point of view of the dimensions of time, in this final stage of providential history the saints cross from the secular into the sacred dimension of time, and this transition corresponds to the transformation of the world into the Kingdom of God. Condemned to destruction, the sinful world suffers God's wrath. After God pours his judgment and brings the world from alienation to reconciliation with him, Christ and his saints reign eternal. This is, indeed, the traditional solution to the paradox of the godly persecuted in God's world.

Yet, the above vision is only one among many such visions in the Book of Revelation. In the others, a "radical" view of the Apocalypse is taken, wherein the earth itself becomes an indispensable part of the cosmic struggle between Christ and Antichrist, or Satan. The theme here is that at a certain point in time, earth and heaven, the secular and the sacred, will intermingle upon the stage of the world, and the discrepancy between them will be resolved through a cosmic apocalyptic struggle that will take place on earth. In this vision Christ appears no more as the slain Lamb; he is now a mighty warrior, engaged in holy war on earth. Alongside Christ in this battle stand the saints, no more patient sufferers of religious persecutions, and no longer passive witnesses to the cosmic spectacle, but active participants in the final and last battle between Christ and Antichrist. The radical implication of this view rests in that new role accorded the saints; they are now fighters in the redemptive drama of all time and history.

This transformation is apparent in the following vision:

> And there was war in heaven: Michael and his angels fought against the dragon.... And the great dragon was cast out, that old serpent, called the Devil, and Satan, which deceiveth the

74

whole world: he was cast out into the earth, and his angels were
cast out with him. (Rev. 12:7-9)

Thrown out of heaven, Satan now turns all of earth into a battleground against
Christ and the Saints. To help him in this war Satan raises many beasts.

[I] saw a beast rise up out of the sea, having seven heads and ten
horns, and upon his horns ten crowns, and upon his heads the
name of blasphemy...and it was given unto him to make war
with the saints, and to overcome them. (Rev. 13:1, 7)

In this clash the cosmic dualism of earth and heaven is broken. By arraying
against the heavenly on earth, Satan and his agents abolish the boundary between
the celestial battle in heaven and the terrestrial history of the Church and saints
in the world on earth. The whole universe becomes the field on which God and
Satan do battle. Against Satan and his beasts who roam the earth, "a Lamb stood
on the mount of Sion," surrounded by her many saints "having his Father's name
written in their foreheads," all ready to aid Christ. As the war wages on, an
angel descends from heaven to proclaim that "Babylon is fallen, is fallen," and
then another voice from heaven is heard to declare before the saints" "Come out
of her, my people, that ye be not partakers of her sins, and that ye receive not
of her plagues." God again pours his wrath on the earth through the seven
angels, yet even with the fall of Babylon the beast continues its war against the
Lamb and the saints. In this moment "heaven opened, and behold a white horse;
and he that sat upon him was called Faithful and True, and in righteousness he
doth judge and make war." The slain Lamb has now been transformed into a
mighty man of war:

His eyes were as flame of fire.... And he was clothed with a
vesture dipped in blood.... And out of his mouth goeth a sharp
sword, that with it he should smith the nations; and he shall rule
them with a rod of iron: and he treadeth the winepress of the
fierceness and wrath of Almighty God.

With this transformation of Christ from a meek Lamb into a warrior, the army
of saints on earth as well as "the armies which were in heaven" fall into step
behind him. Christ now leads his troops to the final skirmish. The beast and

false prophet are overcome and "cast alive into a lake of fire burning with brimstone." And Satan is bound, by "an angel come out of heaven," for a thousand years (Rev. 14:1, 8; 18:4; 19:11-15, 20).

With this last battle won, Babylon fallen, and Satan bound for a thousand years, those who fought and gave their lives for God and his son "lived and reigned with Christ a thousand years" (Rev. 20:4). This is the millennium, the thousand year rule of Christ and his Kingdom on earth. But the cosmic war is still not over; the millennium is only an interval in the larger cosmic struggle. For at the end of the thousand years,

> Satan shall be loosed out of his prison, And shall go out to deceive the nations which are in the four quarters of the earth, Gog and Magog, to gather them together to battle.... And they went up on the breadth of the earth, and compassed the camp of the saints about, and the beloved city. (Rev. 20:7-9)

This, finally, is the last battle. Defeated, Satan and his army are destroyed forever. The world is thereby brought into reconciliation with its Creator and transformed into a divine one. "A new heaven and a new earth" come into being, where "there shall be no more death, neither sorrow, nor crying...for the former things are passed away" (Rev. 21:1, 4). In this new world, "the holy city, new Jerusalem, coming down from God out of heaven, prepared as a bride adorned for her husband" (Rev. 21:2). With this marriage between Christ and his holy city, the Book of Revelation ends.

Viewed from the perspective of sixteenth- and seventeenth-century Puritans seeking guides to meaning and ultimately action, this latter vision of St. John's contains radical implications. As St. John sketches the drama, heaven itself stands no more removed than earth from Satan's threat, for Satan covets sovereignty over the entire universe, heaven included. God's earlier successful expulsion of Satan and his agents from heaven represents but a temporary victory, of no comfort now in the face of Satan's cosmic ambition; thus, earth, Satan's present domain, becomes the scene for history's final reckoning. In this exigency, the role of Christ and his saints in this world must be an active one.

76

In St. John's vision, the meek Lamb and saints are transformed into soldiers of God. And in the process, all dualism in the universe vanishes. Heaven and earth flow into one another; the distinction between secular and sacred time, terrestrial and celestial space, prevalent in St. John's earlier vision, no longer applies. And finally, in this vision's apocalyptic culmination, New Jerusalem descends to earth, where Christ and his saints are united and all live in holiness forever.

The radical setting of this vision, as compared to any previous one, is apparent: in the apocalyptic events precede the establishment of the Kingdom of God on earth, there is no further need for this kingdom to dwell in heaven after the abolition of the dichotomy in the universe between good and evil as mutually exclusive entities, each with its exclusive place in the cosmos. What St. John thus holds out in this vision is nothing less than the possibility for a union of the visible Church on earth with the invisible Church in heaven, or the Militant and Triumphant Church, and the correlation between these two churches on earth. So long as the dualism between earth and heaven is maintained, as was the case in the previous visions, ultimate accommodation between the two was impossible because the visible, or Militant, Church belonged to the secular dimension of time and was thus temporal, while the invisible, or Triumphant Church, belonged to the sacred and was thus eternal. But once, as in St. John's vision, the cosmic drama fused the two dimensions of time and space, the marriage between visible and invisible Church became possible. Indeed, as the history of salvation drew to its conclusion, the predestined union of earthly and heavenly churches became inevitable, as heaven and earth became one in the millennium. Yet, just as the advent of the Kingdom of God, or the millennium, indicated the reconciliation between heaven and earth and the transformation of the world into a divine and holy one, so, also, along with the divine forces, the saints now on earth had themselves to endeavor to fulfill their part in the apocalyptic drama at hand. What is important here, then, in relation to the Puritan movement in England, is that the Book of Revelation pointed to the possibility of perceiving the role of the saints on earth in a radical way - as witnesses in their acts to the divine prophecy.

77

As close readers of St. John's text, many Puritans in England shared this perception. Indeed, they became not just readers of the Book of Revelation but actors in it, that is, active participants in the drama of providential history. As such, they had to assume their proper roles in the cosmic apocalyptic drama of human salvation and redemption. As earthly, secular time wound down towards the millennium, and salvation history reaching its final culmination, they had to perform their final parts. For these English Puritans, the Book of Revelation thus pointed the way toward an active involvement in what they understood as history's final phase. And just around the corner loomed the millennium.

Accordingly, when the Puritan authors of the "General Observations" chose to cite as their first reason for contemplating emigration to America their desire "to rayse a bullwarke against the kingdom of Antichrist," they were not engaging in rhetorical pretense or embellishment, but rather giving expression to their deepest beliefs: beliefs acquired through their reading of Revelation. And when Edward Johnson in Massachusetts Bay wrote on the Puritans' life there, he clearly revealed in what sacred, prophetic historical context the Puritans viewed their emigration into the wilderness and what role Massachusetts Bay would play in raising the Kingdom of God on earth:

> Further know these are but the beginnings of Christ glorious Reformation, and Restauration of his Churches to a more glorious splendor than ever.... And behold the worthies of Christ, as they are boldly leading forth his Troopes into these Westerne Fields, marke them well Man by Man as they march, terrible as an Army ... ther's their glorious King Christ one [on] that white Horse.... Behold his Crown with Carbunkles, wherein the names of his whole army are written.... Listen a while, hear what his herauld proclaimes, Babylon is fallen, is fallen.[18]

Indeed, outside the context of the Book of Revelation, few of the decisions and actions of the emigrating Puritans to America make sense.

III Thomas Brightman and the Millennium at Hand

1. English Apocalyptic Tradition

The Book of Revelation has influenced European history for many centuries, as Norman Cohn shows in his The Pursuit of the Millennium. While confining himself strictly to "the world of millenarian exaltation and the world of social unrest," Cohn vividly traces the "millenarianism that flourished amongst the rootless poor of western Europe between the eleventh and the sixteenth centuries," and the persistent belief in those centuries that "beyond the extermination of all evils lay the Millennium." G.H. Williams, in his The Radical Reformation, shows the power of the millennial impulse among the many religious movements and groups of radical reformers of the sixteenth century, and the connections pertaining between their search for religious and social reform and the prophecies of the Book of Revelation. England was not outside this world of sixteenth century millennial expectations and eschatological visions, in which the struggle for religious reformation against Rome and the Pope was cast along lines derived from a reading of the Apocalypse.[19]

Indeed, from the very beginning of the Reformation in England, Protestants found in Revelation a source for explaining the rift with the Catholic Church. Considering this book as true prophecy, Englishmen, like Protestants on the continent, tended to read out of it the context of their time and history. "Starting in the 1530s with John Bale," according to Paul Christianson, "English reformers found in the apocalyptic mysteries of the Book of Revelation a framework for reinterpreting the history of Christianity and explaining the break from the Roman Catholic Church. Identifying the papacy with Antichrist and the Roman Catholic Church with Babylon, they pictured the reformation as a departure from the false church that derived its jurisdiction from the devil."[20] Applying the prophecies of Revelation to describe the special conditions of the Reformation in England in that time, English Protestant reformers developed through their Biblical exegesis a unique apocalyptic philosophy of history, based on the historical pattern offered

79

by the Apocalypse, in which England occupied a special position in the battle between Christ and Antichrist which would determine the whole course of sacred, providential history.

Most notable among sixteenth century English Protestants attempting to relate contemporary historical events to the Book of Revelation was John Foxe, who used the Apocalypse as the basis for his most popular and influential book, Actes and Monumentes, commonly known as "The Book of Martyrs" (1563). In this religious classic of Elizabethan England, Foxe set his stories within an apocalyptic framework, one which was "clearly based on the Book of Revelation." Tracing the ecclesiastical history of England from apostolic times down until the reign of Queen Elizabeth, Foxe emphasized the unique role England had as Elect Nation in God's divine plan of the future course of sacred, ecclesiastical history.[21]

According to Foxe, England had always fought Antichrist, even from the earliest days when Christianity was planted there. But along with many Marian exiles who had fled from England during the reign of the Catholic Queen Mary, or Bloody Mary, Foxe looked upon his own period as the one in which the fight between Christ and Antichrist would finally reach a climax, or as that time in which the whole mystery of the history of salvation would be resolved. In his monumental book he traced the ecclesiastical history of England from the apostolic times until the reign of Queen Elizabeth and emphasized the unique role of England as the Elect Nation in God's divine plan. In "this account of Church history," wrote William Haller, Foxe showed that a "long succession of the native rulers down to Elizabeth" owed "their authority directly to divine appointment" and "made plain that by all the signs to be found in scripture and history the will of God was about to be fulfilled in England by a prince perfect in her obedience to her vocation, ruling a people perfect in their obedience to her authority."[22]

Indeed, to Foxe, as to many other English Protestants of that time, the early reign of Elizabeth offered renewed evidence of the destiny of England as the Elect Nation: the true reformation in England was being fulfilled through the imperial instrument - the prince - who was leading the fight against Antichrist in the world. But what if the prince failed to fulfill his or her divine mission to lead the true reformation in England and the nation as a whole against Antichrist? "The certainties of one age," noted R.H. Tawney, "are the problems of the next,"[23] and toward the end of the sixteenth century and the beginnings of the seventeenth century, many Protestants and Puritans in England faced nothing but obstacles. For in spite of all their efforts, the prince had failed in the long expected reformation of the Church of England.

"It was of the utmost importance," wrote William Lamont in his important study of religion and politics in England during the seventeenth century,

> that Foxe's work conditioned English Protestants to look to the Book of Revelation for salvation...centrifugal impulses were held in check by Foxe's emphasis on the decisive role to be played by the Christian emperor and his Church. Yet, Foxe's eschatological brinkmanship depended upon faith in Crown and bishop that became increasingly implausible for many in the reign of Charles I. What happened in 1641 was the rejection of Foxe, not the Book of Revelation. Centrifugal millenarianism replaced centripetal millenarianism.[24]

Lamont has here isolated a crucial aspect of the Puritan movement before and during the Puritan Revolution, but with his distinction between the two impulses of millenarianism, he has also provided a much valuable perspective on the Puritan emigration to Massachusetts, for that migration is indeed evidence, along with the behavior of many other Puritan groups before the Civil War, to the centrifugal millennial tendencies that arose in Puritan circles in the early seventeenth century.

Throughout the second half of the sixteenth century, and the first half of the seventeenth century, centrifugal millennial tendencies led those radical religious groups in England who searched after the true reformation to separate from the Church of England or to seek the fulfillment of the premises of reformation outside the established church. Separatist eruptions in England occurred in London, 1566, Norfolk, 1580, and London, 1590. Another wave of separatist activity took place in Norwich in 1605 and 1606.[25] There John Robinson, for example, the minister of the Pilgrim fathers, "believed the time had come to flee the established church, that 'habitation of devils,'" because it "'hold of every foul spirit and...cage of every unclean and hateful bird.'"[26] But for the mass of English Protestants or Puritans the prospect of Separation - the extreme choice available to those dissatisfied with the established church - stood out as an unforgivable heresy. For these people, traditionally, England had been accepted as the stage for the working out of the millennium, with the Church of England and its head, the English monarch, as the central agency in the providential drama. However, with the Puritan failure under Elizabeth, this "orthodox" relationship among the Church of England, the godly Prince, and the millennial prospect came to be reconsidered by many, and millennial expectations focused on the prince began to decline. This shift in the early seventeenth century toward centrifugal millenarianism was conditioned to a large extent by the writing of one of the most famous contemporary commentators on the Book of Revelation - Thomas Brightman.

2. Brightman and Pursuit of the Millennium

Thomas Brightman, 1562-1607, a biblical commentator, celebrated preacher, and one of the most prominent figures in English apocalyptic tradition of the 16th and 17th centuries, was born in Nottingham, admitted a pensioner at Queens' College, Cambridge, in 1576, of which he became fellow in 1584. He graduated B.A. in 1580-81, M.A. in 1584, B.D. in 1591. In 1592 Sir John Osborne gave him the rectory of Hawnes in Bedfordshire. He was celebrated as a preacher, yet his disaffection to the church establishment was no secret, and he frequently discussed the issue of church ceremonies, though he subscribed to the "Book of Discipline." Brightman's commentary on the Book of Revelation, Apocalypsis Apocalypseos, or The Revelation of the Revelation, 1609, which he claimed writing under the inspiration of divine inspiration, had crucially influenced the Puritan movement in England before and during the Puritan Revolution. Ultimately, Brightman's identification in his book of the Church of England with the sinful church of Laodicea of the Apocalypse, was one of the main sources for the Puritan's fears concerning the imminent judgment God's divine providence would inflict upon England as prophecized in the Apocalypse.

Foxe had influenced generations of Englishmen to look on England as the Elect Nation and to look to the Prince as God's instrument in the redemption process. Brightman likewise believed England to be the God's chosen nation, but as he made clear he no longer considered the Prince as occupying the decisive role in the English Reformation. "Brightman argued against expecting too much from a Godly Prince," wrote Lamont, because for him "the Godly Ruler frustrates, not advances, Godly Rule."[27] Behind this turn-about lies the Puritan experience in Elizabethan England, as described so meticulously by Patrick Collinson. The story of "the Elizabethan Puritan Movement," writes Collinson, is in the first place the story of "the politics of the attempt, and of the failure" of Puritans "to secure reform in the whole body of the Church, and by means of public authority...to complete the English Reformation."[28] Brightman's book, on the one hand, can be seen as evidence of the failure, in Puritan terms, to reform the Church of England under Elizabeth. But, on the other hand, his book is more than a mere description of the Prince's failure to lead the religious reformation in England. For his exegesis of Revelation offered, above all a radical interpretation of the Revelation prophecies, an interpretation, moreover, that constituted a unique apocalyptic view or interpretation of history. And up to and during the Puritan Revolution, Brightman's interpretation of Revelation and his philosophy of history greatly influenced Puritans. Indeed, it is Brightman's view of Revelation and apocalyptic interpretation of history that we see reflected in the reasoning and arguments of the "General Observation."

Brightman was the first apocalyptic commentator in England to see in the Book of Revelation the possibility, always present in the text, of a correlation or union between the Visible and the Invisible Church, and he was the first to place this reading within the English historical context. In the English apocalyptic tradition before Brightman, John Bale, in his The Image of Both Churches, 1550, had taken "St. Augustine's idea of the two cities and transformed it into that of the two churches - one headed by Christ and the other by Antichrist."[29] Bale, that is, always kept strictly in time and history the realms between heaven and earth and made this dualism the essential feature of history until the second coming of Christ. Likewise, Foxe in his book followed Bale's dualistic view of history and time, adding to it his stress on England as the Elect Nation. But for both, it should be emphasized, the answer to the mystery of time or the fulfillment of the prophetic revelations in the Apocalypse lay in the future; that is, "Bale awaited the opening of the seventh seal, the opening of that time when the elect would glory in the fall of Babylon and the erection of New Jerusalem," and Foxe likewise foresaw the role of the Elect Nation, led by a Protestant Prince, in fighting Antichrist in future times to come.[30]

With Brightman, the English apocalyptic tradition was transformed. For, according to him, the age of the millennium had already begun in time and history:

> for now is the time begun when Christ shal raigne in all the earth, having all his enemies round about subdued unto him and broken in peeces.[31]

He believed this, in contrast to Bale, for example, because for Brightman the sound of the "last trumpet" had already sounded and blasted in history. Following Revelation, which states that "in the days of the voice of the seventh angel, when he shall begin to sound, the mystery of God should be finished," or more specifically, that

> the seventh angel sounded; and there were great voices in heaven, saying, the Kingdoms of this world are become the kingdoms of our Lord, and his Christ; and he shall reign for ever and ever (Rev. 10:7; 11:15),

Brightman indeed thought himself alive in the time of the seventh trumpet, which came in Revelation after the opening of the seventh seal. That is, he believed himself part of that time in history when the whole mystery of redemption and salvation would be revealed and the Kingdom of God would reign on earth. He

84

identified the year 1555 as "some two or three years before the Seaventh Trumpets blast." Thus, to him the accession of Elizabeth in 1558 was the year in which this trumpet sounded in history. Consequently, from Elizabeth's accession on, the whole holistic drama of history would unfold:

> For now is the last Act, begun of most long & dolefull Tragedy, which shall wholy overflow with scourges, slaughters, destructions, but after this Theater is once removed, there shall come in roome of it most delightfull spectacle of perpetual peace, joyned with aboundance of all good things.[32]

Of course, the millennium might not finally arrive until long after Brightman's lifetime, but the importance of his apocalyptic interpretation lay in the fact that he fixed for himself - and for many Puritans in the early seventeenth century - the early reign of Elizabeth as the period of the blasting of the seventh trumpet. This period, it will be recalled from Revelation, is that time in which the whole dualistic structure of the universe is broken: a war, begun in heaven, spreads to earth, so that earth finally becomes the scene of the whole cosmic drama, out of which emerges the Kingdom of God. This is the period, then, in which after many apocalyptic events, including the destruction of Babylon, the millennium is at hand. Thus, according to Brightman,

> The time is at hand; the Event of things immediately to be done...the things to come are no lesse certaine; But for us, who have seene the consent between the event and the Prophecy for the space of a thousand & five hundred yeares, that is, ever since the dayes of John, we can not possibly doubt, any longer touching those few events which yet remaine to be accomplished.[33]

This sense of the millennium at hand, so characteristic of Brightman's exegesis of Revelation, and so different from previous apocalyptic commentaries, stems from the historical perspective he gave to the prophecies of the Apocalypse. For according to Brightman, with Constantine the Great, who made Christianity a church state in the Roman Empire, "the Divell was bound...for thousand years." in 1300 the Devil or Satan had escaped from his captivity and begun to wage war against Christ and his saints. And he dated the late seventeenth century as the time of the end of Antichrist ("the last end of Antichrist shall expire at the year 1686"). Thus, between these two periods transpired the battle between Christ and Antichrist, in which saints gathered around the Lord in his wars on Mount Sion. Consequently, the church paraded throughout this period as the "Militant Church," a church which gradually spread the kingdom of Christ on earth through religious reformations against Satan and Antichrist. But because Satan and his agents were to wage war against Christ for only 390 years, according to Revelation, Brightman calculated that at the end of the seventeenth century, after the final destruction of Antichrist, the saints with Christ would rule on earth. In this time, "all nations shalbe at the Churches command, & that at a becke, requiring & taking lawes & ordinances from it, whereby they may be governed."[34]

It is evident, then, that Brightman, as it were, immersed the millennium in history. For from 1300 on, the saints and Christ had been engaged in the apocalyptic drama as foretold by Revelation, and world history from that time on revealed the spreading of God's Kingdom on earth. Consequently, by making a revelation of time and history out of the Apocalypse, Brightman emphasized the crucial role of the saints in this world. For the saints, reformation and renewed covenant with the Lord no longer simply signified man's existential salvation alone but became a necessary condition for eschatological salvation as a whole, a vital act in the last and final cosmic battle on earth between Satan and Christ, and ultimately in the all time drama of human salvation and redemption. So when Brightman calculated that the blast of the seventh trumpet proclaiming the coming of the Kingdom of God on earth occurred in the year 1558, he infused a strong eschatological impulse into early seventeenth century Puritan millennial discourse. "This is the last time," wrote Thomas Goodwin three decades after Brightman, "because it is the perfection of the other...and therefore seeing these are the last days, the nigher the day approacheth, the more shall we endeavour to do God service."[35] And Milton, who in his ecstatic vision saw England as "a noble and puissant Nation rousing herself like a strong man after sleep, and shaking her invincible locks," or as "an Eagle muing her mighty youth, and kindling her undazl'd eyes at the full midday beam; purging and unscaling her long abused sight at the foundation it self of heavn'ly radiance" - he, too, was convinced that "thy Kingdom is now at hand, and thou standing at the dore. Come forth out of thy Royall Chambers, O prince of all the Kings of the earth, put on the visible roabes of thy imperial Majesty, take up that unlimited Sceptor which thy Almighty Father hath Bequeath'd thee; for now the voice of thy Bride calls thee, and all creatures sigh to bee renew'd."[36]

By insisting upon the strictest correlation between prophecy and history, Brightman transformed the millennium into an attainable, historical goal to be realized in an immediate future by the saints and Christ under some terrestrial reign; and it was through his historical interpretation of prophecy - his correlation of events described in Revelation with historical events and periods - that he instilled new meaning into the search for reformation in early seventeenth England

Yet in order to infuse the millennium into time and history, Brightman had to interpret Revelation in different ways from his predecessors. According to E.L. Tuveson, "the Protestants of the sixteenth century" accepted St. Augustine's interpretation of Revelation, in which he stressed the view that "the reign of the saints...is not to be earthly; it refers only to their glorified state in heaven."[37] But not Brightman. He in fact replaced St. Augustine's dualistic view of the universe by finding a point in time when history and prophecy, the heavenly city and the earthly city, would coalesce, or when the visible and invisible Church would unite. For this reason he constantly warned against reading Revelation in dualistic cosmological terms: "Heaven here is not distinguished from earth in distance of places, but in the holiness of faith and manner." Or in another place:

> Heaven doth every where in this Book, signify the universal Church...because...it can have no more expresse image than this upon earth.

And when Brightman faced in Revelation the sentence, "And the armies which were in heaven followed" Christ (Rev. 19:14), he glossed, "that is, the Cittizens of the Holy Church uppon earth." Accordingly, to him new Jerusalem was not in heaven and descending to earth from there,

> But as touching this new-Jerusalem...it is not that Citie which the Saintes shall enjoy in the Heaven...but that Church that is to bee looked upon earth, the most noble and pure of all other, that ever have been to that tyme.[38]

By identifying the heaven of Revelation with earthly phenomena, Brightman was able to replace Augustine's dualistic heaven/earth view of the cosmos, with his own view of a cosmos marked by an essential dualism within the earthly realm. Thus, the angels in Revelation were to him "those Ministers of the truth," and "the Person of Antichrist" was "not any certaine & singular man: but a long succession of many men." This reduction to the plane of earth of the dualistic outlook also carried important implications concerning the battle on earth between godly and profane people. When Revelation stated that "the Dragon was cast out upon the earth" (Rev. 13:9), Brightman identified those cast out as all

> out of the borders of true and Holy Church, not only among the profane nations, but also among the rest of Christian people, that was any wayes disagreeing from, or contrary to sinceer piety....
> That which called heaven and earth, was called the Temple and the Court.

Thus the apocalyptic war that characterized the dualism between earth and heaven now enveloped human society on earth. In this new dualism, the Church struggled against those who "disagree to sincere piety" because they belong to Satan. Accordingly, the Dragon or Satan is lurking now within the present church, and the reforming church must cast him out. Thus, according to Brightman, "obstinate sinners, which will not yeald to admonitions, are given up to Satan by the ecclesiastical censure, and are cast out of the Church."[39] With this reformulation, Brightman bestowed upon the next generation of Puritans a formidable weapon. For by replacing the old cosmic apocalyptic dualism of Augustine with his own intra-human society apocalyptic vision, Brightman

88

generated new meanings in the search after true reformation in England in the early seventeenth century.

3. Brightman and the Apocalypse of History

But in order to put the millennium in time and history, as it were, and to uphold his own dualistic view that the apocalyptic struggle between Christ and Antichrist is an immanent struggle within earthly, terrestrial realm, Brightman also had to show that the Book of Revelation described not only sacred revelatory events to come but also contained prophecies with actual historical substance. This he did by arguing that the events in the Apocalypse, or the image of the seven churches there, corresponded to certain, well-defined, historical events in past and present. Hence, his claim that the seventh trumpet had indeed blasted in 1558. "These seaven Epistles," wrote Brightman, "respected not onely the present condition of the seaven Cities, but do...comprehend the ages following for a long tyme."[40] Consequently, if in Revelation the churches, except Philadelphia, moved from the ancient purity of apostolic, primitive, times into decline and degeneration, they also moved in time - according to the holistic pattern of the Apocalypse - toward history's eschatological climax and the apocalyptic events of the Christ's Second Coming. Likewise, according to Brightman, the history of the Church on earth was the story of the Church's approach toward that time when the visible and invisible Church would unite on earth.

It is important to discern Brightman's holistic interpretation of history and its characteristics, because it had enormous influence in England; for through Brightman's apocalyptic interpretation Puritans grasped the meaning of their time and their unique place in history. His book writes Christianson, "gave singular inspiration to the radicals of the early 1640s."[41] His book also gave to Puritan advocates of emigration an apocalyptic historical perspective from which to assess the state of the Church of England and later the redemptive significance of the "Wilderness" in America. For by correlating events described in Revelation with time and history, Brightman envisaged the Kingdom of God to be within the framework of history. And through his construction of the Church's history out of the Apocalypse, from the first until the second coming of Christ, Brightman inspired Puritans to look on their own time as that of the seventh trumpet, a time in which the whole mystery of salvation history would be resolved. Among those he inspired were the Puritans of the "General Observations," who accepted Brightman's identification of the Church of England with Laodicea the sinful Church of the Apocalypse, and used Brightman's fashioning of the term "Church of the Wilderness" in their conceptualizing of their sacred "Errand" into the wilderness in America. It is, then, Brightman's interpretation of history that stood behind the arguments and reasonings for the Puritan planting of the Massachusetts Bay colony.

In his delineation of church history, Brightman endeavored to relate each church in Revelation to an actual historical counterpart. His working assumption in this effort was that each church in Revelation signified a "type," and that each "type" possessed a "counterpaine" - the historical time or period to which the "type" was correlated. In this way, he applied each epistle of Christ to his churches to a particular historical period of time. Thus, in Brightman's presentation, the first church in Revelation, Ephesus, corresponded to that "of the first Christian Church, which taking his beginnings from the preaching of the Apostles, indured until the time of <u>Constantine the Great</u>," that is, until the year 324. The historical period of the second church, Smyrna, spanned from Constantine "until Gratian, about the year of our Lord 382." And the type of the third church, Pergamus, has its "counterpaine" in the period "from the year 400 unto the year 1300."[42]

Similarly, the first church symbolized the time of purity and godliness, though already in this period "godliness languisheth by litle and litle."[43] During the second period Christ's kingdom declined further, and the truth was "despised & troden under the feete of the wicked Hypocrites."[44] The third period was critical, according to Brightman, for during this time the true church almost

90

vanished from the face of the earth under "the Throne of Satan...that is, of Rome." In this city dwelled the "Popes, who all the while...made it plain to the world, that they raigned not in Gods name, but by the helpe and conduct of the Devill." But in this time of almost total decline, the light of the truth began to shine again through "Godly men," among them "the Waldenses, Albingenses," who fought against "them that dwell at Rome in the Throne of Satan." Now, the Kingdom of Christ or the true church began to rise again in time and history.[45]

The fourth church of Revelation, Thyatira, Brightman related to the "time from the year 1300, until the year 1520," or until the Protestant Reformation in Germany. In this period, the true Reformation began, with the freeing of the Church from the tyranny of Rome and Satan. During the time of the fifth church, Sardis, the true Church again appeared visibly in history, with Martin Luther in Germany. Yet, while the churches of Germany "cast away many of the Popish errours," noted Brightman, "their workes were not full, because there was no full reformation made, but one errour was only changed into another."[46]

Brightman's distance from Foxe can be seen in the way he correlates the sixth church of Revelation, Philadelphia, with its historical "counterpaine." This church was the only true and reformed church in Revelation, considered by Christ his only true church on earth. But Brightman, writing almost half a century after the accession of Elizabeth and the Elizabethan Settlement of religion, chose not to identify it with the Church of England, but rather with "the second reformed Church...the Church of Helvetia, Suevia, Geneve, France Scotland." What impressed Brightman about these historical churches was their stubborn fight against heresy, against the "Anabaptists...Arians and such like monsters raised up from Hell," and their "sincere manner of government, whereby men are made partakers of salvation." Above all, these churches signified for him the power of the church to reform itself, for in them "obstinate sinners...are given up to Satan by the ecclesiastical censure and are cast out of the Church." They practiced severe ecclesiastical discipline, and rightly so. Because it was proper that the godly

> bolteth up the gate of heaven against the wicked that are cast
> down to Hell; and no lesse joyfull it is to the godly, which
> unlocke this dore to them, that so they may enter in by it to
> overlasting life.

To the civil magistrate was accorded special power by these churches, for he was responsible "that men might live with all godliness and honestie." In the holy church of Philadelphia, to sum up then, "all these things goe joynely together, the word, discipline, [and] the zeale of the magistrate and people." There the godly "joyned...in Covenant and societie," forming a "company of the faithfull," or "reformed compaynes," and to this church the Lord gave "the whole power of the Keyes."[47]

This holy church, or in Brightman's terms, this "congregation of Saints,"[48] came to be the model on which radical Puritans in England and New England attempted to establish their churches. Within it and outside it the apocalyptic battle between Satan and Christ raged. And through it and around it the whole drama of time and history unfolded.

Although Philadelphia, according to Brightman, "hath but weak power and forces of her defence," this "congregation of saints," had an important role to play "over the papists," in the time when "the Romish Beast" would be thrown into hell. In the eschatological and apocalyptic context of providential history, Philadelphia, being Christ's only true church on earth, would stand "altogether free in the common calamitie of the whole world." In this time of God's wrath on earth, "this one church shalbe preserved from wasting & destruction," for "it seemeth that those Churches which have not regard full reformation, shall at last by Gods judgment come to nothing." In Revelation the Lord promises Philadelphia that he "will write upon" her "the name of my God, and the name of the city of my God, which is new Jerusalem, which come down out of heaven from my God" (Rev. 3:12). To Brightman, now, not recognizing any cosmological dualism between heaven and earth, the church of Philadelphia became in fact the holy city, the "city of my God." "But as toching this New

Jerusalem...that is to bee looked for upon earth, the most noble and pure of all other, that ever have been to that time."[49]

The "heavenly city," then, according to Brightman, rises from time and history, by the actions of the saints; and it is the role of the saints to build Philadelphia on earth, because when the Lord acknowledged their work he would mark this church as the new Jerusalem. Similarly, when William Twisse in England in the 1630s, along with "many grave Divines," asked themselves concerning the Massachusetts Bay colony the question, "Why may not that be the place of New Jerusalem?" they evinced the same understanding. For they, like Brightman, knew that only that place of "the most noble and pure" church would inherit the holy city.[50] But why could not that place be England, the Elect Nation?

4. England and Laodicea

When Brightman refused to accord the Church of England the title Philadelphia, he was left with no further choice: it could only be Revelation"s Laodicea. It caused him much pain and sorrow - "I could not but poure teares and sight from the bottom of my heart" - to admit that "the counterpaine (I say) of Laodicea, is the third reformed Church, namely: Our Church of England." For in Revelation, Christ warned Laodicea that he would "spue thee out of my mouth" (Rev. 3:16). Four decades after the accession of Elizabeth, Foxe's Elect Nation, in the eyes of Brightman, had sunk to such depths which caused him to identify England with Laodicea, the most sinful church of the Apocalypse. "For these forty and two years and more," noted Brightman, "what great abundance of all good things hath he pured upon this Island of Ours." After so many years, "what remayneth now but that he should at length bring forth, his roddes quickly to chasten those, whom he hath been so long in convincing without any fruit or profit?"[51]

At this point in his book, Brightman devoted many pages to cataloging the sin and evil rampant in England, pages which immediately recall the similar

93

cataloging offered by Winthrop and other leaders of the Puritan migration in the "General Observations" of 1629. At the heart of both accounts lies a deep sense of crisis in England: a long-term crisis and of terrifying proportions, both in the Church of England - a church failing to live up to God's word and will - and, in the Elect Nation as a whole, a nation not living up to its divine mission in sacred providential history of fighting Antichrist in the world.

For Brightman, the overt characteristic of Laodicea is its lukewarmness; it is a church indifferent to God's word.

> Now he calleth the man cold, who can well [endure] that the duties of godlines should lie dead, & out of request, litle or nothing at all caring what manner of way he himselfe or others take to worship God. Hee calleth him hott, who boyleth with heat and fervency of Spirit, in his due and full regard of God worship...such an one as can by no meannes indure superstitious and impious religions, but will hazard all he hath, so farre as may bee, to effect reformation.

"The defect" then, "of lukewarmenes...is here found fault with, as being a sinne against God." In a world in which an apocalyptic battle is waged between Christ and Antichrist, the sin of lukewarmness is unforgivable. Thus, continued Brightman,

> In our Realms of England, the matter is more clear, where such a form of Church is established, which is neither cold, nor yet hot, but set in the middest between both... It is not cold, in asmuch as it doth professe the sound, pure, and sincere doctrine of salvation, by which wee have renounced that Antichrist of Rome...greatest parte Antichristian & Romish. In the degrees of clergie men, in elections & or ordinations, & the whole administration of the Church-censures. The which te[m]pering of pure doctrine and Romish regiment maketh this Lukewarmenes, whereby wee stand just in the middest betweene cold and hot, betweene the Romish and the Reformed Churches.[52]

In a world set in the final battle between Christ and Antichrist, such "lukewarmenes" stood as an unforgivable sin.

The "General Observations," it will be recalled, made the same explicit identification of the Church of England with Laodicea. Contemplating the

94

prospect of remaining in England, the authors of the "Observations" pondered: "if we imytate Sodom in her pride and intemperance, if Laodicea in her lukewarmnesse...where is yet the good should content us?"[53] For these men, to remain in England was to risk going down with the rotting ship, a situation appreciated by Edward Johnson in his version of the migration episode: "When England began to decline in Religion, like lukewarme Laodicea...in this very time Christ...raises an Army out of our English Nation" and "creates a New England to muster up the first of his Forces in."[54]

If Laodicea was England, as Brightman believed, then Christ's prophecies about Laodicea applied equally to England. The Lord was demanding from England "a full reformation." Otherwise, said Brightman , "let us know that his punishment shalbe very dreadfull," for Christ "will not fail nor falsifie his word, who hath threatened that hee wilbe avenged of them." A special punishment, then, Brightman foresaw for England - the historical Laodicea - to accompany the general destruction promised by God in the Apocalypse to all who refused to acknowledge him. For in the end, all churches but Philadelphia - "altogether free in the common calamities of the whole world" - "shall at last by God's judgement come to nothing."[55] Included in this final judgment would be Laodicea, which, according to Brightman's formula, faced a double specter: that Christ would cast it from his mouth to Satan, and that it would be consumed in the general conflagration, along with other churches not fulfilling the full reformation.

This anticipation of imminent general destruction, of God's Judgment on England in the very near future, was overwhelmingly present in the writings of the Puritan emigrations before they left England. Winthrop, for example, wrote to his wife in 1629:

> the increasing of our sinnes gives us so great cause to look for some heavye Scquorge and Judgment to be coming upon us: the Lord hath admonished, threatened, corrected, and astonished us, yet we growe worse and worse, so...he must needs gives way to his furye at last...my dear wife, I am veryly perswaded, God will bringe some heavy Afflication upon this lande, and that speedylye.

95

It is common in the historiography of early Massachusetts to associate these fears with events of the Thirty Years' War in Europe in the late 1620s, that is, with the defeat of the Huguenots in France and of the Protestants in Germany against the armies of Ferdinand II and Wallenstein. But Winthrop exhibited these fears for many years, at least from the 1610s on, and he never associated them, at least exclusively, with events in Europe. "The time is at hand," he wrote in 1622, "when they shall call to the (mountains to) hid them from the face of him whom now they slight and neglect." In this letter and many others, Winthrop voiced his fears about corruption in England: "the sinnes bothe our owne and of the whole land doe call for judgmentes rather than blessings."[56]

Indeed, for those Puritans in England who followed Brightman's apocalyptic interpretation in identifying England with Laodicea, the final judgment on England was just a matter of time. "All other Churches of Europe are brought to desolation," wrote the leaders of the Puritan migration in the "General Observations," "and it cannot be, but the like Judgment is coming upon us." Yet, these Puritans also knew, through the writings of Brightman and their own reading of Revelation, that a more glorious destiny was promised by the Lord to Philadelphia, a destiny, though, evidently not to be fulfilled in England. Philadelphia, to these Puritans of the 1620s, would emerge somewhere else: in Massachusetts, the most likely place left for the erection of the true reformed church. And so, in the "General Observations," the authors directed energies away from doomed Laodicea and toward the promise of Philadelphia:

> the service of raysinge and upholdinge a particular Church is to be preferred before the betteringe some small parte of a Church allreadye established.[57]

The identification of the Church of England with Laodicea was, then, the main cause for the rise of Puritan fears over God's pending Judgment on England and ultimately accounts for the attempt by Puritan emigrants to escape this divine, imminent Judgment by removing themselves from the foredoomed church. As yet, though, there is no study that shows the forming of godly covenant societies

96

and companies in England (as we have developed in the first chapter) in the light of Brightman's and others' identification of England with Laodicea. Yet the prevalence and nature of eschatological visions and millennial impulses in England during this period suggests an important connection here. For given the widespread assumption among Puritans that the seventh trumpet had already sounded in history and that England, as Laodicea, would soon face God's boundless wrath, the forming of purified, holy, covenanted societies represented, in part, a predictable response on the part of fearful Puritan saints. Which brings us again to Lamont's important distinction between centrifugal and centripetal millenarianism. For Brightman not only rejected the role of the Prince in the English Reformation; he likewise condemned the Church of England as a sinful Laodicea: "Wee fly away from hearing the word," and "wee cast away Christ from being our guest...wee despise Christ himself who calleth us to his supper." Such behavior indeed left the "godly" with little choice:

> How should it bee that they should not bee afraid, and bethink themselves of flying as fast and as soon as they could from this church, when they should heare that the condition of the ministers was hatefull to Christ, as whom he was about to spew out of his mouth.[58]

Yet Brightman stopped short of preaching separation and he attacked those that stepped over the line:

> The errour...of those men is full of evill, yea of blasphemy, who doe in such manner make a departure from this Church, as if Christ were quite banished from hence, and that there could be no hope of salvation to those who abide here.[59]

Separation and Laodicea, both were to be avoided. A confusing choice, but one accepted by Puritans of the migration, who maintained that to choose between those two evils was still to side with sin. For these Puritans, only by denying both evils, by disclaiming separation from the Church of England while simultaneously renouncing any connection with the sins of Laodicea-England, could personal righteousness be preserved and salvation be attained. In this character the Puritan migration exhibits what Lamont has termed "the centrifugal millenarianism of Thomas Brightman."[60] Disaffected by the Prince's failure to fulfill true reformation, namely, the early Stuarts, King James I and Charles I, the Puritans here arrogated to themselves - the godly - the main responsibility for executing the Reformation. "If any such as are known to be godly," the Puritans argued in the "General Observations,"

> shall...joyn themselves with this church [the future congregational church in New England]...it will be an example of great use both for the removing of scandall and sinister and worldly respect, to give more lyfe to the faith of God's people...and also to encourage others to joyne the more willingly in it.[61]

It was, in part, the fear that God would pour his wrath on England that inspired Puritans to seek their eschatological visions and millennial expectations outside the boundaries of the Church of England in the 1620s as well as in the 1640s. "How horrible a thing is to bee spued out of Christ mouth?"[62] This fear was tangible and real to generations of Protestants and Puritans who looked to the Book of Revelation as God's word and historical prophecy. In this context - wherein the Apocalypse was accepted as real and vital - Brightman's work performed a pivotal role of clarification. Brightman's exegesis of Revelation, notes one historian, "gave singular inspiration to the radicals of early 1640s";[63] yet, as the Puritan emigration to New England indicates, it clearly inspired radical Puritans of the 1620s as well. Brightman's interpretation of Revelation in fact constituted a unique apocalyptic philosophy of history which supplied Puritans with coherent perceptions in relation to the redemptive significance of their time in the entire course of sacred, providential history - past, present, and future. His essential assumption, that through history and time the Kingdom of God, or the true church, would rise on earth, and that this world and not the next was the true field on which the whole mystery of time and history would be revealed, likewise pointed to the crucial apocalyptic role of the saints on earth in executing the true reformation.

At the same time, Brightman's denial of belief in the Godly Ruler and identification of the Church of England with Laodicea deflected millennial expectations away from the king and the established Church of England and focused them on the godly people as the actual instrument through which the reformation would be executed and fulfilled. Thus, wrote John Wilson,

> I am resolv'd, (Consider what I say),
> Out of my mouth to spew thee quite away.

Wilson wrote this poem in the early seventeenth century, many years before he came to Massachusetts with Winthrop to be a minister in Boston's church. And his poem clearly reflected Puritan frustrations with the Godly prince:

> And first, our Queen Elizabeth
> ended her life and Reign;
> To shew that all hope is a breath,
> soon come, soone gone again;
> Unless as children we depend
> on God the surest stay. [64]

When, then, the authors of the "General Observations" approached the pending question of the migration entirely from the perspective and interests of the "godly people" - "the best of the world" - and "God['s] kingdom" - "the best waye in the world" - they were following in a tradition and exhibiting an apocalyptic philosophy of history just recently given renewed meaning by Thomas Brightman. [65]

Thomas Brightman's works were well known among Puritans before and during the Civil War on both sides of the ocean. Yet, concerning the Puritan emigrants to America, they brought with them to New England not only his books but, more importantly, his apocalyptic interpretation of history. Thus, for example, Thomas Hooker based the apocalyptic historical introduction to his A Survey of the Summe of Church Discipline (1648) on Brightman's work, while John Cotton called him "Holy Brightman," and Thomas Shepard cited Brightman as an evidence for the fulfillment of the prophecies of the millennium during the 1640s in relation to the conversion of the "Westerne Indians." As late as 1700,

John Higginson and William Hubbard, contemporaries of John Cotton and Thomas Hooker, who were then in their eighties, wrote that

> The Famous <u>Brightman</u> had foretold...God would yet Reveal more of the true <u>Church-State</u> unto some of His Faithful Servants, whom He would send into a <u>Wilderness</u>, that He might there have Communion with them.[66]

Yet, if it is only natural to find Brightman mentioned by ministers, it is important to note that his identification of England with Laodicea also had been widely used by the lay authors of the "General Observations," by Edward Johnson in his <u>Wonder-Working Providence</u> and by many others who used Brightman's apocalyptic philosophy and interpretation of history as a means to explain and understand their time and life.

Ultimately, Brightman's work raised a new historical consciousness in the early 1600s, a sense of the imminent fulfillment of the prophetic, redemptive revelations of the Apocalypse in time and history, and consequently, of the duty of the saints to execute here and now the premises and principles of religious reformation.   However, by viewing Brightman's apocalyptic interpretation of history as a unique mode of historical thought, it is equally important to see when and how the premises of this apocalyptic ideology led to social and political actions. This attempt to explore the relationship between ideas and the shaping of political and social reality, or between modes of conviction and modes of conduct, will be our main task in the following chapters.   But it can be noted here that, for example, when John Higginson of Guilford wrote in 1654 that "I have thought that the great design of Jesus Christ in this age is to set up his kingdom in particular churches," he made it clear that for the Puritan emigrants the issue of church-government, or Congregationalism, was closely associated with the vision of establishing the Kingdom of God on earth, or with pursuit of the millennium.   That is, given the special dimension of time they had lived in, Puritans believed it to be the saints' duty, as Brightman wrote, to enter into convenanted societies and churches. For the establishment of the true church, or Congregationalism, corresponded to God's divine redemptive plan of history, and it also constituted the best assurance against God's Judgment in the imminent apocalyptic events to come in the near future. Therefore, continued Higginson, "those that with Philadelphia," now established by the saints in New England, "keep the words of Christ's patience" would "undoubtedly be kept (as under the shadow of his wings) in the hour of temptation."[67] In other words, millennial expectations and apocalyptic visions led to such social actions as the forming of covenanted groups and, indeed, the whole Puritan emigration to New England. Without the eschatological and millennial context provided so well by Brightman, the Puritan migration to, and the Puritan commonwealth in, Massachusetts can hardly be completely understood.

The Puritans who emigrated to Massachusetts carried with them not only congregationalism as a system of church-government, but also an apocalyptic philosophy of history, from the premises of which they endeavored to establish the right foundation, both in terms of church and state, for the Christian commonwealth in the wilderness. Indeed, our task in the following chapters will be to see how Puritans attempted to integrate their eschatological visions and millennial expectations within church and society and to form a special and unique relationship between church and state in the holy Puritan commonwealth in New England. Before that, we need to explore the meaning of the term "wilderness" - a notion with special meaning in the Book of Revelation and in Brightman's apocalyptic interpretation.

IV   The Church and the Wilderness

New Jerusalem in Revelation is that city which will descend from heaven at "the end of time," or in the "last time." But in Brightman's exegesis it is that true church on earth that the Lord, after many apocalyptic events, will seal with his name. From this point of view, Brightman's apocalyptic interpreation offered a description of the emergence of God's true church out of the labyrinth of time and history and of the endless human effort involved in the erection of the holy church in purity, according to God's word. In this character, Brightman's exegesis served, at least in part, to take the locus of millennial expectations away from England and place it in the wilderness of Massachusetts Bay. "When you see Jerusalem compassed with armies," preached Francis Higginson in his farewell sermon to his congregation in Leichester in 1629, shortly before he left for Salem in America, "then flee to the mountains."[68] And John Cotton in his farewell sermon before Winthrop's fleet in 1630, declared that

> there be evills to be avoyded that may warrant removal. First, when some grievous sinnes overspread Country that threaten desolation...a wise man forseeth the plague, so in threatning he seeth a commandement, to hide himself from it.[69]

Similarly, in the "General Observations," the eschatological and apocalyptic terms "refuge" and "shelter" defined the immediate goal of the Puritan migration to the wilderness of America. These Puritans thought on themselves as living in the middle of the eschatological and apocalyptic occurrences which marks the final culmination of sacred, providential history, hence they considered themselves "forced to flye into the wildernesse" of America and there "to seek refuge for saftye." Fortunately, they knew, because God "carried his people into the wilderness," he would provide them a "comfortable refuge." Of New England, they believed:

> God hath provided this place to be a refuge for many whom he meanes to save out of the generall callamity, and seeinge the Church hath no place lefte to flie into but the wilderness, what better worke can there be, than to goe and provide tabernacles and foode for her against she come thether.[70]

102

The prevalence of the eschatological terms "shelter," "refuge," and "hiding place" unmistakably points to the fact that these Puritans thought of their migration in an apocalyptic context: they were saints in the midst of an apocalyptic scenario. And as saints in the middle of cosmic occurrences, so to speak, they sought out the best place from which to ride out the storm. What they found was the New England wilderness. Their hope was that "New England might be designed by heaven, as a refuge and shelter for the non-conformists against the storms that were coming upon the [English] nation."[71]

In his important book Puritanism and the Wilderness, Peter N. Carroll offers a comprehensive analysis of the significant role and meaning of the concept of "wilderness" in Puritan New England. According to him, "the Puritans had developed specific views of the wilderness situation prior to their migration." Among them were the identification of the Biblical wilderness with the New England forest, the notion of wilderness as a refuge from worldly corruption and as a place of religious insight, or as a place in which God would test his chosen people. Moreover, "for some, New England signified the New Canaan; others anticipated a barren wasteland; some regarded America as a land of spiritual darkness; and an important segment of the ministry lauded the New World as a refuge." In sum, argues Carroll,

> derived largely from Biblical metaphors, these concepts provided
> New Englanders with elaborate rhetorical devices with which
> they could judge their own experience.[72]

Yet what is missing in Carroll's excellent study is the unique meaning of the concept of the "wilderness" as it appears in the Book of Revelation. "The wilderness," noted Joseph Mede, a famous early seventeenth century commentator on the Apocalypse, is that place where "God is encamping with Israel" and where "God [is] marching before his people" after taking them out of Egypt.[73] It represents, then, an intermediate zone between the corruped past and glorious future, or between Egypt and the Promised Land. Consequently, the wilderness served as that place in time and history where the saints show they deserve to be

God's people; it is the place of trial where faith in the keeping of the covenant is proven. Yet, because the wilderness is in time, it also bears the mark of history. That is, it is still a place within the context of the apocalyptic battle between Christ and Antichrist. That is why "God creates a New England to muster up the first of his Forces in," because "assure your selves the time is at hand wherein Antichrist will muster all his forces, and make war with the people of God."[74] New England was indeed new, but its dimension of time belonged to history, not as yet to the sacred realm of New Jerusalem. The millennium was nearly at hand, as Puritans believed, but until its actual advent, New England still had to play its part in the apocalyptic events. After all, "the Devil with his Instruments have contrived to swallow up that famous Kingdom," wrote John Wilson from Boston, New England,

> and the Church of Christ in it, sonow...all the devils of Hell...busying themselves to batter down the walls of Zion, and to make breaches at the gates thereof, that so they might execute the utmost Butcheries that can be invented, thereby to overthrow the Kingdom of Christ.[75]

Within the apocalyptic visions and the prophetic revelations of the Apocalypse, the wilderness held a unique place.

> And there appeared a great wonder in heaven; a woman clothed with the sun, and the moon under feet, and upon her head a crown of twelve stars.

Being "with a child cried, travailing in birth, and pained to be delivered," the woman has to escape from heaven, because "a red dragon" in heaven aimed "to devour her child as soon as it was born." The woman delivers the child, "who was to rule all nations with a rod of iron," and with him she "fled into the wilderness, where she hath place prepared of God" (Rev. 12:1-6). Later a war breaks out in heaven, wherein, as we saw earlier, Satan is banished from the heavenly realm, "and when the dragon saw that he was cast unto earth, he persecuted the woman which brought forth the man child." Again, with Satan on earth, the woman "fly into the wilderness, into her place, where she is nourished

104

for a time, and times, and half a time, from the face of the serpent." The latter makes every effort to destroy the woman but in vain so

> the dragon was wroth with the woman, and went to make a war with the remnant of her seed, which keep the commandments of God, and have the testimony of Jesus Christ. (Rev. 12:13-17)

In his exegesis, Brightman radically transformed these passages from Revelation concerning the woman and the wilderness by relating them to a concrete historical context. "The woman which is seen," he argues, "doth very fittly carry the image of the Church," and her son, of course, is Christ. Concerning the wilderness, "the place is the wilderness, that is, the Temple." Thus the wilderness is the place in which "the poore handsome of the Elect lurke," and where

> there was a meere solitary wilderness in respect of that place, where that Innumerable company lived, that possessed the holy city.

The woman fled to the wilderness, in Brightman's explanation, because "God car[d] for her," and there he "provide[d] her an hiding place." In the wilderness, the woman, or the Church, "was fed by the helpe of certain men," who maintained her there. Because "this wilderness is that Temple," according to Brightman, "the continuance of banishment in the wilderness is that abode that was made in the Temple."[76]

This is the vision of the Church of the Wilderness, or the "errand into the wilderness," as understood by Brightman and by the Puritan emigrants as well. The Biblical concept of wilderness, as transformed by Brightman, no longer signified the place of trial or the intermediate zone between the corrupted past and the Promised Land, but rather the place in which the church and temple, the house of God, would become one, a solitary place far away from corruption and sin. The flight of the woman into the wilderness occurred in the time of the seventh trumpet, Brightman noted, when the mystery of time and history would be revealed, and in the time of the "sealing of the Elect," when the Lord would elect the saints. Why has the woman fled in these very times, asked Brightman,

105

in which her son and his father have come to conquer the world? "Certainly it could not be the feare of the enemy but the intollerable irkesomenes" because of the lack of "true piety" and the "yoke of tyranny." For once in the wilderness, "she had the leasure to seek out the Reliques of Saints, to consecrate Temples to the Martyrs, and to make supplication of every shrine." In the wilderness, argued Brightman, "there were no outward troubles that did molest men," those troubles that caused men "to corrupt Religion" and "the simple purity which Christ ordained."[77] Likewise for the Puritans of the "General Observations," when the church was "ecclipsed in parte, darkened, or persecuted...it is juste to seeke refuge for saftye, especially where safest hope maye be founde." For them, then, emigration was urgent in 1629 because "nowe the doore is opened, and were a greate forgettfull unthankefullnes to the lorde, to refuse imployment in so hie an ordinance."[78]

An essential feature of Brightman's interpretation, as we saw earlier, was to abolish the Augustinian cosmological dualism between heaven and earth. In so doing, he projected Augustine's heavenly city into the wilderness. For Brightman, that is, the wilderness became a "heavenly place" on earth, a place remote from corrupted history and degenerated human traditions. Consequently, when the woman, or the church, fled to the wilderness, she did so because she "could not endure" the corruption of religion in a nation "where no publike assemblies [were] to be found, wherein the Ordinances of God did not flourish in their integrity." This woman also represented for Brightman the congregation of the faithful, or the company of saints; she "doth not beare the person of the faithfull one by one, but of the whole assemblies of the faithfull."[79]

By this point in his exegesis, Brightman has clearly drawn out the seventeenth century applications of the Apocalypse. He has presented the dragon's persecution of the woman in a way most suggestive for early seventeenth century Puritan readers. Though his immediate Biblical context is the saints' persecution by the "bishops" of historical Rome, seventeenth century readers could not miss the contemporary relevance of the flight of the woman. For according to

106

Brightman's apocalyptic interpretation, the woman is the "whole Church generally" and at the same time "the particular congregation," and the flight into the wilderness signifies, from one view, the migration of the saints from a corrupted nation.

> The Womans flight then is either the dissolution or the depraving of the particular assemblies, so as God should not be porely worshipped in of them according to his will alone, the which thing when once it commeth to passe, the Church fleet away...[80]

But if the woman is the "Holy assemblies of the faithfull," Brightman continued, then "her seede are the faithfull in particular," those who "hold the true Religion," and those "who can not come together to worship God in publike assemblies, because [of] the iniquity of the times." For these saints only the prospect of "nourish[ing] piety in private" remained. Here Brightman has clearly depicted the core of the Puritan experience of the late sixteenth century, as we saw previously in the first chapter: their tendency to withdraw into highly pietistic and religious groups through the forming of covenanted societies or holy fellowships. Against the saints in these godly societies Satan waged a war, "seeing there should be no open assemblies, which should professe the pure and sincere truth according to godlines." Yet, the Church, now the Militant Church, must fight back against Satan and Antichrist.

> Now that is warre, when force is beaten backe with force, and this warre the woman seed should undertake to the end she might defend her selfe against manifest tyranny.[81]

The double meaning of the term wilderness in Revelation, as interpreted by Brightman, constituted the essence of the "errand into the wilderness" as understood by those of the Puritan migration. the wilderness was, first, the place to escape from the corrupted religion of England and, second, the only place in which the true church could flourish in the time of the apocalyptic events foreshadowing Christ's second coming. In eschatological millennial terms, the true church was cast, by force of circumstances, as the militant church, an active agent in the final battle between Christ and Antichrist. Yet, by virtue of the perilous situation of England at that particular time, these saints of the militant church found themselves in the position of having to flee the corrupt nation destined for destruction by God, to flee Babylon for the wilderness. In this vein, the Puritans of the "Observations" argued that "God hath provided this place" - meaning New England - "to be a refuge for many whom he means to save out of the generall callamity." In this formulation, the wilderness served as much needed place for escape, for during that eschatological and apocalyptic moment before Christ's second advent when Antichrist momentarily held the upper hand, the true saints - or Puritans - like the woman, or the church of the wilderness in Revelation, "hath no place lefte to flie into but the wilderness." Yet even in flight, the Puritan migration still represented the militant church, or the true Church's struggle to spread the Kingdom of God in the world. For the end of the flight into the wilderness was "to rayse a bullwarke against the kingdom of Antichrist."[82] Thus, in its second meaning, the wilderness was merely another place in which to carry on the apocalyptic struggle against Antichrist. In this meaning, "these poore New England People" indeed represented "the forerunners of Christ['s] Army," who the Lord had sent "to Preach in this Wildernesse, and to Proclaime to all Nations, the neere approach of the most wonderfull workes that ever the Soones oi men saw": Christ's second coming and his eternal reign on earth.[83]

The Puritan migration and its character as an "errand into the wilderness," to conclude, only acquires full meaning when viewed in the context of these eschatological, apocalyptic and millennial terms - when considered, that is, as evidence of the heightened centrifugal millenarian impulses so prevalent in early seventeenth century England. Similarly, an appreciation of the essential eschatological and apocalyptic impulse in the Puritan migration is crucial for an accurate understanding of the Puritan experience in Massachusetts and the attempt to create there a holy Christian commonwealth. At the same time, discussion of the eschatology and apocalypse of the Puritan migration to Massachusetts is essential for a full understanding of the attitudes of Puritan New England toward

108

England from the very beginnings of the Puritan emigration in the 1620s until and during the Puritan Revolution in England. For a vital determinant of the colony's relationship to England in these decades, as we will soon see, was how the Massachusetts Puritans construed England - and New England - within the unfolding drama of sacred, providential history, or within the prophetic, revelatory course of the history of human redemption and salvation. On opposing sides of the ocean, Puritans supplied differing answers to this important question.

Notes

1. John Foxe, Actes and Monuments (1563), the dedication to Queen Elizabeth I.

2. Thomas Brightman, Apocalypsis Apocalypseos, or A Revelation of the Revelation (Leyden, 1616), p. 528.

3. John Wilson, A Song of Deliverance (Boston, 1680), in Handkerchiefe from Paul, Being Pious and Consolatory Verses of Massachusetts Puritans, ed. Kenneth B. Murdock (Cambridge: Harvard Univ. Press, 1927), p. 43. Wilson wrote this poem in 1603.

4. The Revelation of St. John the Divine, 10:7, 11:15.

5. Thomas Brightman, Apocalypsis Apocalypseos, p. 491.

6. Francis Higginson, "Farewell Sermon: (1629), cited in Magnalia Christi Americana, by Cotton Mather, I, p. 327.

7. "General Observations for the Plantation of New England" (1629), Winthrop Papers, II, pp. 111-149, 114-115. In the following discussion I use the "General Observations" as an inclusive name for a whole series of papers, arguments, objections, letters, etc., which characterized the discussion among Puritans in England in 1629 concerning the plan to settle Massachusetts Bay. In so doing I follow the editors of volume two of the Winthrop Papers. On the relationship between the leaders of the great Puritan migration and Parliamentary leaders during that time, men like Sir John Eliot and John Hampden, who also took an active part in the discussion on the Observations," see: A.P. Newton, The Colonizing Activities of the English Puritans (New Haven: Yale Univ. Press, 1914) and J.H. Hexter, The Reign of King Pym (Cambridge: Harvard Univ. Press, 1948). For the Puritans' involvement in colonization, see: T.K. Rabb, Enterprise and Empire, Merchant and Gentry Investment in the Expansion of England, 1575-1630 (Cambridge: Harvard Univ. Press, 1967).

8. "General Observations," pp. 114, 122.

9. "General Observations," p. 114.

10. George Herbert, "The Church Militant," in The English Works of George Herbert, ed. G.H. Palmer (Boston and New York: Houghton Mifflin, 1905), III, p. 359. For the date in which Herbert composed this poem see Amy M. Charles, A Life of George Herbert (Ithaca: Cornell Univ. Press, 1977), pp. 82, 87, 108, 216, and A.G. Hyde, George Herbert and His Times (New York: G.P. Putnam's Sons, 1906), 305.

11. William Twisse, "Dr. Twisse His Fourth Letter to Mr. Mede," in The Works of...Joseph Mede, ed. John Worthington (London, 1672), p. 799.

110

12. Edward Johnson, Wonder-Working Providence of Sion   Saviour in New England, 1628-1651, p. 23.

13. Perry Miller, The New England Mind: From Colony to Province (Boston: Beacon Press, 1968), p. 185. On Calvin's influence on English and American Puritanism, see R.T. Kendall, "John Cotton - First English Calvinist?", in The Puritan Experiment in the New World, the Westminster Conference (London, 1976), pp. 38-50, and Calvin and English Calvinism to 1649 (Oxford, 1979).

14. Miller, The New England Mind: From Colony to Province, pp. 188, 185, 188; Perry Miller, The New England Mind: The Seventeenth Century (New York: Macmillan, 1939), p. 229. Miller not only took the Book of Revelation from early Massachusetts theology, but also from its early poetry. "The most renowned of New England poets, Anne Bradstreet, being immigrant, wrote only of English streams and English birds," wrote Miller in The New England Mind: From Colony to Province, p. 189. Yet, one could see, for example, in Bradstreet's A Dialogue between Old England and New (1642), how much the "whore" and the "beast" of Revelation had been immersed in her poetry. For Bradstreet's poems, see: J.R. McElrate and A.P. Robb, eds., The Complete Works of Anne Bradstreet (Boston: Twayne, 1981).

15. Perry Miller and Thomas H. Johnson, eds., The Puritans (New York: Harper Torchbooks, 1963), I, p. 82.

16. In the following discussion on the Book of Revelation I owe much to William Lamont's important study, Godly Rule, Politics and Religion, 1603-1660 (London: Macmillan, 19619), which shows how essential Revelation was to the Puritan movement in England in the early seventeenth century, and to the excellent study of J.G.A. Pocock, "Time, History and Eschatology in the Thought of Thomas Hobbes," in his Politics, Language and Time (New York: Atheneum, 1973), pp. 148-201. See also Pocock's essay "Modes of Action and Their Pasts in Tudor and Stuart England," in National Consciousness, History and Political Culture in Early Modern Europe, ed. Orest Ranum (Baltimore: Johns Hopkins Univ. Press, 1975).

17. Paul Christianson, Reformers and Babylon: English Apocalyptical Visions from the Reformation to the Eve of the Civil War (Toronto: Univ. of Toronto Press, 1978), p. 5. St. Augustine's distinction between the City of God and the Earthly City appears in his De Civitate Dei. "St. Augustine," wrote George H. Sabine, "made the distinction a key to the understanding of human History, which is and always must be dominated by the contest of the two societies. On the one side stands the earthly city, the society that is founded on the earthly, appetitive and possessive impulses of the lower human nature; on the other hand stands the City of God, the society that is founded in the hope of heavenly peace and spiritual salvation. The first is the kingdom of Satan.... The other is the kingdom of Christ." See, George H. Sabine, A History of Political Thought, 3rd ed. (New York: Holt, Rinehart and Winston, 1961), pp. 189-190. An excellent study of the appearance of the theme of the city of God in the eighteenth century is Carl L. Becker, The Heavenly City of the Eighteenth Century Philosophers (New Haven: Yale Univ. Press, 1933).

18. Edward Johnson, Wonder-Working Providence, pp. 49-50.

19. Norman Cohn, The Pursuit of the Millennium Revolutionary Millenarian and Mystical Anarchists of the Middle Ages, rev. ed. (New York: Oxford Univ. Press, 1980), pp. 17, 213; George H. Williams, The Radical Reformation (Philadelphia: Westminster Press,

1962), passim. On the role of the Apocalypse in the Protestant Reformation, see: Rubin B. Barnes, Prophecy and Genosis: Apocalypticism in the Wake of the Lutheran Reformation (Stanford, 1988), and A.G. Dickens and John M. Tonkin, The Reformation in Historical Thought (Cambridge, Mass., 1985). On millennial expectations and apocalyptical visions in England during the sixteenth and seventeenth centuries, see: Bryan W. Ball, A Great Expectation: Eschatological Thought in English Protestantism to 1660 (Leiden: E.J. Brill, 1975); Peter Toon, ed., Puritans, the Millennium and the Future of Israel: Puritan Eschatology (Cambridge: James Clark, 1970); Katharine R. Firth, The Apocalyptic Tradition in Reformation Britain 1530-1646 (Oxford Oxford Univ. Press, 1979); and Charles Webster, The Great Instauration: Science, Medicine and Reform 1626-1660 (London: Duckworth, 1975); Richard Bauckham, Tudor Apocalypse: Sixteenth Century Apocalypticism, Millenarianism and the English Reformation, from John Bale to John Foxe and Thomas Brightman (Oxford, 1978); Bernard S. Capp, The Fifth-Monarchy Men: A Study of Seventeenth Century English Millenarianism (London, 1972); William Lamont, Richard Baxter and the Millennium (London, 1989); Tai Liu, Discord in Zion: The Puritan Divines and the Puritan Revolution (The Hague, 1973(); G.J.R. Parry, A Protestant Vision: William Harrison and the Reformation of Elizabethan England (Cambirdge, 1987); Chrisopher Hill, Antichrist in Seventeenth Century England (Oxford, 1971), and The World Turned Upside Down: Radical Ideas during the English Revolution (New York, 1972). For the association between millennial and utopian thought, see: Ernest Lee Tuveson, Millennium and Utopia: A Study in the Background of the Idea of Progress (Berkeley and Los Angeles: Univ. of California Press, 1949) and J.C. Davis, Utopia and the Ideal Society: A Study of English Utopian Writing 1516-1700 (Cambridge: Harvard Univ. Press, 1981), and James Holstun, A Rational Millennium: Puritan Utopias of Seventeenth-Century England and America (Oxford, 1987). There are many studies of millennial thought in America in general and New England in particular. See: Joy B. Gilsdorf, "The Puritan Apocalypse: New England Eschatology in the Seventeenth Century," Diss. Yale 1964; James W. Davidson, The Logic of Millennial Thought: Eighteenth Century New England (New Haven: Yale Univ. Press, 1977); W. Clark Gilpin, The Millenarian Piety of Roger Williams (Chicago: Univer. of Chicago Press, 1979); Cecelia Tichi, New World, New Earth: Environmental Reform in American Literature from the Puritans through Whitman (New Haven: Yale Univ. Press, 1979); John Seelye, Prophetic Waters: The River in Early American Life and Literature (New York: Oxford Univ. Press, 1977); Theodore D. Bozeman, To Live Ancient Lives: The Primitivist Dimension in Puritanism (Chapel Hill, 1988); Philip F. Gura, A Glimpse of Sion's Glory: Puritan Radicalism in New England, 1620-1660 (Middletown, Conn., 1984); Helmut R. Nieburh, The Kingdom of God in America (Hampden: Shoe String Press, 1955); Sacvan Bercovitch, The Millennium in America (New York, 1975); David H. Watters, "With Bodilie Eyes": Eschatological Themes in Puritan Literature and Gravestone Art (Ann Arbor, 1981); Mason I. Lowance, Jr., The Language of Canaan: Metaphor and Symbol in New England from the Puritans to the Transcendentalists (Cambridge, Mass., 1980); J.A. de Jong, As the Waters Cover the Sea: Millennial Expectations in the Rise of Anglo-American Missions, 1640-1810 (Kampden, 1970); Nathan O. Hatch, The Sacred Cause of Liberty: Republican Thought and the Millennium in Revolutionary New England (New Haven, 1977); Clark Gilpin, The Millenarian Piety of Roger Williams (Chicago, 1989); Ruth H. Bloch, The Visionary Republic: Millennial Themes in American Thought, 1756-1800 (Cambridge, 1985). See also the bibliographical essay by Leonard I. Sweet, "Millennialism in America: Recent Studies," Theological Studies, XL, (Sept. 1979), pp. 510-531. On the relationship between millennial thought and social actions, see two excellent studies: Kenelm Burridge, New Heaven New Earth: A Study of Millenarian Activities (New York: Schocken, 1969) and Michael Barkun, Disaster and the Millennium (New Haven: Yale Univ. Press, 1974).

20. Christianson, Reformers and Babylon, book jacket.

21. Ibid., p. 39.

22. William Haller, Foxe's Book of Martyrs and the Elect Nation (London: Jonathan Cape, 1963), pp. 224-225. See also, V. Norskov Olsen, John Foxe and the Elizabethan Church (Berkeley, 1973), and David Cressy, Bonfires Bells: National Memory and the Protestant Calendar in Elizabethan and Stuart England (Berkeley, 1989).

23. R.H. Tawney, Religion and the Rise of Capitalism (New York: Mentor), p. 231.

24. Lamont, Godly Rule, p. 25.

25. B.R. White, The English Separatist Tradition (Oxford, 1971), pp. 20-90. See also, J.W. Martin, Religious Radicals in Tudor England (London, 1989), and Stephen Barclow, The Communion of Saints: Radicals Puritan and Separatist Ecclesiology, 1570-1625 (Oxford, 1988).

26. Stephen Brachlow, "John Robinson and the Lure of Separatism in Pre-Revolutionary England," Church History, L (Sept., 1981), p. 291.

27. Lamont, Godly Rule, p. 51.

28. Patrick Collinson, The Elizabethan Puritan Movement (Berkeley and Los Angeles: Univ. of California Press, 1967), p. 13.

29. Gilsdorf, "The Puritan Apocalypse," p. 33.

30. Christianson, Reformers and Babylon, pp. 15, 18.

31. Thomas Brightman, Apocalypsis Apocalypseos, pp. 491, 502. (All quotations from Brightman are from the Leyden, 1616, edition.).

32. Ibid., pp. 491, 502.

33. Ibid., p. 1135.

34. Ibid., pp. 519, 569, 852, 1119. On Brightman, see also my essay, "Thomas Brightman and English Apocalyptic Tradition," in Menasseh Ben-Israel and His World, eds. Yosef Kaplan, et al. (Leiden, 1989), pp. 31-44.

35. Thomas Goodwin, "Three Sermons on Heb. I, 1, 2," in The Works of Thomas Goodwin, ed. J.C. Miller (Edinburgh, 1861-1865), V, pp. 533-534.

36. John Milton, cited in Douglas Bush, English Literature in the Earlier Seventeenth Century, 1600-1660 (New York, 1952), p. 373; Milton, Animadversions, cited in Haller, The Rise of Puritanism, p. 357.

37. Tuveson, Millennium and Utopia, p. 17.

38. Brightman, Apocalypsis Apocalypseos, pp. 526, 300, 1118, 115.

113

39. Ibid., pp. 618, 585, 520, 143. In Chapter Eleven of Revelation, an angel says to St. John: "Rise, and measure the temple of God.... But the court which is without the temple leave out, and measure it not; for it was given unto the Gentiles: and the holy city they tread under foot" (Rev. 11:1, 2).

40. Ibid., p. 155.

41. Christianson, Reformers and Babylon, p. 100. A holistic interpretation of history is one that sees history as moving toward a redemptive, eschatological goal in or beyond history. That is, a view that charges history with religious significance and, given the fact that history has been created by God, is guided by Divine Providence from beginnings to an end. See, in relation to this kind of historical interpretation, K.R. Popper, The Poverty of Historicism (London: Routledge & Kegan Paul, 1969) and Sir Isaiah Berlin, Historical Inevitability (London: Oxford Univ. Press, 1955).

42. Brightman, Apocalypsis Apocalypseos, pp. 74, 86.

43. Ibid., p. 60.

44. Ibid., p. 75.

45. Ibid., pp. 86, 92.

46. Ibid., pp. 97-09, 100, 118, 113, 126-127.

47. Ibid., pp. 139, 140, 142-145, 155.

48. Ibid., p. 140.

49. Ibid., pp. 147-149, 151, 155.

50. William Twisse, "Dr. Twisse His Fourth Letter to Mr. Mede, The Works of...Joseph Mede, p. 799.

51. Brightman, Apocalypsis Apocalypseos, pp. 159, 161, 199.

52. Ibid., p. 166-168.

53. "General Observations," p. 122.

54. Johnson, Wonder-Working Providence, p. 23.

55. Brightman, Apocalypsis Apocalypseos, pp. 169, 171-172, 149, 151.

56. "John Winthrop to his Wife," Winthrop Papers, II, p. 91; I, pp. 271, 286.

57. "General Observations," pp. 124-125.

58. Brightman, Apocalypsis Apocalypseos, pp. 204-205.

59. Ibid., pp. 204-205.

114

60. Lamont, Godly Rule, p. 52.

61. "General Observations," p. 118.

62. Brightman, Apocalypsis Apocalypseos, p. 208.

63. Christianson, Reformers and Babylon, p. 10.

64. John Wilson, "A Song of Deliverance for the Lasting Remembrance of Gods Wonderful Works," Handkerchiefe from Paul, Being Pious and Consolatory Verse of Puritan Massachusetts, ed. K.B. Murdock (Cambridge: Harvard Univ. Press, 1927), pp. 29, 43. This poem was written in 1603.

65. "General Observations," pp. 134-136.

66. Thomas Hooker, A Survey of the Summe of Church-Discipline (London, 1648), preface; John Cotton, An Exposition Upon the Thirteenth Chapter of Revelation (London, 1656), p. 90; John Higginson and William Hubbard, A Testimony to the Order of the Gospel in the Churches of New-England (1700), in A Vindication of the Government of New-England Churches (1717), by John Wise, ed. Perry Miller (Gainesville, Fla., 1958), p. 3.

67. John Higginson, "Part of Mr. John Higginson's Letter of Guilford, dated 25 of the 8th month, 1654, to his Brother the Rev'd Thomas Thatcher of Weymouth," Connecticut Historical Society, Collections, III (1895), p. 319.

68. Francis Higginson, cited in Magnalia Christi Americana, by Cotton Mather, I, p. 327.

69. John Cotton, "Gods Promise to His Plantation," p. 9.

70. "General Observations," pp. 114, 116, 125, 128, 136, 129, 139.

71. Francis Higginson, cited in Magnalia Christia Americana, by Cotton Mather, I, p. 328.

72. Peter N. Carroll, Puritanism and the Wilderness: The Intellectual Significance of the New England Frontier, 1629-1700 (New York, 1960), pp. 2, 8. On the "wilderness" in America, see: R. Nash, Wilderness and the American Mind, rev. ed. (New Haven: Yale Univ. Press, 1973). On the concept of the "wilderness" in Christianity, see the excellent study of George H. Williams, Wilderness and Paradise in Christian Thought (New York: Harper, 1962).

73. Joseph Mede, The Brief Meaning or Summary Exposition of the Apocalypse, in The Works of Joseph Mede, pp. 917, 918.

74. Johnson, Wonder-Working Providence, pp. 23, 33.

75. John Wilson, "A Song of Deliverance," p. 26.

76. Brightman, Apocalypsis Apocalypseos, pp. 503, 512, 514-515.

77. Ibid., pp. 512-516.

78. "General Observations," pp. 128-129.

79.   Brightman, Apocalypsis Apocalypseos, pp. 517, 526.

80   Ibid., pp. 517, 526, 533.

81.   Ibid., pp. 526, 533.

82.   "General Observations," p. 139.

83.   Johnson, Wonder-Working Providence, pp. 60-61.

CHAPTER THREE:
REFORMATION AND SEPARATION:
MASSACHUSETTS' RELATIONSHIP WITH ENGLAND
DURING THE 1630s

The first of these political sense of freedom or liberty...I shall call the 'negative' sense, is involved in the answer to the question 'What is the area within which the subject...is or should be left to do or be what he is able to do or be, without interference by other person?' The second, which I shall call the 'positive' sense, is involved in the answer to the question 'What, or who, is the source of control or interference that can determine someone to do, or be, this rather than that?'
-- Sir Isaiah Berlin[1]

We do not go to New England as separatists from the Church of England; though we cannot but separate from the corruptions in it: but we go to practise the positive part of church reformation, and propagate the gospel in America.
-- Rev. Francis Higginson, 1629[2]

Fourth ingratitude among many of them toward their native country of England callinge it Babilon, Egipt, Rome the land of idolatry etc.
-- Richard Sadler, 1640[3]

Be not unmindful of our Ierusalem at home, whether you leave us, or stay at home with us.
-- Rev. John Cotton, 1630[4]

Reject not the wombe that bare you nor the paps that gave you sucke: till Christ gives us a bill of divorcement, do not you divorce yourself from us.
-- John Cotton, 1631[5]

117

My brethren, cast your thoughts afar off, and see what is become of those famous Churches of Pergamun and Thyatira and the rest mentioned, Rev. i:11...glory is departed from England; for England hath seen her best days...God begins to ship away his Noahs...and God makes account that New England shall be a refuge...a rock and a shelter for his righteous ones to run unto.
-- Rev. Thomas Hooker, 1631[6]

In the New Jerusalem...are none of the men of Gibea the sonnes of Belial knocking at our doors disturbing our sweet peace or threatening violence. Here...our eares are not beaten nor the aire filled with Oaths. Swearers nor Railers, Nor our eyes and eares vexed with the unclean Conversation of the wicked.
-- Rev. Thomas Welde, 1633[7]

I. Two Concepts of Liberty

The two previous chapters have attempted to discern two essential features of the Puritan experience in England in the late sixteenth and early seventeenth centuries, which may be considered as well as the essential conditions for the Puritan migration to New England. Through their forming of godly covenanted societies, the Puritans expressed their pietistic impulse to deny the "profane" any part in the "true church" and to transform the parish church into a society of visible saints only. Furthermore through their particular pattern of interpreting history according to the Book of Revelation, the Puritans declared their belief both that they lived in "the end of time" in the midst of the final battle between Christ and Antichrist and that they had an active part to play in the last act of providential history.

How these Puritans chose to act in England and New England was related to how they read the Bible and, more specifically, how they understood the Book of Revelation. This fact is illustrated by Richard Sadler's description, written in Massachusetts in the late 1630s, which clearly illuminates how Puritan modes of social and religious conduct were informed by powerful eschatological visions and millennial expectations.

After some 3 or 4 persons in a new

> plantacion or els where [have been engaged in a discourse]
> concerning some new things preacht out of the Revelation about
> constitution of churches and church discipline, subversion of Anti
> Christ and the Romish Babilon, erection of new Jerusalem Christ
> reigning personally a thousand years etc., begot a conceite of
> themselves and knowledge to be above others.... Wherefore
> they conclude to enter into a covenant to serve the Lord in a
> church way according to Christs rule as they think etc.[8]

First New England generally, and then Massachusetts in particular held out to some Puritans what was denied them in England: the prospect of the advancement of religious reformation and the advent of the Kingdom of God on earth. "Corruptio unius est generatio alterius; and God makes the ruines of one church to bee the raysing of an other," wrote Richard Saltonstall in the early

1630s concerning England and Europe's religious decline. And Francis Higginson declared in his farewell words, upon leaving England for Salem, that Puritan emigrants sought in America "to practise the positive part of church reformation." From the early 1620s, then, the Puritan emigration to New England was, to use Sir Isaiah Berlin's distinction between the two concepts of liberty, carried out in the "positive sense" of liberty; the Puritans desired the freedom to realize their own modes of conviction and reflection, and to fulfill their own religious aims and goals. At the same time, however, the migration was carried out in the "negative sense" of liberty as well; the Puritans desired to be free from the sins and corruptions overspreading the Church and state of England.

> Must wee study some distinctions to slave our Consciences in complying with so manifold corruptions in Gods Worship? or should wee live without Gods ordinances, because wee could not partake in the corrupt administration thereof? or content our selves to live without those ordinances of Gods Worship and Communion of Saints which hee called us unto, and our souls breathed after?[9]

The following chapter examines the Puritan migration to New England as a movement to achieve in America what had been denied of the Puritans in England. From this point of view, the very act of emigration defined the immediate relationship between the Massachusetts Puritans and England during the 1630s. For in America the Puritans came to exercise, from the point of view of the established church in England, the stand of non-conformity that no King or bishop was willing to allow at home. By the very act of removing themselves to the new world, Puritan emigrants had declared implicitly and explicitly, attitudes they held toward England. Yet, again, these attitudes concerned not only the Crown or the bishops; they concerned equally those segments in English society opposed to Puritan notions of religious reformation. Those who came to Massachusetts left England in order to escape Laodicea. In Massachusetts they set about to build a New Jerusalem, the name promised by

God to his true church Philadelphia. By their very act of emigration they set the terms for what would become New England's "controversy" with England.

II   Religion and the Colonization of New England

Long before 1629, when Winthrop and other leaders of the Puritan migration joined the Massachusetts Bay Company, New England had been viewed by some English Puritans as the only place in which to fulfill the premises of religious reformation. The pilgrims of New Plymouth, after all, betook themselves from Holland to America in 1620. But they were not the only ones in the 1620s interested in New England for religious ends. In 1624 Captain John Smith, who had been well acquainted with colonization efforts in that area, noted that

> by Cape Anne there is a Plantation a beginning by the Dorchester men...who...have set a fishing worke; some talke there is some other pretended Plantations, all whose good proceedings the eternal God protect and preserve.

Smith did not elaborate in his "The Present State of Plymouth" on the other plantation enterprises contemplated for New England at that time. But he recognized, concerning New Plymouth, that the adventurers of that plantation in London constituted "not a corporation, but...a voluntary combination in a society...aiming to doe good and to plant Religion."[10]

In the past it has been argued that only with the entrance Winthrop and other Puritans from eastern England was the Massachusetts Bay Company transformed from a mere commercial company into a religious enterprise. Yet, there is much evidence to show that from 1620 on some Puritans in England already held distinct religious goals concerning the New England wilderness and that not only the Bay Company but the New England Company as well was designed for religious purposes. In this context, the activities of the Council for New England, and especially of the New England Company of 1627/8, should be examined in order to consider Puritan expectations concerning New England before the entrance of the Massachusetts Bay Company leaders in the spring of 1629. Specifically, it is important to view both the New England Company and the Bay Company in the context of the religious aims developed by Puritans in England toward New England during the 1620s.

122

The Council for New England was incorporated by James I on November 3, 1620. Among the Puritans interested was John White of Dorchester, recognized by the seventeenth century historians of the Bay colony as a central figure in early attempts during the early 1620s to establish a plantation in New England for religious reasons. Thus, William Hubbard wrote, "Mr. White of Dorchester in Old England," was the first to "contrive...the carrying on of a plantation of sober and religious person," whose "chiefest intentions and aims were to promote religion, and if it might be, to propagate the Gospel, in this dark corner of the world." Similarly, Cotton Mather declared that

> the news of the good progress made in the new plantation of Plymouth, inspired the renowned Mr. White...to prosecute the settlement of such another plantation here for propagation of religion.[11]

The Records of the Council for New England also suggest the religious character of this early migration, for they reveal the attempt by English authorities to interdict religious non-conformist traffic to this area. "It is thought fit," reads the Council entry for May 22, 1622,

> that there shall bee an order procured from the Lords of his Magesty Councel for sending for such as have in contempt for authority gone for New England this last yeare.

Nevertheless, the Council's attempt to stop such emigration did not halt White's attempt to plant New England. His intention concerning New England, writes his biographer, was "to provide a refuge to which the churchmen could flee" from persecutions in England. Eventually, White's first attempt, the settlement in Cape Anne, failed, and with this failure in 1626 the Dorchester Company dissolved. But White himself continued in Dorchester and London all through the 1620s to promote the idea of a plantation in New England for religious purposes. Indeed soon after the failure of the Dorchester Company, he and other Puritans from the west country made an appeal to Puritans in London and together procured a patent from the Council for New England in March 1627/8. Thus was formed the New England Company by the joint efforts of the western people from Dorchester and the easterners from London.[12]

The New England Company lasted, in fact, only one year, from March 19, 1627/8, until March 4, 1628/9, the period in which the Massachusetts Bay Company gained incorporation by royal charter.[13] But the importance of the New England Company in relation to the Puritan migration was great, for this company, with its clear and distinct religious program for the colony, first imparted to the New England plantation its character as "a shelter" for non-conformist Puritans. In the summer of 1628, for example, the company sent John Endecott to Salem to be its governor in America. He landed on September 6 and quickly established that he was in New England not as a mere agent for an economic enterprise but as a crusader. "This worthy gentleman Mr. John Endicott," recorded William Bradford in his history of Plymouth, "shortly after he came over [to Salem] visited Merry-mount," the site established by Thomas Morton. In Merry-mount, continues Bradford, Thomas Morton and his company had

> set up a maypole, drinking and dancing about it many days
> together, inviting Indian women for their consorts, dancing and
> frisking together like many fairies, or furies, rather, and worse
> practices. As if they had anew revived and celebrated the feats
> of the Roman goddess Flora, or the beastly practices of the mad
> Bacchanalians.

Morton's manners had proved hateful to the pious Puritans of Plymouth, and they had consequently sent him back to England before Endecott's arrival. But when the staunch Puritan Endecott arrived on the scene in 1628, he wasted no time in going up to Merry-mount and there "caused that the maypole...be cut down" and rebuked Morton's company "for their profaneness and admonished them to look [that] there should be better walking." In England, as we saw earlier, Richard Baxter could do nothing about the maypole tree in his village. But in New England, "in His holy sanctuary," the godly magistrate did not have to suffer

124

such affairs. Consequently, the name of Merry-mount was changed to "Mount Dagon," after the god of the Philistines.[14]

While Endecott had been engaged in preparing the settlement at Salem, the New England Company had begun to choose ministers for its colony. "It is fully resolved, by God's assistance," wrote Matthew Cradock, governor of the company on February 16, 1628/9, "to send over two ministers." Upon the "approbation of Mr. White of Dorchester, and Mr. Davenport," the company chose Samuel Skelton and Francis Higginson.[15] We have already reviewed Higginson's reasons for emigrating, but about Skelton's life almost nothing is known, except that he preached in Lincolnshire and was considered a separatist. That fact alone indicates that the New England Company chose for its first church in the colony at Salem two non-conformist ministers.

Although the Massachusetts Bay Company was incorporated on March 4, 1628/9, Cradock's letters to Endecott concerning the ministers bear the name "The Governor and Deputy of the New England Company," and Higginson himself wrote that he was sent by "the Company of New England." With the sending of the ministers and the fleet of April 1629, Cradock assured Endecott that the company had "been careful to make plentiful provision of godly ministers." In the same letter, the company made it clear what Endecott and the people of Salem should expect from Skelton and Higginson:

> For the manner of the exercising their ministry...we leave that to themselves, hoping they will make God's word the rule of their actions, and mutually agree in the discharge of their duties. And because their doctrine will hardly be well esteemed whose persons are not reverenced, we desire that both by your own example, and by commanding all others to do the like, our ministers may receive due honor.[16]

Two months later, the Salem church was founded on a congregationalist basis. "Nothing is said of any church being then formed," wrote Thomas Hutchinson,

> but on the 6th of August, the day appointed for the choice and ordination of the elders and deacons, thirty persons entered into covenant in writing, which is said to be the beginning of the church, and that the ministers were ordained or instituted anew.[17]

"Undoubtedly," writes Perry Miller, "the crucial moment in the religious history of Massachusetts was the founding of the church of Salem in 1629." Arguing against the theory of "the free air" as the source for the erecting of a congregational church there, Miller calls the attention of historians to the fact that "the action at Salem can be seen to be the outcome of a long and matured program" of ecclesiastical polity that emerged on the other side of the ocean decades before 1629. He consequently traces the background of the events in Salem in relation to "a certain school of ecclesiastical thinkers," or in his term, the "non-separatist congregationalists."[18] This account is a true but incomplete view of the situation. For the circumstances of the establishment of the church in Salem expressed many features of the Puritan experience in England beyond the specific issue of ecclesiastical polity, including the forming of covenant groups, the attempt to identify the church with the visible saints, and, concomitantly, the exclusion of the ungodly or profane from the church. Puritans had attempted to satisfy these concerns in England many years before the Puritan emigration only to fail because the established church - and most important many segments of established society there as well - resisted their efforts.

With the coming of the fleet in 1629, the population of Salem reached about two hundred people. The newly-arrived ministers, Higginson and Skelton, wrote a contemporary,

> in pursuance of the end of their coming into this wilderness, acquainted the Governour, Mr. Endicott, and the rest of the godly people...with their professed intentions, and consulted with them about settling a reform congregation.

Consequently, they settled on August 6 as the day "for their entering into solemn covenant with God, and one another," and on that day "thirty persons" established the first church in Salem. A week before the formation of the church, Charles Gott, who came to Salem with Endecott, wrote to William Bradford in Plymouth that "a company of believers" in Salem had "joined together in covenant to walk together in all the ways of God."[19]

126

In England, godly people could join themselves to form a covenant society but not a church. But in America the long hoped for creed of reformation could be finally realized; a godly congregation could be constituted, based exclusively on visible saints. Once in Massachusetts, then, Puritans could fulfill their long cherished goal to reform the particular church and transfer it into a place of holiness. "All men," wrote William Ames, "ought...by all lawful meanes to endeavor that they may live in those Churches, where the precious is separated from the vile." Thus, Salem, the first church to be erected on New England's shore (for those of Plymouth, wrote John Cotton, "came over in church estate, and only renewed their covenant when they came hither"), was a realization of Ames' ideal.[20]

As had usually happened in England, however, the attempt at reformation in Salem in 1629 did not pass without opposition. "Some of the passengers that came over at the same time" with the fleet of 1629, wrote Nathaniel Morton,

> observing that the ministers did not, at all, use the book of common prayer, and that they did administer baptism and the Lord's supper without the ceremonies, and that they professed also to use discipline in the congregation against scandalous persons, by a personal application of the word of God...and that some that were scandalous were denied admission into the church, they began to raise some trouble.

At the forefront of those contesting the Salem way were the two brothers, Samuel and John Browne, the first a lawyer and the other a merchant, and "both of them amongst the number of the first patentees, men of estates, and men of parts and port in the place." Upon learning of the ecclesiastical tendency prevailing in Salem's church, the Brownes "gathered around them a company together, in a place distinct from the public assembly, and there, sundry times, the book of common prayer was read unto such as resorted thither." Soon Endecott noticed "the disturbance that began to grow among the people." And when the Brownes were called before Endecott, they

> accused the ministers as departing from the orders of the church of England, that they were separatists, and would be anabaptists,

127

& but for themselves, they would hold to the order of the church of England.[21]

In answering these accusations, Higginson and Skelton declared that "they were neither separatists nor anabaptists," because they

> did not separate from the church of England nor from the ordinances of God there, but only from the corruptions and disorders there; and that they came away from the common prayer and ceremonies, and had suffered much for their non-conformity in their native land, and therefore being in a place where they might have their liberty, they neither could nor would use them, because they judged the imposition of these things to be sinful corruption in the worship of God.[22]

However, to separate from the Book of Common Prayer was indeed separation from the Church of England, no matter what Bay Puritans said.

The story of the Brownes' struggle in Salem is from Nathaniel Morton, a contemporary from Plymouth, who obviously shared the views of the godly in Salem and not those of their opponents. According to him,

> the governour and council, and the generality of the people, did well approve of the ministers answer; and therefore finding those two brothers to be of high spirits, and their speeches and practices tending to mutiny and faction, the governour told them, that New England was no place for such as they.[23]

The Brownes, consequently, were sent back to England that same summer, and upon their arrival they immediately registered a complaint with the Massachusetts Bay Company in London against Endecott. But the Bay Company proved no more receptive than Salem authorities to the Brownes and dismissed the complaint out of hand. Indeed, among the leaders of the company was Thomas Dudley, who after his arrival to America wrote back to England in 1631 and declared in plain words that New England was no place for profane and ungodly people.

> I do more willingly use this open and plaine dealeinge least other men should fall short of their expectation when they come hether as wee.... If any godly men out of religious ends will come over to helpe us in the good worke wee are about I think they cannot dispose of themselves nor of their estates more to God's glory and the furtherance of their own reckoninge.... And for profaine

128

and deboshed persons their oversight in comeinge hether is wondered at, where they shall find nothing to content them.[24]

Massachusetts, then, was destined for the "precious" and not the "vile." The Brownes were the first, but many others following in their path returned to England because Puritan New England "was no place for such as they." From this cross-traffic, authorities in England, as well as the Puritan brethren there, gained first hand evidence of the nature of the holy experiment taking place during the 1630s in the wilderness. In this slowly-evolving comprehension on the part of the Crown - and English Puritans - in the 1630s about the actual nature of the religious reformation underway at Salem lay the basis for England's subsequent relationship with Massachusetts. For the Crown was not about to suffer abroad what it had taken great pains to suppress at home: religious non-conformism. Nor were many English Puritans about to support what in their eyes had no warrant in the word of God.

Yet for the Puritans of the migration, only the overseas prospect held out hope; England was no place for true reformation. Years before the establishment of the church in Salem, John Robinson, the Pilgrim's pastor in England and Holland, noted that

> if the old Puritans were secure of the magistrate's sword and go on with his good licence, they would shake off the prelate's yoke, and draw no longer in spiritual communion with all the profane in the land, and though they then preached and wrote against the separatists, yet if they were in a place where they might have their liberty, they would do as they did.[25]

Salem proved to be, as later did the entire Bay colony, as the sober Robinson foresaw. There the godly magistrate secured and administered the true reformation. In England of course there were many godly magistrates too, but they had to deal with the established Church, its ecclesiastical courts and jurisdiction. In 1632, for example, when John Cotton was summoned to appear before an ecclesiastical court in England for his practices, he first looked

> to his friends in power for relief, but he was quickly informed that the days of their influence in ecclesiastical matters had

passed. The Earl of Dorset bitterly remarked...that the only solution for nonconformists was "to fly for your safety."[26]

Many ministers who came to the Bay colony were at one time or another under the protection of a "Puritan earl," including the Earls of Lincoln, Warwick, and others. But with the failure of such Puritan lords to protect the godly, the saints, as the Early of Dorset advised them, had "to fly" for their "safety" outside the boarders of England. Holland, of course, was only a temporary refuge, as Bradford and his company discovered when they arrived there. "The manifold temptations of the place" led many future Pilgrims to take "some worse courses tending to dissolution and the danger of their souls...to the great...dishonour of God." Bradford and his people learned that Holland was not the appropriate place to raise "the kingdom of Christ," for there "they like skillful and beaten soldiers were fearful either to be entrapped or surrounded by their enemies so as they should neither be able to fight nor to fly."[27] Likewise, as Hooker wrote to Cotton in an attempt to prevent the latter from coming to Holland, "the state of these provinces to my weak eye, seems wonderfully ticklish and miserable." The native Dutchmen, he informed Cotton, "content themselves with every forms" of religions, "though much blemished; but the power of godliness...they know not."[28]

Thus, in England the godly magistrate could not exercise his power to assure the true reformation, while in Holland the native magistrate's policy of religious toleration offended the English Puritans' sense of religious reformation. Furthermore, in England, as Robinson wrote, the Puritans, in order to take any effective actions, first had "to secure...the magistrate's sword." Yet in Puritan New England there was no need for that, for the godly magistrate came precisely and mainly to secure there the conditions of religious reformation: to build the true church, to protect it against heresy, and to nurse it. Thus, when Endecott wrote to Bradford in the summer of 1629 that the congregationalist form of church government "is, as far as I can gather, no other than is warranted by the evidence of the truth. And the same which I have professed and maintain[ed]

130

ever since the Lord in mercy revealed Himself to me," he clearly signaled his primary reason for emigrating.[29] Like Robinson, Endecott understood that without political power the godly magistrate, as the Puritan experience in England had shown so clearly, could do little to exercise his godliness in defending and supporting the true church.

But what would happen if the godly magistrate succeeded in procuring a royal charter or patent for land in America, in which he acquired, as the agent of a commercial company, extended rights for self rule and the authority to execute them? Then, clearly, the godly magistrate could assume power and exercise his godliness. In England, Endecott had no power to exclude such "profane" people as the Brownes, people who used the Book of Common Prayer and the traditional rites and ceremonies of the Church of England from the parish church; but in Salem he possessed the political power to do much what he liked. Evidently, migration leaders understood this, and so precisely one year after the erection of the Salem Church, John Winthrop, the godly magistrate, had the royal charter of the Massachusetts Bay Company transferred to America. To the extent that Massachusetts Bay was a commercial company, its interest was to have its administrative body in London, the business hub of the expanding empire. In its character as a non-conformist religious enterprise, however, the Company's definite interest was to have its charter and government far away from the hands of the king and bishops, who could easily vacate the charter and convert Massachusetts into a royal colony, as James I had in fact earlier done with the Virginia Company in 1624. Accordingly, when the Bay Company transferred the charter to America, it did so because the charter provided exactly what the company wanted: extended rights for self-rule. Through the charter, the godly Puritan magistrate would possess political authority and power to exercise his godliness: to defend, protect, and nurse the true church.

Events in Salem, and later in Massachusetts Bay, did not refute John Robinson's prognosis concerning the "old Puritans." Emigration to the Bay colony did indeed turn out to be a way to "shake off the prelate's yoke," a way to escape from Establishment ecclesiastical jurisdiction. But there is more to Robinson's description of the "old Puritans." For he claimed, as we saw earlier, that if the old Puritans "might have their liberty, they would do as" the separatists did concerning church polity. The case of New England, at least, where there was much cooperation between Salem and Plymouth, and between Massachusetts and Plymouth on ecclesiastical matters, would seem to bear out Robinson's prediction. This development is not surprising because the Bay churches and the Plymouth church essentially shared the same premises of church-government, and there is much additional evidence that ministers who came to the Bay colony exercised a close relationship with Plymouth all through the 1620s. For example, when Plymouth people had trouble with Rev. John Lyford in 1624 because he tried to send letters protesting Plymouth ecclesiastical polity back to England, both parties appealed to the Adventurers in London, each choosing "two eminent men for moderators in the business. Lyford's faction chose Mr. White, a counselor at Law; the other part chose Reverend Mr. Hooker, the minister." This was Thomas Hooker, then rector of Esher, Surrey, and later a founder of Connecticut. "This incident," wrote the biographer of Hooker, "also establishes that comparatively early in his career," Hooker "was willing to be on friendly terms with the separatists." John Cotton, too, could be on friendly terms with Plymouth, for Deacon Fuller, in his letter to Bradford in 1630, wrote that he met in Boston, New England, "a gentleman, one Mr. Cottington...who told me, that Mr. Cotton's charge at Hampton was, that they [that is, the fleet of 1630] should take advice of them at Plymouth, and should [do] nothing to offend them." And in New England in 1629, "letters did pass between Mr. Higginson, and Mr. Brewster, the reverend elder of the church of Plymouth," wrote a contemporary, "and they did agree in their judgments, viz. concerning the church-membership of the children with their parents."[30]

III Reformation and Separation

However, if there had been no essential differences between the congregationalists in the Bay and the separatists at Plymouth concerning religious creeds and practices, could it be as well that there had not been so crucial and essential a difference between Plymouth and Massachusetts on the issue of separation? In his Orthodoxy in Massachusetts, Perry Miller powerfully argues that the issue of separation or non-separation from the Church of England divided essentially the Puritan movement in England in the decades before the great Puritan migration, and that the subsequent migration itself was carried out by the non-separatist congregationalists. Among the evidence he adduces as to the non-separating character of the planters of the Bay colony is the famous sailing words of Higginson. On May 1, 1629, prior to setting sail for New England, Francis Higginson gathered the passengers of his ship for a final view of England. While all gazed at the disappearing shore, Higginson told them:

> We will not say as the separatists were wont to say at their leaving of England, Farewell Babylon! Farewell the Church of God in England, and all the christian friends there! We do not go to New England as separatists from the Church of England; though we cannot but separate from the corruptions in it: but we go to practisc the positive part of church reformation, and propagate the gospel in America.[31]

Clearly, Higginson's words can be interpreted in many ways and not just in the manner chosen by Miller.

Indeed, there is much evidence that Massachusetts did not diverge so sharply from Plymouth on the issue of separation as Miller contended. "This absolute cry, only of the Elect, holding all (but themselves) reprobates and cast-awaies," wrote Captain John Smith on Winthrop's fleet of 1630. "Babel [i.e. Babylon] they tearmed England," he wrote of the Puritan emigrants. These characterizations are significant, because Smith totally denied that these emigrants were "Separatists," or that they were even, according to him, "Puritans."[32] And Richard Sadler, who came over to New England in 1638, recorded in his account

133

of the colonial churches that there had been "ingratitude among many of them toward their native contry of England calling it Babilon, Rome, the land of idolatry etc."[33] And Anne Hutchinson, at her trial, in Massachusetts, testified to the powerful lure of the colony's religious liberty for people, who like the separatists, were convinced of England's utterly corrupt state. "When I was in old England," she confessed, "I was much troubled at the constitution of the churches there, so farre, as I was ready to have joyned the Separation." But although she did not join the separatists, she did maintain that "God discovered unto me the unfaithfulness of the churches [of England] and the danger of them, and that none of those Ministers could preache the Lord Jesus aright." Thus, without being separatist herself, Anne Hutchinson remembered that "then it was revealed to me that the Ministers of England were these Antichrist...." Consequently, she found that after John Cotton and her brother Wheelwright were silenced, "there was non in England that I durst here [hear]," and so betook herself to the Bay colony.[34]

Theologically speaking, the issue of separation related to the question of whether the Church of England was a true church. Separatists denied while the Congregationalists of the Bay colony affirmed that it was. So runs the common interpretation. But, as Higginson's words suggest, the issue was not so clear cut. Consider the intellectual position of William Ames and the actions of his disciples. Ames, as Keith Sprunger explains, maintained that "visible instituted churches are congregations of gathered believers, and that each particular congregation is truly a complete church." Yet his premise - viz., that the church was made up of visible saints - was not, as we saw earlier, attainable in England, for there both the established Church and a great number of people as well were opposed to the Puritan conception of reformation. On the other hand, each particular church, or congregation, according to Ames was a part of "the mystical invisible church," that is the invisible catholic church, or the universal church, to which the saints of all times and places belonged.[35] When congregationalists declared that they were not separatists, they meant that they did not separate from

134

this invisible, catholic, and universal church, and that they counted the Church of England to belong to this invisible universal church. But what about separation from the "visible" corrupted Church of England?

For the Puritan emigrants, the distinction made by Ames between the invisible and visible church - once an effective means of assuaging Puritan disappointment over the sorry state of religion in England - did not serve their needs. Because of their eschatological visions and millennial expectations, Bay colony Puritans, tired of an intellectual stance that rested upon faith in the eventual reformation of the present Church of England, demanded immediate and throughout reformation. But they well knew by the early seventeenth century that this goal was not immediately attainable. As it turns out, not even Ames himself could any longer maintain his previous distinction. For while formally condemning separation and schism, Ames actively supported Puritan efforts to remove from England and in fact came in 1630 to justify such emigration in his book Conscience:

> If any one either wearied out with unjust vexations, or providing for his edification, or for testimony against the wickedness, shall depart from such a society to one more, without condemnation that Church which he leaves, he is not therefore to be accused of Schism of any sinne.[36]

Such casuistry, in fact, lay behind much of the Bay colony's public expression in the 1630s. On the basis of such sophistry the Puritans in the wilderness had appealed to England not to consider them as separatists. In actuality, however, the tension between reformation and separation had been more real and acute. For according to Ames, "Although we may joyne to one [Church], in which many defects are necessarily to tolerated, yet not to one in which we must of necessity partake in any sinne."[37] Thus, in 1630, when he came to justify the great Puritan migration, Ames himself had disavowed his earlier distinction between the visible and invisible church. To stay in England meant explicitly that the saints did not live up to their promised covenanted relationship with God. That is why many colonists broke with Ames' caution not to call England what, given their millennial expectations, it surely was: Babylon, Rome, the place in which the Antichrist reigned. On this important issue of separation, then, actions often spoke louder than words.

Furthermore, separation was not merely a theological question - one concerned with fine distinctions between visible and invisible churches - but an acute social question. As the seventeenth century historian William Hubbard said of the Plymouth Separatists, and their counterparts in the Bay colony, they "did strangely jump very near together, into one and the same method and idea of church discipline." And Skelton, the minister at Salem, "did not, in some things, not only imitate and equal, but strongly endeavour to go beyond, that pattern of Separation set before them in Plymouth," as in the matter of "enjoining all women to wear veils, under the penalty of non-communion...as well as in refusing communion with the Church of England."[38]

The social context of separation, involving the refusal to take communion with the Church of England and its members, was a grave issue, as John Winthrop and his fleet learned immediately upon their arrival in America. When members of Winthrop's fleet came to Salem in the summer of 1630, some of them requested admission to the sacraments (e.g., the Lord's Supper or Baptism) in the Church of Salem. This request Skelton strongly denied on the grounds that the new emigrants were not members of any particular reformed church, organized on the basis of an explicit covenant. When news of this event reached John Cotton in Boston, England, he wasted no time in rebuking Skelton. "It not a little troubled me," wrote Cotton to Skelton in 1631,

> that you should deny the Lords Supper to such godly & faithfull Servants of Christ as mr governour mr Johnson, mr Dudley...my griefe increased upo[n] mee when I heard you denyed Baptisme unto mr Codingtons child...because hee was no member of any particular church, though of the Catholike.

To Cotton, refusal to admit the new emigrants to the sacraments suggested that Skelton thought "that none of our congregations in England are particular reformed churches."[39] Skelton's action, that is, indicated clearly that he practiced a separatist stance visa-a-vis the Church of England.

The crucial difference, then, between Skelton and Cotton in 1631 was on the issue of whether the covenant was to be considered a necessary condition for any particular or visible church. "I answer," wrote Cotton in his letter to Skelton, "that this explicite & solemne covenant is rather a solemne vow to bind the members of the church together...then any such essential cause of the church without which it can not bee."[40] Earlier we saw that cotton attempted to base his church in Boston, England, on a covenant group, but made no effort at that time to identify his church exclusively with this godly group, for this indeed would have meant separation. But in 1636 Cotton came to Salem to preach and in his sermon he confessed that his letter of 1631 was in error. What caused Cotton in 1636, as he said, "to alter my judgment" concerning Skelton's action in 1630? For one thing, in 1636 he was no longer willing, as he had been in 1631, to defend the Church of England on the basis of his eschatological visions and millennial beliefs, as can be seen, for example, in his An Exposition Upon the Thirteenth Chapter of the Revelation, a series of sermons on the Apocalypse which he preached in Boston in the late 1630s. The crucial difference between his stands of 1631 and 1636, however, lay in his changing view of the role of the covenant. In 1631 the covenant was not for Cotton a necessary condition for the true church. But in 1636 he plainly argued for

> the necessity of a church covenant to the institution of a
> church...that which doth make a people a joined people with
> God, that doth make a church: What is that? The covenant of
> grace doth make a people, a joined people with God, and
> therefore a church of God.

Now viewing the true church or congregation as necessarily based upon an explicit covenant, Cotton began to preach freely on the duty of separation. "You would have no fellowship with them, that did allow of false assemblies," Cotton told the people of Salem. Furthermore, "The Lord in heaven will speak a blessing to your separation," from those who "do reject the word of life," or those who "put the word of God from them."[41]

The transformation of cotton's views concerning the covenant and hence of separation is crucial to our understanding of the Puritan migration, for many in England - Puritan and non-Puritan alike - criticized the Bay colony exactly as Cotton did in 1631. "Heare is a muttering of a too palpable separation of your people from our church government. Allas, alas," lamented a friend of the colony in England in the early 1630s.[42] To these Englishmen, the Bay colony's churches, as Cotton saw in 1631 concerning Salem's church, simply denied the right hand of fellowship to members of English congregations. From this English perspective, not the distinction between visible and invisible churches, but rather the actual fact of the exclusion of members of the Church of England from colonial church membership and the sacraments, constituted indeed the crucial point of separation. After all, as noted Dr. John Burgess in 1631, the pursuit of reformation "carry some men that they scarce will give a friendly countenance or salutation to any of different minde...as if Christ were (I say not) divided betwixt us, but wholly taken away from us to them."[43]

Radical Puritans in England had always mourned the impurity of the parish communion, but in the face of the established church their options were limited. No such limitations, though barred Puritans in America from executing the positive part of their premises of religious reformation: to found the church upon a necessary covenant basis and thereby to identify the church solely with visible saints. In this context, as Roger Williams pointedly reminded Bay colony Puritans, Ames' fine theological distinction between the visible and invisible church quickly unraveled, ultimately becoming irrelevant. For example, in a letter to Williams, John Cotton claimed that Massachusetts Puritans "practise[d] separation in peace" from England, and that "the Revelation, speake of locall separation, which...we have made" upon emigration. To this Williams answered that if Cotton "call the Land Babel mystically...how can it be Babel, and yet the Church of Christ also?" Here Williams had put his finger on the essentially

138

ambiguous nature, theologically considered, of the Puritan emigration. For if the Puritan emigration defined its departure from England in eschatological and millennial terms according to the Book of Revelation, which Cotton and the Bay Puritans did in fact, then contrary to Cotton's claim, the Puritan emigration was not "of local Separation." "I could not well have beleeved," wrote Williams in his examination of Cotton's letter,

> that Mr. Cotton or any would make the comming forth of <u>Babel</u> in the antitype. Rev. 18, 4, to be <u>locall</u> and <u>material</u> also. What civill State, Nation or Countrey in the world, in the antitype, must now be called <u>Babel</u>?"

In other words, Williams had pinpointed the central contradiction of the Puritans on separation: if England was Babel and it was necessary to separate from it and remove to New England, how could the church in England still be counted a true church?[44]

Of course, the issue of separation is at bottom of a matter of definition. Obviously, the Puritan emigrants strove at all times to avoid the taint of separation. Nonetheless, we must be skeptical about their claims, for too often in their words and actions in the wilderness, both on the subject of church government in the New World and on the status of the Church of England in the Old World, these Puritans exhibited their kinship to the self-proclaimed separatists. And indeed, this was precisely how many in England viewed their colonial venture from the very beginning. For all the while the Bay Puritans dissociated themselves from separation, the ships that stocked the Bay colony with its godly population returned to England loaded with those like the Brownes who had been judged by Bay authorities as unfit for the holy experiment in the wilderness. These returnees brought their own stories back to England on the actual state of ecclesiastical affairs in New England. To understand the relationship between England and Massachusetts in the 1630s, then, it is necessary to appreciate the fact that, although the Puritans in America presented themselves as non-separatists, the Crown and those Puritans still in England viewed them otherwise: namely, as people who had in actuality separated themselves from the Church of England.

IV   The "Call" to New England

We left Salem's settlers in the summer of 1629, when they had just laid "the right foundation" for their church there. For Francis Higginson, those first months in Salem had been dedicated to the completion of a work for the future emigration from England. He completed his "A true relation of the last voyage to New England" in July 1629 and immediately sent it off to "His Friends in England" who had "earnestly requested to be truly notified in these things." Tracing the origins of his own voyage to "the Company of New England, consisting of many worthy gentlemen in the Citty of London, Dorchester, and other places, ayming at the glory of God," Higginson directed this book to a select audience: to those godly people already inclined to emigrate.

> This I write not for boasting and flattery; but for the benefit of
> those that have a mynd to come to New England hereafter, that
> if they looke for and desyre to have as prosperous a voyage as
> we had, they may use the same meanes to attayne the same.

Describing for these readers his own "pious and   christian-like passage," Higginson related how he and his fellow passengers aboard the ship that carried them to New England had "constantly served God morning and evening by reading and expounding a chapter singing and prayer."[45]

In July 1629, Higginson also sent a letter to "His Friends at Leicester," advising immediate emigration. This letter clearly reveals how eschatological visions so powerfully informed the godly migration to New England. "Such of you as come from Leister, I would counsell you to come quickly," Higginson wrote, for "if you linger too long, the passages of Jordan through the malice of Satan, may be stopped, that you cannot come if you would." Higginson informed these friends that "there are certainly expected here next spring the coming of 60 familyes out of Dorcettershire," who had already requested Endecott "to appoint them place of habitation; they bringing their ministers with them." This was the group with which Roger Clap came, as we saw earlier, along with the ministers John Warham and John Maverick. "Also many families are expected out of

141

Lincolnshire," Higginson added, "and a minister with them, and a great company of godly christians out of London." As much as he could, then, Higginson tried to convey the actual conditions prevailing in the colony. "Once parted with England," he detailed,

> you shall meete neither with taverns nor alehouse, nor butchers, nor grossers, nor apothecaries shops to helpp what things you need in the midest of the great ocean, nor when you are come to land here.

A daunting prospect, but one full of promise, as Higginson expressed in another work of that year, "New Englands Plantation," intended for interested English readers: "that which is our greatest comfort and means of defence above all others, is, that we have here the true religion and holy ordinances of Almighty God among us."[46]

Higginson's writings were widely read by "His Friends" in England. Three editions of his "New Englands Plantation" appeared in 1630. In October of that year Winthrop sent Higginson's book to his friend John Forth, requesting him to "reade the book" to his wife, and also to copy it in order to "shewe it to mr. Mott, my neighbour and others that have a minde to N:E; especially that gratious latter in the end" - that is, Higginson's letter to his friends in Leicester - "which I wish thee and the rest to read seriously over." Thomas Mott, though, does not appear to have needed this extra stimulus. Already in June 1629 he had written Winthrop that his mind "stands inclinable" to emigrate, informing the latter that "many will goe" to New England.[47]

Thus, while the Salem colonists had begun to fulfill the positive part of the reformation, "the call" to New England was sounded in many parts of England. In May 1629, Winthrop wrote to his wife that the Lord "hath smitten all other Churches" in Europe "before our eyes, and made them to drinke of the bitter cuppe of tribulation, even unto death," and that now the Lord "is turninge the cuppe toward us also," namely England, "and because we are the last, our portion must be, to drinke the verye dreggs which remaine." God's imminent Judgment was approaching England, Winthrop was sure. Yet, he applied this eschatological and apocalyptic vision evidently only to the old world, for the Lord, Winthrop wrote his wife, "will provide a shelter and hiding place for us and ours." In July of the same year at the "Commencement in Cambridge...many reverend Divines" assembled and listened "to Consider of mr Whites call" for New England. Probably in August, the "General Observations for the Plantation of New England" were composed and circulated, and on August 26 the leaders of the Puritan emigration of 1630 signed the Cambridge Agreement in which they promised to emigrate to New England, on the condition that "the whole government together with the Patent for the said plantacion bee first by an order of Court legally transferred and established to remayne with us" in New England.[48]

The basis of the Agreement was the royal charter to establish a commercial colony in New England, given to the Bay Company on March 4, 1628/9. The Puritans could legally discuss the transfer of this charter because nowhere in this document did it say that the government of the Massachusetts Bay Company should remain in England. This loophole provided the leaders of the emigration with a great opportunity. Who was responsible for this? Was the omission the Crown's oversight or the Bay Company's foresight? Not much has been written about the issuing of the Massachusetts Bay Company's charter, but one study that does deal with this question reveals an interesting fact. According to Charles Deane, the original draft of the proposed charter was written by the New England Company through its counselor, a Mr. Whyte.[49] This suggests that the original draft by the Company eventually served as the basis of the royal charter. We should not ask, therefore, why the Crown failed to stipulate that the government of the Bay Company remain in England, but rather what the New England Company intended to gain by not mentioning the location of the government in its request for the charter. Lack of further information on this subject makes a conclusive answer to this question impossible. Yet it is clear that if the Bay Company intended to establish non-conformist churches in New England, it needed to have absolute control over the colony. For the precondition for

143

religious reformation in the colony was indeed noninterference by King and bishops. Without this, Bay Puritans could hope for no better prospects than they had met in England. This was, in fact, the nature of the powers that the Company thought it had procured. On April 30, 1629, immediately after procuring the royal charter, the Company declared that "we have...thought fit to settle and establish an absolute government at our Plantation in the Massachusetts Bay, in New England."[50]

What happened in August 1629, as represented by the Cambridge Agreement was that Puritan leaders decided that their de facto monopoly of government in the colony was not enough; in addition, they wanted the royal charter and the main body of the Company's government switched from England to the colony, so that the Crown could not do to their holy enterprise in Massachusetts what it had done to the Virginia Company. For in 1624 the crown had vacated the charter of the Virginia Company, thereby establishing royal government in Virginia. "His Majesty's ayme," ran the royal proclamation on Virginia, "was only to reduce the Government into such a Course as might best agree with that Forme which was held in the rest of his Royall Monarchie." Consequently, the King ordered that "the Government of the Collonie of Virginia shall immediately depend uppon Our Selfe, and not be commytted to anie Companie or Corporation."[51]

In the Virginia case, the commercial interests of the colony were not necessarily injured by this transfer of administrative control. But for Massachusetts Bay, with its professedly religious aspirations, such a transfer, considering the Crown's views on religious unity and conformity, could only prove fatal to the colony's original intention. Accordingly, to help ward off such a situation, Puritan leaders had the Massachusetts Bay charter and government transferred to America. The charter was the legal basis on which the godly magistrates in the colony exercised the political authority essential to the fulfillment of the premises of reformation. All during the 1630s the Crown had tried to bring the colony to surrender its charter, and by this to take the

144

government there into the King's hand. But the Puritans consistently refused to give up the legal basis of their government in Massachusetts, for the charter was indeed the necessary constitutional means by which they could execute their holy experiment. Even in the face of armed intervention, the Puritans, as we will see later, were unwilling to surrender the charter.

This, then, is the importance of the Cambridge Agreement. Without some form of self-rule, as the charter provided, the imperative of religious reformation could not be realized. In England the hands of the godly magistrates were tied by ecclesiastical courts and jurisdictions, and not the less by the policy of the Crown. But in the colony the godly magistrate was free to become what Puritans had long sought: the nourishing father of the true church. However, the radical plan of the Cambridge Agreement had to be affirmed by the General Court of the Bay Company. Thus, only two days after the agreement was signed the members of the Court were notified that on August 28

> the espetial cause of their meeting was to give answere to divers
> gent, intending to goe into New England, whether or noe the
> chiefe govnmt of the plantacon, togeather wth the pattent, should
> bee settled in New England, or heere.

One day latter the Company passed a resolution concerning the transfer of the charter and the government made in favor of those who signed the agreement: "it appeared by the genall consent of the Company, that the govnmt & pattent should bee settled in New England, & accordingly an order to bee drawne upp."[52]

With this resolution, the way was cleared for Winthrop's fleet of 1630. Earlier the Cambridge Agreement had set also the time table for emigration:

> To embarke for the said plantacion by the first of march next, at
> such port or ports of this land…to the end to passe the Seas
> (under God protection) to inhabite and continue in New
> England."[53]

Less than a year was left for the Puritans to prepare the great fleet, too little time for such a great undertaking. Only a few had waited for them in Salem, but the leaders of the emigration of 1630 were sure many would follow from England. For many had already declared their intentions to go, even before the resolution

145

of the General Court concerning the transfer of the charter and government. Many others soon heard about the errand into the wilderness.

> Sir, we conceite you may have heard of the resolution of divers of us to engage our person and estates in the planting of a Colony in New England for divers ends concerning the glory of God and the service of his Church,

wrote Winthrop and other leaders to inform Puritans of their plans. It was a call to come to Massachusetts and erect there the true church: "We are in hand with for the establishing of a Church in N:E."[54]

An urgent task facing the leaders of the Puritan migration in late 1629 and early 1630 was to find a sufficient number of ministers to serve the many laymen who had already decided to emigrate. "Unto the furthering of this work," wrote these leaders,

> we finde the L[orde] strongly overwaying and enclining the spirits of many of his servants to offer themselves willingly unto him for his service, only we want hitherto able and sufficiant Ministers to joyne with us in the worke.

On this disproportionate situation, the leaders continued:

> The reason whereof we find to be the Conscience of the Obligacion by which they stand bound unto this Church for the services in which most of them are employed att present and want of sufficient calling unto the employment for which we desire them.[55]

The Puritan migration, that is, in the eyes of its primary organizers, was mainly a laymen's enterprise; ministers were slow to respond to the call, arriving in New England only after the first waves of laymen had already established themselves there. When Isaac Johnson wrote to Winthrop in December 1629, he informed him that Hooker, Cotton, and Ames had still not given positive answers on the upcoming sailings in 1630. Ames never removed to New England, and Hooker preferred at that time to go to Holland. Cotton hesitated until 1633, when he finally sailed for the colony. Yet, if "able" ministers, "bound unto this Church [of England]," found it sometimes difficult to join the migration, many

146

laymen responded to the venture with enthusiasm. Thus, Arthur Tyndale wrote to Winthrop:

> I had absolutelie resolved...to live under the Hierarchie of your church and civill government, purposed and concluded among your selves...oh, if I obtain the happines, to laye but one stone in the foundacion of this new Syion, I shalbe ravished with high content.[56]

In March 1630, Puritans began to gather at the port of Southampton. In April, John Cotton came from Boston to preach a farewell sermon before these members of Winthrop's fleet. "The placing of a people in this or that Country," Cotton told the godly emigrants, "is from the appointment of the Lord." The Lord "carrieth them along to it, so that they plainly see a providence of God leading them from on Country to another." Within a theocratic universe, ruled directly and immediately by divine providence, the time, the place, and the destiny of the Puritan migration, Cotton instructed, was from God. "You have seene how I have borne you as on Eagles wings," Cotton quoted from Exodus, "and brought you unto my selfe." On the present occasion, New England was awaiting the godly seafarers, for of their general plight the Lord said "I will appoint a place for my people Israell, and I will plant them, that they may dwell in a place of their owne, and move no more." On the shore across the ocean, Cotton assured the emigrants, there "is a land of promise," because there "God wrappes us in with his Ordinances, and warmes us with the life and power of them as with wings." And why the necessity for such a removal of God's people from England to New England? Because when "grievous sinnes overspread Country," they "threaten desolation." Therefore, "a wise man foreseeth them," and "he seeth commandement to hide himself from it." In Cotton's words, the Puritan migration became an essential element in the unfolding Christian drama:

> Here is then an eye of God that openes a door there [New England], and set him loose here [England], inclines his heart that way, and outlookes all difficulties. When God makes roome for us, no binding here, and an open way there.[57]

147

In his farewell sermon Cotton blessed his brethren Puritans' errand into the wilderness. But by 1631, disturbed by the ecclesiastical tendencies in Massachusetts Bay, he was almost ready to revoke that blessing. It was in this spirit that he hastened the letter, discussed earlier, to Rev. Skelton in Salem, condemning the separatist tendency evident in that colony. "Reject not the wombe that bare you," Cotton warned Skelton, "nor the paps that gave you sucke: till Christ gives us a bill of divorcement, do not you divorce yourself fro[m] us."[58] Cotton was angry in 1631, apparently because he considered recent events in Salem to be a rejection of what he had preached before the emigrants in 1630, when he had advised:

> be not unmindfull of our Jerusalem at home, whether you leave us, or stay at home with us.... As God continueth his presence with us...so be ye present in spirit with us, though absent in body: Forget not the wombe that bare you and the brest that gave you sucke.[59]

Cotton, like many other Puritans in England during the 1630s, was especially angered by the separatist tendencies evinced by the Bay Colony because these departures stood in sharp contrast to the declaration made by the emigrants of 1630 before they left England. Aboard the Arbella, on April 7, 1630, before their departure for America, Winthrop, Saltonstall, Johnson, Dudley and other leaders of the migration had written "The Humble Request." As Cotton had advised them in his sermon, these Puritan leaders declared in this declaration that their "solemne Enterprise" was not aimed at separation from the Church of England. Addressing themselves to "the rest of their brethren in and of the Church of England," these leaders of the migration asked that their departure from England not be considered as a movement seeking separation.

> We desire you would be pleased to take notice of the principals, and body of our company, as those who esteeme it our honour to call the Church of England, from whence wee rise, our deare Mother, and cannot part from our native Country, where she specially resideth, without much sadness of heart, and many tears in our eyes, ever acknowledging that such hope and part as wee have obtained in the common salvation, we have received in her

148

bosome, and suckt it from her breast: wee leave it not therefore, as loathing that milk wherewith we were nourished there.[60]

Yet, despite this appeal of "The Humble Request," the actions of Winthrop and his godly Puritan company in America signified precisely the very thing these men strove to disavow: separation. For these emigrants knew that the Crown and church in England would not allow in New England what they banned at home - namely, a non-conformist church. Something of the complicated political nature of the Puritan declaration was caught by John Rous, who wrote in his diary entry of June 7, 1630:

> Some little while since the company went to New England under Mr. Winthrop. Mr. Cotton, of Boston in Lincolnshire, went to their departure...and preached to them, as we heare, out of Samuel, vii, 10...I Sawe a book at Bury at bookseller's, conteining a declaration of their intent who be gone to Newe England, set out by themselves, and purposed for satisfaction to the King and state...because of some scandalous misconceivings that rune abroade.[61]

Rous well understood the nature and purpose of "The Humble Request," and the situation surrounding it. However they chose to present themselves, the emigrating Puritans were Separatists.

As the "Humble Request" was written, in part, to refute "the generall rumour of this solemne Enterprise,"[62] John White published his own The Planters Plea in 1630, again to scotch rumors of Separation associated with the Massachusetts Bay. "It is objected by some," wrote White,

> that religion indeede and the colour thereof is the cloake of this work, but under it is secretly harboured faction and separation from the Church. Men of ill affected mindes (they conceive) unwiling to joine any longer with our assemblies, meane to draw themselves apart, and to unite into body of their owne, and to make that place nursery of faction and rebellion, disclaiming and renouncing our Church as the limbe of Antichrist.

White was a long-time activist in the cause of establishing a colony for religious purposes in New England, and in The Planter's Plea he set out to record and refute much of the contemporary criticism relating to the Puritan migration.

This book supplies the best evidence we have on some of specific contemporary objections against the Puritan migration. As one of these ran:

> yet they dislike our discipline and ceremonies, and so they will prove themselves semi-separatists at least; and that is their intention in removing from us, that they may free themselves from our government.[63]

The arguments against the Puritan migration, cited by White in The Planter's Plea, indeed capture the essential religious dimensions of the future holy experiment in the wilderness. The central feature of the migration, as White quotes his contemporaries, was that the emigrants were not willing "to joine any longer in our assemblies," or churches in England, and wanted "to draw themselves apart, and to unite into body of their owne." And indeed the Puritans in America sought not to repeat the ecclesiastical polity of the motherland. In New England "into the dark mists," as wrote Sumner Chilton Powell in his Puritan Village, "had disappeared articles of visitations, Book of Common Prayer, presentments, commissary, archdeacon, church courts, purgation, certificate of penance, and holy days."[64] Puritans, after all, did not travel to New England to make it old England; they traveled to make it "new." Most important, of course, was the fact that in New England Puritans were finally free from the presence of the "ungodly" and "profane" people who troubled so much the Puritans in England prior to their emigration to America. "Here," wrote Thomas Welde of Puritan Massachusetts in 1633 to his friends in England,

> are none of the men of Gibea the sonnes of Belial knocking at our doors disturbing our sweet peace or threatening violence. Here blessed be the Lord God for ever Our eares are not beaten nor the aire filled with Oaths. Swearers nor Railers, Nor our eyes and eares vexed with the unclea[n] Conversation of the wicked.[65]

Ultimately, the Puritans in their own justifications, as well as their antagonists' many accusations, point up two pivotal factors instrumental to the decision to emigrate to New England. These Puritans desired to fulfill in America "the gospel of Reformation" as they understood it, and they believed that they lived in a special dimension of time. A contemporary satirical poem against the Puritans vividly caught this aspect:

> My Brethren all attend,
> And list to my relation:
> This is the day, mark what I say,
> Tends to your renovation;
> Stay not among the Wicked,
> Lest that with them you perish,
> But let us to New England go
> And the Pagan People cherish[66]

Likewise the Puritan author of Good News from New England in 1648:

> When England by Elizabeth began a Reformation
> It was a joyful day to all, the godly of that
>   Nation.
> Proh Dolor [unhappily], it did not goe on with
>   joyfull acclamation,
> But hierarchy and lordly throne of Prelacy invading,
> The government of Christs dear flocke, the godli-
>   ness was fading.
> Some men impute it to the pride of Bishops, others
>   say,
> The loosenesse of the Laity did carry most away.
> But sure it is that godlinesse, and purity deriding,
> Mov'd many godly ones to seek, a place of new
>   abiding.[67]

By and large, then, from the apologetic and equivocal nature of the emigrants' departing declarations and from the concern of their friends in England to defend the emigration and the ecclesiastical polity in the colony, we can conclude that many in England understood the essentially separatist character of the Puritan migration. Accordingly, official eyes in England were trained upon the colony's system of ecclesiastical polity. At once, therefore, the issue of ecclesiastical polity in the colony and its non-conformist character became the crucial point in Massachusetts' relationship with England all during the 1630s. The ultimate goal of the Puritans in the Bay colony was indeed to maintain their unique ecclesiastical way in the wilderness according to their creed and millennial expectations. But at the same time they had to be exceptionally cautious that their practice of religious non-conformism and their explicit separation from the rites and ceremonies of the Church of England would not result in political and social separation from England, which would present indeed a real danger to the young colony. By all means, they had to avoid being officially adjudged separatists by the Crown, for such a judgment would spell the end of their holy experiment in the wilderness of America. This was the reason why Bay Puritans constantly denied that they were separatists, even while they were explicitly separating themselves from the Church of England. In order not to raise the anger of authorities in England, Bay Puritans had to dissociate themselves from separation.

V   The Struggle Over the Charter

Already in 1631, Thomas Dudley was writing that many who had left the Massachusetts Bay colon

> out of their evill affections towards us, have raised many false and scandalous reports against us, affirming us to be Brounists in religion and ill affected to our state at home and that theirs vile reports have wonne credit with some who formerly wished us well.

But the task of defending the colony against these rumors became harder and harder if not impossible indeed, even for the friends of Dudley and Winthrop in England. For the Puritans in the Bay colony in truth were asking the impossible. For example, when Dudley wrote that

> for our further cleareinge I truely affirm that I know noe one person who came over with us the last yeare to be altered in his judgment and affection eyther in ecclesiastical or civill respects since our comeinge hether,

he uttered only a half-truth. What he failed to mention was that the Book of Common Prayer had been banned in the colony, along with the traditional rites and ceremonies of the Church of England. Dudley had asked "our friends" in England to "bee more ready to answer for us, then we heare they have beene."[68] But, considering the circumstances, this was no easy chore. A sailor returning from Massachusetts to England in that year, wrote Edward Howes to Winthrop,

> would give none of you a good word but the governor...al the rest were Heriticks and they would be more holy than all the world, they would be a peculiar people to God, but goe to the divell...that your preachers in their publique prayers, pray for the governor before they praye for our kinge and state...that you never use the Lords prayer, that your ministers marrie none, that fellowes which keepe hogges all the weeke preach on the Saboth...that you count all men in England, yea all out of your church...in the state of damnacion.

For Howes these rumors were evidence that Satan, unable to reign fully in England, was trying to gain a foothold in Massachusetts. "Here by," he concluded his letter to Winthrop,

153

you may partly see howe the Divell stirrs up his instruments where his kingdome is so mightily opposed he setts upon you with all [h]is might and maine and would have you to be like himself.[69]

Howes was a loyal friend of the holy experiment in America, but many in England had a wholly different view of Puritan activities in Massachusetts and the non-conformist, or congregational, church established there.

Authorities in England were of course well acquainted with the Puritan migration from its very beginnings. When Charles Chauncey, Vicar of Ware, Hertford, was charged in 1630 by the Ecclesiastical Commissioners with omitting "the surplice, the cross in Baptisme," he was additionally accused of speaking "in praise of the Puritans, in disparagement of the authority of the church," and "in expectations whereof he asserted that some families were preparing to go to New England." And many local authorities could not avoid first hand experience with the Puritan migration. For example, in 1630 the Lord Mayor of London complained about shortages and scarcities in his city because "the people which lately gone for New England and other plantations have carried with them great store of victuals." Likewise with the Mayor and Aldermen of Bristol, who complained that "the late furnishing of a ship for New England has in some measure unfurnished their market" from corn. And ecclesiastical authorities also faced on the local level serious problems in relation to the Puritan migration. In 1632, for example, Dr. Samuel Collins, of Braintree, wrote that the bishop of London, Laud, was angry with him because he had failed "to reform the error of sundry in this town" - that is, of non-conformist Puritans who had demanded from Collins "toleration of their wonted inconformity." Apologetically, Collins wrote to his friend that

it is no easy matter to reduce a numerous congregation into order that has been disorderly these 50 years, and for the last seven years has been encouraged in that way by all the refractory ministers of the country by private meetings and leaving schismatical books among them.

154

"These persons," continued Collins on the Puritans of Braintree, "have laboured to make his person and ministry contemptible and odious, because he would not hold correspondence with them." Yet, Collins admitted, he had few choices open to him on the matter, for

> if he had suddenly fallen upon the strict practice of conformity he had undone himself and broken the town to pieces. Upon the first notice of alteration many were resolving to go to New England.[70]

Circulation of rumors about, and the general growth of information on, the Puritan migration and the ecclesiastical situation in Massachusetts led English authorities in the early 1630s to take a closer look into the entire Puritan holy enterprise in the wilderness. In early November 1632, the Council for New England decided that "no ship passingers nor goods be permitted to be transported for New England without License" from the Council for New England. At the end of that month, the Council was pleased to note that "his Majesty...was gratiously pleased to referre the Examinacon of abuses complained of in the plantacons in New England, should bee speedily moved and entreated to meet." And in November, apparently, Sir Christopher Gardiner, Thomas Morton of Merrymount, and Philip Radcliffe, all with objections to the Massachusetts patent, petitioned the Privy Council, describing Bay Puritans as scandalous people and requesting that Massachusetts Bay Company be deprived of its royal charter. In response to this action, Edward Winslow, Plymouth's agent in London and now Massachusetts' agent there as well, petitioned the Privy Council in November 1632 on behalf of "the planters in New England." He declared in his petition that the Puritans left England because of "disliking many things in practice here in respect of Church ceremony" and that they had chosen "rather to leave the country than to be accounted troublers of it." He strongly denied that the colonists were "Brownists, factious Puritans, and schismatics" and asked the Privy Council to consider "the characters of their adversaries," Morton, Gardiner, and others. Finally, almost two years after the departure of Winthrop's fleet, the Massachusetts Bay colony's case came to Whitehall. On December 19, 1632, "upon reading this day several Petitions preferred by some Planters of New England...and upon long debate of the whole carriage of the Plantations of that Country," the Privy Council decided to set up a committee from among its members to "examine how the Patentes for the said Plantation, have been graunted, and how carried," and in general to evaluate "Informations" contained in the petitions concerning ecclesiastical matters in the Bay colony.[71]

The resolution of the Privy Council's Committee for New England appeared as an order on January 19, 1632/3:

> His Majesty hath lately been informed of great distraction and much disorder in that plantation in the parts of America called New England, which if they be true, and suffered to run on, would tend to the dishonour of his Kingdom, and utter ruine of the plantation.

Yet, as the Privy Council's order continued, the Committee finding "most of the things informed" against the colony "being denied, and resting to prove," "his Majesty" decided

> not only to maintain the liberties and privileges heretofore granted, but supply anything further that might tend to the good government, prosperity and comfort of his people there of that place.[72]

Upon receipt of this decision, Winthrop hastened a letter off to Bradford in Plymouth.

> The cause was heard before the Lords of the Privy Council, and afterwards reported to the King; the success whereof makes it evident to all, that the Lord hath care of his people here...the conclusion was against all mens expectations, and order for our incouragement, and much blame and disgrace upon the adversaries.

In celebration of this victory, Massachusetts appointed "a day of thanksgiving to our merciful God," who "hath lifted us up, by an abundant rejoycing in our deliverance out of so desprate a danger."[73]

But Winthrop's elation over the Privy Council's order was premature. For, as C.M. Andrews noted, the committee established in late 1632 by the Privy Council, entitled "the Committee on the New England Plantations," was a special

156

body created by the Crown to deal with Puritans in Massachusetts. Its creation marked an inauspicious precedent. For the Crown, by creating this committee, declared its intention to deal directly with the Puritan non-conformists across the ocean. In 1632, the archbishop of York sat at the head of this committee, but in 1633, with the accession of William Laud to the See of Canterbury he gained the committee's chairmanship. And Laud wasted no time in treating the Bay Puritans differently. "Two commissions were almost simultaneously created under his presidency," and these, as his biographer H.R. Trevor-Roper wrote, "for the express purpose of dealing with New England Puritanism." The first was the Committee on the New England Plantations, revived by Laud in 1633 and now called the "Committee for New England."[74] On February 21, 1633/4, this committee issued "an Order made at the Council Table...about the Plantation in New England," which showed clearly that "Religion" stood at the center of the relationship between old and New England.

> Whereas the Board is given to understand of the of the frequent transportation of great numbers of his Majesty's subject out of this Kingdom to the Plantation of New England, amongst whom divers persons known to be ill affected, discontented not only with civil but ecclesiastical government here, are observed to resort thither, whereby such confusion and distraction is already grown there, especially in point of Religion, as, beside the ruin of the said Plantation, cannot but highly tend to the scandal both of Church and State here.

Consequently, the Lords of the Privy Council ordered that "divers ships in the River Thames, ready to sail," for New England, be held up "until further order from this Board." In the same order the Lords also requested "that Mr. Cradock," in the past governor of the Massachusetts Bay Company, "be required to cause the Letters-patents for the said Plantation to be brought to this Board."[75] Thus, in early 1633/34, authorities in England began to move to regulate the Puritan emigration and to reconsider Massachusetts Bay's royal charter.

The second committee created by Laud to deal with the non-conformist Puritans in Massachusetts Bay was "The Lords Commissioners for Plantation in

157

General," or "The Commission for Foreign Plantations." This committee, established in 1634, was a royal commission, and the extensive powers accorded it clearly reflected the Crown's growing resolve to confront head-on the problem of religious non-conformity in Puritan New England. "The Lords Commissioners," by an order of April 28, 1634, were given the power "to make laws, constitutions and ordinances pertaining...to the public state of these colonies," as well as authority "for the settling, making and ordering of the business for the designing of necessary ecclesiastical and clergy portion." The Lords furthermore had the power "to remove and displace the governors or rulers of those colonies," and "to change, revoke, and abrogate" the laws of the colonies, along with "power and special command over all charters, letter patents and rescripts royal of the regions...in foreign part," all so that the committee could determine which colony was "in rebellion against us, or withdrawing from our allegiance."[76]

Thus, Puritans in America found themselves directly responsible to a royal commission with their nemesis Archbishop Laud at its head. What they had left England to escape now confronted them in America. As of 1634, Laud, in theory,had the same power over the English churches in America as he had over the Church in England. As of 1634, it would then appear, the Crown had decided that its fight against Puritan non-conformity at home was linked with the practice of Puritan non-conformity abroad. In Laud's opinion, as he wrote in that year to the Lord Viscount Wentworth, "Protestants, and popishly affected, do for factious ends worke one upon another, and then join against the State." Of "the New Englanders," Laud had no illusions. "Certainly," he wrote about the Puritans in Massachusetts, "wherever they come they'll root out that which is far better than what they plant. A miserable time the while it is, that so many poor men...should be misled as they are." Official attitudes such as these were widely sensed in England. For example, Henry Dade, a commissary of Suffolk, presiding over an ecclesiastical court at Ipswich, England, in 1635, stated "that he knew the King and his Council would be glad that the thousands

[Puritans] who went to New England were drowned in the sea."[77]

Religious conformity and unity in the seventeenth century were important not only for the church, but for the well-being of the state or commonwealth as well. Hence, religious non-conformism, such as the Puritan refusal to obey the established church, threatened the foundation of all political obligation. "The Church and the commonwealth...are one society," Richard Hooker, the famous apologist of the Elizabethan Settlement of 1559, argued in The Laws of Ecclesiastical Polity (1594). Both were identical in membership. Therefore, not to obey the church's laws was, ipso facto, not to obey the laws of the kingdom. For, "we hold, that...there is not any man of the Church of England but the same man is also a member of the commonwealth; nor any man a member of the commonwealth, which is not also of the Church of England."[78] Hooker raised this argument against the Puritans and Catholics at the end of the sixteenth century. By the mid-1630s, the argument was still being applied, but, as a contemporary poem exhibits, the social and religious climate had greatly altered:

> A learned Prelate of this land
> Thinking to make Religion stand,
> With equall poise on either side,
> A mixture of them thus he try's;
> An ounce of Protestant he singleth,
> And then a Dram of Papish mingleth,
> With a scruple of the Puritan,
> And boyled them all in his brain-pan;
> But when he thought it would digest
> The scruple troubled all the rest.[79]

Throughout the 1630s Laud continued to bring "the scruple" to conformity in England, but he well knew that his efforts were compromised by the example of the Puritan experiment in New England. On this point, Henry Dade, the commissary of Suffolk, wrote to Laud in early 1633/4:

> about the 10th of March two ships are to sail from Ipswich, with men and provision, for their abiding in New England, in each of which ships are appointed to go about six score passengers, whom he suppose are either indebted persons or persons

159

discontented with the government of the Church of England. Hears that as many more are expected not long after to go altogether will amount to 600 persons. If suffered to go in such swarms, it will be a decrease of the King's people here, and increase of the adversaries to the episcopal state, and also will be an overthrow of trade, for as soon as any one purpose to break, he may fly to New England, and be accounted a religious man for leaving the kingdom because he cannot endure the ceremonies of the church.[80]

Laud, as head of the Church of England, was well informed about the Puritan emigration and the nature of the ecclesiastical polity in Massachusetts. For example, his agent in Holland in early 1633/4 wrote to him that Davenport "came out of England as desertor ecclesia" and that in Holland Davenport forsook "his king and church." Laud also knew, through his agent in New England, that "Mr. Cotton and his son (born a-shipboard and therefore called Sea-born), and Mr. Hooker are safely arrived" at Boston, Massachusetts. And in February, 1633/4, Laud received a complaint from "Subjects of his Majesty" in England on the Puritans "having of their owne country and religion out of the King's dominions, upon any discontent may fly to New England whence they cannot be avocated by reason of the largeness of that continent."[81] Surely none of these reports came as a surprise to Laud.

It is also evident that English authorities well understood the millennial and eschatological dimension of the Puritan migration, a dimension that singled out Puritan New England, and not England, as the Promised Land for God's people. They could not have not been aware of the many Puritan public pronouncements to this effect. "God is packing up his gospel," preached Thomas Hooker, like many others Puritan emigrants, in his sermon "The Danger of Desertion" in 1631, "because none will buy his wares" in England. Therefore, continued Hooker,

God begin to ship away his Noahs, which prophesied and foretold that destruction was near; and God makes account that New England shall be a refuge for his Noahs and his Lots, a rock and a shelter for his righteous ones to run into.

160

Because God is leaving England, declared Hooker, the destruction of that state is imminent. "My brethren, cast your thoughts afar off, and see what is become of those Famous Churches of Pergamum and Thyatira and the rest mentioned" in the Book of Revelation. "Glory is departed from England; for England hath seen her best days, and the reward of sin is coming on apace." The time, Hooker argued before his congregation, is the time of the sound of the trumpets as foretold in Revelation;

When thou shalt hear the trumpets sound, and when thine ears shall tingle with the sound of war; then depart forever.[82]

In the knowledge of such aspirations, Laud and other authorities in England created their Committee and the Lords Commissioners for the Bay colony. They were not prepared to permit the non-conformist Puritans in Massachusetts "their owne country and religion." But first they moved to limit and regulate the Puritan migration from England.

In February 1633/4, the Lords Commissioners sent out an order from Whitehall "to all Captains and Masters of his Majesties Shipps, officers of his Majesties Customes &c." to stop and hold "Shipps...bound for New England," with the instructions "not to suffer them or any of them to departe" until they had received further word from the Privy Council. In addition, the Masters and Captains of the ships so detained were ordered to see that their passengers used "the Prayers contayned in the Book of Common Prayers established in the Church of England" and that each emigrant had a "Certificate from the officers of the Port where he is imbarqued that he hath taken both the oaths of Allegiance and Supremacie." In sum, ship masters were required to see that only loyal subjects sailed for New England. And "Bailiffes and officers of the Customes" in the ports of England were required to execute and keep the above order. From now on, ship masters, before sailing, were to bring "a list of the name of all the Passengers" intending to emigrate, "with certificate" that they "had duly taken the oaths."[83]

161

The increasingly critical posture of English authorities toward Massachusetts led Edward Howes, who had witnessed in England the proceedings against the colony, to write to a friend in America: "Sir, I am more sensible hereof, in regard I was daylie and houerly auditor and spectator of all the passages" in England against the colony "that your plantation hath need of some hartie and able friends to back you upon all occasions." And another friend of the colony told Bay Puritans: "your frend heer who are members of your plantacion have had much to do to answer the unjust complaints made to the Kinge and counsell of your gevernment there."[84] Nonetheless, when Sir Simonds D'Ewes advised Winthrop and New England Puritans to conform to the Church of England, Winthrop sharply rejected the advice:

> for your counsell of Conforminge ourselves to the Ch[urch] of E[ngland]...I dare not thank you for it; because it is not conformable to Gods will revealed in his worde: what you may doe in E[ngland] where things are otherwise established, I will not disput, but our case heere is otherwise: being come to clear light and more Libertye...we may freely enjoye it.[85]

In 1635, after Massachusetts' persistent refusal to conform in ecclesiastical matters, Sir John Banks, attorney-general of England, issued "A Quo Warranto" against "the Company of Massachusetts Bay." This warrant ordered the Company to come and answer fourteen questions relating to its government in Massachusetts Bay. By what right, asked Banks, had "the said Company in New England" - "without any warrant or royal grant" - "the soul government in that country," there "to make such lawes and statutes...against the laws and customes of England." By no right, argued Banks in this official document, for the "liberties" of the colony 'do usurp in contempt of his majesty."[86]

Banks issued the "Quo Warranto" after the Privy Council had decided to begin legal proceedings against the Bay colony's charter and after Gorges had moved that the Council for New England "surrender to his Majesty of the great Charter," originally received from James I in 1620. On April 25, 1635, the members of the Council for New England appealed to the Privy Council for the

King to return New England affairs to his own jurisdiction because Massachusetts Puritans had presumed upon their authority to the point of instituting "new laws, new conceits of matters of religion, and forms of ecclesiastical and temporal government." Thus, "the Privy Council finding matters so desperate" in Massachusetts, "saw a necessity for the King to take the whole business into his own hands." One day later, on April 26, Gorges offered himself as 'his Majesty's Governor or Lieutenant of New England," and the King accepted immediately. "We have resolved," declared the King, "to imploy our servants Sir Ferdinando Gorges...[and] to second him with Our Royal & ample authority" in New England. And in October of that year, Captain John Mason, a long time friend of Gorges and enemy of the Puritans in New England, was appointed by the "Lords of the Admiralty" to be "Vice-Admiral of New England."[87] In 1634-1635, then, the Crown took three major steps against the Puritan holy experiment in the wilderness of America. It initiated procedures to regulate the Puritan migration, began legal proceedings designed to abolish the Massachusetts Bay Colony's charter, and appointed Gorges and Mason as Crown representatives invested with extensive powers, at the Bay.

With regard to these measures, the Crown's attempt to regulate emigration to the Bay colony did not stop an average of two thousand emigrants from making the voyage each year throughout the 1630s, and the legal proceedings against the charter would draw out for some more years before the Crown abandoned his plan to revoke the Massachusetts Bay Colony's mandate. But the appointment of Gorges and Mason represented an immediate threat to the whole Puritan experiment in the wilderness. Equipped with royal authority, Gorges and Mason could now invade Massachusetts, or so thought the Puritans in the colony, and dismantle the whole Puritan enterprise. "This plantation and that of Virginia," wrote Emmanuel Downing to the secretary of state Sir John Coke, "went not forth upon the same reason nor for the same end. Those of Virginia went for profit...." These of Massachusetts went "to satisfy their one curiosity in point of conscience." And Henry Vane, Jr., wrote to his father, Sir Henry Vane, that "it

163

is not trade that God will set up in these parts" of New England "but the profession of his truth." In Massachusetts, "in the New Jerusalem," wrote Thomas Welde to his parishioners in England, "we shall enjoy together sweet society in all fullness of perfection to all eternity."[88] The appointment by the Crown, then, of Gorges and Mason to govern all New England was interpreted by Bay Puritans as an attempt to destroy their "new Jerusalem." From this point on, as a result, tensions between Massachusetts and England could only escalate. The colonists had been well acquainted with the proceedings against them in England. "It is in diverse mouths that you are, and your plantation and planters hath often lately bin preached against at Paul Crosse etc.," a friend wrote to the colony from England.[89] So far, indeed, proceedings against the Puritan colony had been restricted to England. But now, with the appointment of Gorges and Mason to rule in New England, the Crown, in its attempt to bring Massachusetts Puritans to conformity, had decided to shift the struggle into the colony itself.

Evidently, information concerning the new developments in England reached the colony immediately. John Humfrey came to Massachusetts in June 1634 and carried with him news about the regulation of the emigration, the contemplated recalling of the royal charter, and the creation of the Lords Commissioners. "The archbishop," wrote Winthrop, "and others of the council...sent out a warrant to stay the ships, and to call our patent." Around the same time, Cradock sent to the colony the Privy Council's order demanding the return of the charter and the stoppage of Massachusetts-bound ships in England. On the question of returning the charter, wrote Winthrop to Cradock, only "a general court" could decide. One month later, Winthrop received a letter from England filled "with many railing speeches and threats against" the Massachusetts Bay Colony.[90] This letter informed him of the recent appointment of the general governor of the colony. In September, the General Court assembled at Newtown, but rather than answer Cradock's letter on the matter of the charter, as it was supposed to do, the Court decided to fortify Castle Island, Dorchester, and Charlestown. All three locations, one can easily observe, represented key strategic points overlooking the entrance to Boston harbor. This sudden action by the General Court, it would then seem, reflected the Puritans' growing fear of armed intervention in their affairs, presumably by England.

It was around the same time that Massachusetts Bay received "a copy of the commission granted to the two archbishops and ten others of the council to regulate all plantations." Winthrop and the other Puritan leaders had no illusions as to the aims of the Lords Commissioners:

> This being advise from our friends to be intended specially for us, and that there were ships and soldiers provided, given out as for the carrying the new governour, Capt. Woodhouse, to Virginia, but suspected to be against us, to compel us, by force, to receive a new governour, and the discipline of the church of England, and the laws of the commissioners.

The heightened peril, wrote Winthrop "occasioned the magistrates and deputies to hasten our fortification, and to discover our mind to each other; which grew to this conclusion." Hence, unfortunately, at this point, a large blank intervenes in the manuscript of Winthrop's history. The story picks up, though, a few weeks later, when

> all the ministers...met at Boston, being requested by the governour and assistances, to consider...what we ought to do if a general governour should be sent out of England.

According to Winthrop, "they all agreed, that, if a general governour were sent, we ought not to accept him, but defend our lawful possession (if we were able); otherwise to avoid or protract."[91]

Military preparations in the colony showed without doubt that the Puritans had decided to defend themselves, by armed resistance if necessary, against any attempted intervention by England. "A beacon" was set "on the sentry hill att Boston, to give notice to the country of any danger." A committee of military affairs was appointed, "to dispose of all" military "companyes," with authority "to make either offensive or defensive warr," and "whatsoever may be further...for the good of this plantacon." To this committee was given the "power to imprison or confine any that shall judge to be enemyes to the

165

commonwealth." Concurrently, militias were called up in each town. How well the colony was prepared to face armed intervention from England can be seen from the following example. In early 1634/5 unidentified ships were sighted near Cape Ann. Immediately, "an alarm was raised in all our towns," wrote Winthrop, "and the government and assistants met at Boston." Soon these ships were identified as harmless and the alarm was called off, but the incident exhibits the colony's resolve to resist outside interference in its essential affairs.[92]

In the midst of all this apprehension, a significant event took place in Salem. In late 1634, John Endecott "defaced" the cross from "the ensign at Salem." In Massachusetts the militia in each town had its "ensign bearer," who carried the ensign with "the King's colors" and "red cross." What Endecott did was cut "the red cross out of the King's colors." He did this because "the red cross was given to the King of England by the Pope, as an ensign of victory, and so indeed by him as a superstitious thing, and a relic of Antichrist." The case of the red cross was soon before the General Court, for "many soldiers refused to follow the colors so defaced," and many argued that in existing circumstances this act "might be interpreted [as] a kind of rebellion." The soldiers, of course, were perfectly right in their complaints, and in England Endecott would have been charged with treason. But in Massachusetts the General Court "could not agree about the thing" - indicating that Endecott was not alone in his sentiments. As happened so often, a compromise was offered for the time being, and accepted. For the present, it was decided, "all the ensigns should be laid aside." Following this, a committee was formed to deal with the case and to discipline Endecott. Yet Endecott told the committee that "he, judging the cross, etc., to be a sin, did content himself to have reformed it at Salem." This, of course, was the essential issue, namely, how far any person in authority, or the colony as a whole, could go with its religious radicalism. Whether, in short, it could defy symbols of the king's authority. The committee, accordingly "disabled" Endecott "for one year from bearing any public office" for his offense. But the issue was far from over. For the court, subsequent to the sentencing of Endecott, requested that "every

166

man...deal with his neighbors, to still their mind, who stood so stiff for the cross, until we should fully agree about it." That is, the community was charged with further dissipating the problem. Meanwhile, "the ministers had promised to take pains about it,"[93] to the point even of seeking advice about this issue from England. Apparently, judging from the lack of evidence, no advice came out of England on the issue of the cross, and so the Bay Puritans were left to decide for themselves.

Much evidence suggests that the issue of the cross sharply divided the Puritan commonwealth and that this division revolved around the issue of the Puritans' application of eschatological visions and millennial expectations and their views concerning the means for attaining religious reformation. Thus, many in the colony were not prepared to suffer such "a relic of Antichrist" as the cross in the midst of their holy experiment. This issue of the cross, wrote Israel Stoughton in 1635,

> hath already caused no little alienation of affection, strife
> ...censuring on their parts who are so zealous for the cross its
> rejection against, almost condemning their brethren that have not
> been so opinionated and affected as themselves.

Two parties formed on the matter. One "washed their hand of" Endecott's action. Another, made up of "some of the magistrates with some ministers and divers of the people," viewed the cross as "an idol, unlawful to be continued in so honorable a place and time." On the latter side was Winthrop, who, Stoughton informs us, "was so zealous against the cross, for he esteems it a gross idol." At first, according to Stoughton, "the greater part of ministers and country" had opposed Endecott's act, but eventually Endecott's and Winthrop's party triumphed on the issue, and their stand became the official stand of the colony throughout the 1630s.[94] "At the last general court," wrote Winthrop in 1635, "it was referred to the military commissioners to appoint colors for every company; who did accordingly, and left out the cross in all of them."[95] Religious radicalism, at least as illustrated by this case, thus led eventually to political radicalism in

167

Massachusetts, to the inevitable detriment of that colony's relationship with England.

Meanwhile, Massachusetts' sensitivity on the question of the cross continued on into the late 1630s. When a ship came to the colony from England in 1636 with the red cross emblazoned on its flag, "the lieutenant" of Castle Island "went aboard her, and made her strike her flage." But then, a patriotic sailor from another ship, seeing that "we had not the king's colors at our port," accused the Puritans of being "traitors and rebels, etc." When the master of the ship asked the governor why the King's colors were not displayed at the port, Winthrop replied "that for our part we are fully persuaded, that the cross in the ensign was idolatrous, and therefore might not set in our ensign." Yet, this seemingly minor incident was a serious one, as Winthrop and company fully understood. As a result, to avoid serious political repercussions they contrived a compromise, deciding that "the port was the king's and maintained in his name" and therefore that the king's colors "might be spread there." (There is historical irony in the fact that during the 1640s, while the Parliamentary arms continued the use of red cross in their ensigns, Massachusetts had restored the red cross to its ensigns. But this restoration was on the condition that the colony restored them "till the state of England shall alter the same, which we much desire.")[96]

Massachusetts' readiness to resist English force with force, and the free hand assumed by the Puritans in the cross cutting incident, reflected the colony's growing sense of sovereignty vis-a-vis England. What had begun as essentially a religious debate had now escalated into a major political struggle concerning Church and State. But again, as the cross episode shows, out of religious considerations and millennial expectations Massachusetts developed its stand concerning political obligation. The religious controversy between old and New England thus led to political struggle.

By the middle of the 1630s the overt struggle between Massachusetts and the English Crown and church was well recognized on both sides of the ocean, and there is evidence that Puritan fears of invasion from England had been based on actual preparations that took place in England for this purpose. In the summer of 1636 Lord Say wrote to Winthrop "that Capt. Mason and others, the adversaries of this colony, had built a great ship to send over the general governour, etc., which, being launched, fell in sunder in the midst."[97] Likewise, Sir Simonds D'Ewes, a famous antiquarian and Winthrop's friend, wrote that

> Episcopal enemies of New England had at several times given out reports that a bishop and governor should be sent amongst them to force upon them the yoke of our ceremonies and intermixtures, so to deter others from going. And, indeed, at this time [1634, 1635?], the same report was more likely to be fulfilled than ever before or since; for one, Sir Fernando Gorges, was nominated for governor, and there was a consultation to send him thither with a thousand soldiers: a ship was now in building, and near finished to transport him by sea, and much fear there was amongst the Godly lest that infant Commonwealth and Church should have been ruined by him; when God that carried so many weak and crazy ships thither, so provided it, that this strong, new-built ship in the very launching fell in pieces, and so preserved his dear children there at this present time, from that fatal design.[98]

And Peter Heylin, in his biography of his master, William Laud, wrote too that during the 1630s, "it was once under Consultation" by the Privy Council and

> those who were to take special care of the Church Health, to send a Bishop over to them, for their better Government; and to back him with some Forces to compel, if not otherwise able to perswade Obedience.[99]

With the failure of Gorges to launch his ship, the immediate threat dissipated, but the colony's fear of a general governor assisted by an army nonetheless continued. Thus, for example, when in 1638 Davenport led his people to New Haven, he justified the move in part by pointing out that the western site offered "more safety...from danger of general governour, who was feared to be sent this summer."[100]

By the end of the 1630s, the confrontation between England and Massachusetts had boiled down to a clash between two uncompromising demands. English authorities were determined to force Massachusetts churches and government to submit to English rule, and the colony was bent on defending, to whatever extreme necessary, its particular religious beliefs and liberties of self-government. For its part, the colony's struggle against the Crown and Church of England was a continuation of the earlier non-conformity battles fought by Puritans when they were still in England. That at least, according to Heylin, was how Laud understood the Puritans' American colony.

> For how unsafe must it be thought both to Church and State, to suffer such constant Receptacle of discontented, dangerous, and schismatical Person, to grow up so fast: from whence, as from the Bowels of the Trojan Horse, so many Incendiaries might break out to inflame the Nation?[101]

And as Laud learned from George Burdett, his agent in New England, "the truth" about the Massachusetts Puritans was that they

> have long since decreed to spend their blood in maintaining their present way and humour, and are using all diligence to fortify themselves.[102]

Meanwhile, in England legal proceedings against the colony's charter ended in July 1637 and "the King took the whole management of Massachusetts Bay into his own hands." By the same order, the King declared that "none be permitted to go" into New England "without Gorges' knowledge or licence." A year later, in 1638, the King issued "A Proclamation to Restrain the Transporting of Passengers and Provision to New England without Licence." According to this order, "all Merchants, Masters and Owners of Ships...from henceforth" could not sail to New England without first obtaining "special License from his Majesty, or such of the Lords and others of his Privy Council." The King's Proclamation of May 1638 was necessitated by

> the frequent resort to New England, of divers Persons ill-affected to the Religion established in the Church of England, and to the good and peaceable Government of this State... His Majesty well knowing the factious disposition of the People...in that Plantation.[103]

Yet, viewed as a whole, the Crown exhibited nothing so much by these actions against the Puritans' American enterprise as its own incapacity to enforce its rule on the distant colonists. For all their apparent threat, Captain Mason was dead by 1635 and Gorges was without the financial means to assume his governorship of New England. And in any event, by the late 1630s the prime energies of the English crown were being drawn into a situation taking place in Scotland.

VI Covenant and Revolt

On July 23, 1637, at St. Giles' Cathedral in Edinburgh, the first attempt to impose on Scotland and the Kirk the English Prayer Book led to riots. One year later, in 1638, the Scots resisted the imposition of the English Prayer Book, along with the Church of England's canons and liturgy, by creating a "National Covenant." "There being no other way left unto us," declared the Scots in that year,

> we were necessitated to renew the National Covenant of this Kirk and Kingdom, and thereby to reconcile us to God...[and] against the Service-Book and Book of Canons, as main Innovations of Religion and Laws, and full of Popish Superstition.[104]

Thus began "the Troubles," as contemporaries referred to the rising of Scotland against Charles I and his attempt to impose on that kingdom religious conformity. This new situation immediately affected the relationship between England and Massachusetts. "Many ships arrived this year," wrote Winthrop in 1638,

> with people of good quality and estate, notwithstanding the council's order, that none [such] should come without the king's license; but God so wrought, that some obtained [license], and others came away without. The troubles which arose in Scotland about the book of common prayer, and the canons, which the king would have forced upon the Scotch, did so take up the king and council, that they had neither heart nor leisure to look after the affairs of New England.[105]

There is reason to think that the King who crossed the border into Scotland with his army to enforce the Book of Common Prayer had earlier contemplated a similar action in reference to Massachusetts. For Heylin wrote that Charles and Laud had a plan to send a bishop with an army to Massachusetts, but that "this Design was strangled in the first Conception, by the violent breaking out of the Troubles in Scotland."[106] In the late 1630s, that is, armed conflict between England and the colony was probably prevented because of the troubles in Scotland. Likewise coming to an end was the Crown's attempt to inhibit and regulate the Puritan migration. "Gone into New England" now became a common phrase in local authorities' accounts to the Privy Council. "I find,"

172

wrote Archbishop Neil of York to the King in 1638, "that too many of your Majesty's subjects inhabiting in these parts of Yorkshire are gone into New England."[107]

Charles I's failure against the Scottish Covenanters in the First Bishops' War, 1639, compelled him, after eleven years of rule without Parliament, to summon the Short Parliament of 1640. The king needed money for his campaigns, but the Parliament he needed it from turned out to be more interested in questions of Tonnage, Poundage, and Ship Money. The king dissolved this Short Parliament after three contentious weeks. In the Second Bishop's War, 1640, Charles proved no more successful than in the first. This second engagement ended with the Scots once again triumphant and now in possession of a part of England. In the circumstances, Charles had no choice but to reassemble Parliament in order to meet the Scots' financial demands. This was the Long Parliament, gathering November 1640. And this time, its members were not prepared to allow the King to dismiss them. The struggle between King and Parliament dragged out eventually into the Civil War and the execution of Charles.

The struggle of the Puritans in Massachusetts was inseparable from the Puritan cause in England before and during the Civil War. Naturally the colony associated itself with the Long Parliament's struggle with the King during the 1640s. At the same time, the Scottish debacle and the subsequent Parliamentary crisis served to remove the Crown's threat to the political and ecclesiastical autonomy of the Bay colony. Yet the Bay Puritans' problem in this regard was far from over. For all through the 1630s emigrant Puritans had disagreed with the majority of Puritans in England on basic theological and ecclesiastical matters, albeit these differences had been held in check by their greater common cause against Laud. But now Laud was off the scene, and, for the first time, Puritans in England had the opportunity, which the Massachusetts Puritans had already taken during the 1630s, to infuse their religious ideas into state and society, to create a Puritan commonwealth in England. Yet, the majority of Puritans in England had not accepted the "New England Way" as a model of ecclesiastical

173

polity and civily policy for England during the 1640s. Thus, on both sides of the ocean, Puritans had been engaged in a bitter controversy over theological matters, over the application of millennial expectations, and over the nature and foundation of a Christian commonwealth. As a result, Massachusetts Puritans in the 1640s discovered that its relationship with a Puritan England could be as bitter and fractious as a relationship with the England of Charles I and Archbishop Laud. But before turning to explore the Puritan colony's relationship with the long Parliament during the 1640s, it is necessary to examine first the nature and foundation of the Puritan commonwealth in New England, or the "theocracy in Massachusetts."

Notes

1.   Sir Isaiah Berlin, "Two Concepts of Liberty," in Four Essays on Liberty (New York, 1970), pp. 121-122.

2.   Francis Higginson, a sermon upon his sailing to Salem (1629), cited in Magnalia, by Mather, I, p. 328.

3.   Richard Sadler, cited in "Richard Sadler's Account of the Massachusetts Churches," by Richard Simmons, NEQ, XLII (1969), p. 416.

4.   John Cotton, "Gods Promise to His Plantation," preached before Winthrop's fleet (1630), Old South Leaflets (Boston, N.D.), III, No. 53, pp. 53, 14.

5.   John Cotton, cited in "John Cotton's Letter to Samuel Skelton," by David Hall, WMQ, XXII (1965), p. 484.

6.   Thomas Hooker, "The Danger of Desertion" (1631), in Thomas Hooker: Writings in England and Holland 1626-1633, eds. George H. Williams, et al. (Cambridge, Mass., 1975), pp. 230, 245-246.

7.   Thomas Welde, "A Letter of Master Wells from New England to Old England to His People at Tarling in Essex...1633," Massachusetts Colonial Society, Transactions, XXIII (1910-11), pp. 130, 131.

8.   Richard Sadler, cited in "Richard Sadler's Account of the Massachusetts Churches," by Richard C. Simmons, NEQ, XLII (1969), p. 417.

9.   Richard Saltonstall, "Richard Saltonstall Jr. to John Winthrop Jr." (April, 1633), in The Saltonstall Papers, ed. Robert E. Moody (Boston, 1972), I, p. 121; Francis Higginson, cited in Magnalia, by Mather I, p. 328; Sir Isaiah Berlin, "Two Concepts of Liberty," pp. 121-122; Thomas Shepard and John Allin, A Defence of the Answer (London, 1648), p. 6 (preface).

10.   Captain John Smith, "The Present Estate of New Plymouth," in Travels and Works of Captain John Smith, ed. E. Arber, 2 vols. (Edinburgh, 1910), II, p. 783.

11.   Frances Rose-Troup, John White (New York, 1930), p. 50; William Hubbard, A General History of New England (Boston, 1848), p. 116; Cotton Mather, Magnalia, I, p. 162.

12.   "Records of the Council for New England," American Antiquarian Society, Proceedings (1867), p. 59; Frances Rose-Troup, The Massachusetts Bay Company and Its Predecessors (1930), p. 13.

13. "The Records of the New England Company" are included among the Records of the Governor and Company of the Massachusetts Bay in New England, ed. Nathaniel B. Shurtleff, 5 vols. (Boston, 1853-1854), I (hereafter cited as MA. Records). The New England Company's Records can be found also in Alexander Young, ed., Chronicles of the First Planters of the Colony of Massachusetts Bay (Boston, 1846); they are printed along with letters the company sent to Endecott in Salem. On John Endecott, see: Lawrence S. Mayo, John Endecott (Cambridge, 1936).

14. William Bradford, Of Plymouth Plantation, ed. Samuel Morison (New York, 1967), pp. 205-206; Robert Keayne, The Apology of Robert Keayne, ed. Bernard Bailyn (Gloucester, 1970), p. 2; Bradford, Of Plymouth Plantation, p. 206. On the episode of the maypole in Merrymount and the relationship between Plymouth and Massachusetts with Thomas Morton, see Michael Zuckerman, "Pilgrim in the Wilderness: Community, Modernity, and the Maypole at Merry Mount," NEQ (1977), p. 1.

15. "Gov. Cradock's Letter to John Endicott" (Feb. 16, 1629), in Chronicles, ed. Young, pp. 134-135. The New England Company sent in fact three ministers in 1629. The third, along with Higginson and Skelton, was Rev. Francis Bright. Though a non-conformist Puritan, Bright was not willing to renounce his allegiance to the Church of England or to give up the Book of Common Prayer, and thus he moved immediately, after his coming to Salem, to Mishawum, later Charleston.

16. "The Company's Instruction to Endicott and His Council" (April 17, 1629), in Chronicles, ed. Young, pp. 142, 144, 168; Francis Higginson, "A True Relation of the Last Voyage to New England" (July 24, 1629), in A Collection of Original Papers Relative to the History of the Colony of Massachusetts Bay, comp. Thomas Hutchinson, 2 vols. (New York, 1865 [1967]), I, p. 35 (hereafter cited as Collection, comp. Hutchinson). "The company of New England," wrote there Higginson, "consisting of many worthy gentlemen...ayming at the glory of God...furnished 5 ships to go to New England." It is clear, then, that Higginson thought that he was sent by the New England Company, and given the fact that this company and not the Massachusetts Bay Company sent the ministers in 1629, it is evident that the formation of the church in Salem was indeed the New England Company's enterprise.

17. Thomas Hutchinson, The History of the Colony and Province of Massachusetts Bay, ed. Lawrence S. Mayo, 3 vols. (Cambridge, 1936), I, p. 12 (hereafter cited as History, by Hutchinson).

18. Perry Miller, Orthodoxy in Massachusetts, pp. xiii-xiv.

19. Mayo, John Endecott, p. 37; Nathaniel Morton, New England Memorial (Boston, 1826), pp. 145-146; "Charles Gott to William Bradford" (1629), in Of Plymouth Plantation, by Bradford, p. 225.

20. William Ames, Conscience, with the Power and Cases Thereof (London, 1630 [1641]), p. 63; John Cotton, The Way of the Congregational Churches Cleared (1648), in John Cotton on the Churches of New England, ed. Larzer Ziff, (Cambridge, Mass., 1968), p. 193. According to Cotton there, "neither did that company which came over to Plymouth erect here a new church...for by the consent of the church which they left, they came over in church estate, and only renewed their covenant when they came hither."

21. Nathaniel Morton, New England Memorial (Boston, 1826), pp. 147-148.

176

22. Ibid., pp. 147-148.

23. Ibid., p. 148.

24. Thomas Dudley, "Gov. Thomas Dudley's Letter to the Countess of Lincoln, March 1631," in Tracts and Other Papers Relating Principally to the Origin, Settlement and Progress of the Colonies in North America, ed. Peter Force, 4 vols. (Washington, 1836-1847), II, p. 12 (hereafter cited as Tracts, ed. Force).

25. John Robinson, cited in History, by Hutchinson, I, p. 353.

26. Larzer Ziff, The Career of John Cotton (Princeton, 1962), p. 66.

27. Bradford, Of Plymouth Plantation, pp. 24-25.

28. Thomas Hooker, "Letter to John Cotton from Rotterdam" (1633), in Thomas Hooker, Writings in England and Holland, 1626-1633, ed.s, George H. Williams, et al., p. 297.

29. John Endecott's letter to Bradford, May 11, 1629 in Of Plymouth Plantation, by Bradford, pp. 223-224.

30. Bradford, Of Plymouth Plantation, pp. 167, 168; Frank Shuffelton, Thomas Hooker, 1586-1647 (Princeton, 1977), p. 72; Samuel Fuller's letter to Bradford appears in "Governour Bradford's Letter Book," Massachusetts Historical Society, Collections, III, (1794), p. 75.

31. Francis Higginson, cited in Magnalia, by Mather I, p. 328; Perry Miller, Orthodoxy in Massachusetts, p. 137.

32. John Smith, Advertisement for the Unexperienced Planters of New England, 1631, in Travels and Works of Captain John Smith, ed. E. Arber, II, pp. 954, 926.

33. Richard Sadler, in Richard Simmons, "Richard Sadler's Account of the Massachusetts Churches," NEQ, XLII (1969), p. 417.

34. Anne Hutchinson, in John Winthrop, A Short Story of the Rise, Reign, and Ruine of the Antinomians, Familists & Libertines (London, 1644), in The Antinomian Controversy, ed. David Hall (Middletown, 1968), pp. 271-272.

35. Keith L. Sprunger, The Learned Doctor William Ames (Urbana, 1972), p. 185.

36. Ames, Conscience, pp. 62-63.

37. Ibid., pp. 62-63.

38. William Hubbard, A General History of New England, p. 117.

39. John Cotton's letter to Salem, in "John Cotton's Letter to Samuel Skelton," by David Hall, WMQ, XXII (1965), pp. 480-481, 479, 483.

40. Ibid., pp. 479, 483.

41. John Cotton, "A Sermon Delivered at Salem, 1636," in John Cotton on the Churches of New England, ed. Larzer Ziff, pp. 42, 45, 55, 58-59.

42. "Edward Howes to John Winthrop, Jr." (Nov. 1631), in Winthrop Papers, III, p. 54.

43. John Burgess, cited in Thomas Hooker, Writing in England Holland, 1626-1633, eds. George H. Williams, et al., pp. 9-10, n. 21.

44. John Cotton, "A Letter of Mr. John Cotton...to Mr. Williams," in The Complete Writings of Roger Williams, eds. Reuben A. Guild, et al. 7 vols. (New York, 1963), I, pp. 15, 17; Roger Williams, "Mr. Cottons letter Lately Printed, Examined and Answered...." (1644), in The Complete Writings of Roger Williams, I, pp. 52, 76.

45. Francis Higginson, A True Relation of the Last Voyage to New England, 1629, in Chronicles, ed. Young, pp. 214-238; "Some brief collections out of a letter that Mr. Higginson sent to his friends at Leicester" (July 1629), in Collection, comp. Hutchinson, pp. 52, 54.

46. Higginson, "New Englands Plantation..." (Sept. 1629), in Collection, comp. Hutchinson, p. 52. In the above discussion of Higginson's writings I accept Everett Emerson's distinction between Higginson's "A True Relation" and his "New Englands Plantation" as two different works. Concerning the latter, Emerson wrote that "one suspects that Higginson was aware of the controversial nature of the church arrangement" in Salem, and "so avoided discussing it." See Everett Emerson, ed., Letters from New England (Amherst, 1976), pp. 11-39, esp. 12, 29.

47. MA. Records, I, p. 51; "John Winthrop to His Wife" (Oct. 9, 1629), in Winthrop Papers, II, p. 157; "Thomas Mott to John Winthrop" (June 13, 1629), in Winthrop Papers, II, p. 97.

48. "John Winthrop to His Wife" (May 15, 1629), in Winthrop Papers, II, p. 91; "Isaac Johnson to Emmanuel Downing" (July 8, 1629), in Winthrop Papers, II, p. 103; "The Agreement at Cambridge" (August 26, 1629), in Winthrop Papers, II, p. 152.

49. Charles Deane, "The Forms in Issuing Letters Patents by the Crown of England," MHSP (1869-70), pp. 169, 182.

50. "The Form of Government for the Colony" (1629), in Chronicles, ed. Young, p. 193.

51. "Establishment of Royal Government in Virginia," in Great Britain and the American Colonies, 1606-1673, ed. Jack P. Greene (New York, 1970), pp. 35-36.

52. MA. Records, I, pp. 50-51; "The Agreement at Cambridge," p. 152.

53. "The Agreement at Cambridge," p. 152.

54. "John Winthrop and Others to..." (Oct. 27, 1629), in Winthrop Papers, II, p. 163; "John Winthrop and Others to William Cager" (Jan (?) 1629/30), in Winthrop Papers, II, p. 199.

55. "John Winthrop and Others to..." (Oct. 27, 1629), in Winthrop Papers, II, pp. 163-164.

56. "Isaac John to John Winthrop" (Dec. 17, 1629), in Winthrop Papers, II, p. 178; "Arthur Tyndal to John Winthrop" (Nov. 10, 1629), in Winthrop Papers, II, p. 166.

57. John Cotton, "God's Promise to His Plantation," pp. 5-10.

58. David Hall, "John Cotton's Letter to Samuel Skelton," p. 484.

59. John Cotton, "Gods Promise to His Plantation," p. 14.

60. "The Humble Request of His Majesties Loyall Subjects...," Winthrop Papers, II, pp. 231-232.

61. John Rous, "Diary of John Rous," ed. M.A.E. Green, Camden Society (1861), pp. 53-54.

62. "The Humble Request," p. 231.

63. John White, The Planters Plea, (1630), pp. 59, 61.

64. Sumner Chilton Powell, Puritan Village, the Formation of a New England Town (New York, 1965), p. 183.

65. Thomas Welde, "A Letter of Master Wells from New England to Old England...1633," Massachusetts Colonial Society, Transactions, XXIII (1910-11), pp. 130-131. On the transfer of English culture to Puritan New England, see, David Grayson Allen, In English Ways, the Movement of Societies and Transfer of English Local Law and custom to Massachusetts Bay in the Seventeenth Century (Chapel Hill, 1981), and David Cressy, Coming Over: Migration and Communication Between England and New England in the Seventeenth Century (Cambridge, 1987).

66. "The Zealous Puritan" (1639), in The Literature of America: Colonial Period, ed. Larzer Ziff (New York, 1970), p. 25.

67. Edward Johnson (?), Good News from New England (1648), in Seventeenth-Century American Poetry, ed. Harrison T. Meserole (New York, 1968), p. 157. Meserole, after Harold S. Jantz, ascribes this work to Edward Johnson.

68. Thomas Dudley, "Gov. Thomas Dudley's Letter to the Countess of Lincoln" (March 1631), in Tracts, ed. Force, II, pp. 15-16.

69. "Edward Howes to John Winthrop, Jr.," (Nov. 1632), in Winthrop Papers, III, pp. 100-101.

70. Calendar of State Papers, Domestic Series of the Reign of Charles I IV, pp. 233, 266, 384 (hereafter cited As CSPD); CSPD V, p. 255.

71. "Records of the council for New England," p. 111; Calendar of State Papers, Colonial Series, 1574-1660, I, pp. 156-157 (hereafter cited as CSPC); "Records of the Council for New England, p. 113; CSPC, I, pp. 156-157; Acts of the Privy Council of England, Colonial Series, 1613-1680, I, p. 83 (hereafter Cited as APCC). For an excellent study of the political relationship between Massachusetts and England in the seventeenth century, see Charles M. Andrews, The Colonial Period of American History (New Haven, 1936-8).

72.   "Copy of an Order of his Majesty's Council" (Jan. 19, 1632/3), in Collection, comp. Hutchinson, pp. 58-59. The Privy Council's Order also appears in Bradford, Of Plymouth Plantation, p. 421.

73.   "A Copy of Letter from Mr....to Mr. Bradford...," in Collection, comp. Hutchinson, pp. 57-58.

74.   Charles M. Andrews, British Committees, Commissions, and Councils of Trade and Plantation, 1622-1675 (Baltimore, 1908), p. 15; H.R. Trevor-Roper, Archbishop Laud, 1573-1645 (London, 1940), pp. 260-261.

75.   "The Copy of an Order Made at the Council Table, February 21, 1633...," in A General History of New England, by Hubbard, p. 153; and in APCC, I, p. 199.

76.   "Royal Commission for Regulating Plantations" (April 28, 1634), in Of Plymouth Plantation, by Bradford, pp. 422-425.

77.   "William Laud to the Lord Viscount Wentworth" (Jan. 12, 1634), in The Works of... William Laud (Oxford, 1850-1860), VII, p. 100 (hereafter cited as Works, by Laud); "William Laud to the Lord Viscount Wentworth" (June 22, 1638), in Works, by Laud, VII, 448; CSPD, VIII, p. 86. On the project to establish episcopal control over the colonies, see Arthur Lyon Cross, The Anglican Episcopate and the American Colonies (New York, 1902). Laud's policy against Massachusetts was part of his overall attempt to bring the English nonconformist congregations in Europe, the foreign congregations in England, and the whole Church of England, under religious uniformity and conformity. On this aspect of Laud's attempts, see H.R. Trevor-Roper, Archbishop Laud.

78.   Richard Hooker, The Laws of Ecclesiastical Polity (London, 1594), in The Works of...Richard Hooker, ed. Isaac Walton, 2 vols. (Oxford, 1850), I, pp. 488, 485. On Hooker's thought, see Robert K. Faulkner, Richard Hooker and the Politics of Christian England (Berkeley, 1981).

79.   Peter Heylin (Heyelin), Observations on the History of the Reign of King Charles (London, 1656). The poem appears in Heylin's book, pp. 50-51.

80.   CSPD, VI, p. 450. Conrad Russell in his excellent study, "Arguments for Religious Unity in England, 1530-1650," Journal of Ecclesiastical History, XVIII (1967), traced many of contemporaries' reasons not to allow religious nonconformism.

81.   CSPD, VI, pp. 449-450.

82.   Thomas Hooker, "The Danger of Desertion" (April, 1631), in Thomas Hooker, Writings in England and Holland, eds. G.H. Williams, et al., pp. 246. 230, 245, 242.

83.   APCC, pp. 200-201, 206.

84.   "Edward Howes to John Winthrop, Jr." (March, 1632/3), in Winthrop Papers, III, p. 111; Francis Kirby to John Winthrop, Jr." (March, 1632/3), in Winthrop Papers, III, p. 117.

85.   "John Winthrop to Sir Simonds D'Ewes" (July 21, 1634), in Winthrop Papers, III, p. 172.

86. "A Quo Warranto Brought Against the Company of the Massachusetts Bay...," in Collection, comp. Hutchinson, pp. 114-116.

87. "Records of the Council for New England," p. 115; CSPC, I, pp. 204-205; "Records of the Council for New England," pp. 119, 121; CSPC, I, p. 214. On Sir Ferdinando Gorges and Captain John Mason, see, Ferdinando Gorges and His Province of Main, ed., James Phinney Baxter, 3 vols. (New York, 1967 [1890]), and J.W. Dean, ed., Capt. John Mason the Founder of New Hampshire (New York, 1967 [1887]).

88. Emmanuel Downing, cited in Letters from New England, ed. Everett Emerson, p. 93; "Henry Vane Jr. (?) to Sir Henry Vane" (July 28, 1636), in Letters from New England, ed. Everett Emerson, p. 209; Thomas Welde, "A Letter of Master Wells from New England to Old England" (1633), pp. 128-129.

89. "Edwards Howes to John Winthrop, Jr." (March 18, 1633/4), in Winthrop Papers, III, pp. 111, n. 1.

90. John Winthrop, The History of New England, ed. James Savage, 2 vols. (Boston, 1853), I, pp. 161, 164, 166 (hereafter cited as Winthrop, History); MA. Records, I, pp. 136-139.

91. Winthrop, History, I, pp. 171, 183; MA. Records, I, pp. 136-139.

92. MA. Records, I, pp. 137-138; Winthrop, History, I, 186, 188.

93. Winthrop, History, I, p. 175; Hubbard, A General History of New England, p. 164; Winthrop, History, I, pp. 186, 188-189, 191; MA. Records,I, pp. 137, 146.

94. Israel Stoughton, "Israel Stoughton to John Stoughton" (1635), in Letters from New England, ed. Everett Emerson, pp. 144-145, 151.

95. Winthrop, History, I, p. 215.

96. Winthrop, History, I, pp. 222-225, 215, n. 2.

97. Winthrop, History, I, p. 192.

98. Sir Simonds D'Ewes, Autobiography and Correspondence of Sir Simonds D'Ewes, ed. J.O. Halliwell (London, 1845), II, p. 118.

99. Peter Heylin Cyprianus Anglicus or The History of...Lord Archbishop of Canterbury (London, 1668), p. 369.

100. Winthrop, History, I, p. 313.

101. Peter Heylin, Cyprianus Anglicus, p. 369.

102. CSPC, I, pp. 283-284, 256.

103. Thomas Rymer, ed., Foedera, Conventions, Litera, Acta Publica, Regis Anglica (London, 1726), XIX, p. 223; John Rushworth, Historical Collections (London, 1659-1701), II, pp. 718, 721. On Puritan colonial activities during the 1630s in America, apart from

Massachusetts Bay, see Arthur P. Newton, The Colonising Activities of the English Puritans (New Haven, 1914).

104. Rushworth, Historical Collections, II, pp. 756-759.

105. Winthrop, History, I, pp. 319-320.

106. Peter Heylin, Cyprianus Anglicus, p. 369.

107. CSPD, XIII, p. 430.

CHAPTER FOUR:
THEOCRACY IN THE WILDERNESS
THE PURITAN HOLY EXPERIMENT IN NEW ENGLAND

We chose not the place for the land, but for the government, that our Lord Christ might raigne over us, both in Churches and Commonwealth...the upholding of the truths of Christ, is chief cause why many have hitherto come: and further if the servants of Christ be not much mistaken, the downfall of Antichrist is at hand, and then the Kingdome[s] of the Earth shall become the Kingdome of our Lord Christ...and surely godly civill government shall have a great share in that work.
   -- Edward Johnson, 1654[1]

Theocratic, or to make the Lord our Governour, is the best Form of Government in a Christian Common-wealth, and which men that are free to chuse (as in new Plantations they are) ought to establish.
   -- John Davenport, 1639[2]

Yet so as referreth the soveraigntie to himself...Theocracy [is] the best forme of government in the common-wealth, as well as in the church.
   -- John Cotton, 1636[3]

Whereas the way of God hath always been to gather his churches out of the world; now, the world, or civill state, must be raised out of the churches.
   --John Winthrop, 1637[4]

> Until the time drew nigh wherein
> The glorious Lord of hosts
> Was pleasd to lead his armies forth
> Into those forrein coastes...
> Here was the hiding place, which thou,
> Jehova didst provide
> For they redeemed ones, and where
> thou didst thy jewels hide.
>   -- Michael Wigglesworth, 1662[5]

Throughout the 1630s thousands of Puritans had crossed the ocean to reach New England where they intended to dedicate their lives to God and His word. They believed themselves as living in the time in which sacred, prophetic revelations would be fully realized and when the whole mystery of providential history, or salvation history, is resolved. So, according to Thomas Hooker,

> These are the times drawing on, wherein Prophecies are attain their performances: and it is a received rule and I suppose most sane, when Prophecies are fulfilled they are best interpreted, and the accomplishment of them is the best commentary.... These are the times, when the knowledge of the Lord shall cover the earth as the waters the Sea; and these waters of the Sanctuary encrease from the ankles unto the knees, thence into the loins, and thence become a river that cannot be passed.[6]

They came with the belief that the millennium was at hand and that the saints would have a decisive role in the apocalyptic events of the cosmological drama of all time. "The great design of Jesus Christ in this age," wrote John Higginson from Guilford, Connecticut, to Thomas Thatcher of Weymouth, Massachusetts,

> is to set up his Kingdom in particular churches, and yet the great duty of such as are in church fellowship, is to conform themselves to those primitive patterns.[7]

The raising and establishing of congregational churches, Puritans thus believed, was the great work of their time and history, and as soon as they arrived in New England they immediately began this divine work.

But, in the time of the millennium at hand and the realization of sacred, prophetic revelations, it was not enough only to constitute true churches in the wilderness. Obviously, in the apocalyptic drama of all time and history, the Puritan migration had a larger goal: "to rayse a bullwarke against the kingdom of Antichrist" that would help to insure that Christ and not Antichrist would reign in this world.[8] If Massachusetts was the site for establishing the true church, it was also, and even more importantly, for creating a holy Christian commonwealth in which Christ would reign over his saints in both church and state. For in the providential drama a Christian commonwealth was inextricably connected with

184

the existence and well being of the true church. "We chose not the place for the land," wrote Edward Johnson on the cause and origins of the Puritan migration to Massachusetts Bay,

> but for the government, that our Lord Christ might raigne over us, both in Churches and Common-wealth...the upholding of the truths of Christ, is chief cause why many have hitherto come: and further if the servants of Christ be not much mistaken, the downfall of Antichrist is at hand, and then the Kingdome[s] of the Earth shall become the Kingdome of our Lord Christ.

In this transformation of the world into the Kingdom of God, the godly civil magistrate had a crucial role. "Godly civil government," continued Johnson, "shall have a great share in the worke" of the upcoming millennium. In Massachusetts, he happily noted,

> our Magistrates being conscious of ruling for Christ, dare not admit of any of bastardly brood to nurse up upon their tender knees, neither any Christian of a sound judgment vote for any, but such as earnestly contend for the Faith.[9]

Church and state, then, in the early years of Massachusetts were but two complementary instruments through which Puritans hoped to defeat Antichristian institutions and realize their pursuit of the millennium. For the Puritans, the nature of a Christian commonwealth had always been a crucial issue in the struggle for religious reformation. Not surprisingly, therefore, the relationship between church and state has been a persistent issue in the historiography of the early years of the Massachusetts Bay colony. Historians have debated whether church and state were isomorphic during the formative years of the Puritan colony or whether they were almost completely separate. Yet neither of these extreme characterizations is true. The aims and thought of the Puritans in Massachusetts were neither to separate church from state nor to make them one. Rather, they tried to shape the relationship between church and state in terms of models of the ancient Christian churches and the Old Testament.

Clearly, the type of political system the puritans succeeded in creating in the American wilderness would largely determine both their degree of success in

185

effecting the religious and social reformation they had been unable to achieve in England, as well as the fulfilment of their providential mission to defeat Antichristian institutions and usher in the Kingdom of God. Precisely what was the nature of the Puritan commonwealth in New England, however, remains one of the most persistent questions in the historiography of American Puritanism. In the many works dealing with the Puritan colonies in America, whether or not the Puritans actually intended to and succeeded in creating a theocracy in New England, remains one of the essential questions not yet conclusively resolved.[10]

I   The Politics of Covenant

Those Puritans who emigrated to Massachusetts had long been attempting to reconstruct the church as a spiritual society based on holy covenant and in that way to separate themselves from profane and ungodly people admitted to membership by parish churches in England. The wilderness had offered, therefore, a unique opportunity to realize this longstanding goal. As Edmund Morgan has shown in his important book Visible Saints, "the English emigrants to New England were the first Puritans to restrict membership in the church to visible saints, to persons, that is, who had felt the stirrings of grace in their souls, and who could demonstrate this fact to the satisfaction of other saints."[11] At the same time, the wilderness also provided the possibility of forming a godly Puritan commonwealth in which the proper relationship between church and state might be achieved.

The pursuit of reformation, as we saw earlier, led as well to the forming of civil and social covenants in England in the early seventeenth century. A social covenant, as Winthrop preached in his lay sermon "A Model of Christian Charity," upon sailing to New England in the summer of 1630, was the foundation of the Puritan holy enterprise in the wilderness. Accordingly, when the godly reached New England, they immediately covenanted among themselves before settling a town or establishing a church. A social or civil covenant was something distinct and different from a church covenant; the first related to civil and social affairs, while the second pertained to a holy spiritual fellowship. Both, however, were essentially religious covenants intended to further the premises of reformation in church and state alike. While one regulated the saints in the commonwealth, or in the civil sphere, the other governed them in the church. This distinction is an important one because the problem of the relationship between the social or civil covenant and the church covenant lies at the root of the whole issue of the relationship between church and state in early Massachusetts. By and large, the civil covenant can be seen as the expansion of

187

a religious covenant, or at least of religious aims and ends, into the political realm. Thus, in state, as in the church, the covenant was a devise to exclude those who were not visible saints from participation.

In both church and state Bay colony Puritans sought to follow God's word. Given the fact that their intention was to constitute both church and state on the basis of covenants, it was no surprise that in both realms covenants served to exclude the ungodly from fellowship with the saints. "Here the churches and commonwealth are coinplanted together in holy covenant and fellowship with God," wrote John Davenport, and therefore "the people that choose civil rulers are God's people in covenant with him, that is members of churches."[12] By this rule Puritans linked the civil covenant and the church covenant in a radical way, so as to exclude those who were not saints not only from the church but also from political power in the Puritan commonwealth in New England.

Two of the most prominent New England ministers, John Cotton and John Davenport, asserted that the best form of government for a Christian commonwealth was a theocracy, a form that assumed a special relationship between church and state, clergy and magistracy, and, above all, the social covenant and the church covenant. Cotton, reported Rev. John Norton in <u>Abel Being Dead Yet Speaketh</u>, had advised the Massachusetts General Court in 1636 "to persist in their purpose of establishing a <u>Theocracy</u> (i.e. Gods Government) over Gods people" so that the godly "be governed conformably to the Law of God."[13] "Theocracy," wrote Cotton to Lord Say and Sele in 1636, is "the best forme of government in the common-wealth, as well as in the church."[14] To the same effect, John Davenport had argued that "<u>theocratic</u>, or to make the Lord God our Governour, is the best Form of Government in a Christian Common-wealth, and which men that are free to chuse (as in new Plantations they are) ought to establish."[15] To understand the nature of the Puritan holy commonwealth in Massachusetts, it is thus first necessary to explore the concept of "theocracy."

"Of English-speaking communities," wrote R.H. Tawney in Religion and the Rise of Capitalism,

> that in which the social discipline of Calvinist church-state was carried to the further extreme was the Puritan theocracy of New England. Its practice had more affinity with the iron rule of Calvin's Geneva than with the individualistic tendencies of contemporary English Puritanism. In that happy, bishopless Eden...men desired only to worship God 'according to the simplicities of the gospel and to be ruled by the laws of God's word'...those who escaped the judgment of Heaven had to face the civil authorities and the church, which in the infancy of the colony, were the same things.[16]

Although many studies have followed Tawney's interpretation of the relationship between church and state in early Massachusetts, it is basically misleading. For the modern concept of "theocracy" as used by Tawney differs fundamentally from that employed by seventeenth century Puritans to describe their experiment in America.

Few concepts have changed more radically over time. According to The Shorter Oxford English Dictionary, theocracy is "a form of government in which God (or a deity) is recognized as the king or immediate ruler...a system of government by a sacerdotal order, claiming a divine commission." This is the meaning intended by Tawney and those who have followed his lead. The Massachusetts "theocracy," they implied in using the term, was a state in which priests exercise political power, or, more precisely, a state ruled by ministers. But this meaning of theocracy is in fact a quite modern one. For according to the Encyclopedia of Religion and Ethics, "the term 'theocracy' was coined by Josephus...to denote a certain kind of national polity. Any tribe or state that claims to be governed by God or Gods may be called a 'theocracy.'" To understand the difference between these two meanings of theocracy is important. While the first implies that the sacerdotal order exercises dominant political power, the latter requires ministers to assume no political power at all. Bay colony Puritans used the latter - and older - meaning of theocracy.

II Covenant and Theocracy

The truth of this assertion can be seen in John Davenport's Discourse about Civil Government in a New Plantation Whose Design is Religion (1639). In the past, this work was ascribed to John Cotton, and, as Larzer Ziff has argued, it was certainly "represeatative of Cotton's opinions on that subject." Recently, however, Bruce E. Steiner demonstrated authoritatively that it was indeed Davenport who wrote this tract. In fact, the views and arguments in the Discourse were not limited to Davenport and Cotton but were central to "the Puritan mind." The importance of Davenport's Discourse lies in its unusually full exposition of the precise meaning of theocracy during the early years of the Puritan experiment in New England.[17]

In the summer of 1638, immediately after Davenport and his company reached their destination in New Haven, where they set about to establish a new settlement, "all the free planters assembled together in a ge[neral] meeting to consult about the settling of civill Government according to God" and also to nominate the people who would lay the foundation of the church there. Concerning civil government, their aim was to establish "such civill order as might be most p[leas]ing unto God." Before taking this step, all the "freeplanters" assembled to make a solemn covenant, "called a plantation covenant to distinguish itt from [a] church covenant." In New Haven, as in Massachusetts, a civil or social covenant thus preceded a church covenant. During the meeting, "Mr. Davenport propounded divers quaeres" concerning the nature of a Christian commonwealth and exhorted the gathering to "consider seriously in the presence and fear of God the weight of the business they met about." What Davenport argued in these queries was that "the civil power" in Christian commonwealth should be "confined to church members." But another minister, Rev. Peter Prudden objected to Davenport's motion. To answer Prudden, Davenport composed his Discourse to show the necessity of confining the civil power only to church members.[18]

Davenport's aim, in his words, was

> to prove the Expediency and Necessity...of entrusting free
> Burgesses which are members of Churches gathered amongst
> them according to Christ, with the power of Chusing from
> among themselves Magistrates, and men to whom the
> Managing of All Public Civil Affairs of Importance is to be
> committed. And to vindicate the Same from an Imputation of
> an underpower upon the Churches of Christ.

As this passage suggests, Davenport argued that limiting the choice of civil magistrates to church members would not lead to theocracy in its modern meaning. Rather, he contended, "the Church so considered" was "a Spiritual Political Body" and could not interfere in any civil affairs. He did not argue that every church member had the right to choose magistrates, but only those who were "free Burgesses" or freemen. "Though they may be, and are Church-Members," "Women and Servants" were obviously not free burgesses. As was the case in Massachusetts, in New haven one had to be both a freeman and a church member to have the right to vote for civil magistrates. But this was not to suggest that the "Rights and Powers of Chusing Civil Magistrates belong[ed   only] unto the Church of Christ" but just that in a Christian commonwealth no one who was not a church member could be permitted to exercise that right.[19]

Davenport premised his work upon a basic distinction between civil and ecclesiastical affairs. "Ecclesiastical Administration," he contended, was "a Divine Order appointed to believers for holy communion of holy things," while "Civil Administration" was "an Human Order appointed by God to men for Civil Fellowship of Human things." Thus, any attempt to unite both orders could transform "the Spiritual Power, which is proper to the Church, into the hand of the Civil Magistrate, as Erestus [Erastus] would have done in the matter of Excommunication." (Thomas Erastus, 1524-83, the Swiss theologian who argued for the state's right and duty to exercise jurisdiction in all matters, whether civil or ecclesiastical. Hence the term, Erastianism - the ascendary of the state over the church in ecclesiastical matter. Both in England and New England Puritans

191

strongly denounced Erastus' views.) On the other hand, there was the possibility, as had been the case with the Romish tyranny, that the church would usurp civil authority in the state.[20]

Either of these dangers, Davenport was aware, could result form unification of church and state: spiritual power could be transferred to the state or ministers would assume political power in the commonwealth, and he was concerned to prevent both. But he also was fearful of yet another, even more important danger: that of separating church and state so completely as to set "these two different Orders, Ecclesiastical and Civil...in opposition as contraries, that one should destroy the other." What he wanted, ultimately, was for church and state to be in a "co-ordinate state, in the same place reaching forth help mutually each other for the welfare of both, according to God."[21] In shaping a Christian commonwealth in the wilderness, Puritans thus aimed neither at unification nor at complete separation of church and state. Rather, they thought of church and state as two different means to the same end.

In New Haven in 1638, as in Massachusetts in 1630, the wilderness provided an opportunity for Puritans to create a Christian commonwealth according to their own premises of religious reformation. In thus "laying the foundation of a Christian Common-wealth," they could choose what kind of rulers would reign over them. In these unique circumstances, argued Davenport, godly people had to choose godly magistrates:

> Men that profess the fear of God, if they be free to make
> Choice of their Civil judges (as in this new plantation we are)
> they should rather chuse such as are members of the Church
> for that purpose, than others that are not in that estate.

There had been two sorts of people in the colony, "free Burgesses," or freemen, and "inhabitants." To exclude the latter from political power was natural because they were not citizens and were "never likely to be numbered among...Rulers." Confining civil power to church members did not, therefore, deprive these inhabitants of any civil right they would otherwise have had. "When we urge, the magistrates be Chosen out of free Burgesses, and by them, and that those free

192

Burgesses be Chosen out of such as are members of these Churches," said Davenport, "we do not thereby go about to exclude those that are not in Church-Order, from any Civil right or Liberty that is due unto them as Inhabitants and planters." The only group which lost any civil rights, Davenport made clear, were those freemen who were not church members and could not, therefore, in a godly Christian commonwealth be permitted either to choose magistrates or to exercise political power in the colony. In other words, they, as non-members of the church, retained their passive but lost their active political rights. On the other hand, only those "free Burgesses" who were in the "fellowship of the Church," contended Davenport, could have the "power of chusing from among themselves Civil Magistrates, and men to be intrusted with transacting all publick Affairs of Importance."[22]

Davenport, thus advocated disenfranchisement of all freemen who were not church members, and his rationale for doing so was to prevent ungodly magistrates from reigning over godly people. For, he believed, only godly magistrates could be entrusted with preserving civil and church covenants properly. It was his belief, and that of other Puritans also, that the covenant was the foundation of state as well as Church, and that by its very nature it belonged only to the "saints," who "by virtue of their Covenant" were "bound" to serve "God and his ends." To invest those who were not saints with civil power would therefore necessarily mean breaking the covenant with God. In this manner, Davneport transformed the religious obligations of the covenant into political obligations in the Christian commonwealth. Because the ungodly were not "consecrated to God and his ends," they could not be given civil power.[23]

It was precisely for this reason that Davenport and other Puritans argued that "Theocratic, or to make the Lord God our Governour" was "the best form of Government in a Christian Commonwealth." Only in this unique political system, according to the Puritans, could there be absolute assurance that the civil covenant in society and the church covenant in the church would be adhered to.

193

Davenport spelled out precisely what he meant by theocracy. A theocracy, he wrote, was that

> Form of Government where 1. The people that have the power of chusing their Governors are in covenant with God: 2. Wherein the men chosen by them are godly men, and fitted with a spirit of Government: 3. In which the Laws they rule by are the Laws of God: 4. Wherein Laws are executed, Inheritances allotted, and civil differences are composed, according to Gods appointment: 5. In which men of God are consulted with in all hard cases, and in matters of Religion.

This, said Davenport, was "the Form which was received and established among the people of Israel whil'st the Lord God was their Governour...and is the very same with which we plead for."[24]

Davenport gave here the true and comprehensive meaning of Puritan theocracy; that is, neither to unify nor to separate church and state, but to establish a special relationship between them in order "to make the Lord God our Governour." According to this meaning, theocracy clearly did not invest ministers with political power. Rather, it emphasized the necessity for civil magistrates to govern according to God's words and will. Although Puritans did not believe ministers should assume civil power, they strongly stressed the obligation of godly magistrates to seek to make civil society conform to God's purposes. Religious reformation was necessary not only in the church but in society as a whole. Because civil magistrates were charged with such weighty responsibilities, it was essential for them to be saints.

A theocratic government, then, was one which gave "Christ his due preheminence," and godly people were obliged to make sure that "all things and all Government...should serve...Christs ends, for the welfare of the Church whereof he is the Head." To meet this obligation civil authorities had to be "wise and learned in matters of Religion," which in turn meant that they had to be church members. The presence of ungodly magistrates in England had been a crucial reason why many Puritans emigrated to New England. Now that they were in a "new plantation" in America and were "free to chuse" they had no

194

choice but to take every step possible to prevent the true church from coming under persecution from ungodly magistrates. Thus, in the name of purity and sainthood, the Puritans excluded people not only from the church covenant but also from the civil and social covenant. In both church and state, they believed, the covenant was the foundation, and by its very nature the covenant belonged only to the godly, who "by virtue of their Covenant" were "bound" to serve God and his ends. To invest those who were not saints with civil power would therefore necessarily mean breaking covenant with God. In this way of reasoning, the covenant became the necessary foundation not only of the spiritual society of the church but of civil society as well. Thus did Davenport transform the religious obligations of the covenant into political obligations in the Christian commonwealth. Precisely because the ungodly were not "consecrated to God and his ends," they could not be given civil power.[25]

For Davenport, as for many other Puritans in New England, the reason for excluding those who were not considered saints from civil power was thus "evident of itself." First, men who were "out of the church" and therefore were "unsanctified" were by their very nature, according to Davenport, "unsuitable to Gods ends in Civil Administration." Only those who were "Saints by calling," or visible saints, and "according to Christ's appointment" were "in Covenant with God, and one with another, whereby they are most strictly bound to do faithfully whatsoever they do to God or men," were suitable managers of public affairs. Thus, since political society, no less than the church or holy fellowship, was confined to those capable
of preserving the covenant, the exclusiveness of church fellowship led directly to the exclusiveness of the political system. Besides, to delegate political authority to the ungodly, warned Davenport, would ruin the entire holy experiment in the wilderness and would jeopardize the saints' capacity to assist Christ in the apocalyptical battle against Antichrist. To commit power into the hands of those "worldly spirits," who "hate[d] the Saints and their communion" was indeed to

provide Satan with an instrument for "resisting and fighting against Christ and his Kingdom and Government in the Church."[26]

Davenport addressed these arguments to the new colony of New Haven, but they were by no means peculiar to him. In fact they had been the policy in Massachusetts from its very beginnings. In 1631, "to the end that body of commons may be preserved of honest and godly men," the Massachusetts General Court had ordered "that for the time to come no man shall be admitted to the freedom of this body politic, but such as are members of some of the churches." By this action, the General Court limited the right to participate in civil affairs to saints. Also, in 1634 in Guilford, later part of Connecticut, "the inhabitants believed that only verified saints ought to vote or hold government offices and the verification was the function of the institutional church."[27]

When Connecticut towns drew up their Fundamental Orders in 1638/9, they did not explicitly stipulate that "church membership was...a prerequisite for the franchise." But as Mary J.A. Jones found in her Congregational Commonwealth: Connecticut 1636-1662, this condition was implicit in the colony's constitution. "The purpose of the Fundamental Orders was to provide a legal guide for the government of the holy and regenerate."[28] In Connecticut, no less than in Massachusetts and New Haven, a social covenant preceded the establishment of the Puritan commonwealth. The Fundamental Orders were a civil covenant in which the godly declared that "the word of God requires" that "there should be an orderly and decent Government established according to God" and pledged themselves to

> associate and conjoyne our selves to be as one Publike State or Commonwealth...to mayntayne and presearve the liberty and purity of the gospel of our Lord Jesus wch we now professe, as also the disciplyne of the Churches, wch according to the truth of the said gospel is now practised amongst us.[29]

As Jones remarks, this was

196

a covenant between the godly property owners of Hartford, Windsor, and Wethersfield, not between all the residents on the Connecticut River, just as the church covenants were the agreement between the saints only. Civil rights were the privilege of the few.[30]

Similarly, in New Haven, "the practice championed in Davenport's Discourse had [also] triumphed." A "generall meeting of all the free planters" in New Haven in 1639 agreed

> thatt church members onely shall be free bourgesses, and they onely shall chuse among them selves magistrates and officers to ha[ve] the power of transacting all publique civill affayres of this plantation.[31]

If, then, the essence of theocratic government was maintaining the political realm as the sole and exclusive domain of the saints, the system of government in all these New England Puritan colonies, Massachusetts, Connecticut and New Haven may justifiably be defined as theocracy.

The Puritans' rigid insistence upon excluding the ungodly from political power was thus a crucial element in shaping the relationship between church and state in the early years of Puritan New England. To realize their premises of religious reformation, Puritans believed, they had to keep their covenants, in the civil as well as in the religious realm, with God, and that obligation required that only the godly be entrusted with civil power. With religious reformation going hand in hand with social and political reform, the same drive for reformation that led to the admission into the church of only the "visible saints," led, in the political realm, to the establishment of theocratic government, a political system which entrusted authority only to those in the Puritan colonies who belonged to the "gathered churches" or the saints. Thus, in their drive to achieve religious reformation through establishment of a Christian commonwealth, Puritans did everything in their power to make sure that magisterial authority would be confined only to the godly.

But the concept of the covenant and aspirations for religious reformation were not the only sources for Puritan ideas about the role of the godly Christian magistrate.   Those ideas also derived from the unique premises of Congregationalism which Puritans carried with them into the wilderness. How the principles and assumptions of congregational church-government affected the relationship between church and state and accorded the godly magistrate such a crucial role in the beginning and formative years of the Bay colony will be analyzed in the next section.

III   Magistrates and the Pursuit of Religious Unity and Conformity

The Puritans came to America in order to create a theocracy, or to make the Lord their governor, in the wilderness. In such a political system, as we have seen, ministers in the Bay colony had no intention of assuming political power. In fact, they voluntarily left the political realm to the civil authorities in the colony because they intended to renew the ancient meaning of the church as a spiritual entity. This voluntary withdrawal from state affairs, combined with the view that it was the duty of the state, or the magistrate, to uphold the true church, were among the basic premises of Congregationalism as a system of church-polity in the Puritans' attempts to erect the church upon the model of the ancient churches in early Christianity.

The cornerstone of Congregationalism was its emphasis upon the independence of each particular church in order to achieve the highest purity of Christian faith and life. The model for the early congregationalists was the voluntary gathering of the ancient Christian congregations, consisting only of true believers, whose churches, though independent of each other, were directly related through their mutual covenants with God. For the congregationalist, then, the primary motivation "was not a desire to establish a novel polity, but to foster the spiritual development of the believer by his separation from communion with the non-faithful whom all the state churches allowed a place in the church." Only visible saints could gather and establish a church; others, who had no proof of their being elected by God, were excluded from membership.[32]

As a result of its covenant with God, each particular congregation stood in direct relationship to God and held the keys to the Kingdom of Heaven or salvation. According to Thomas Hooker in his A Survey of the Summe of Church Discipline, in 1648,

> A Church Congregation is the first subject of the keys. Each Congregation compleatly constituted of all Officers, hath sufficient power in her self, to exercise the power of the keys, and all Church discipline, in all the censures thereof.[33]

And John Cotton likwise declared in The Keys of the Kingdom of Heaven, in 1644, that each particular congregation was "the first subject of the power of the keys" and thus had "independent power in the exercise thereof."[34] What all these exponents of Congregationalism thus argued was that each particular church possessed in itself the means and modes of salvation.

The implication of this kind of church polity was revolutionary from the point of view of the concept of a national church, such as the Church of England which theoretically possessed the sole means of salvation within the nation. With its insistence on the independence of each congregation, Congregationalism contributed to the breakdown of the notion of national church by arguing that each particular church, over which any kind of ecclesiastical power was denied, held the means of salvation through its possession of the keys to the Kingdom of Heaven derived from its covenant with God. Thus, Puritans came to realize, the notion of a national church was incompatible with the premises of Congregationalism. "In the Old Testament indeed," wrote Cotton, "we read of a national church...but we read of no such national church...in the New Testament."[35] But Cotton did not mean to imply that Massachusetts Puritans objected to all concepts of a church state. On the contrary, as we will see later, all they argued against was any kind of national or church state that would exercise ecclesiastical jurisdiction over particular churches or congregations.

In Massachusetts, from its beginnings, only the congregationalist church was permitted to exist. "And the general Court," wrote Thomas Lechford, who was in the colony in the late 1630s, would "not allow of any Church otherwise gathered."[36] From the time of the creation of the church in Salem in 1629, many (but only congregationalist) churches were established there. Thus, the problem faced by congregationalists in the wilderness was how to sustain both the principles of the independence of each congregation without sacrificing the necessary conformity and unity within the ecclesiastical polity of the colony.

Congregationalism was in fact a church-state in the early years of the Bay colony, but only in the sense that congregationalist churches alone were allowed

200

to be established; it was not, however, a church-state in the sense that each congregation was dependent on a hierarchical ecclesiastical order, as was the case with the Church of England during that time. Who, then, was to be charged with maintaining the conformity of all the congregations in the colony and who was to oversee the unity in ecclesiastical matters in the Puritan commonwealth according to the congregational way? The lack of an ecclesiastical order above the particular congregations and the inability of a ministers to interfere with another church's affairs indicate that this task could not be assumed by the colony's clergy. As will be seen, the civil magistrates would acquire this responsibility and role. It was, therefore, the very premises of Congregationalism's rigid insistence on the independence of each particular congregation that led to the involvement of the godly magistrate in the colony's ecclesiastical affairs.

The establishment of a new settlement and the creation of a new congregation went hand in hand in the early years, for it seeming "as unnatural for a right N.E. men to live without an able minister as for a Smith to work his iron without a fire." The formation of a new body of believers and of holy fellowship took place under the eyes of ministers of other churches who oversaw and ascertained that the congregational way was adhered to. However, the creation of new congregations was not observed only by ministers:

> Also it is the duty of the Magistrate (in regard of the good and peace of the civil government) to be present, at least some of them (not only to prevent the disturbance might follow in the Commonwealth by any, who under pretence of Church-Covenant, might bring in again those cursed opinions…to the great damage of the people) but also to countenance the people of God in so pious a work, that under them they may live a quiet and peaceable life, in all godliness and honesty.

The Elders of other churches also witnessed the creation of a new Church, and after the ordination of its officers, the elders of neighboring congregations would "give the New Officers the right hand of fellowship, taking them by the right hand, every one severally, or else, sometimes, one...in the name of all the rest, with a set speech unto them."[37]

Of all those involved, the role of the magistrate in the process of the creation of a new congregation was decisive. In 1642, with the establishment of Woburn's church, civil magistrates present at the ordination of the minister, Rev. Thomas Carter, censured the church for not conforming to the congregational way. Instead of adhering to the imposition of hands by elders or ministers, as required in a congregational minister's ordination, the imposition of hands upon Carter was performed by lay members: "Two persons in the name of the Church laid their hands upon his head, and said, We ordain thee Thomas Carter to be Pastor unto this Church of Christ." The Woburn church had rejected the alternative of having ministers from other churches perform this ceremony because its members feared that such a procedure would diminish the independence of the church. As Winthrop wrote,

> Some advised, in regard they had no elder of their own, nor any members very fit to solemnize such ordination, they would desire some of the elders of the others churches to have performed it; but others supposing it might be an occasion of introducing a dependency of churches, etc. and so presbytery, would not allow it.[38]

Paradoxically, because ministers of other churches could not interfere in the affairs of other churches, and because there was no ecclesiastical court to deal with such matters, the magistrates were the ones who censured the congregation in Woburn.

Rev. Thomas Welde described thus the relationship among the churches in the colony in a 1644 tract. "With the creation of a new congregation," wrote Welde,

> the churches indeed send messengers (commonly their elders) to lend them a word of counsell if they need.... The messengers never arrogated to themselves such power...as to forbid their entrance into church state. The most they do...is, to desire leave to be faithfull in interposing their counsell, and

202

that only when they see very great cause: and withall leave them to their Christian liberty.[39]

Similarly, in his description of the creation of the church at Weymouth in January 1639, Winthrop wrote that the congregation was gathered "with the approbation of the magistrates and elders." The power of the elders was limited only to advice, but magistrates did not hesitate to interfere in the affairs of a particular church as the example of the censuring of the ordination of the Woburn church shows.[40]

That magistrates had power over the colony's churches was indeed embodied in the colony's laws. In 1641 the Bay colony adopted "The Body of Liberties" composed by Nathaniel Ward of Ipswich. The "Civill Authoritie hath power and libertie," it was stated there, "to see the peace, ordinances and Rules of Christ observed in every church according to his word, so it be done in a Civill and not in an Ecclesiastical way." The churches, then, were absolutely dependent in the colony on the civil power. Likewise, An Abstract of the Laws of New England, published in London in 1641, listed one of the main duties of civil magistrates as the preservation of religion through punishment of "blasphemy," "Idolatry," "Witchcraft," and "Heresy."[41]

203

IV   The Struggle Against Heresy: The Antinomian Controversy

The Antinomian controversy in 1636-1638 revealed sharply the weakness of the congregationalist way against the challenge of heresy and how decisive and crucial was the role of the godly magistrate in the religious affairs of the colony. The theological conflict revolved around the issue whether the Bay Colony ministers were in fact preaching the "covenant of works" in contrast to "covenant of grace" which ought to be regarded as the sole requisite for salvation. The Antinomians, Anne Hutchinson and her faction in the Boston Church, claimed that assurance of salvation lay solely in the internal testimony of the Holy Spirit, and denounced the majority of ministers in Massachusetts of preaching a "covenant of works" - namley, that the commandements are prerequisite for salvation.   But in terms of ecclesiastical and social control, the unity and conformity of the Massachusetts churches was at stake.   The ultimate problem was how to deal with a particular church, the Boston church, situated in the heart of the colony, and to whom belonged Ann Hutchinson and the Antinomians, and whose majority dissented from the prevailing views in the colony, had to be resolved.[42]

When the controversy developed, it was the magistrates, or more specifically, the Massachusetts General Court, who called a synod to be assembled in the summer of 1637 to deal with the opinions of Hutchinson and other Antinomians. The synod met in Newton, now Cambridge, and consisted "not only [of] the ministers and messengers of churches, but the magistrates also, who Mr. Welde says...were not only hearers but speakers also, as they thought fit." Among those present was the governor, John Winthrop, who seemed to "have a controuling power" over the synod.[43] This was no surprise, indeed, for given the stress upon the independence of each congregation, the actual power of the synod, as illustrated in the case of the Antinomians, was limited to giving advice or counsel.   Such a synod, wrote Hooker, could "counsell and admonish other

Churches, as the case may require, but they have no power of excommunicate. Nor do their constitutions binde formaliter & juridice."[44]

The Puritans did not object to synods or clerical church consociations as such. Such ecclesiastical bodies had been often assembled in Massachusetts. "Consociation of Churches...and Synods we hold to be lawful and in some cases necessary," wrote Richard Mather in his Church-Government and Church-Covenant Discussed in 1643. And it was stated in "The Body of Liberties" in 1641, that

> It was allowed and ratified, by the Authoritie of this Generall Court as a lawfull libertie of the Churches of Christ. That once in every month of the year...it shall be lawfull for the ministers and Elders...to assemble by course in each severall Church one after an other.

But, it should be stressed, the most synods or other ecclesiastical assemblies could do was to renounce the "right hand of fellowship" with a church that deviated from the congregational way.[45]

Thus, Congregationalism had no efficient means for dealing with a local church which differed from the other churches in the colony, as did the Boston church during the Antinomian controversy. Later, the historian Thomas Hutchinson clearly defined and explained the meaning and role of the synod in Newton concerning the Antinomians: "This spiritual court did not pronounce particular persons to be hereticks, but it determined what was heresy, and made the way plain for the secular power to proceed." Ministers had no right to interfere in other churches' affairs, only to give advice, but godly Christian magistrates had ample power and authority over each particular church in the colony. Consequently, when the court decided to banish the leaders of the Antinomians, despite the fact that their followers constituted the majority of the Boston church, it was not a decision of an ecclesiastical court but of the civil authority, whose justification was that Anne Hutchinson and her faction "disturbed the civil peace." The premises of Congregationalism left in fact no other way of handling such a case. To preserve the independence and spirituality of each congregation, the ministers were willing to pay the price entailed in delegating responsibility for maintaining unity and conformity in the colony to the godly magistrate.[46]

The Antinomians had, in fact, challenged the very basis of the Puritans' holy experiment in New England, and more particularly, in Massachusetts. The central issue posed by antinomianism, according to R.A. Knox, concerns the question of whether "the natural law of morals is binding on a soul which has emancipated itself from the natural, and lives now by the law of grace." For the antinomians in the Hutchinson controversy, the godly were predestined for salvation through a "covenant of grace" bestowed upon them by God and revealed to them through the operation of His Holy Spirit within them. According to this view, there was no need for the godly "to be troubled by the Law" as that law was represented by either the Scriptures or by written covenants with God. Quite the contrary, so far from being a route to salvation, adherence to such law, antinomians argued, was "of no use at all...to drive man to Christ" because a man could be "united to Christ...only...by the work of the Spirit upon him" and not by "any act of his" own. Salvation could not, they declared, be achieved through performing good works and living according to the "letter of the Scripture" and the covenant. Hence, antinomians insisted, there was no need for the godly to be "bound to the Law [of scriptures and covenant] as a rule" of their lives and conversations. Indeed, they contended, adherence to that law and efforts to gain salvation through what they contemptuously denounced as a "covenant of works" was actually "Antichristian" and an aid to Satan in his war with Christ. To "put any worke of sanctification in a legall frame," declared Ann Hutchinson's lieutenant John Wheelwright in a Boston fast-day sermon in 1637, was to kill "the spirit of Gods [true] children," and Wheelwright condemned all proponents of such "legal frame[s]" as "enimyes to the Lord." By thus substituting private revelation of the Holy Spirit for the covenant as the essential feature of man's relationship with God and by denouncing "all covenants to God expressed in words" as "legall workes" subversive of Christian societies, the

206

antinomians thus challenged the very foundations of church and state in Massachusetts. They thereby threatened destruction to the Puritan vision of establishing a tightly-ordered city upon a hill upon the basis of binding covenants with God, covenants that were scrupulously enforced by civil authorities.[47]

If the Antinomian crisis illustrated how closely theology was associated with the political and social life in the colony and presented a serious threat to the foundation of a Christian commonwealth in New England, it also revealed to what a great extent ecclesiastical order in the colony depended upon civil authority. Notwithstanding its continuing commitment to the belief that each particular congregation was sufficient unto itself in determining the means and modes of salvation, the Massachusetts clergy happily welcomed the interposition of the state to purge the church of such a menace. Thus did the antinomian crisis contribute to establish and to define the power of magistrates over the churches in the Puritan commonwealth in Massachusetts in its early years.

The distinction made by the early congregationalists between the spiritual realm and the civil realm, between church and state, has led historians to conclude that the Puritans separated church from state. As applied to seventeenth century Congregationalism, however, these interpretations are somewhat misleading. Winthrop S. Hudson has rightly cautioned historians about confusing the concept of separation of church and state with "the doctrine of 'the spirituality of the church.'"[48] Hudson's distinction is an important one, for it points to the essential intention of the Puritans in Massachusetts in distinguishing between church and state and that they considered both as a means to the same religious end. For they contended that both church and state had a common mission with a single aim - a providential mission to defeat Antichristian institutions. By contrast, the concept of separation of church and state implies that each has a unique aim to fulfill that differs from that of the other. But such a view was unacceptable both to Puritans in England and New England. On both sides of the Atlantic Puritans wanted to establish a religious society and Christian commonwealth according to God's word. Thus, the omnipresent attempt to

207

achieve the highest purity of the church did not lead to separation of church and state. To the contrary, by the very premises of congregationalism, as the case of the Boston church during the antinomian controversy showed, ministers in the colony fully acknowledge the magistrate's power over the church. In Massachusetts, as Perry Miller wrote, "the fundamental law was the Bible. The magistrates were to have full power to rule men for the specific purposes to which society was dedicated."[49]

V   In Defense of Theocracy

Although the pursuit of the spirituality of the church rather than the separation of state and church was their primary concern, the founders of Massachusetts Bay left the church itself bereft of any worldly means to maintain order, unity, and conformity in religious affairs.   Rather, both ministers and magistrates favored placing the duty of preserving the well-being of the churches in the colony in the hands of civil authorities.   As C.H. George and K. George have pointed out in their The Protestant Mind and the English Reformation, this was an essential feature of the Puritan movement before the Puritan Revolution. Therefore, the Puritans' pursuit of "liberty and Reformation" had been closely associated with order, and "the way to the New Jerusalem" had all along been involved with warnings not "to let loose the golden reins of discipline and government in the Church."[50] Thus, "the Grand Remonstrance" of December 1, 1641, announced that:

> we do here declare that it is far from our purpose or desire to let loose the golden reins of discipline and government in the Church, to leaven private persons or particular congregations to take up what form of Divine Service they please, for we hold it requisite that there should be throughout the whole realm a conformity to that order which the laws enjoin in the Word of God.[51]

This was indeed the very issue upon which "Young Henry Vane" and John Winthrop clashed sharply in 1637.   An important consequence of the antinomian controversy in Massachusetts was   an order, enacted by the General Court in 1637, "that no town or person shall receive any stranger resorting hither," nor "shall allow any lot of habitant to any...except such person shall have allowance under the hands of some one of the councile, or two other of the magistrates."[52] In other words, civil authorities intended to restrict the entrance of those "profane persons" who held antinomian views into the Bay colony.   "A family is a little common wealth," Winthrop wrote in defense of the order of 1637, "and a common wealth is a great family. Now as a family is not bound to entertaine all

209

comers...no more is [a] common wealth."[53] The Court's order intended to protect the churches as well as the commonwealth as a whole by preserving the colony as a covenanted society against the heresy of the antinomians.

But to Henry Vane the Court's order revealed an alarming tendency which stood in a clear contrast to the Puritan vision of the holy refuge and shelter in the wilderness. And this

> because here is a liberty given by this law to expell and reject those which are most eminent christian, if they suite not with the disposition of the magistrates, whereby it will come to passe, that Christ and his members will find worse entertainment amongst us than the Israelites did amongst the Egyptians and Babilonians.... Now that law, the execution whereof may make us more cruell and tyranicall over Gods children.

Christ, argued Vane, citing Rev. 1:5, "is the head of the church, and the prince of the kings of earth," but the colony's law by giving magistrates power to expell whomever they wanted, contradicted "many lawes of Christ." More tolerant of diversity of belief, Vane warned that

> Christ commands us to do good unto all, but especially to them of the household of faith. Many other lawes there are of Christ, which this law dasheth against, and therefore is most wicked and sinnefull.[54]

Winthrop's answer to Vane's charges clearly reveals the character of the Puritan theocracy in Massachusetts. It illustrated both how closely the Puritans associated church and state and how the social and church covenant were so tightly interwoven in the early years of the colony. In response to Vane's argument that the court's order gave Massachusetts magistrates unlimited power to determine what sorts of Christians could reside in the colony, Winthrop replied that the magistrates were "members of the churches here and, by that covenant" could not act in opposition to but were required and "regulated to direct all their wayes by the rule of the gospell." This law, furthermore, was not a new policy. For Vane should have known, continued Winthrop, that it was "an established order" in Massachusetts "that none should be received into cohabitation there, except they be allowed by certain men appointed to judge of their fitness for church-fellowship."[55] During the 1630s, as mentioned earlier, Laud and the Crown had tried to regulate the Puritan emigration to Massachusetts, but Winthrop's words clearly showed that the Bay Puritans themselves also had been engaged in controlling the emigration into their holy experiment.

Winthrop's aim in his reply to Vane was more than an attempt to justify the Court's order. His primary concern was to vindicate the establishment of theocratic government in Massachusetts by confirming the Puritans' adherence to their eschatological visions and millennial expectations and to their belief that they were living in a special dimension of time. Winthrop maintained that the providential process which was to culminate in the reign of Christ and his church or saints on earth had already begun. Therefore he justified the Court's order in a radical way:

> whereas the way of God hath always beene to gather his churches out of the world; now, the world, or civill state, must be raised out of the churches.[56]

The radicalism embodied in this view should not be overlooked. While John Davenport had argued in New Haven that the political realm should be the exclusive domain of the saints, who alone were proper governors in a Christian commonwealth, or theocracy, Winthrop here declared that the body politic as such was the outcome of the gathering of churches, or more precisely, that the holy society of the churches in Massachusetts constituted the political body of the colony. With this radical approach, he clearly implied that the boundaries of the church covenant were exactly congruent with those of the civil covenant.

But this stand did not signify that church and state were one, but only reaffirmed the principle that church membership, participation in the church covenant, was a prerequisite to participation in the civil covenant and membership in the colony's body politic. That was why Winthrop took pains to refute Vane's claim that magistrates, by the Court's order, operated against God's law. For, according to Winthrop,

211

the magistrates are limitted both by their church covenant and by their oath, and by the dutye of their places, to square all their proceedings by the rule of Gods word, for the advancement of the gospell and the weale publick...for whatsoever sentence the magistrate gives, according to these limittations, the judgment is the Lords, though he do it not by any rule particularly prescribed by civill authority.[57]

Winthrop therefore concluded the Court's rule that "none should be received to inhabit within the jurisdiction" of Massachusetts Bay "but such as should be allowed by some of the Magistrates" was necessary for preservation of both civil and church covenants and to the well-being of church and state in the colony. If Vane objected that the order was directed against some Christians, some members of "the household of faith," Winthrop made it clear that he considered the colony's religious welfare to be more important than the possible damage to the antinomians. "Better it is some members should suffer the evill they bring upon themselves," he wrote, "than that, by indulgence toward them, the whole familye of God in this country should be scattered, if not destroyed."[58]

Congregationalism, then, having left the church bereft of any worldly means to maintain unity and conformity in religious affairs, led Massachusetts Puritans to give the ultimate responsibility for preserving the ecclesiastical order to the civil magistrates. "A Model of Church and Civil Power," composed by the Bay ministers and published in 1636, explicitly revealed the clergy's view concerning the relationship of church and state. In the preface, the ministers declared that

> God hath given a distinct power to Church and Common-weale, the one Spiritual (called the Power of the Keyes) the other Civill (called the Power of the Sword), and hath made the members of both Societies subject to both Authorities, so that every soule in the Church is subject to the higher powers in the Commonweale, and every member of the Commonweale (being member of the Church) is subject to the Lawes of Christ Kingdome, and in him to the censure of the Church.[59]

However, as a spiritual society which could assume only spiritual power, the Church had to turn to the godly Christian magistrate so that the latter, by his power of the sword, could preserve religious peace. Thus did

> Magistrates have power given to them from Christ in matters of Religion, because they are bound to see that outward peace be preserved...in all godlinesse and honesty, for such peace God aymes at. And hence the Magistrate is custos of both the Tables of godlinesse, in the first of Honesty, in the second for Peace shake.

Without honesty, the ministers declared, "the subject will not be bonus Civis"; without godliness, "the subject will not be bonus vir, who is the best bonus Civis." As custodians of the two tables, the magistrate thus had responsibility to see that honesty, the necessary quality for the good citizen, and godliness, the essential condition for a good man, would be maintained. Above all, the magistrate "must see that godlinesse and honesty be preserved, or else himself will not be bonus Magistratus." Just as godliness transformed a subject into a good man and hence into the best citizen, so also did it make a magistrate godly. In that way, indeed, the godly magistrate became Defensor Fidei, the defender of the faith. "Civill peace," Puritans believed, could not "stand intire, where Religion is corrupted." Despite this close interrelationship, however, the civil and religious realms were not conflated: "Lawes, though conversant about Religion, may still be counted Civill Lawes, as on the contrary, an Oath doth still remaine Religious, though conversant about Civill matters."[60]

As this passage shows, however, Puritan ministers found it extremely difficult to maintain the distinction between spiritual and civil power. This was precisely what so angered Roger Williams, and in his The Bloody Tenant of Persecution, for Cause of Conscience, published in London in 1644, he sought to refute the "Model of Church and Civil Power" section by section. Knowing too well the Bay Puritans' intentions concerning state and church, Williams argued that they never intended to make "a true difference between the Church and the World, and the Spiritual and the Civill State." By giving civil magistrates power over religious matters, Williams charged, Massachusetts Puritans had stopped in the middle of the pursuit of "the spirituality of the church." Denying that Christ had ever, as the ministers' "Model" had suggested, "sent any of his Ministers or Servants to the Civill Magistrate for help in spiritual matters," Williams argued that by adopting this policy Massachusetts Puritans in fact came nearer to acting as Satan's agents by stirring "up the Kings of the Earth to make warre against the Lambe Christ Jesus, and his Followers" than to helping Christ in his fight against Antichrist.[61] But John Cotton took precisely the opposite view in The Powring Out of the Seven Vials, published two years earlier, where he reaffirmed his belief that the civil sword should be employed on God's side against Antichrist for God-given ends. "Cursed is he that does the work of the Lord negligently," wrote Cotton, "and cursed is he who keeps his sword back from blood when the Lord call us to use the sword of authority."[62]

Obviously, then, what seemed to Williams to be "the bloody tenent of persecution," that is, the involvement of magisterial power in religious matters and men's conscience, was in Massachusetts an essential attribute of the good or godly ruler. A godly society had to have godly means, and what the churches with their exclusively spiritual powers could not achieve, became the holy duty of the civil power to preserve. That is, the godly ruler had to make sure that no breach would occur between God and his people and that the covenant would be strictly maintained. Although both Williams and Bay colony Puritans both considered themselves to be living within a special dimension of time, the millennium at hand, their millennial expectations concerning the establishment of the Kingdom of God on earth led them to two different views about the saints' role in the world. As Jesper Rosenmeier has noted, "Williams believed that Christ's coming had signified an end to Christian calling; Cotton considered a Christian calling rich with possibilities. For Williams, redemption lay beyond the present world; for Cotton, it was located in the complex world around him."[63]

In the Cambridge Synod and Platform of 1646-1648, the Massachusetts clergy reiterated its stand and view, formerly revealed in "A Model of Church and Civil Power" of 1636, that they advocated not separation of state and church but the dependence of the church upon the state. "The Cambridge Platform," wrote Williston Walker,

> is the most important monument of early New England Congregationalism, because it is the clearest reflection of the system as it lay in the mind of the first generation...after nearly twenty years of practical experience. The Platform...urges the right of the civil magistrate to interfere in matters of doctrine and practice, because Congregationalism then believed that such right was his.[64]

The articles of the Platform concerning the relationship of the church and state reveal how far the clergy in the colony had moved from the views of Roger Williams and other sectarians in England who raised the "case of the conscience" against the magistrate's power in matters of faith, and how far the clergy had developed reasons of state concerning the role of civil authorities in religion:

> It is the duty of the Magistrate, to take care of matters of religion, & to improve his civil authority for the observing of the duties commanded in the first, as well as the second table. They are called Gods. The end of the Magistrates office, is not only the quiet & peaceable life of the subject, in matters of righteousness & honesty, but also in matters of godliness, yea, of all godliness.

In the case of a congregation which inclined to different ecclesiastical views and ways, the clergy left no doubt about the role they expected the magistrate to play:

> If any church one or more shall grow schismatical, rending it self from the communion of other churches, or shall walke incorrigibly or obstinately in any corrupt way of their own, contrary to the rule of the word; in such case, the Magistrate is to put forth his coercive power as the matter shall require.[65]

During the early years of the Puritan commonwealth, there were many examples in which magistrates interfered in religious affairs of churches in order to maintain unity and bring conformity to the congregational way. For example, in 1631,

> the governor, and deputy, and Mr. Nowell, the elder of the Congregation at Boston, went to Watertown to confer with Mr. Phillips, the pastor, and Mr. Brown, the elder of the congregation there, about an opinion, which they had published, that the churches of Rome were true churches. The matter was debated...and, by the approbation of all the assembly, except three, was concluded an error.[66]

Winthrop, then the governor, did not give us a full account of the case and how he convinced the Watertown church; what is important, however, is the fact that the civil authority, not the clergy, took steps to correct the "error." In Watertown in 1631, as with the churches at Weymouth in 1639, Woburn in 1642, and elsewhere at other times, interference by civil authorities in church matters exemplifies a situation in which the clergy in the colony almost always conformed to the decisions of the magistrates. The clergy's acceptance of civil authority's power in religious matters contrasted sharply to the non-conformist stand of those ministers in old England before they came to the colony. Once the congregational polity became dominant in the colony, however, the very premises of congregationalism as a system of church-government dictated that the clergy not be permitted to enforce unity and conformity in ecclesiastical matters. As David Hall has noted, while the clergy had formerly "prophesied against the standing order" in England, they became in New England advocates "for the reigning values, men whose principles became translated into practice."[67]

A striking example of the conformity of the clergy to the magistrates' decision concerned the quantity of ministers' lectures. When in 1634 civil authorities asked ministers to reduce the number of their lectures from four to two per week, the latter acquiesced. On the other hand, when ministers tried to interfere in political affairs, the magistrates did not hesitate to assert their authority. In 1631, the ministers of Watertown raised their objections to the magistrates' decision to tax each town in the colony for the fortification of Newton, later Cambridge. It was not long before the governor summoned the

216

ministers and others from Watertown to appear before the governor and council, where, "after much debate, they acknowledge[d] their fault, confessing freely, that they were in error, and made a retraction and submission under their hand, and were enjoined to read it in the assembly the next Lord's day."[68]

The transformation of the clergy's stand from non-conformism in old England to conformism to the civil authority in Massachusetts is attributable both to the premises of congregationalism and to the changing conditions in which the ministers operated. On the one hand, the Puritans who came to America had closely identified a particular structure of church government with their millennial expectations concerning the imminent Second Coming of Christ and the establishment of the Kingdom of God within time and history. To preserve each congregation independent from any ecclesiastical jurisdiction above it, as John Cotton noted in 1656, had been an essential issue in the fight between Christ and Antichrist.

> Leave every church Independent; not Independent from brotherly counsell; God forbid that we should refute that; but when it comes to power, that one Church shall have power over the rest, then look for a Beast [Rev. 13:2], which the Lord would have all his people to abhor.[69]

By such reasoning, the clergy in the colony delegated to the civil power the whole responsibility to maintain ecclesiastical unity and religious uniformity among each of the independent and particular congregations within the colony. On the other hand, looking at the clergy in the colony as "intellectuals," their activities in old English prior to emigration and their role in Massachusetts assume a different coloring from that connoted by Mark H. Curtis' depiction of them as "alienated intellectuals." On both sides of the ocean, the ministers' role had been, like that of all intellectuals as defined by Edward Shils,

> to locate the individual, his group, and the society in the universe; to interpret, explain, and attempt to control the occurrence of evil; to legitimate authority and define its responsibilities; to interpret the society's past experiences; to instruct the youth in the traditions and skills of the society; to facilitate and guide the aesthetic and religious experiences of

217

various sectors of the society; and to offer assistance in the control of nature.[70]

Once congregationalism was ascendant in the churches of Massachusetts, the clergy's role, given the political and ecclesiastical context in which the Puritans operated in the wilderness, became even more important. Thus, both clergy and magistrates defended the Massachusetts polity against any attempt of the English Crown to bring the congregations there into conformity with the Church of England, and both clergy and the magistrates worked hand in hand against any attempt to establish in the colony any different kind of church. The combined effort of clergy and magistracy to defend and sustain the congregational way led Robert Child, who tried to initiate a movement against the established order, to call the clergy "masters rather than ministers." Child was fully justified, because the clergy had not intended to separate church and state, but rather to renew the ancient meaning of theocracy in which church and state "may be close and compact, and coordinate one to another."[71]

The theocracy in Massachusetts had confused many in England because of its unique relationship between church and state. Even William Fiennes, Viscount Say and Sele, and Robert Greville, Baron Brooke, all long time friends of the Puritan emigration to America, found themselves puzzled by the holy experiment in the wilderness. In 1636, both Lord Say and Sele and Lord Brooke, along with other English nobles, considered emigration to Massachusetts, as did so many other Puritans during the 1630s. Being noblemen, however, they sent "Certain Proposals...as conditions of their removing to New England." In their answer, Massachusetts Puritans revealed that they could meet almost all of the legal and constitutional demands of the Puritan lords, with the notable exception of the issue of the relationship between church and state, an exception that finally determined that the lords abandoned their plain to join the Puritan holy commonwealth in America.[72]

What the Puritans lords had demanded was that they be permitted to continue in New England to exercise the privileges of their noble rank. Thus, their first "demand" before emigrating to New England was that "the common wealth should consist of two distinct ranks of men," the one "gentlemen of the country" and the other "freeholders." In their answer, the Bay Puritans declared that they "willingly acknowledge" the lords' proposal about "two distinct ranks." The second condition was that "the chief power of the common-wealth shall be placed" in the hands of the "gentlemen and freeholders," which the colonists acknowledged already characterized the situation in the colony. When, however, the lords demanded that they should be admitted as freemen without being church members, Bay Puritans would not assent. For this demand, obviously, could not be granted without destroying the very foundation of their theocracy. Thus they answered the lords that though they would "receive them with honor and allowe them pre-eminence and accommodations according to their condition, yet" they would "not, ordinarily, call them forth to the power of election, or administration of the magistracy, until they be received as members into some of our churches."[73]

A Christian commonwealth, as Winthrop had made clear in "A Model of Christian Charity," was based upon the law of grace as well as upon the law of nature. "There is likewise," Winthrop argued, "a double lawe by which we are regulated in our converscion one toward the another...the lawe of nature and the lawe of grace, or the morall lawe or the law of the gospel." The law of nature came to regulate civil society as such, while the law of the gospel, or that of grace, came to regulate Christian society. Thus when the lords demanded admission to freemenship in the colony according to their noble status, the Bay Puritans answered that "hereditary authority and power standeth only by the civil law" and not upon the law of grace, or the gospel. For "if God should not delight to furnish some" of the lords' heirs "with gifts fit for magistracy," the colonists argued, Massachusetts could not "call them forth" to assume the power of magistracy "when God doth not."[74]

Although they were valid in the realm of the civil law, hereditary privileges and the communion of saints were thus incompatible according to the law of grace. Consequently, when the lords demanded that "the rank of freeholders shall be made up of such, as shall have so much personal estate there as shall be thought fit for men of that condition" and thereby to limit the status of freemanship to property owners, the colonists replied that they had to "confess our ordinary practice to be otherwise." Not material property and hereditary privileges, but spiritual saving grace was the essential prerequisite for admission to freemanship in the Puritan theocracy according to custom in Massachusetts. "None are admitted freemen of this commonwealth," declared the Puritans in their response to the lords, "but such as are first admitted members of some church or other in this country," and only out of those were their "magistrates...Chosen." The ultimate justification for such a custom, continued the colonists, was "a divine ordinance (and moral) that none should be appointed and chosen by the people of God, magistrates over them, but men fearing

220

God...chosen out of their brethren...saints." For the "joy of a commonwealth" was "when the righteous are in authority, and the calamity thereof, when the wicked bear rule." The Puritans of course did not deny that there were "carnal men whom God hath invested with sundry eminent gifts of wisdom, courage, justice," so as to "fit [them] for government." But they argued that such qualities were by themselves insufficient for the assumption of civil power in a Christian commonwealth. For

> the best gift and parts, under a covenant of works (under which all carnal men and hypocrites be) will at length turn aside by crooked ways, to depart from God, and, finally, to fight against God, and are therefore, herein, opposed to good men and upright in heart.[75]

The most striking element in the Puritans' answer to Viscount Say and Sele and Baron Brooke is the assertion that the exclusion of the ungodly from political power was "a divine ordinance." Davenport in his Discourse never went so far as to call this premise of theocracy a divine ordinance. But we have already seen that Winthrop in his answer to Vane in 1637 argued that "now, the world, or civill state, must be raised out of the churches," so that the body politic was in fact congruent with the holy society of the church and the church covenant tightly interwoven with the civil covenant.[76] A Christian commonwealth, through such reasoning, took on the dimensions of the earthly domain in which the saints should exercise their holiness. Although complete identification of the church and civil covenants would occur only in the millennium, when the earthly kingdoms would become the Kingdom of God, Puritan New England would seek meanwhile to link the purity of the church with the holiness of the Christian commonwealth as two means of achieving the New Jerusalem. Only in the New Jerusalem would the church and the civil covenant be completely identified. In the meantime, however, in Puritan Massachusetts the pursuit of the spirituality of the church and the holiness of a Christian commonwealth would be closely linked as two ways to the end of achieving a heavenly city in time and history on earth. Only a theocratic political system could give saints exclusive political authority, to the exculsion of the ungodly from all political and ecclesiastical participation in the holy experiment in the wilderness.

Here again one can see the grounds on which the Puritans so strongly insisted that magistrates be godly; for, given the fact that the church's means were only spiritual, only the civil power could transform society into a godly and holy one. For the same reason, to reiterate, the Puritans confined membership in the political body only to godly people:

> Now, if it be a divine truth, that none are to be trusted with public permanent authority, but godly men, who are fit materials for church fellowship, then from the same grounds it will appear, that none are so fit to be trusted with the liberties of the commonwealth as church members. For, the liberties of the freemen of this commonwealth are such, as require men of faithful integrity to God and the state, to preserve the same.[77]

Neither wealth nor property nor heredity, but faith and godliness were thus the conditions of citizenship in the Puritan commonwealth in Massachusetts. Without doubt, this assertion sounded very strange indeed to Lord Say and Sele, Lord Brooke, and those other persons of "quality" who considered emigrating to New England in 1636. The Puritans clarified their position in their answer to the lords and warned that if they accorded magisterial power "to men not according to their godliness, which maketh them fit for church fellowship, but according to their wealth" they would themselves be "no better than worldly men." Such an alternative was unthinkable, since "in case worldly men should prove the major part" of the magistrates, the Bay Puritans warned, they soon might "turn the edge of all authority and laws against the church and the members thereof, the maintenance of whose peace is the chief end which God aimed at in the institution of Magistracy."[78] Thus the Massachusetts Puritans finally and definitely rejected the noble lords' proposals to join the holy experiment in the wilderness of America.

The colony's answer to the lords had affirmed, then, the practice in Massachusetts from its beginnings, in which, by the law of 1631, the General

Court had restricted the franchise to church members who became freemen. And it is significant that when the law of 1631 was revised in 1664, the change occurred only because of "the insistence of the English government" after the Restoration. The new statute of 1664 gave "the vote in provincial elections not only to church members...but to all other 'English men' at least twenty-four years of age, who presented a certificate from the minister of the town that they were orthodox." But even this new statute, as royal commissioners later condemned, was little more than a paper compliance with metropolitan demands. In practice, Michael Zuckerman has noted, "until 1692 the colonial suffrage extended only to freemen," though "by the time non-freemen had been voting in towns' affairs for almost half a century." Nevertheless, in early seventeenth-century Massachusetts, the essential question, as we have seen in the colony's response to the Puritan lords, had been who should "be trusted with public permanent authority" in a godly Christian commonwealth? For Bay Puritans, the goals of a holy Christian commonwealth could not possibly be achieved unless godly magistrates were appointed by godly people to direct society, state, and church towards God-given ends.[79]

VIII Theocracy, Monarchy, Aristocracy and Democracy

"Those who only consider Calvin as a theologian," wrote Jean-Jacques Rousseau in The Social Contract (1762), "do not understand the extent of his genius." For according to Rousseau, the drawing up of the "wise edicts" of Geneva "does him as much honor as his Institutes," and therefore he placed Calvin aside Lycurgus as a legislator, as a man who "constitutes the republic."[80] One of the essential features of Geneva under Calvin had been the relationship between the temporal and the spiritual power, or between church and state. Thus, according to Calvin,

> It is the purpose of temporal rule, as long as we live among men, to foster and support the external worship of God, to defend pure doctrine and the standing of the church, to conform our lives to human society, to mold our conduct to civil justice, to harmonize us with each other, and to preserve the common peace and tranquility.[81]

Secular institutions, then, according to Calvin, had more than worldly importance - they were among the "external" means of salvation. Massachusetts Puritans understood well the theological as well as the legislative "genius" of Calvin, and, although the Puritan commonwealth differed in many ways from Calvin's Geneva, both Protestant communities had sought a close association between church and state. Thus, excommunication in Geneva had deprived a citizen from holding public office, just as in Massachusetts, where freemanship had been conditioned by membership in a church.

The nature of the relationship between church and state in Massachusetts was further revealed in 1636 in John Cotton's letter on the subject to Lord Say and Sele. Apparently surprised by the colony's answer to his proposals, Lord Say and Sele wrote directly to Cotton. Although this letter no longer exists, Cotton's answer makes it clear that Lord Say and Sele had accused Massachusetts Puritans of having created a "theocracy" in its modern meaning, namely, in the sense of a state ruled by the church, much in the same way as would Tawney three centuries later. But Cotton flatly denied that in Massachusetts "all things [were]

224

under the determination of the church." The colony's magistrates, Cotton pointed out, were neither

> chosen to office in the church, nor doe governe by direction from the church, but by civill lawes, and those enacted in generall courts, and executed in courts of justice, by the governors and assistants.

Moreover, Cotton insisted, the church had no formal role in the civil realm other than to prepare "fitt instruments both to rule, and to choose rulers, which is no ambition in the church, nor dishonor to the commonwealth." Cotton did not, however, deny that the state was subject to religious influence. On the contrary, because "the word, and scripture of God do conteyne a short...platforme, not onely of theocracy but also of other sacred sciences," including "ethicks, economicks, politicks, Church-government, prophecy, academy," Cotton firmly believed that men should follow God's word in the state as well as the Church.[82]

What Cotton argued, in fact, was that God had actually prescribed the proper relationship between church and state:

> It is very suitable to Gods all-sufficient wisdome...not only to prescribe perfect rules for the right ordering of a private mans soule to ever-lasting blessedness with himself, but also for the right ordering of mans family, yea, of the commonwealth too so farre as both of them are subordinate to spiritual ends, and yet avoide both the church usurpation upon civill jurisidictions, in ordine ad spiritualia, and the commonwealth invasion upon ecclesiastical administrations, in ordine to civill peace, and conformity to the civill state.

Because all human experiment ought thus to be subordinate to spiritual ends, Cotton contended against Lord Say and Sele, the spiritual and temporal realms could hardly be completely separated. Moreover, a certain degree of overlapping (as opposed to usurping) of authority was inevitable: "Gods institutions (such as government of church and of commonwealth be)" should "be close and compact, and coordinate one to another, and yet not confounded." The subordination of the state to spiritual ends required that the body politic act to preserve the church and the true faith. To make sure that this requirement would be met, Cotton explained, was why the colony restricted freemanship only to church members: "When a commonwealth hath liberty to mould his own frame," he wrote, "I conceyve the scripture hath given full direction for the right ordering of the same, and that, in such sort as may best mainteyne the euexia [good] of the church."[83]

God's word, then, according to Cotton, gave full warrant to the constitution of the Puritan commonwealth in Massachusetts, and theocracy was the proper term of the colony's government, for "it is better than the commonwealth be fashioned to the setting forth of Gods house, which is His church, than to accommodate the church frame to the civill state."[84] In the sixteenth century, Calvin had left Zurich because Zwingli's reformation there had brought about a union between church and state, and he came to Geneva to constitute a Christian commonwealth without such a union. In New England, not only Massachusetts Puritans, but as was seen earlier, those of Connecticut and New Haven as well, had fashioned the state in such a way that it might preserve the church and to ensure that the commonwealth would be subordinated to spiritual ends, without attempting to unite church and state. Theocracy faciliated their purpose by providing an arrangement by which God, the true sovereign in both church and state, would reign over both.

It is worthwhile examining here the famous passage in Cotton's letter to Lord Say and Sele concerning democracy, monarchy, and aristocracy:

> Democracy, I do not conceyve that ever God did ordeyne as a fitt government eyther for church or commonwealth. If the people be governors, who shall be governed? As for monarchy, and aristocracy, they are both of them clearly approved, and directed in scripture, yet so as referreth the soveraigntie to himself, and setteth up Theocracy in both, as the best forme of government in the commonwealth, as well as in the church.

This passage is especially significant, not for Cotton's consideration of the relative merits of democracy, aristocracy, and monarchy, but rather for his treatment of the term "soveraigntie." Cotton's prime concern here is clearly the issue of whom to invest with sovereignty, or who should reign and rule over

226

church and commonwealth. He rejects democracy, not only because it had no warrant in scripture, but mainly for its failure to provide God with immediate and direct sovereignty over His saints within a theocratic universe. Likewise, despite their full warrant in scripture, Cotton rejects aristocracy and monarchy for not providing God with sovereignty over His people. Consequently, Cotton declares "theocracy," the system in which God is the immediate sovereign of both Church and state, to be the "best forme of government in the commonwealth, as well as in the church."[85]

State and church in Puritan Massachusetts were thus under the common headship of the Lord. Separation between church and state was unthinkable to the Puritans, for it implied to them that each had a unique destiny that differed from that of the other. At the same time, a people who insisted over and over that church and state were different instruments in the sweep of providential history could not accept the principle of a union of church and state as a proper foundation for a Christian commonwealth. To a large extent, Cotton's letter was an attempt to refute Lord Say and Sele's accusation that church and state were united in Massachusetts. The foundation of the holy experiment in the wilderness, then, was theocracy, which by its very ancient meaning invested the Lord with the headship of both church and state and thus subordinated both to spiritual, God-given ends. But being both "God's institutions," church and state in Puritan New England had to be "close and compact, and co-ordinate one to another."[86]

Massachusetts' insistence upon adhering to the law of 1631 "that none shall be chosen to magistracy among us but a Church member" was the main reason, "if not the only one," according to Cotton, why the colony declined the lords' proposals in 1636. To Lord Say and Sele's angry charge "that if such a rule were necessary, then the church estate and the best ordered commonwealth in the world were not compatible," Cotton responded that in Massachusetts, as was the case in the time of the early Christian churches, "the church submitteth itself to all the laws and ordinances of men, in what commonwealth soever they come to

227

dwell." The church in Massachusetts, Cotton continued, rather was compatible with the state, for

> these three things doe not undermine, but doe mutually and strongly mainteyne one another (even these three which wee principally aime at) authority in magistrates, liberty in people, purity in the church. Purity, preserved in the church, will preserve well ordered liberty in the people, and both of them establish well-balanced authority in the magistrates. God is the author of all these three, and neyther is himselfe the God of confusion, nor are his wayes the wayes of confusion, but of peace.[87]

The controversy between Massachusetts and Lord Say and Sele, Lord Brook and other Puritan noblemen in England, was not a theological one. Rather, it concerned the appropriate political and social premises for a Christian commonwealth. Although these lords shared with Bay colony Puritans the principles of congregationalism as a system of church-polity, and although many of them later played an important role in the English Civil War and contemporary ecclesiastical controversies in England, they and Massachusetts clashed sharply over the political and social implications of religious reformation and what the relationship between church and state should be in a Christian commonwealth. In church and state, then, what was formed in Massachusetts had been a new exercise in holiness, something very strange and radical to many contemporaries in England at that time.

IX   Magistrates as "Nursing Fathers and Mothers to the Church"

An important consequence of the theocracy in Massachusetts was the total
dependence of the colony's churches upon the civil authority. For by stressing
that each congregation held "the keys of the Kingdom of Heaven," the New
England way deprived the churches there of all means of exercising central
political power. According to Cotton, in The Keys of the Kingdom of Heaven,
those keys were

> neither sword nor scepter; nor sword, for they convey not
> civil power of bodily life and death; nor scepter, for they
> convey not sovereign or legislative power over the church, but
> stewardly and ministerial.

Consequently, the colony's clergy always stressed that the well-being of their holy
congregations depended upon the state: "We willingly acknowledge a power in
the civil magistrates, to establish and reform religion, according to the word of
God." As magistrates are "nursing fathers and mothers to the church," the
church was "subject to the power of the sword in matters which concern civil
peace."[88]

Civil peace, however, according to Cotton, included "the establishment of
pure religion, in doctrines, worship and government, according to the word of
God: As also the reformation of all corruptions in any of these." Again,
therefore, congregationalism limited the church's power to spiritual matters and
delegated the decisive role of maintaining religious unity and conformity to the
magistrates. "It is true," wrote Cotton, that

> the establishment of pure religion, and reformation of
> corruptions pertain also to the churches and synodical
> assemblies. But they go about it only with spiritual weapons,
> ministery of the word, and church censures upon such as are
> under church power. But the magistrates address themselves
> thereto, partly by commanding, and stirring up the churches
> and ministers thereof to go about it in their spiritual way:
> partly also by civil punishments upon the wilfull opposers,
> and distrubers of the same.[89]

It has been argued that Independent (Congregationalist) Divines in England during the Puritan Revolution, because of the circumstances of the Civil War, began to embrace different ideas from their brethren in America concerning the role of the magistrate in religious matters and that during the 1640s congregationalists on both sides of the ocean engaged in a bitter struggle over the issue of religious toleration. According to this argument, opposition to toleration became an essential part of "orthodoxy in Massachusetts," while English Independents became advocates of religious toleration.[90] However, when Philip Nye, one of the leaders of the Independent divines in English, defined the role of magistrates in ecclesiastical matters, his words showed that congregationalists on both sides of the ocean were much closer to each other than this argument suggests:

> Though we affirm that Church-Government is independent and immediately derived from Christ; yet we affirm also, that the Civil Magistrate is even therein (there is, in Ecclesiastical Matters) Supreme Governor civilly. And though nothing may be imposed on the Christian Churches against their will by any spiritual Authority...yet we affirm withall, that the Civil Magistrate may impose on them spiritual Matters, by Civil Power, yea whether they like or dislike, if it be good in his eyes, that is if he judge it within his Commission from God.[91]

The theological premises of congregationalism, therefore, yielded almost identical positions in both England and New England concerning the power of magistrates in religious affairs.

Dialectically, then, the doctrine of the spirituality of the church led to the direct involvement of the civil authority in church affairs, and by denying the church any temporal means, congregationalism brought the civil authority into ecclesiastical matters. Thus Cotton declared that "the church is not to refuse subjection to the civil magistrate, in the exercise of some spiritual administrations, which may advance and help forward the public good of civil state according to God." Among these "spiritual administrations," said Cotton, were lawful proclamations for fasts and calling synods. "If the magistrate call for a synod, the churches are to yield him ready subjection herein in the Lord." Finally, the church also had to yield to civil authority, according to Cotton, in the following instance: "wherein the church is not to refuse subjection to the civil magistrate, is in patient suffering their unjust persecutions without hostile or rebellious resistance." Such submission to the state even in the face of persecution was necessary because the church had "received the power of the keys, not of the sword, to the power of the keys they may and ought to administer, but not of the sword."[92]

Do Cotton's words justify the interpretation that church and state became identical? Not at all. They indicate, rather the voluntary withdrawal of the church from civil and political affairs in order to achieve the highest purity and spirituality of the church. A comparison of the churches in the colony with the Church of England during that time shows clearly that the congregationalists in the Bay colony tried to create a totally different relationship between church and state. In his Economic Problems of the Church, Christopher Hill thus describes the involvement of the church with civil affairs in England before the Puritan Revolution:

> It would have to consider the church as political, judicial, and educational organisation. Bishops formed a solid government phalanx in the House of Lords. They had nearly a majority of the vote there under Elizabeth, never less than a quarter under James. They were civil servants and administrators, and under Laud they came to hold key posts in the government.[93]

In New England, on the other hand, the church, modeled on the ancient Christian churches which lacked political means and power, was stripped of all involvement in political affairs and was totally under the power of the civil authority. Moreover, like the ancient Christian churches, the congregational churches in the Bay colony did not develop any ecclesiastical order. The Puritans in Massachusetts, therefore, thought that the "weakness" caused by a lack of an hierarchical ecclesiastical order should be corrected by the magistrates' use of coercive means.

231

The power over church affairs and religious matters Massachusetts Puritans invested in the magistrates had been an essential feature of the Puritan theocracy. The ultimate aim was indeed to create a theocracy as it appeared in the Bible, one in which godly secular authority rather than priests maintained religious society. Magistracy, then, acquired a divine commission, to rule religious Christian society according to God's word. Such a divine commission made the godly ruler a "part of the history of salvation" by giving him the duty to keep "the members of the community within providential history."[94] That was why in the early years of the colony, both the clergy and magistrates appeared so well-acquainted with each other's roles. From the point of view of the ministers, said Rev. Ezekiel Rogers, "godly wisdom should teach us both not to intermeddle where we have no call, and to know what respect belongs to Christian Magistrates."[95]

On the other hand, when members of the Boston church in 1637 tried to call Winthrop to account for his role in banishing Antinomians from the colony, Winthrop informed them that "a church has not power to call any Civil Magistrate, to give Account of his Judicial proceeding in any Court of Civil Justice." There is a distinction, Winthrop argued, between the power of the church and that of the civil government. For Christ,

> as he is King of Kings and Lord of Lords he has set up another kingdom in this world, wherein magistrates are his officers, and they are to be accountable to him, for their miscarriage in the way and order of this kingdom.

But, if magistrates and clergy did not maintain this proper distinction, and if the church usurped civil authority and vice versa, Winthrop warned that the result would be

> Christs kingdom divided, one Ordinance against another, not to moderation but to destruction: and here is no means to reconcile them: but if the rule of Christ be observed, Resist not evil, and submitt yourself to the higher power.

Moreover, any encroachment of the church as a holy spiritual fellowship upon the civil realm, Winthrop reminded members of the Boston church, would make that church little less than "the supreame Court" in the colony "and so in trueth meerly Antichrist, beinge exalted above all, that is called God," or the magistrates.[96]

John Hull of Boston, a goldsmith, clearly revealed how contemporaries in the colony understood the nature of their theocracy. Writing in his diary Hull explained that

> the civil government framed so as none might bear any weightly office, civil or military, but such as were members of some particular church, gathered and in order, neither might any elect unto such choice employment but members of churches, who had also sworn fealty to the Commonwealth.

By making sure that only godly people have political power in the Puritan colony, "the churches and civil state" in the Massachusetts Bay colony, Hull claimed, were always "thus mutually embracing and succoring each other."[97]

So far as the ministers were concerned during the early years of the colony, the clergy strictly followed Winthrop's demand: "submitt yourself to the higher power." They had no intention to establish a theocracy in its modern meaning, that is, as a form of government in which ministers would assume and exercise political power. On the contrary, they knew and accepted that in a holy Christian commonwealth the church must submit to "the higher power": "Let every soul be subject unto the higher powers. For there is no power but of God: the powers that be are ordained of God." Rulers were "not a terror to good work, but to the evil" (Rom. 13:1, 3). This was the colony's policy in relation to the godly magistrate, one who had commission to rule a godly society according to God's word. For this reason, ministers and the people as a whole acknowledged the magistrate's decisive power concerning civil and religious matters. In this context, indeed, the fulfillment of the premises of religious reformation were indispensably associated with the right constitution of a godly commonwealth, not less than with the establishment of the true church.

"Know this is the place," wrote Edward Johnson in praise of New England, "where the Lord will create a new Heaven and a new Earth in, New Churches, and a new Common-wealth together." He reminded new Puritan emigrants upon their arrival in Massachusetts that "purity in Religion" should be "preferred above all dignity in the world." Therefore, "at your landing" in the colony, he advised,

> see you observe the Rule of the Word...[and] search out the mind of God both in planting and continuing Church and civill government, but be sure they be distinct yet agreeing and helping one to the other.

Concerning the magistrates, Johnson wrote, "make choyce of such as are sound both in Profession and Confession," for the magistrates' "commission is not onely limitted with the commands of the second Table," the last six Commandments which deal with the duties to one's fellow men, "but they are to looke to the Rules of the first also," namely, the first four Commandments which deal with duties to God. It was the magistrates' duty, he explained, to maintain purity in the churches and holiness in the Christian commonwealth, while it was the duty of the godly, "once safely set on the shore of America," to set and constitute such a "civill government" as would insure that godly magistrates would be "the Eyes of Restraint set up for Walles and Bulworks, to surround the Sion of God." Such an arrangement was necessary, according to Johnson, because only by selecting the godly ruler in such a way could

> the people of and under your Government...live a quiet and peaceable life in all godlinessse and honesty, and to the end that you may provoke Kings, Princes, and all that are in authority to cast down their Crones at the Feet of Christ, and to take them up againe at his command to serve under his Standard as nursing Fathers and Mothers to the Churches and people of Christ.[98]

At this moment it is necessary to examine the momentous political consequences of the ideological premises laid down by the Puritan theocracy in America.   Those who advocated theocratic government which explicitly acknowledge Christ as sole ruler over them, were presenting the revolutionary view that no one, neither bishop nor king, could stand between God and His people. Furthermore, with the political realm considered the exclusive domain of the saints by virtue of their covenanted relationship with God both in Church and state, theocratic government entailed a denial that any rights based on the privilege of property, heredity and wealth could determine eligibility to participate in the political life.

The revolutionary character of theocracy is best seen in the barring of unbelievers from any participation in the system of civil government. Since the covenant, the foundation of both Church and state, belonged strictly to the godly, religious obligations were transformed into political obligations in the Christian commonwealth in New England, and the exclusiveness of the holy fellowship of the church led directly to the exclusiveness of the political system.

As long as England had bishops and kings, the establishment of a theocracy similar to that of New England remained an impossibility. But conditions changed radically in England during the 1640s: the office of bishops was totally abolished and King Charles I was beheaded. When confronted with this new reality, English Puritans also began to consider the idea of erecting a godly civil government in England based on the premises of theocracy. In 1649, for example, shortly after the king's execution, "Certain Queries" were presented to Thomas Lord Fairfax, Lord General of the Army, and to the General Council of War, "by many Christian people" from the county of Norfolk and the city of Norwich who wondered if indeed the time had come to establish a theocratic government in England. These people asked the leaders of the Army to ponder the question of "the present interest of the Saints and people of God." If indeed "the time (or near upon it) of putting down that worldly government, and erecting this new kingdom" of God on earth had arrived, as the authors of "Certain Queries" believed, the saints would have to assume their important role in the providential drama. Millennial expectations thus led to the demand for social and political action. According to this particular group, the saints' duty was to begin "to associate" themselves "together into several church-societies" in accordance with "the congregational way." The convening of all these gathered churches in "general assemblies, or church-parliaments, choosing and delegating such officers of Christ, and representatives of the churches, as may rule nations and kingdoms", would in turn result in God giving them "authority and rule over the nations and kingdoms of the world" and "the kingdoms of the world" becoming "the churches." Fearing that their aims would be thwarted by the election of the ungodly to positions of authority, this group questioned the "right or claim mere natural and worldly men have to rule and government" in a holy Christian commonwealth and advocated a form of government strikingly similar to the theocracy which had already been founded by the Puritans in the wilderness.[99]

Even before the king's death, millennial expectations and apocalyptical visions had led Puritans in England to propose barring the ungodly from political life and to argue for the exclusive right of the saints to rule in a Christian commonwealth. Thomas Collier, for example, in his sermon, A Discovery of the New Creation (1647), contended that "as formerly God hath many times set up wicked men to rule and govern," so now "he will give it into the hands of the Saints." Using similar arguments during the Whitehall debates in 1649, Colonel Thomas Harrison expressed the belief that the day had come, "God's own day," in which "the powers of this world shall be given into the hands of the Lord and his saints." Harrison tried to calm his opponents who believed that "our business is...only to get power into our own hands, that we may reign over them," with the claim that putting the reins of government into the hands of the saints was not usurpation, but rather the necessary consequences of God's "coming forth in glory in the world."[100]

236

Only after the king was executed, however, did the Puritans in England seriously undertake putting into action the theocratic ideas. This was especially true of the Fifth Monarchists, who sought to clear the way for the approaching millennium by political measures. Thus the author of A Cry for the Right Improvement of all our Mercies (1651) "called for the restriction of membership of Parliament to those who were 'in church fellowship with some one or other congregation.'" In the same year, the author of another tract, A Model of a New Representative, argued that "borough M.P.s should be replaced by 'two or more members' of the Congregational churches in their respective towns and that county M.P.s should be elected by the gathered churches of their shire."[101]

Nor was the conviction that theocratic government should be established in England limited to radicals such as the Fifth Monarchists. Many Puritans shared their beliefs and their desire for action. "A hundred and fifty-three members of Morgan Llwyd's Independent church at Wrexham," for example "urged" that "the new representative should be elected by the gathered churches."[102] Those who strove, then, to establish theocratic government in England, like the Puritans in America, assumed the ultimate association between the church covenant and the civil covenant, and therefore claimed the political realm as the exclusive domain of the saints.

Puritan theocratic impulses reached their peak in England during Barebone's Parliament in 1653. Never before had England been so close to the ideal of theocratic government as with this parliament with its revolutionary social and religious reforms. Many of its nominees had been elected upon the recommendations of the gathered churches, and the combination within it of Fifth Monarchists, radical Independents and Baptists, clearly revealed how serious the saints were in their intentions to play their role in providential history. As Woolrych writes, many members of Barebone's Parliament "were not looking for a mere caretaker government to educate the people in the benefits and responsibility of a self-governing republic. They wanted a sanhedrin of the saints, a dictatorship of the godly that would prepare for the millennium by

237

overturning every vestige of the old 'carnal' government." The radical goals of these saints were probably no better understood than by the anonymous author of A True State of the Case of the Commonwealth (1654); he warned that in "this last Assembly" (Barebone's Parliament), "there was a party of men...who assumed to themselves only the name of Saints, from which Title they excluded all others," and by "pretense to an extraordinary Call from Christ himself" did "take upon them to rule the Nation by virtue of a supposed Right of Saintship in themselves." Their "dangerous attempts," he continued, "extended not only to the abolition of Law, but to the utter subversion of civil Right and Property." Finally, this commentator on the radicals of the Barebone Parliament admonished against the dangers which would ensue should their policy succeed: "it would have utterly confounded the whole course of Natural and Civil Right, which is the only Basis of foundation of Government in this world."[103]

Gradually but inevitably, in their attempts to constitute all dimensions of human life on the basis of a covenant relationship with God, the Puritans reached the conclusion that only one's covenant relationship as manifested in one's membership in the church could provide one with political rights. Those who emigrated to New England in the 1620s and 1630s made this premise the basis of their theocracy in the wilderness. When political conditions were ripe in England during the 1640s and 1650s, when English Puritans could seize the opportunity to create a theocratic system of government, they embarked on the very same policy.

The notion of a common ground shared by English and American Puritans concerning theocracy is supported by the case of Richard Baxter. A moderate Puritan, the Presbyterian Baxter clearly did not belong to the lunatic fringe of Puritanism; yet it was he who proposed the establishment of theocracy in England with arguments strikingly similar to those of the Puritans in America. In his book A Holy Commonwealth, or Political Aphorisms Opening the True Principles of Government (1659), Baxter demonstrates "how a Commonwealth may be reduced to this theocratical temper" by instituting the rule, among others, that "no

238

persons...none as Cives (or free subjects, commonly called burgesses or enfranchised persons)" but only "those who have publicly owned the Baptismal Covenant, personally, deliberately and seriously" should have the right to vote in a holy Christian commonwealth. He continues by emphasizing the need to exclude "ordinary despisers of God's public worship, or neglecters of it, and of the guidance of God's ministers", from the body of electors. Above all, Baxter reiterates the principle that the foundation of theocratic government demands that the proper relationship between church and social covenants be maintained:

> But that which I mean is, that the same qualification [that] maketh a man capable of being a member both of a Christian Church and Commonwealth...is his Covenant with God in Christ, or his Membership of the Universal Church.[104]

Clearly, then, Puritans of widely differing persuasions were equally concerned with establishing theocracy, and they all agreed that, to reach their goal, a revolutionary approach to defining the political body was absolutely essential. It was partly in response to this extreme Puritan design to reshape the political system that Thomas Hobbes wrote his refutation in the Leviathan (1651).[105]

Hobbes began by attacking what he perceived as pretentiousness in the Puritan claim to hold sole spiritual authority to exercise and impose the will of God:

> For if every man, should be obliged, to take for God's law, what particular men, on pretence of private inspiration, or revelation, should obtrude upon him, in such a number of men, that out of pride and ignorance, take their own dreams, and extravagant fancies, and madness, for testimonies of God's spirit; or out of ambition, pretend to such divine testimonies, falsely, and contrary to their own consciences, it were impossible that any divine law should be acknowledged.

Hobbes goes on to deny "that the present church now militant, is the kingdom of God," and therefore that "the Church and commonwealth are the same persons." Such identification of the Kingdom of God with the church, argued Hobbes, is unwarranted because "by the kingdom of God, is properly meant a

239

commonwealth, instituted by the consent of those which were to be subject thereto, for their civil government." Contrary to Puritan belief that this was the time in which the kingdoms of the Earth would become the Kingdom of God, Hobbes asserted that "the kingdom of God is a civil kingdom," and as such should be ruled only by "civil sovereigns" and not by the church or its saints. Comparing advocates of Puritan theocracy to the "Roman clergy," Hobbes denounces them as "a confederacy of deceivers" who seek power on the basis of "dark and erroneous doctrines."[106]

While Puritans on both sides of the Atlantic strove equally to achieve theocratic government, the Puritan experience on each side differed significantly. In New England, Puritans could, and did in fact, try to fully implement the premises immediately upon their arrival. In England, on the other hand, Puritans were given a similar opportunity only during the 1640s and 1650s, and even then faced such strong opposition that their holy scheme was never implemented. Only in light of the experience in England can one sufficiently appreciate the achievement of the New England Puritans in creating a theocracy in the wilderness.[107]

XI   Theocracy and the Millennium

Theocracy, "or to make the Lord God our Governour," was, then, the ultimate aim of the Puritan migration and an essential component of the Puritan errand into the wilderness in America. This goal was moreover reinforced by its close association with the Puritans' eschatological visions and millennial expectations concerning the Kingdom of God on earth. Given the fact that God's Kingdom would rise in time and history according to Puritan belief, the erecting of the true church along with the establishment of theocracy in New England, accorded the American Puritans a special role in providential history. For "these poore New England People" were, as a result of their situation, "the forerunners of Christs Army." The time of the millennium was at hand, a time in which "Christ the great King of all the Earth is now going forth in his great Wrath and terrible Indignation to avenge the bloud of his Saints," a time "for the great and bloudy Battell of Gog and Magog." In this "dreadfull day, when the patience and long-suffering of Christ, that hath lasted so many hundreds of years, shall end," Puritan New England had a special role. The hand of Providence sent the Puritans to Massachusetts to be "the forerunners of Christs Army," to "Preach in this wilderness, and to proclaime to all Nations, the neere approach of the most wonderful workes that ever the Sonnes of men saw." Situated in the middle of the apocalyptic drama that would mark the end of time and history, New England not only engaged in battle with Antichrist, it also became God's herald in announcing the Second Coming of Christ to the whole world. The colony's singular place in sacred, providential history then was the necessary result of its success in fulfilling the prophecies of Revelation. In establishing theocracy in New England the Puritans made God the immediate and direct ruler of the Puritan commonwealth and so set an example in their providential mission of the upcoming of the millennium and the advent of the Kingdom of God on earth.[108]

Before the Puritan emigration, wrote Michael Wigglesworth in his God's Controversy with New England, 1662, America had been

A country where no English foot
In former ages past:
A waste and howling wilderness
Where none inhabited
But hellish fiends, and brutish men
That Devils worshipped.

But then, when

The time drew nigh wherein
The glorious Lord of hosts
Was pleasd to lead his armies forth
Into those forrein coastes
At whose approach the darkness sad
Soon vanished away
And all the shaddows of the night
Were turnd to lightsome day.

Thus, New England had became a special place in divine history:

Here was the hiding place, which thou
Jehova, didst provide
For thy redeemed ones, and where
Thou didst thy jewels hide.[109]

Well aware of Massachusetts's place and presence in history, Ann Bradstreet had admonished England, in A Dialogue Between Old England and New in 1642, to "bring forth the beast that rule the world with his beck, and tear his flesh, and set your feet on his neck." And when England did "to Gog as thou hast done to Rome," then

No Canaanite shall then be found in the land
And holiness on horses' bells shall stand.[110]

And John Cotton proclaimed time and again that "now is the time when the Church is militant," and the "time hast'neth fast when it shall be Tryumphant." In the context of this belief that the millennium and the apocalyptic events entailed with the rise of the Kingdom of God were at hand, one can see the meaning and nature of theocracy in Massachusetts.[111]

The aim of the Puritan migration, wrote the author of Good News from New England (1649), was

242

to set up government, not only for the orderly execution of judgment and justice among themselves, but also for the suppressing of all malignant adversaries of the kingdome of Christ, that at any time should invade or disturb this government.

Therefore, he continued, in Massachusetts "both Magistrates and Ministers joyne heart at hand herein, yet the latter meddle not with Civill Justice."[112] It was left then to civil authorities to deal with all the enemies of the Kingdom of God on earth, and thus in fact one of the primary duties of magistrates was to fulfill the will of God within the political body. In that way magistracy became an essential instrument in providential history which would finally bring God's rule over a redeemed world. Massachusetts had been the first, with its theocracy, to acknowledge God's rule over its church and commonwealth. Therefore there the magistrates,

> Who, Ruling in the fear of God
> The righteous cause maintained,
> And all injurious violence,
> And wickedness, restrained.

At the same time, because church and state in the colony both aimed "to praise...that King of Kings," it was in Massachusetts that "Gods throne was here set," and "This was the place, and these the folk/In whom he took delight."[113]

When the magistrates came to believe that their primary duty and obligation was to maintain and fulfill the will of those who selected them rather than to fulfill God's will, the unity between religion and politics began to decline. But in the early years of the colony, as Winthrop assured Hooker, "the magistrates are members of the churches here, and by their covenant are regulated to direct all their ways to the rule of the gospel."[114] The clergy, in turn, acknowledged and praised the "godly rule" of the magistrates:

> We cannot but with thankfulness acknowledge the goodness
> of God in our gracious magistrates, and their assistance to us
> in the work of the Lord.... Though they sometimes consult
> with us in matters of conscience; yet they take our counsel no
> further than they see it clear from the word.[115]

By God's commission and by God's word the godly magistrate ruled in the theocracy of Massachusetts.

However, with the rise of Puritanism in England during the 1640s, it became clear on both sides of the ocean that the ecclesiastical model of the colony, Congregationalism, was not acceptable to the majority of Puritans in England. Similarly, many Puritans in England rejected many other features of the Puritan theocracy in Massachusetts, a fact that to a large extent determined Massachusetts' relationship with England during the Puritan Revolution and to which we will turn in the next two chapters.

No autocratic ruler in England caused the Puritan emigration to America. Rather, the call of the wilderness had motivated them in part because the wilderness itself, to use Erik H. Erikson's words, was "an autocratic tempter," a place in which they could hope to realize the full premises of the reformation in church and state, with Congregationalism and with theocracy.[116] To submit to the autocratic rule of God was a prime motive of the Puritan migration. The essential function of theocracy was indeed to constitute the autocratic or unlimited authority of God over the godly people by investing God with the sole authority in the colony. It was, of course, a divine autocracy. But in terms of the Puritans' millennial expectations, heaven and earth would intermingle at one moment in time so that the Lord of heaven would come to rule on earth. Edward Johnson thus captured the essence of the Puritan holy experiment in the wilderness:

> I am now prest for the service of our Lord to re-build the most glorious Edifice of Mount Sion in a Wildernesse...for behold hee is comming againe, he is comming to destroy Antichrist, and give the whore double to drinke the very dregs of his wrath. Then my deare friend unfold thy hands, for thou and I have much worke to doe, I[ay] and all Christian Souldiers the World throughout.[117]

244

Notes

1. Edward Johnson, Wonder-Working Providence, p. 146.

2. John Davenport, A Discourse about Civil Government in a New Plantation whose Design is Religion (Cambridge, 1663), p. 34.

3. John Cotton, "Copy of a Letter from Mr. Cotton to Lord Say and Seal in the Year 1636," in History, by Hutchinson, I, p. 415.

4. John Winthrop, "A Reply to an Answer Made to a Declaration of the Intent and Equity of the Order..." (1637), in Collection, comp. Hutchinson, I, p. 101.

5. Michael Wigglesworth, God's Controversy with New-England (1662), in Seventeenth-Century American Poetry, ed. Harrison T. Meserole (New York, 1968), pp. 44-45.

6. Thomas Hooker, A Survey of the Summe of Church-Discipline (London, 1648), the preface.

7. John Higginson, "Part of John Higginson's letter, of Guilford, dated 25 of the 8th Month, 1654, to his Brother the Rev'd Thomas Thatcher of Weymouth," in Connecticut Historical Society, Collections, III (1895), p. 319.

8. "General Observations for the Plantation of New England" (1629), in Winthrop Papers, II, p. 114.

9. Johnson, Wonder-Working Providence, p. 146.

10. Among the many works dealing with the political nature and foundation of the Puritan commonwealth in New England and the special relationship between church and state there, see: Paul E. Lauer, Church and State in New England (Baltimore, 1892); Aaron B. Seidman, "Church and Society in the Early Years of the Massachusetts Bay Colony," New England Quarterly, Vol. XVIII, 1945; Perry Miller, "Puritan State and Puritan Society," in Errand into the Wilderness (Cambridge, 1976) and "The Theory of State and Society," in The Puritans, Perry Miller and Thomas M. Johnson (eds.) (New York, 1963); Edmund S. Morgan (ed.), Puritan Political Ideas (Indianapolis, 1965); T.H. Breen, The Character of the Good Ruler: A Study of Puritan Political Ideas in New England 1630-1730, (New Haven, 1970); T.J. Wertenbaker, The Puritan Oligarchy: Authority in Early Massachusetts (New York, 1960); Paul R. Lucas, Valley of Discord: Church and Society Along the Connecticut River (Hanover, 1976); Mary Jeanne Anderson Jones, Congregational Commonwealth, Connecticut 1636-1662 (Middletown, 1968); Isabel M. Calder, The New Haven Colony (New Haven, 1934). George L. Mosse put American Puritan political ideas in the context of English Puritanism in a series of studies: The Holy Pretence: A Study

245

in Christianity and Reason of State from William Perkins to John Winthrop (Oxford, 1957); "Puritan Political Thought and the 'Case of Conscience'", Church History, Vol. XXIII (June, 1954); and "Puritanism and Reason of State and Old and New England," William and Mary Quarterly, Vol IX (June 1966). For the Protestants' general view of Church and state, see the important article by Winthrop S. Hudson, "Protestant Concept of Church and State," Church History, Vol. XXXV (June, 1966).

11. Edmund S. Morgan, Visible Saints: The History of a Puritan Idea (Ithaca, 1975), p. 113.

12. John Davenport, in Collection, comp. Hutchinson, I. p. 184.

13. John Norton, Abel Being Dead Yet Speaketh, or, the Life & Death of the Most deservedly Famous Man of God, Mr. John Cotton, Late Teacher of the Church of Christ, at Boston in New England (London, 1658), pp. 35-41.

14. John Cotton, "Copy of a Letter from Mr. Cotton to Lord Say and Seal in the Year 1636," in Thomas Hutchinson, The History of the Colony and Province of Massachusetts Bay, I, p. 415.

15. John Davenport, A Discourse about Civil Government, p. 14.

16. R.H. Tawney, Religion and the Rise of Capitalism: A Historical Study (New York, 1954), pp. 111-112.

17. Bruce E. Steiner, "Dissension at Quinnipiac: The Authorship and Setting of a Discourse about Civil Government in a Plantation Whose Design is Religion," WMQ, XXXVIII (1981), pp. 14-32; Larzer Ziff, The Career of John Cotton, p. 97, p. 35.

18. Charles J. Hoadly, ed., Records of the Colony and Plantation of New Haven, from 1638 to 1649 (Hartford, 1857), pp. 11-12 (hereafter cited as New Haven Records); Steiner, "Dissension at Quinnipiac," p. 126.

19. Davenport, A Discourse about Civil Government, pp. 3-5.

20. Ibid., pp. 6-8

21. Ibid., pp. 6-8.

22. Ibid., pp. 9-11, 14.

23. Ibid., pp. 19-20.

24. Ibid., pp. 14-15.

25. Ibid., pp. 15-16, 19-20.

26. Ibid., pp. 20-23.

27. MA. Records, I, p. 87; Paul R. Lucas, Valley of Discord: Church and Society along the Connecticut River, 1636-1725 (Hanover, 1976), p. 33; Frank Shuffleton, Thomas Hooker, 1586-1647, p. 231.

28. Mary Jeanne Anderson Jones, Congregational Commonwealth, Connecticut, 1636-1662, p. 77.

29. J. Hammond Trumbull and Charles J. Hoadly, eds., The Public Records of the Colony of Connecticut, 10 vols (Hartford, 1850-1890), I, p. 21.

30. Mary J.A. Jones, Congregational Commonwealth, p. 70.

31. Steiner, "Dissension at Quinnipiac," p. 32; New Haven Records, pp. 14, 17, 21.

32. Williston Walker, ed., The Creeds and Platforms of Congregationalism (Boston, 1960), p. 14.

33. Thomas Hooker, A Survey of the Summe of Church Discipline Wherein the Way of the Churches of New England is Warranted Out of the Word (London, 1648), "Preface," xvii-xix. These principles and others which appeared in Hooker's "Preface" in his book above had been written earlier in 1645. See: Walker, "Hooker's Summary of Congregational Principles, 1645," The Creeds and Platforms of Congregationalism, pp. 132-148.

34. John Cotton, The Keys of the Kingdom of Heaven (London, 1644), in John Cotton on the Churches of New England, ed. Larzer Ziff, p. 124.

35. Cotton, The Keys of the Kingdom of Heaven, p. 128.

36. Thomas Lechford, Plain Dealing or News from New England (London, 1642), in Lechford's Plain Dealing, ed. J. Hammond Trumbull (Boston, 1867), p. 16.

37. Johnson, Wonder-Working Providence, pp. 214, 215; Lechford, Plain Dealing, p. 14.

38. Johnson, Wonder-Working Providence, p. 217; Winthrop, History, I, pp. 103-110.

39. Thomas Welde, An Answer to W.R., His Narration of the Opinions and Practices of the Churches Lately Erected in New England; Vindicating those Godly and Orthodoxal Churches (London, 1644), pp. 34-35.

40. Winthrop, History, I, p. 346.

41. "The Body of Liberties," in Massachusetts Historical Society, Collections, 3rd Series, VIII, p. 226 (Hereafter cited as MHSC); An Abstract of the Lawes of New England as They are Now Established (London, 1641), MHSC, 1st Series, V, pp. 173-187, 173, 182, 174.

42. Many works deal with the Antinomians in Massachusetts and a partial list can be found in J.F. Maclear, "Anne Hutchinson and the Mortalist Heresy," NEQ 54 (1981), pp. 74-103. See also: Ronald D. Cohen, "Church and State in Seventeenth Century Massachusetts: Another Look at the Antinomian Controversy," Journal of Church and State, XII (Autumn, 1970), and Amy S. Lang, "Antinomianism and the 'Americanization' of Doctrine," NEQ (June, 1981). Antinomianism played a significant role in the sweep of Puritan history in England. See, for example, Gertrude Huehns in Antinomianism in English History (London, 1951) and Christopher Hill in The World Turned Upside Down, Radical Ideas during the English Revolution (London, 1972).

43. Hutchinson, History, I, p. 60.

44. Thomas Hooker, A Survey of the Summe of Church-Discipline, "Preface,"xvii-xix.

45. Richard Mather, Church-Government and Church-Covenant Discussed, In an Answer of the Elders of the Severall Churches in New-England to Two and Thirty Questions, Sent over to Them by Divers Ministers in England (London, 1643), p. 43. "The Body of Liberties," pp. 235-236, made it clear that "no thing be concluded and imposed by way of" ecclesiastical "Authority from one of more churches upon an other, but onely by way of Brotherly conference and consultations." On the practice of clerical consociation in the Bay colony, see the important article of Robert F. Scholz, "Clerical Consociation in Massachusetts Bay: Reassessing the New England Way and its Origins," WMQ, 3rd Series, XXIX (1972), p. 3.

46. Hutchinson, History, I, p. 61.

47. R.A. Knox, Enthusiasm (Oxford, 1962), p. 583, 19, 110; "John Wheelwright, a Fast-Day Sermon" (1937), in The Antinomian Controversy, 1636-1638, ed. Hall, pp. 169, 161, 162, 164, 163 165; Thomas Welde's "Preface" to John Winthrop, A Short Story of the Rise, Reign, and Ruine of the Antinomians, Familists & Libertines (London, 1644), in The Antinomian Controversy, ed. David Hall, pp. 203, 207, 204, 203, 202. Recently Stephen Foster put the antinomian controversy in Massachusetts, as well as other heresies, within the context of Puritanism in old and New England. See: S. Foster, "New England and the Challenge of Heresy, 1630-1660: The Puritan Crisis in Trans-atlantic Perspective," WMQ 38 (1981), pp. 624-60.

48. Winthrop S. Hudson, "Protestant Concept of Church and State," Church History 35 (1966), p. 229; Hall, The Faithful Shepherd, pp. 122-123; Aaron B. Seidman, "Church and State in the Early Years of the Massachusetts Bay Colony," NEQ, 18 (1945), p. 233.

49. Miller and Johnson, eds., The Puritans, I, p. 189.

50. C.H. George and K. George, The Protestant Mind of the English Reformation (Princeton, 1961), pp. 174-210.

51. "The Grand Remonstrance, with the Petition Accompanied it," in The Constitutional Documents of the Puritan Revolution, 1625-1660, ed. Samuel R. Gardiner (Oxford, 1906), p. 229 (Herafter cited as Gardiner, Const. Documents).

52. MA. Records, I, p. 196.

53. John Winthrop, "A Defence of an Order of Court Made in the Year 1637," in Collections, comp. Hutchinson, I, pp. 79, 81.

54. Henry Vane, "A Brief Answer to a Certain Declaration..." (1637), in Collections, comp. Hutchinson, I, pp. 81, 85, 95, 88, 96. Henry Vane's life and role in Puritan Massachusetts and England are best described in J.H. Adamson and H.F. Holland, Sir Henry Vane: His Life and Times (1613-1662) (Boston, 1973). For Vane's political ideas see Margaret Judson, The Political Thought of Sir Henry Vane the Younger, (Philadelphia, 1969).

55.   John Winthrop, "A Reply to an Answer Made to a Declaration..." (1637), in Collections, comp. Hutchinson, I, pp. 111-112, 100-101.

56.   Ibid., pp. 100-101, 111-112.

57.   Ibid., pp. 111, 113, 79, 113.

58.   Ibid., pp. 79, 113.

59.   "A Model of Church and civil Power, Composed by Mr. Cotton and the Ministers of New England," in The Bloudy Tenent, of Persecution, for Cause of Conscience, by Roger Williams (1644), in The Complete Writings of Roger Williams, ed. Samuel L. Caldwell, III, pp. 118, 222, 232-233, 247. There are several studies on Roger Williams: Perry Miller, Roger Williams: His Contribution to the American Tradition (Indianapolis, 1953); Edmund S. Morgan, Roger Williams: The Church and the State (New York, 1967); Ola E. Winslow, Master Roger Williams (New York 1957); Samuel H. Brockunier, The Irrepressible Democrat: Roger Williams (New York, 1940). Two excellent studies deal with Williams' millennial views: W. Clark Gilpin, The Millenarian Piety of Roger Williams (Chicago, 1979); and Jesper Rosenmeier, "The Teacher and the Witness: John Cotton and Roger Williams," WMQ, XXV (1968).

60.   "A Model of Church and Civil Power," pp. 232-233, 247.

61.   Roger Williams, The Bloudy Tenent, pp. 118, 234, 243, 228.

62.   John Cotton, The Powring Out of the Seven Vials (London, 1642), p. 19.

63.   Rosenmeier, "The Teachers and the Witness: John Cotton and Roger Williams," p. 431.

64.   Walker, The Creeds and Platforms of Congregaionalism, p. 185.

65.   "The Cambridge Synod and Platform, 1646-1648," in The Creeds and Platforms of Congregationalism, ed. Williston Walker, pp. 236-237.

66.   Winthrop, History, I, p. 70.

67.   Hall, The Faithful Shepherd, p. 121.

68.   Winthrop, History, I, pp. 172, 84. In 1636 the court had ordered "that no church, etc., should be allowed, etc., that was gathered without consent of the churches and the magistrates." See, Winthrop, History, I, p. 220.

69.   John Cotton, An Exposition upon the Thirteenth Chapter of Revelation (London, 1656), pp. 30-31. Cotton's book consists of a series of sermons Cotton preached in new Boston in 1639-1640, according to Larzer Ziff, The Career of John Cotton, p. 266.

70.   Mark H. Curtis, "The Alienated Intellectuals of Early Stuart England," in Crisis in Europe, 1560-1660, ed. Trevor Aston (London, 1965), pp. 295-316; Edward Shils, "Intellectuals," in International Encyclopedia of the Social Sciences, ed. David L. Sills, VII, p. 400.

71. Robert Child, cited in The Faithful Shepherd, by Hall, p. 121; John Cotton, "Copy of a Letter from Mr. Cotton to Lord Say and Seal, in the Year 1636," in History, by Hutchinson, I, p. 415.

72. "Certain Proposals Made by Lord Say, Lord Brooke, and Other Persons of Quality, as Conditions of Their Removing to New-England, with the Answers thereto," in History, by Hutchinson, I, pp. 410-413.

73. "Certain Proposals...," pp. 410-412.

74. John Winthrop, "A Model of Christian Charity," Winthrop Papers, p. 294; "Certain Proposals...," pp. 412-413.

75. "Certain Proposals...," pp. 412-413.

76. Winthrop, "A Reply to an Answer...," p. 101. On Puritan political thought, see two excellent studies by George L. Mosse, who attempts to put the American Puritans in the English context of that time: The Holy Pretence: A Study in Christianity and Reason of State from William Perkins to John Winthrop (Oxford, 1957); and "Puritan Political Thought and the 'Case of Conscience," Church History, XXIII (1954).

77. "Certain Proposals...," p. 413.

78. "Certain Proposals...," p. 413.

79. B. Katherine Brown, "The Controversy over the Franchise in Puritan Massachusetts, 1954 to 1974," WMQ, XXXIII (1976), pp. 233, 237; Michael Zuckerman, "The Social Context of Democracy in Massachusetts," WMQ, XXV (1968), p. 525, and Michael G. Hall, The Last American Puritan: The Life of Increase Mather (Middleton, Conn., 1988), pp. 264-271.

80. Jean-Jacques Rousseau, On the Social Contract, ed. R.D. Masters (New York, 1978), p. 68.

81. John Calvin, "On Civil Government," in Institutes of the Christian Religion, IV, xx, p. 2.

82. "Copy of a Letter from Mr. Cotton to Lord Say and Seal, in the Year 1636," in History, by Hutchinson, I, pp. 414-417.

83. Ibid., pp. 414-417.

84. Ibid., pp. 414-417.

85. Ibid., pp. 414-417.

86. Ibid., pp. 414-417.

87. Ibid., pp. 414-417.

88. John Cotton, The Keys of the Kingdom of Heaven (London, 1644), in John Cotton on the Churches of New England, ed. Ziff, pp. 88, 152-156.

89.   Ibid., pp. 152-156.

90.   On the supposed controversy between the congregationalists in Massachusetts and the Independents in England concerning toleration, see: Perry Miller, Orthodoxy in Massachusetts, p. 273.   I shall deal more fully with the relationship between these two groups in Chapter VI.

91.   Philip Nye, cited in "Philip Nye on Church and State," by D. Nobbs, The Historical Journal, 5-6 (1935-1940), p. 55.

92.   Cotton, The Keys of the Kingdom of Heaven, pp. 154-156.

93.   Christopher Hill, Economic Problems of the Church: From Archbishop Whitgift to the Long Parliament (London, 1968), p. x.

94.   Sacvan Bercovitch, The Puritan Origins of the American Self (New Haven, 1978), p. 47.

95.   Ezekiel Rogers, cited by Hall, The Faithful Sheperd, p. 132.

96.   "John Winthrop's Essay Against the Power of the Church to Sit in Judgment on the Civil Magistracy," Winthrop Papers, III, pp. 505-506.   On the role of the state in Puritan thought, see: George L. Mosse, "Puritanism and Reason of State in Old and New England," WMQ, IX (1952), pp. 66-80.

97.   John Hull, "The Diaries of John Hull," American Antiquarian Society, Transactions, III (1857), p. 168.

98.   Johnson, Wonder-Working Providence, pp. 25, 30, 32.

99.   "Certain Queries Presented by Many Christian People" (1649), in A.S.P. Woodhouse, Puritanism and Liberty (Chicago, 1951), pp. 241-247.   The similarity of the political proposals of this group to theocracy in America is readily apparent.   As Austin Woolrych wrote: the people of this group tried to establish in England "a government based not on the people as a whole but on the 'gathered churches', that is to say those congregations which had been voluntarily formed by a company of 'visible saints'."   See, Austin Woolrych, "Oliver Cromwell and the Rule of the Saints', in The English Civil War and After, 1642-1658, R. H. Parry (ed.), (Berkeley and Los Angeles, 1970), p. 63.

100.   Thomas Collier, "A Discovery of the New Creation" (1647), in Woodhouse, Puritanism and Liberty, pp. 290-296; Thomas Harrison's words appeared in "The Whitehall Debates" in Woodhouse, Puritanism and Liberty, p. 178.

101.   Michael R. Watts, The Dissenters (Oxford, 1978), pp. 135-6, 143; B.S. Capp, The Fifth Monarchy Men: A Study in Seventeenth-Century English Millenariansm (London, 1972), pp. 51, 230-1.   On the relationship between the Fifth Monarchists and the American Puritans, see J.F. Maclear, "New England and the Fifth Monarchy: the quest for the Millennium in Early American Puritanism," William and Mary Quarterly, Vol. 32 (1975), pp. 223-260.

102.   Watts, The Dissenters, pp. 137, 142.

103. Woolrych, "Oliver Cromwell and the Rule of the Saints," p. 68; "The True State of the Case of the Commonwealth" (1654), in The Puritan Revolution: A Documentary History, Stuart E. Prall (ed.) (New York, 1968), pp. 264-5. Thus far the best study of Barebone's Parliament is Tai Liu, "Saints in Power: A Study of the Barebone Parliament," PhD. Thesis, University of Indiana, 1969.

104. Richard Baxter, A Holy Commonwealth, or Political Aphorisms Opening the True Principles of Government 1659, pp. 241, 219, 247, 249, 218. For an excellent study of Baxter's life and his millennial expectations see William M. Lamont, Richard Baxter and the Millennium: Protestant Imperialism and the English Revolution (London, 1979).

105. Thomas Hobbes, Leviathan, or the Matter, Forme and Power of a Commonwealth Ecclesiastical and Civil (1651), Michael Oakeshott (ed.) Oxford. On Hobbes' thought see the brilliant study by J.G.A. Pocock, "Time, History and Eschatology in the Thought of Thomas Hobbes" in his book Politics, Language and Time (New York, 1973). For the general ideological context of Hobbes' writings, see the series of articles by Quentin Skinner: "Hobbes' Leviathan," The Historical Journal, Vol. VII, 1964; "The Ideological Context of Hobbes's Political Thought," The Historical Journal, Vol. IX, 1966; "Conquest and Consent: Thomas Hobbes and the Engagement Controversy," in The Interregnum, G.A. Aylmer (ed.), Hamden 1972, and "History and Ideology in the English Revolution," The Historical Journal, Vol. VII, 1965.

106. Hobbes, Leviathan, pp. 254-5, 451, 268, 295, 399, 233, 298, 306, 459, 452, 397.

107. For evident of this theocratic quest among Dutch Calvinists in Holland during the first half of the seventeenth century, see Douglas Nobbs, Theocracy and Toleration: A Study of the Dispute in Dutch Calvinism from 1600 to 1650 (Cambridge, 1938).

108. Johnson, Wonder-Working Providence, pp. 60-61.

109. Michael Wigglesworth, "God's Controversy with New England" (1662), in Seventeenth-Century American Poetry, ed. H.T. Meserole, pp. 43-45.

110. Anne Dudley Bradstreet, "A Dialogue Between Old England and New Concerning Their Present Troubles, Anno 1642," Old South Leaflets, No. 159, pp. 1-8.

111. John Cotton, cited in Meserole, Seventeenth-Century American Poetry, p. 382.

112. Edward Johnson (?), Good News from New England, With an Exact Relation of the First Planting... (London, 1648), p. 11. 112.

113. Wigglesworth, "God's Controversy with New England," p. 46.

114. John Winthrop, cited in "Rev. Thomas Hooker Letter, in Reply to Governor Winthrop," Connecticut Historical Society, Collections, I, p. 17.

115. John Cotton, The Way of the Congregational Churches Cleared (London, 1648), in John Cotton on the Churches of New England, ed. Ziff, pp. 258-259.

116. Erik H. Erikson, "Reflections on the American Identity," in Childhood and Society, p. 296.

117. Johnson, Wonder-Working Providence. p. 52.

CHAPTER FIVE:
MASSACHUSETTS AND THE LONG PARLIAMENT
DURING THE 1640s

Some lost their livings, some to prison pent,
Some, fined, from house and friends to exile went.
-- Anne Dudley Bradstreet, 1642[1]

Let us be every day confessing of our old England sinnes, of its high pride, Idolatry, superstition, blashpemies, blood, cruelties, Atheismes, &c., and let us never goe to our secrets without our Censors in our hands for old England, deare England still in divers respects, left by us in our persons, but never yet forsaken in our affection.
-- William Hooke, 1641[2]

If we should put ourselves under the protection of the parliament, we must then be subject to all such laws as they should make, or at least such as they might impose upon us; in which course though they should intend our good, yet it might prove very prejudicial to us.
-- Massachusetts General Court, 1641[3]

Will you be gone again to Egypt (God forbid I should count all our Native Country as Egypt) but if you go thither, you will have much adoe to escape the paws of the Bear; If you be once incorporated into any of their Parishes, you will finde such beastly work in Church Government that you...must worship the beast or the Image of the beast.
-- John Cotton, early 1640s[4]

For the laws of England...by our charter we are not bound to them...whereas our allegiance binds us not to the laws of England any longer than while we live in England, for the laws of the parliament of England reach no further, nor the king's writs under the great seal go any further.
-- Massachusetts General Court, 1646[5]

253

> There is at this time a great battle between Michael and the
> Dragon, and the Angels. The Beast and the Kings of earth, and
> their Armies have gathered themselves together to make war with
> the Lambe. All the Principalities, and Powers, and Rulers of the
> Darknesse of the World, and Spirituall wickednesses in High
> places are up in Armes this day, and there is scarce a Davill left
> in Hell...O let us all enter into Covenant with England.
> -- William Hooke, 1645[6]

The history of England in the late 1630s and early 1640s was shaped not only by the English people within England but also by historical events that took place outside England. That was, at least, how Archbishop Laud understood the relationship between events in Scotland and their influence on England. "The tumults in Scotland, about the Service-Book offered to be brought in," he wrote in his diary, "began Juli 23, 1637, and continued increasing by fits, and now hath brought that kingdome in danger. No question, but there is a great concurrence between them and the Puritan party in England."[7] In Scotland, at that time, Robert Baillie, a moderate presbyterian and professor of divinity at Glasgow, was confused by the riots and revolt of his people against the Book of Common Prayer. "The whole people thinks poperie at the doores," he wrote. "No man may speak any thing in publick for the king's part, except he would have himself marked for sacrifice to be killed one day. I think our people possessed with a bloody devill."[8]

Among the many zealous Puritans in England "possessed with bloody devill," was Thomas Goodwin, who had just returned from exile in Holland. When in 1641 Goodwin heard news of events in England and Scotland, shortly before his return to England, he preached a fast sermon, "A Glimpse of Sion Glory," to his congregation of English exiles in the Netherlands. "Babylons falling is Sions raising, Babylons destruction is Jerusalems salvation," he told his people. "It is the work of the day," he continued,

> to cry down Babylon, that it may fall more and more, and it is
> the worke of the day to give God no rest, till he sets up

254

Jerusalem as the praise of the whole World. Blessed is he that dasheth the brats of Babylon against the stones.

The millennium, according to Goodwin, was at hand, and saints were duty bound to return to England "to bring forth more and more the voice of our PARLIAMENT as a voice of Thunder...to the Antichristian party."⁹ Goodwin, therefore, led his people from their temporary exile in Holland back to England, the Elect Nation, where they expected to create the Kingdom of God. For another English community across the ocean and far from England, the choice was much harder and more complicated.

When the overt struggle between the king and parliament broke out in England, only a decade had passed since the Puritans came to Massachusetts, and the saints in the wilderness were still in the middle of establishing and realizing their holy experiment, attempting to shape their covenanted societies into a holy Christian commonwealth. Unable to fulfill in England the gospel of reformation, the Puritans had voluntarily emigrated from England to establish the Kingdom of God in the wilderness, where they hoped their eschatological visions concerning the millennial rule of Christ upon earth would be realized. Unlike Puritan exiles in Holland, howevever Massachusetts Puritans chose the wilderness not as a temporary refuge, but as a place that would everlastingly be blessed by God. Thus, while they shared with Goodwin and other Puritans in England the belief in the millennial kingdom of Christ upon earth, the Bay colony's Puritans looked back to England with many conflicting expectations. Obviously one source of the complexity of New England Puritans' attitudes toward England during the 1640s was the difficult task of defining the place of England in providential history. During the 1620s and 1630s, the Puritans emigration was animated to a large extent by the belief that only exile could save the saints from the day of Judgment and God's wrath soon to fall on England. But from the early 1640s, many Puritans in New and old England thought that given the Long Parliament's acts, England was on the road to true reformation. Thus, for the Puritans in the wilderness, the events in England presented a difficult choice, whether to return

255

as had Goodwin, to aid in the saints' holy war in England, or to stay in the wilderness to continue the establishment of the Kingdom of God there.

This choice was difficult because returning to England had serious implications for the Kingdom of God in the wilderness. To return could imply that one had given up on the hope that Massachusetts would occupy an important place in providential history as the site on which the New Jerusalem would be built. Events in England thus compelled New England Puritans to re-evaluate and redefine their attitudes toward and relationship with England during the 1640s. At the same time, events in England had a crucial influence on colony's economic and social life; for once the saints in England began to embark on the road to reformation, the Puritan emigration to Massachusetts almost totally stopped, and the colony immediately experienced a severe economic recession. This chapter will explore, therefore, the complexity of the attitudes Massachusetts Puritans had toward England during the ascendancy of Parliament and define the colony's relationship with England during the Civil War.

I   "New England's Tears for Old England's Feares"

Almost immediately, Massachusetts felt the consequences of events in Scotland and England. Shortly after the Long Parliament had assembled, Winthrop wrote in 1640 that because of

> the Scots entering into England, and the calling of a parliament, and the hope of through reformation...some among us began to think of returning back to England. Others desparing of any more supply from thence, and yet not knowing how to live there, if they should return, bent their minds wholly to removal to the south parts, supposing they should find better means of subsistance there, and for this end put off their estates here at very low rates.[10]

At the same time, friends of the colony in England wrote that, given the war, Massachusetts could expect almost nothing now from England. "It beeing a very dead and hard time for money generally," wrote John Tinker from England to Winthrop, adding that

> they are like to come but small quantyty of Passengers over, in comparison of what hath been formerly, and the reason I conceive to be the hope of some reformation in England by the intended parliament, the which cann hardly be expected per judicious and wise men...but rather see a troublesome time approaching both within and without the Kingdome.[11]

This gloomy picture of circumstances in England and their serious consequences for the colony, including economic shortages and emigration, frightened Bay Puritans. For in an age in which every event was interpreted as evidence of God's providence, any economic or social failure in Massachusetts could also be seen as a commentary on its role in providential history. After all, the New Jerusalem in Revelation had been a model of utopian order in Christina thought for many centuries, a utopian society that God had promised to sustain. New Jerusalem was therefore supposed to be "a city upon a hill," to which all eyes would look, and not, as happened in Massachusetts in the early 1640s, a place from which people escaped. The tension between the Puritans' millennial expectations and the poor economic conditions the colony could offer to its

257

inhabitants continued to cause many problems for Massachusetts during the 1640s. At the same time, however, events in England could be interpreted as an affirmation of the Bay Puritans' eschatological expectations and long-expected fears concerning the imminent calamities England would undergo, and thereby helped to counteract adverse conditions in New England.

The news about the First Bishops' War of 1639 evoked many different attitudes among Massachusetts Puritans. In July 1640, after the dissolution of the Short Parliament, the churches in New England appointed "a day of Publike Humiliation...in behalf of our Native Country in a time of feared dangers." On this occasion, the Rev. William Hooke preached a sermon before his congregation in Taunton, entitled "New Englands Teares for Old Englands Feares."[12] In this sermon, Hooke considered the relationship between Massachusetts and England, with special attention to Puritan interpretations of England's calamities at that time. The sermon provides much evidence, and here lies its importance, of how divided Puritan feelings were toward England in the early 1640s.

The main theme of Hooke's sermon was that civil war (for him the Bishops' War between England and Scotland was such a war) was the worst thing a nation could suffer, and he admonished his congregation against the view that England's misfortune should be a cause of joy. "It is commonly observed," warned Hooke, "that men and women who have turned Witches" and have been "in league with the devill...grieveth at the Prosperity, and rejoyceth at the misery of others." Hooke attempted to dissuade his hearers from acting like witches and from rejoicing in the "afflications and miseries in England." "Though I am not able to charge any of you with this cursed affection," Hooke declared,

> yet I doe wish you to looke into your owne hearts; for this I am
> sure, here are strong temptations sometimes, leading toward it in
> this land, which when they meet with an heart voyd of grace,
> must needs stirre up the disposition in it, and not only emulations
> and envyings, but witchcraft itself is a worke of the flesh.[13]

Though the English Civil War had only begun in 1642, Hooke foresaw that the war between England and Scotland was a prologue to an extended and bloody

258

struggle yet to come. Many who came to Massachusetts in the previous years came because of the fear that God would soon visit His divine wrath upon England. But Hooke told his listeners that this Judgment would be not a blessing but a terrible disaster. "Let us therefore, I beseech you," pleaded Hooke,

> lay aside the thoughts of all comfort this day, and let us fiten our eyes upon the calamaties of our brethren in old England, calamities, at least, imminent calamities dropping, swords that have hung along time over their heads by twine thread, judgement long since threatened as a foreseene by Gods Messengers in the causes...heavy judgement in all probability when they fall, if they are not fallen already.

To Hooke the war between England and Scotland was a gloomy development: "between the two Sister Nations (Sister-Nations? ah, the word woundeth), let us look this day simply on the event, a sad event in all likelihood, the dividing of a King from his Subjects, and his from them, their mutual taking of Armes in opposition and defence."[14]

The breach between the King and his subjects, according to Hooke, would lead only to a horrible war, and "even the gloomy and dark consequences thereof, are killing and slaying, and sacking and burning, and robbing and rifting, cursing and blaspheming." For when each side took up arms, war was imminent and in war death "reign[ed] in the field." A civil war, he admonished, could give no joy to God's people. Rather, "a day of battle" was " day of harvest for the devill." Yet, though every war was horrible, there were none "so cruel, so unnaturel, so desolating, as civill warres," argued Hooke.[15]

Although Hooke acknowledged that there were "no warres that Englands sinnes have not deserved," he argued that New England could not rejoice at "the feared sorrowes of our Countrymen" because he contended, "that Land first bore us" and New Englanders stood "in spiritual relation to many, yea very many in that Land." Following the prophetic visions in the Apocalypse, Hooke declared, none could deny that England was "neither hot nor cold" and that its inhabitants included many "drunkennesses... another Lukewarnesse many a Laodicena." Nor was it untrue that New England had "done enough and enough to overwhelme

259

old England with the wrath of God." To Hooke, however, England's manifold sins rather demanded that "our hearts at this moment" be "over shadowed with clouds of sorrow" and not that "we would be glad to heare of Judgments upon our native Country." Above all, Hooke warned his people, without peace in England, New England's churches could not expect to "have peace, and therefore in the misery in that Land, we shall never be happie."[16]

William Hooke's sermon reflected the deep ambivalence of New England Puritans towards England. The issue Hooke tried to face was indeed an essential feature of the Puritan migration. As the movement was carried forward to a large extent on the basis of eschatological visions and millennial expectations, the belief in the imminent judgment England would undergo in the near future was an essential motive for the Puritan migration to America. On the other hand, obviously, the migration was not an emigration of one nation out of another, but merely an English migration out of the English nation, and the relationship between the Puritan emigrants and Englishmen at home had always been rooted in the ground of common nationality. Nationality, of course, is hard to define in the early seventeenth century. But when Hooke described the proper relationship of New England with England, it is clear that he thought of common national values. "There is no Land that claimes our name, but England," he asserted, "we are distinguished from all the Nations in the world by the name of England." Furthermore, argued Hooke, there was "no Potentate breathing" in the world "that wee call our dread Soveraigne, but King Charles, nor Lawes of any Land have civilized us, but Englands." Nor was there any "Nation that calls us Countrey-men, but the English."[17]

However one might define nationality at that time, then, Hooke's sermon revealed how national sentiments were combined with anticipation of calamities among New England Puritans to shape their attitudes toward England. The last means to correct England was indeed God's judgment upon it. With all his might, however, Hooke attempted to convince his people that the Puritans in the wilderness should pray for their native country and not rejoice at its sorrows.

260

"Let us be every day confessing of our old England sinnes, of its high pride, Idolatry, superstition, blasphemies, blood, cruelties, Atheismes," he declared, "and let us never goe to our secrets without our Censers in our hands for old England, deare England still in diverse respects, left by us in our persons, but never yet forsaken in our affections."[18] With these words Hooke concluded his sermon, a marvelous expression of brotherly love towards England and a sermon full of fear of the worst kind of war - civil war.

II Massachusetts' Commission to the Long Parliament

Hooke preached his sermon in July 1640, following the First Bishops' War and the dissolution of the Short Parliament the previous May. At the Short Parliament, the King demanded money for his war against the Scots and, having failed to achieve it, dissolved that Parliament. Without money to raise an adequate army, Charles could only lose in the Second Bishops' War during the summer of 1640. In this war, the Scots took the initiative, crossed the Tweed in August and, after defeating the English army, encamped on English land. In subsequent years, the Scots played a crucial role in England's religious and political struggles. The treaty the Scots forced upon Charles clearly implied that Parliament should give its assent to the final settlement with the Scots. Consequently, the Long Parliament was summoned and assembled in November 1640. Under the leadership of John Pym and John Hampden, this parliament immediately began to initiate legislative programs to abolish ship-money, arminianism, and the High Commission and Star Chamber; to secure the continuity of the Parliament with the Triennial Act; to impeach the King's ministers; and to exclude bishops from the House of Lords. By their acts and attacks, therefore, Parliamentary leaders showed their ambition to have some share in the executive power.

These events did not go unnoticed in New England which followed political religious developments in England closely.

> New England is preparing a-pace,
> To entertain King Pym, with his Grace...
> No surplisse nor no Organs there,
> Shall ever offend the Eye, or the Ear,
> But a Spiritual Preach, with a 3. hours Prayer.[19]

So ran an English poem in which the author associated the leader of the Long Parliament with New England Puritans. Across the ocean, however, the Puritans immediately felt the consequences of the rapid changes in England. Once the Long Parliament's acts had brought new hope of reformation in England, most English Puritans now preferred to stay at home and to engage there in God's war.

As Winthrop wrote in 1641, Parliament's "setting upon a generall reformation both of church and state...caused all men to stay in England in expectation of a new world" there. In 1641, emigration to the colony slowed to a trickle, a development that worsened the economic recession that began the previous years. "Few coming to us, all foreign commodities grew scarce, and our own of no price," complained Winthrop, "Corn would buy nothing: a cow which cost last year 20 might now be bought for 4 or 5,... and many gone out of the country, so as no man could pay his debts, nor the merchants make return into England for their commodities." Viewing the gloomy consequences of the economic crisis in the colony along with the migration of some from Massachusetts to Virginia, the West Indies, and England, Winthrop wrote resignedly that "God taught us the vanity of all outward things."[20]

Apparently, the colony's friends in England knew the circumstances in Massachusetts well and tried to help. Many of them had been members of the Long Parliament and thus for the first time provided a direct link between the revolutionary Parliament and the colony. "Upon the great liberty which the king had left the parliament in England," wrote Winthrop in early 1641, "some of our friends there wrote to us advice to send over some to solicit for us in the parliament, giving us hope that we might obtain much." Apparently, these men were the Earl of Warwick, Lord Say and Seale, Lord Robert Brooke, Thomas Barrington, Arthur Haselrig, and many more who during the 1630s had done so much to help Massachusetts. This invitation from the Parliament aimed to reverse the policies which the Crown and Laud had directed against the colony in previous years, and the colony's friends showed that the Long Parliament would consider the colony's complaints along with other charges against Laud and others of the king's ministers. But this invitation to send a commission from the colony to the Parliament created much controversy in Massachusetts. Eventually, the colony declined to accept it on the grounds that "if we should put ourselves under the protection of the parliament, we must then be subject to all such laws as they should make, or at least such as they might impose upon us; in which

263

course though they should intend our good, yet it might be prove very prejudicial to us." [21]

Ever obliged to define and re-define its relationship with England according to changing circumstances, Massachusetts persistently resisted any arrangement that might threaten its liberties and self rule. The very existence of the Puritan commonwealth in America was based on the power of self rule, which as we saw earlier, Puritans regarded as the necessary condition for religious reformation there. Thus, when the Crown during the 1630s attempted to infringe on Massachusetts' liberties, the colony was ready to defend itself by armed force. Now, with the invitation from England, Massachusetts was careful not to bring itself under Parliament's power and authority. An essential part of Massachusetts' attitudes towards England during the 1640s was the colony's determination not to be "subject to all such laws as they should make" in the Long Parliament. [22]

The invitation from England was the first public encounter between the enthusiastic Puritans of England, embarking now finally on the road to reformation, and the Puritans in the wilderness, who refused to risk their religious enterprise by submission to the Parliament. Persuaded that in order to maintain the uniqueness of religious reformation the colony had to have a large degree of political autonomy, Massachusetts declined to send a commision to represent its interest in Parliament; in view of the recession in the colony, however, the colonists did decide to send a commision "to satisfy our countrymen" about the economic situation of Massachusetts, explain why the colony could not fulfill its financial "engagements" with England, and seek out some way by which the colony might recover from its recession. The commissioners were both to carry out these economic assignments and to advise "in furthering the work of reformation of the churches" in England. The General Court chose three people as commissioners: Rev. Hugh Peter, pastor of the Salem church, Rev. Thomas Weld, pastor of the Roxbury church, and Mr. William Hibbins of Boston. Winthrop and other magistrates wrote to the churches of Salem and Roxbury asking them to give permission for their ministers to go to England. Weld got the permission from his church without any problem, but Peter's case was much more complicated because many in Salem strongly opposed sending a commission. "Agitation" concerning the commission began in Salem but "was soon about the country" so that the whole idea had to be dropped for a while.[23]

The nature of "the agitation" in the colony is revealed in a letter John Endecott wrote to Winthrop in February 1640/41. Endecott was strongly opposed to a commission, which, he predicted, might "prove more hurtfull than helpefull unto us divers wayes." First, Endecott feared that it might give credibility to those people in England who, already aware that many in the colony were removing to the West Indies because they could not "heere maintayne their families," believed that "New England can no longer subsist without the helpe of old England." By encouraging such beliefs, the commission could hurt the image of Puritan Massachusetts and thereby further divert people and money from the colony; it could contribute to discredit the Puritan experiment in New England and in that way "dishonour...God." Instead of sending agents, Endecott urged the colonists "to look amongst ourselves" and to see "how unprofitable the monies we have had have been layd out, as namelie in wines and liquors, and English provisions of dyett and unnecessarie braverie in apparell: all which tends to the scandal of religion and povertie." In the early 1640s, as in the 1630s, Endecott affirmed, the colony should depend upon "God's providence" and eschew all ungodly means. After all, he argued, the short history of the colony had already proved that God had "hitherto bene verie good unto us beyond expectation."[24]

Endecott was not blind to the colony's economic problems, but he regarded them as evidence of the colony's need to live more frugally according to the premises of the reformation so that "our scarcitie of money" should lead the colony "rather to some more frugall course heere at home and to strict reformation of mispending of money than to seek abroad for more to maintain us in our disorders." But lack of frugality was not the only sin committed by Bay Puritans; they had, in Endecott's view, manifested too much "distrust" in God's

265

providence and skepticism concerning the colony's unique place in providential history. Hugh Peter, Endecott pointed out, was one of those who had been guilty of distrust, arguing, along with Lord Say, that New England was not a place fit to live in and that removing the colony to the West Indies was desirable. All of those chosen for the commission, noted Endecott, were "men well-affected to the West Indies," and he expressed the conviction that the colony would gain "more peace...and blessing...in a patient waiting upon God, than in a (seeming at least) distrust of his providence." Thus, Endecott thought nothing more should be done concerning the colony's economic needs than for a few "Godlie wise men" in Massachusetts to write privately to those godly people in England who are most "likelie to do us good," in order to seek help "to further the worke of the Lord" in New England.[25]

Again and again, events in England exerted powerful influences upon Massachusetts. The economic decline in the colony, caused by the developments in England, produced severe strains within the holy experiment in Massachusetts. The expectations of reformation in England had not only stopped the emigration to Massachusetts, they had also again thrust England back to the center of providential history, and thus directed the attention of English Puritans away from the holy experiment in the wilderness. Most seriously from the point of view of Massachusetts, was the emigration of inhabitants to other places. For those who emigrated from the colony to the West Indies and England left behind them, among other things, the godly vision of Massachusetts as the promised land and denied the colony's uniqueness in divine history.

In June 1641, after much delay, the General Court in Massachusetts reached a final decision concerning the commission to England. Rejecting Endecott's arguments, it delegated Peters, Weld, and Hibbens to proceed to England, where they were "to congratulate the happy success" of reformation in England and "to satisfy our creditors of the true cause" of the inability of the Puritans in the Bay colony to pay their debts on time. The court also charged the commissioners "to be ready to make use of any opportunity God should offer for the good of the country here." To allay the fears of those who thought the commmissioners would appear to be begging, the court stipulated that the commissioners "should not seek supply of our wants in any dishonorable way, as by begging or the like, for we were resolved to wait upon the Lord in the use of all means which were lawful and honorable." Lest anyone in England think that the commission meant that the colony had given up on its divine mission, the court directed the commissioners to offer English Puritans the benefit of New England's experience in the ecclesiastical realm, specifically ordering the commissioners to "give any advice, as it should be required, for the settling of the right form of church discipline" in England.[26] Despite the court's actions, Endecott's warning against the members of this commission proved to be right: Hugh Peter and Thomas Weld never again saw the shores of New England.

When it sent its commission to England, Massachusetts had every reason to expect that the Long Parliament would look favorably on its request for abolishing the limitation and regulation of emigration and commodities to the colony issued by Crown commissioners during the 1630s. "The Parliament of England," wrote Winthrop at that time, was proceeding "readily to reform all public grievances," and its acts seemed to closely reflect the interests of New England.[27] In late 1640, the "Root and Branch Petition" to abolish the government of "archbishops and lords bishops, deans and archdeacons" had been submitted to Parliament, and many of its articles bore a marked similarity to the "General Considerations" of the Puritan emigration of 1629, with its attacks on the "great corruption" in church and state in England. The Parliament had abolished the Court of Star Chamber and the Court of High Commission, and the Commons had issued "The Protestation," in which they "vow and protest to maintain and defend...the true reformed Protestant religion expressed in the doctrine of the Church of England, against all Popery and popish innovation within this realm." And while the House of Lords considered a "bill on Church Reform," the commons issued its resolution concerning "Ecclesiastical Innovations." By this resolution, the Commons intended to nullify Laud's

267

ecclesiastical policy of previous years, including his permission of "dancing or other sports" on the Lord's day. The close association between Parliament's acts and Massachusetts' interests was nowhere more clear than in the articles of "The Grand Remonstrance" of December 1641, in which the Commons decried the "great numbers" of people who in order to "avoid their miseries departed out of the kingdom," because of the King's and his ministers' policy, "some into New England and other parts of America, others to Holland."[28]

Even before the colony's commissioners arrived in England, Parliament displayed its favor to Massachusetts. "Some of our people being then in London," wrote Winthrop in September 1641, "preferred a petition to the Lords' house for redess of that restraint which had been put upon ships and passengers to New England" during the 1630s, and Parliament responded by ordering that Massachusetts "should enjoy all" its "liberties." At the same time, the colony's patent or charter "which had been condemned and called in upon an erroneous judgment in a quo warranto" by the Crown in 1635, "was now implicitly revived and confimred" by the Parliament. Winthrop did not specify the names of those friends of the colony who appealed to the Parliament on its behalf, but he noted that "this petition was preferred without warrnant from our court." Thus, Parliament during its struggle with the King overturned the Crown's policy against the colony of the 1630s. When news of these events arrived in Massachusetts Bay, Puritans held "a day of thanksgiving" in "all our churches for the good success of the Parliament in England."[29] Massachusetts, moreover, was soon informed of another act of Parliament that favored it. In March 1642, the Commons declared that "whereas the plantation in New England" had been "very beneficial and commodious to this kingdom and nation," "all merchandizing goods" to and from New England should "be freed and discharged of and from paying and yeilding any custom, taxation, or other duty."[30]

Parliament's decisions affirming the colony's liberties and attempts to help its economic needs brought to an end almost ten years of struggle between Massachusetts and the Crown. Parliament's sympathy towards New England could also be seen in the trial of Archbishop Laud. In his speech in the Parliament in February 1642, Lord Say and Sele accused Laud of pursuing an ecclesiastical policy that caused many "to be thrust out of the land, and cut off from their native country." Because these actions wounded "the consciences" of the Puritans in the Church of England, Say and Sele charged, Laud had by them "offend[ed] and sin[ned] against Christ."[31] To these charges Laud answered that he had "some very good grounds to think" that Lord Say and Sele "hath been and is the great cause and enlarger of all the separation that now is in Church affairs." But more particularly concerning the "cause" of the Puritan migration, Laud sharply and correctly denied that the Puritans "have been banished, or 'thrust out of the land,' or 'cut off from their native country,'" as Say and Sele had charged. To the contrary, Laud argued, "they have thrust themselves out, and cut themselves off, and run a-madding to New England, scared away, as they say, because certain gross corruptions not to be endured in this Church." Historically speaking, Laud's understanding of the Puritan migration was right, but the Puritans in old and New England wanted justice and revenge, not truth.[32]

By its acts and proceedings, then, the Long Parliament redressed the Crown's policy against Massachusetts and executed its chief enemy - William Laud. To a great extent, then, the Puritans' struggle in England in the early 1640s represented a culmination of a common struggle of Puritans on both sides of the ocean. But Parliament's relationship with the colony did not stop with these favorable measures. For while Parliament renewed the colony's legal rights and liberties, it did not affirm the whole Puritan holy enterprise in the wilderness: it adopted neither the New England model of church government nor the premises of theocracy in New England with its unique relationship between church and state. Nevertheless, Parliament's decisions concerning New England showed clearly that it regarded the saints' tribulations on both sides of the ocean as part of a common struggle and thereby encouraged American Puritans to identify with the Parliament's cause in England. Once Massachusetts had made this identification, however, New England Puritans could not avoid taking sides in the

269

bitter theological and religious controversies in England over the correct premises of the true reformation. And Massachusetts was soon to learn that these theological struggles could be as dangerous to the foundations of the Puritan commonwealth in America as had been the Crown's threats of the 1630s.

III Massachusetts and Religious Reformation in England

The first session of the Long Parliament ended in the summer of 1641, but its acts had a profound influence upon the whole kingdom. "The crucial happening in 1641," writes William Lamont, "was the destruction of Laudianism. Away went censorship, away went Star Chamber and the Court of High Commission, away went imposition of oaths, away went searching visitation, away went the claim that bishops ruled by divine right - and away went the archbishop himself to a prison cell." In the country, parliamentary ordinances concerning the removal of all remnants of Popery from parish churches caused "angry disputes" between Puritans and non-Puritans. In Puritan districts, "stone saints were shattered from reredos and tomb" and "village crosses overturned." Religious reformation also stimulated large-scale efforts at social reformation. "To attempt reform of the English Church in the seventeenth century," wrote William Haller, "was to attempt the reorganization of society."[33]

Concering religion, the Commons plainly declared in the Grand Remonstrance of 1641 that it was "far from our purposes or desire to let loose the golden reins of discipline and government in the Church, to leave private persons or particular congregations to take up what form of Divine Service they please." Consequently, Parliament ordered that "for the better...to effect the intended reformation" of the Church of England "there may be a general synod of the most grave, pious, learned and judicious divines of this island," along with participants from "foreign parts" as Scotland and Holland which professed "the same religion with us." Thus did Parliament begin to think of an assembly of divines to define the principles through which genuine religious reformation could be realized, "the result of their consultation" to be submitted to Parliament "to be there allowed of and confirmed, and receive the stamp of authority." After affirming the assembly's resolutions, Parliament, on its own part, promised to "find passages" to enforce them "throughout the kingdom."[34] In these circumstances an invitation was sent in early 1642 to "Mr. Cotton of Boston, Mr. Hooker of Hartford, and

Mr. Davenport of New-haven, signed by several of nobility, divers members of the house of commons, and some ministers, to call them or some of them...to assist in the assembly of divines" that Parliament proposed to call in England.[35]

According to Winthrop, the signers of the invitation "stood for the independency of churches." But an analysis of the list along the lines of J.H. Hexter's distinction in The Reign of King Pym shows that the group was considerably more diverse. Many had long been connected with the Puritan emigration to Massachusetts and other parts of America: The Earl of Warwick, Lord Say and Sele, Lord Brooke, Sir Arthur Haselrig, Sir Thomas Barrington, Sir Henry Darley, and several others. All of these people belonged to the Middle Group in Parliament. Most important, at least three signers were presbyterians and therefore did not, as Winthrop claimed, "stand for the independency of churches." These three were John Gurdon, Sir William Massham, and Sir Nathaniel Barnardiston. Given the fact that almost all of the people who signed the invitation had been connected with Puritan migration for many years, the finding of "presbyterians" among them strongly suggests that in 1640s, as in the 1620s and 1630s, Puritans of different persuasion worked together side by side to develop the Puritan shelter and refuge in Massachusetts. Finally, among the signers were Oliver Cromwell and Oliver St. John.[36]

An understanding of the reaction in New England to the invitation to attend the future Westminster Assembly of Divines, 1643-1653, is crucial to a comprehension of the relationship between Puritans on both sides of the Atlantic during the 1640s. According to Winthrop, immediately after the letters of invitation came to Massachusetts, "the magistrate and elders...met together, and were most of them of opinion that it was a call from God." Consequently, they sent messengers to Connecticut and New Haven to inform Hooker and Davenport about the invitation. When these messengers returned, however, "it was found that Mr. Hooker liked not the business, nor thought it any sufficient call for them to go 3,000 miles to agree with three men, (meaning those three ministers who were for independency, and did solicit in the parliament)." Davenport, on the other hand, "thought otherwise," but his congregation, "seeing the church had no other officer but himself," refused to give permission for him to go to England. As for Cotton, he "apprehended strongly a call of God" in this invitation but finally also decided to decline. Thus ends Winthrop's account of the reaction of the three ministers.[37]

But Winthrop's account is more complex than it may appear. The reactions of both Hooker and Cotton both repay closer analysis. Hooker was not willing to cross the sea, one of his biographers has written, only for the purpose of agreeing with "the small nucleus of Independents among the English delegates" to the Westminster Assembly. But it would be more than a year before the Westminster Assembly first convened in July 1643, and because the Lords and Commons still disagreed about which divines to choose for the assembly, Hooker obviously could not have known in 1642 that the Presbyterians would constitute a majority at the future assembly. At this date he could not even have known which divines the Lords and Commons were considering summoning. Clearly, all Hooker knew in 1642 and what his stated objection implied was that the New England way, congregationalism, had been accepted in England by only three prominent ministers in the whole kingdom. If this is true, Hooker's decline of the invitation revealed something very profound concerning New England's ecclesiastical way: that is, how little sympathy it had among English Puritans by the early 1640s.[38]

Although Winthrop reported Cotton's reaction as positive, there is far too much additional evidence to show that his account of Cotton as one who wanted to go back to England to help in its reformation stood in sharp contrast to Cotton's views on England at that time. For Cotton was one of the most persistent and powerful critics in Massachusetts concerning the emigration back to England. In his book The Church Resurrection, published in 1642, he declared plainly that "if men be weary of the Country and will [go] back again to England because in their heart they are weary...I fear there is no spirit of Reformation." Why Cotton opposed emigration back to England so strongly can

273

be seen from his contemporary sermons and exegesis of the Book of Revelation. During 1639/40 Cotton preached a series of sermons in Boston on the thirteenth chapter of the Apocalypse. These sermons appeared in London in 1655 as An Exposition Upon the Thirteenth Chapter of the Revelation. In 1642, he also published in London The Powring out of the Seven Vials. Out of these works one could see exactly what Cotton thought about the Puritans' providential mission in the wilderness and their relationship to England.[39]

In the thirteenth chapter of Revelation there is a description of a beast rising up from the sea with "seven heads and ten horns" and "the name of blasphemy" imprinted upon his heads. The duty of this beast was "to make war with teh saints" (Rev. 13:1, 7). In accord with the apocalyptic interpretation as a mode of historical thought, Cotton in An Exposition Upon the Thirteenth Chapter of the Revelation, identified the beast with Antichrist. But in fact, Cotton went further than that to identify the beast with a particular ecclesiastical order - "from the tumult of particular Churches did this beast arise." In Christ's time, argued Cotton, the Church consisted of many particular visible churches. But over time these congregations had been organized as "diocesan," and "from diocesan, to Metropolitan; from Metropolitan to Patriarchal, from Patriarchal to Oecumenical." Thus, "it came to pass, all Churches must be gathered into one Sea, that is the Catholick Church." It was from this sea of ecclesiastical confusion, then, according to Cotton, that the beast had arisen, that is, from all the forms of church government that had been established above the particular visible church. "The Beast did arise out of them all," Cotton declared, because none of these church organizations from the diocesan to the ecumenical had been founded on "pure doctrine, or worship, or Discipline." On the other hand in New England, proclaimed Cotton, no other church was accepted but the congregational. By identifying the beast in Revelation with certain forms of church government, Cotton interpreted the apocalyptic struggle as the battle between contrasting views of church government. That is, any kind of church that was not congregationalist in its constitution, in Cotton's words, made "a

274

beast of the Church."[40]

Out of his premises of church government, Cotton thus developed a unique view of the Beast in Revelation. Although he acknowledged his debt to "Holy Brightman," Cotton radically transformed Brightman's interpretation. For although Brightman always insisted on the importance of the visible church, he never infused into the issue of church government, as did Cotton, the whol cosmological and apocalyptical dimension of Revelation. The implications of Cotton's views for his attitude towards England are not hard to find. The whol Puritan migration became, according to Cotton's exegesis of Revelation, a deliverance "from this Monster...[and] from the remnants of the Image of this Beast, from all Diocesan and National Churches." On the other hand, looking at the churches in the Bay colony, Cotton identified them with the vision of "the Lambs" in Revelation "that stood on mount Sion" and with the saints who came to aid Christ in his war against Antichrist. New England, not England, declared Cotton, was therefore the place for God's saints. And for the "many poore creatures that came hither to this Country, and will be ready to go back again" to England, Cotton preached, "such man hath not an eare, nor an eye open" and "he knows not where he goes." "Will you be gone back againe to Egypt?" Cotton admonished his people in an effort to dissuade them from going back to England. God "forbid I should count all our Native Country as Egypt," he admitted, but at the same time he made it clear that "if you goe" back to England "you will have much adoe to escape the paw of the Bear: if you be once incorporated into any of their Parishes, you will finde such beastly work in Church Government." Thus, the Beast still explicitly existed in England and was vividly present there in the government of the Church of England. Consequently, Cotton warned that anyone who went back "must worship the beast or the image of the beast." For "a Diocesan, or National Church," as the Church of England indeed was, was "but an Image of the great beast."[41] The whole drama of salvation and redemption, then, in Cotton's interpretation, divided New England from old England, and it was the duty of the saints in the wilderness not to return

275

to England.

In these sermons one can find Cotton's real reason for not accepting the invitation to go back to England to help in realizing the reformation of the Church of England. On the other hand, accepting Brightman's view concerning the time of the seventh trumpet "when the Kingdomes of this world became the Kingdomes of our Lord, and of his Christ," Cotton calculated that this event would take place in 1655. "I will not be two [sic] confident," explained Cotton, "because I am not a Prophet, nor the Son of Prophet to foretell things to come; but so far as God helps by Scripture light, about the time 1655, there will be then such a blow given to this beast."[42] Cotton also included his claculation of the prophetic Revelations in The Powring Out of the Seven Vials. Looking at events in England and Scotland at the time of the Bishops' Wars Cotton argued that according to Revelation the Scots' rising was evidence of the time of the fifth vial, when "the fifth angel poured out his vial upon the beast" (Rev. 16:10). In this book, he argued as he did in his Exposition Upon the Thirteenth Chapter of Revelation, that "congregational only" is "the true Church of God," and all others - "Cathedral," "Provinciall" or "Diocesan" - should be counted as the beast of the Apocalypse.[43]

Eschatological visions and millennial expectation had played a crucial role both in the Puritan migration and in the attitudes of New England Puritans toward England during the 1630s and 1640s. Massachusetts, argued Cotton, should thank God "that he hath delivered us from the power of this Beast" in England, and "that he hath freed us from making an Image to that Beast." Moreover, any emigration back to England, Cotton admonished his congregation, was returning to the Beast's paw. For, given the structure of the Church of England, as national and diocesan, it was necessarily the instrument of the Beast or Antichrist. Essentially, then, Cotton had developed Brightman's interpretation of Revelation in a radical way; along with "Holy Brightman" he argued that the beast and Antichrist fought with the saints and the true church, but Cotton went one step further. With him the very structure of the church was evidence of its being

276

either of the Beast or of Christ, and thus all those who did not accept the congregational way of church government put themselves on the side of Antichrist. By this way of reasoning, Cotton placed the debates among Puritans in England and New England over the principles of church government within the eschatological and apolcalyptic dimensions of the Apocalypse.[44]

This is the context in which one should consider New England's refusal of the invitation to aid England with its reformation of church-government. This analysis does not suggest that Massachusetts had lost all interest in the reformation of the Church of England, but it does contain serious implications for Perry Miller's concept of "the errand into the wilderness." "The large unspoken assumption in the errand" of the Puritan migration, wrote Perry Miller in his marvelous essay "Errand Into the Wilderness," was that if the Puritan emigrants would realize the true reformation in America Jehovah "would bring back these temporary colonials to govern England." Thus if the first sense of the Puritan errand was to fulfill the positive part of reformation, the second one, according to Miller, was to influence the reformation in England. The Puritan migration, he argued.

> was an organized task force of Christians, executing a flank attack on the corruption of Christendom. These Puritans did not flee to America; they went in order to work out that complete reformation which was not yet accomplished in England and Europe, but which would quickly be accomplished if only the saints back there had a working model to guide them.[45]

Did Puritan emigrants assume this second sense of the errand? That is, did they emgirate in order to influence the reformation in England? Miller could argue this only by overlooking the eschatological visions and millennial expectations that had been so essential a part of the whole migration, visions and expectations in which the anticipation of God's wrath and his judgment led the Puritans to emgirate from England and in which the ultimate need was the prophetic flight of "the woman" in Revelation, or the true church, into the "wilderness." Viewing the Puritan migration in the light of these eschatological and apocalyptic dimensions it is clear that the two poles of time and history were Babylon and the New Jerusalem; bewtween these two the whole apocalyptic drama of the history of salvation and redemption occurred; Babylon would soon be destroyed, hence it was the saints' duty to depart from it.

On the other hand, Massachusetts Puritans knew already at the time of their emigration and in the next decade that their model of church-government was not acceptable to most English Puritans. The emigration, then, could hardly have been a temporary enterprise, as Miller argued, but a permanent and absolute departure from Babylon. For, if Miller was right, there is no way to explain Hooker's and cotton's declining invitation to return to England in 1642. But Hooker knew already that the congregational way had been accepted only by three people, according to his specific words, in all England, while Cotton, as his sermons on Revelation reveal, attacked all those in Massachusetts who considered emigrating back to England in the early 1640s on the grounds that the Beast and its Image were inextricably tied to the very structure of the Church of England. And, as Cotton knew, the main body of the Puritans in England wanted to preserve the Church of England as a national church. By and large, then, any attempt to apply Millers' concept of "the errand into the wilderness" to the Puritan migration to, and existence in, New England during the 1630s and 1640s is inadequate to explain the origins and assumptions of this migration.

IV   Crisis in the "City Upon the Hill"

On the other side of the ocean, in England, radical political developments took place in 1642 which repeatedly required Massachusetts to define and redefine its relationship with England.   While Parliament imposed step-by-step constitutional and ecclesiastical changes in the kingdom, the King refused to let Pym, Hampden, and others in the Parliament deprive him of his power and alienate him from his people.   Thus, in January 1642 Charles had tried to impeach and arrest five parliamentary leaders, Pym, Hampden, Holles, Haselrig and Strode, but failed in his attempted coup De'etat.   At that moment, the city of London, already on Parliament's side, decided to direct the train-bands and the seamen of the ports to defend Parliament against the King.   In March the Parliament passed the "Militia Ordinance," asserting its "power to assemble and call...His Majesty's subjects...that are meet and fit for the wars."   The control of the militia became the crucial issue in the confrontation between the King and Parliament and the essential cause for the outbreak of the English Civil War.   In May the King issued a proclamation condemning the Militia Ordinance of the Parliament and forbidding anyone in the kingdom to obey Parliament's orders concerning the militia.   To reach some sort of compromise with the King, Parliament in June sent to him the "Nineteen Propositions."   But Charles refused to accept these propositions on the grounds that they would "anihilate the royal power and leave nothing but the empty forms of majesty."   With the denial of the "Ninetten Proposition," nothing stood between King and Parliament but war.   In August 1642, the King raised his royal standard in Nottingham, and his army clashed with the Parliament army in the first major battle of the Civil War at Edgehill in October 1642.[46]

The continuity of the struggle in England, now becoming an open and armed breach between King and Parliament, had deepend the economic crisis in Puritan Massachusetts and raised severe inner strains in the colony.   Emigration to the West Indies and England continued, and some even considered accepting a Dutch

279

invitation to move to Long Island. "The city upon the hill" was being abandoned by many of its inhabitants. "The sudden fall of land, and the scarcity of foreign commodities, and money," wrote Winthrop in 1642, "with the thin access of people from England, put many into an unsettled frame of spirit...they began to hasten away, some to the West Indies, others to the Dutch, at Long Island...and others back to England." The "saints" emigration out of Massachusetts was followed by anxiety and controversies among the godly who preferred to stay in the colony. "Much disputation there was about the liberty of removing for outward advantage, and all ways were sought for an open door to get out at," lamented Winthrop, "but it is to be feared many crept out at a broken wall." There is no evidence that authorities in the colony considered trying to stop this emigration, but at the same time many in Massachusetts were angry that some Puritans England were attempting to draw people from the colony to other plantations. Lord Say and Sele, who persistently attempted to convince Bay Puritans to move to the West Indies and Providence Island, raised Winthrop's ire against him. "God would never have sent so many of his people" to Massachusetts, wrote Winthrop to Say and Sele, "if he had not seen the place sufficient to maintain them" there. But Say and Sele answered that Massachusetts was a "place appointed only for a present refuge, and that, a better place being now found out, they ought all to remove thither."[47]

For Winthrop the colony's economic and social crises and their implications for his vision of the "city upon the hill" provided an occasion to go back to the principles he had preached in 1630 in his "A Model of Christian Charity." If in 1630 Winthrop attempted in his lay sermon to encourage Puritan emigrants embarking on the work of establishing the true church and Christian commonwealth in the wilderness, all he could do in 1642 was to beseech his brethren not to leave the "holy refuge":

> Ask thy conscience if thou wouldst have plucked up thy stakes, and brought thy family 3000 miles, if thou hadst expected that all, or most, would have forsaken thee there. Ask again, what liberty thou hast towards others,which thou likest not to allow

others towards thyself; for if one may go, another may, and so the greater part, and so church and commonwealth may be left destitute, in a wilderness, exposed to misery and reproach, and all for thy ease and pleasure.[48]

One could imagine Winthrop's disappointment in 1642 upon seeing "many crept out at a broken wall" of what was thought to be only a decade ago "a city upon a hill." What was left to him was to raise once again the covenant principle set down in his lay sermon of 1630. "Such as come together into a wilderness," declared Winthrop, "confederate together in civil and church estate, whereby they do, explicitly at least, bind themselves to support each other, and all of...that society, whether civil or sacred." Because Puritan Massachusetts was a covenanted society, some colonists doubted whether they had "liberty of removing" from it. Eventually, Winthrop reaffirmed the liberty to emigrate, but the very consideration of emigration put in doubt the Puritan vision of a holy experiment in the wilderness. For a covenanted civil and church society, the emigration was a serious blow to Massachusetts' dreams for itself, and Winthrop could only plead with those who were considering emigration "to choose rather to suffer afflications with thy brethren" in Massachusetts "than to enlarge thy ease and pleasure by furthring the occasion of their ruin."[49]

"Societies, like individuals," wrote R.H. Tawney in Religion and the Rise of Capitalism, "have their moral crises and their spiritual revolutions," and if one is about to consider the state of the Puritan colony in 1642, it seems that Massachusetts at that moment was at its lowest level of any point between 1630 and 1660.[50] "The main cause for alarm" in the Puritan colonies, wrote William L. Sachse in his study of "the Migration of New Englanders to England," was not the number that returned, but their quality." In 1642, for example, "seven of the nine graduates in Harvard's first class" returned to England, and overall "more than a third of the graduates before 1656 crossed over to England." Developments in England had opened many ecclesiastical positions in England, and at least "sixty New Englanders" went back to England to obtain religious posts there. Other ministers returned from America to resume their ministry in their parent towns or to recover their previous ecclesiastical posts, and some would have an important role in England during the next two decades. Thus was New England "drained of many of their most enterprising and gifted men."[51] Moreover, these people had left not only church and commonwealth in New England but also the dream and vision of a holy society that had so deeply motivated many Puritans in the previous decade to come to New England. What views of Massachusetts and New England did these emigrants to England carry with them? Not much is known on this subject, but Winthrop wrote in 1642 that when John Humfrey, who was one of the leaders of the Great Migration, "and four ministers, and a schoolmaster" went back to England, all of them except one spoke "evile of this good land and the Lord's people here."[52] If so, then, the rise of Puritanism in England during the 1640s had opened the way back to England for many Puritans who had been disappointed by the holy experiment in the American wilderness.

In the midst of the colony's economic recession and spiritual crisis, Parliament took further steps to ease the colony's burden. In March 1643 the Commons passed a resolution declaring that because "the plantations in New England" had proved "very beneficial and commodious for this kingdom and nation...all merchandize, goods exported, etc., into New England...be free of all custom, etc., in England and New England, and all other ports." Parliament reaffirmed this resolution in late 1644. Declaring that New England Puritans "were well affected to the Gospel of Truth, and the Honourable Proceedings of Parliament," Parliament granted the Puritan colonies "free liberty to trade and traffick from New England into any places of this Kingdome within the Jurisdiction of Parliament... without any payment of Customes whatsoever." There were many reasons for Parliament's decision, but not the least of them was an acknowledgment that the Puritans in the wilderness were part of Parliament's cause during the Civil War. "Though they are gone from us, yet were of us, and still are; only removed a little in distance of Climate; absent in body, present in spirit, and brotherly affection."[53]

When news of the Common's resolution of March 1643 reached Massachusetts, the General Court happily acknowledged "so great a favor from that honorable assembly" and decided to put the Commons' order among the colony's records "in perpetuam rei memorian." At the same time, the General Court passed an important resolution indicating that for the first time the colony had decided to take a side in the struggle between King and Parliament. The Civil War forced all Englishmen to reconsider their political obligations, and in this sense Massachusetts was no exception. Because the King "had violated the privileges of Parliament and made war upon them, and thereby had lost much of his kingdom and many of his subjects," the Court decided "to omit that part" of the oath in which civil officials in Massachusetts swore allegiance to the King upon taking office. This was the first time in which Massachusetts explicitly identified itself with Parliament.[54] By omitting that part of the oath, Bay Puritans declared that they no longer considered Charles I as their sovereign. This defiance of royal sovereignty, complained one roaylist in England in his A Preter-Pluperfect (1643), was the essence of the "new Publique Faith" in England, and "it hath transform'd our land...old England into New England spiritually." Puritans and Parliament, he lamented, out of the "new Publique Faith" had brought total anarchy in church and state and transformed England into New England.[55]

Massachusetts had identified its interest with that of Parliament in 1643, but the colony could not expect too much from Parliament at that time. For during 1643 royal and Parliamentary armies engaged in a a series of battles, none of which led to a decisive victory for either side. In that year, Parliament finally came to an agreement with the Scots, the "Solemn League and Covenant" of September 1643, in which the Scots had made their entrance into the war on Parliament's side conditional upon reforming the Church of England and Ireland "in doctrine, worship, discipline and government, according to the word of God, and the exmaple of the best reformed Churches," among which the Scots, naturally, considered their Kirk to be the very best.[56] Earlier, in July, in an effort to meet the demands of both Scots and Puritans, the Westminster Assembly of Divines began its work. Given the circumstances in England, the Puritans on the other side of the ocean had to reckon themselves alone with rival colonial powers and Indians in the New World. Surrounded by the French in New France, the Dutch in New Netherland, the Swedes in New Sweden and the Indians, and without a central power in England available to protect them, New England Puritans found that only by their acts could they protect themselves.

The problem of protecting themselves from other colonial powers and the Indians first arose for Massachusetts and other Puritan colonies during the 1630s. In that decade Charles I was too weak to defend the English coloneis in America. Even if he could have protected them, however, Massachusetts, as we saw earlier, by all means wanted to avoid English force that could suppress its non-conformism. Thus, already in the 1630s, first from New Haven in 1637, and then from Connecticut in 1638, came an initiative to establish a defensive confederation of all the Puritan colonies in New England. After much dealy, on May 29, 1643, four colonies signed and established the "United Colonies of New England." "No event of our early history," noted one historiarn, "is more significant than the confederation of the four colonies, Massachusetts, Plymouth, Connecticut and New Haven, a distinct foreshadowing of the great American Union."[57] The main condition for admission to this confederation, it should be stressed, was religious: the maintaining of congregationalism. Williams' Providence and other English platnations in New England were neither "received nor called into the confederation," Winthrop noted, "because they ran a different course from us both in their ministry and civil administration."[58]

According to the articles of the confederation, mutual protection was the ultimate cause for the United Colonies of New England, but events in England during the early 1640s certainly were also a contributory factor. "We all came into these parts of America with one and the same end and aim, namely, to advance the kingdom of our Lord Jesus Christ, and to enjoy the liberties of the gospel in purity and peace." Because the Puritan colonies were "encompassed with people of several nations and strange languages, which...may prove injurious to us or our posterity," and because "the sad distraction[s] in England" had deprived the colonists of any "comfortable fruits of protection" from England, the colonies had "to enter into present consociation amongst ourselves for mutual help and strength." Consequently, the four Puritan colonies, "jointly and severally" entered into "a firm and perpetual league of friendship and amity, for offence and defence." Each colony had kept its "peculiar jurisdiction and government," but as a Puritan league, the confederation was also intended to provide "mutual advice and succor upon all just occasions, both for preserving and propagating the truth and liberties of the gospel."[59] On both sides of the ocean, then, Puritans during the same year entered into united leagues; in England and Scotland with the Solemn League and Covenant, and in New England with the United Colonies. Revealingly, nowhere did the confederation's articles mention the saints' cause in England and Scotland.

From its beginnings, the confederation created considerable anxiety among the other English settlements in New England that had been excluded from it. Situated between the borders of the Puritan colonies, the English planters of Narragansett, many of whom had been victims of Massachusetts' persecutions, men like Roger Williams, Samuel Gorton, and William Coddington, feared that the united Puritan colonies would try to expand their jurisdiction over what was later called Rhode-Island. Their fears were not unjustified, for Parliament was at that time establishing Commissioners for Plantations, among whom were many friends of Massachusetts, including Lord Say and Sele, Sir Arthur Haselrig, Oliver Cromwell, and others, and had appointed Robert Earl of Warwick as "Governor-in-Chief and Lord High Admiral of all the Plantations in America." "Both Houses have passed an Ordinance," informed The True Informer, Parliament's newspaper, "whereby they doe constitute and ordain" the Earl of Warwick "Governour in chiefe, and Lord high Admirall of...Plantation," along with other "Commissioners," with power and authority "to provide for, order, and dispose all things" in the English colonies, though <u>Mercurius Aulicus</u>, the royalist newspaper, argued that the new Commissioners for Plantations had really been created to provide "a secure and convenient place, whither the members" of "the pretended House" might "speedily retreat" when their "plot tailes" in England.[60]

Within a year after the establishment of this commission, Warwick, in December 1643, granted the Narragansett country to Massachusetts. In these circumstances, and against the menace of the United Colonies, Roger Williams went to England in 1643 to try to secure a Parliamentary charter for his settlement in Providence. During his stay in England he published <u>The Bloody Tenent fo Persecution,</u> an attack on Massachusetts's proceedings against him during the 1630s, which may have had some influence upon his success in persuading Warwick to grant in 1644 "to the inhabitants of the towns of Providence, Portsmouth, and Newport...a free and absolute charter of incorporation," under the title of "Providence Plantation."[61] There was historical irony, indeed, in the fact that the creation of the United Colonies forced Williams to seek a charter from Parliament and thus caused English authorities to secure his settlements against the Puritan confederation in New England. This outcome was, of course, far from Massachusetts' intentions in accepting the offer to constitute the confederation. From now on Parliament would be part of the internal politics of the Puritans in the wilderness in many unanticipated ways.

V   Transfer of the Civil War to America

In 1644 both sides in the Civil War in England transferred their struggle to the colonies in America. The Parliamentary commissioners sent a commission to Virginai to "free" the people there "of all former taxation" and give "them liberty to choose their governor." At the same time, the King sent a countermand to Sir William Berkeley not to obey Parliament's order but "to maintain the Kings's authority." Virginia now, in Winthrop's eyes, was "like to rise in parties, some for the king, some for the Parliament."[62] To avoid such a gloomy development, Massachusetts now took occasion to proclaim an official stand on the Civil War. In May 1644 the General Court declared that

> whereas the civill warrs & dissention in our native country...cause devisions in many places of government in America, some professing themselves for the king, & others for the Parliament, not considering that the Parliament themselves professe that they stand for the king & Parliament against the malignant Papists & delinquents in all that kingdome, it is therefore ordered, that [any] person soever shall, by word, writing, or action, endeavor to disturbe our peace, directly or indirectly, by drawing a party, under pretence that he is for the King of England...against the Parliament, shalbe accounted as an offender of high nature against this common wealth.

This resolution, the court declared, did not apply to "any merchant, strangers, & shipmen that come hither meerly for matter of trade." The colony declared any open door for anyone from any part of England, even such as had been "against the Parliament," on the condition that while in the colony they refrained "from raising or nurishing any faction, mutiny, or sedition."[63]

Massachusetts' support of Parliament was followed immediately by a strict policy within the colony. When one Captain Jenyson, "an able man" and one of the founders of Watertown, "in private conference, questioned the lawfulness of the parliament's proceeding in England" agains the King, he was summoned to the court and examined concerning his opinions. He contended that he ws "assured that those of the parliament side were the more godly and honest part of the kingdom" in England. But at the same time he argued that "if he were in

287

England, he should [be] doubtful whether he might take their part against their prince." In other words, like Englishmen in England, Jenyson questioned the right of subjects to bear arms against their sovereign. But eventually, acocrding to Winthrop, Jenyson "ingenuously confessed his scruple" and admitted "he was now satisfied that the parliament's cause was good, and if he were in England he would assist in defence of it."[64]

The transfer of the Civil War to the colonies combined with Massachusetts' need to keep trade open obviously created many problems for Bay Puritans. As long as the war was far away, Massachusetts could easily declare its support of Parliament, but with the transfer of the struggle to the colonies beginning in 1644, Massachusetts found that its support of Parliament could hurt its interests. In July 1644, two ships arrived in the colony, a Parliamentary one from London and a royal one from Bristol. When the captain of the Parliamentary ship heard about the presence of the royalist ship, he sent an ultimatum to surrender or fight. Being a commerical ship, the captain of the Bristol ship yielded. But what in England at that time would have been a rightful act of war, in Massachusetts stimulated much confusion and debate. One merchant who had stock in the Bristol ship "began to gather a company and raise tumult" so that Winthrop, as deputy governor, had to ask the captain of the Parliamentary ship by what warrant he had seized the royalist ship. The captian showed Winthrop his commission from the Earl of Warwick, permitting him "to take all vessels in or outward bound from Bristol" and declaring it "lawful for all men" to seize these ships.[65]

Parliament's commission to seize Bristol ships raised the old and crucial issue of Massachusetts' relationship with England - that is, whether the colony should submit to English authority within its jurisdiction. "Some of the elders...exhorted the magistrates...to maintain the people's liberties, which were, they said, violated by this act" of seizure. They based their arguments upon the contention that a Parliamentary "commission could not supersede a patent," or the Massachusetts' charter. Consequently, they demanded that the master of the

288

Parliamentary ship restore the royalist ship to the captain. But his view, according to Winthrop, was confined to that minority among the elders and magistrates who refused to admit that Parliament had any authority in Massachusetts.[66]

Against this minority group, a majoirty of elders and magistrates argued that the colony could affirm the Earl of Warwick's commission within Massachusetts' jurisdiction and thus permit the captain to seize the royalist ship. Affirmation of the commission, they held, "could be no precedent to bar" the colony "from opposing any commission or other foreign power that might indeed tend to our hurt and violate our liberty." Another reason to affirm the commission was that, given the fact that "the king of England was enraged agasint" the colony along with "all the popish states in Europe," Parliament and Massachusetts both were necessarily involved on the same side in the same battle. Therefore, if the colonists now opposed Parliament, the colony "could have no protection or countenance from any" against the Popish party and would thus "lie open as a prey to all men."[67]

Still another reason for not rejecting Parliament's commission related to the colony's charter. "We might not deny the parliament's power in this case," the majority argued, without denying the "foundation of our government by our patent; for the parliament's authority will take place in all peculiar and privileged places, where the king's writs or commission will not be of force." The Crown had given Massachusetts its charter, and for reasons of expediency, according to this view, the colony should now admit the commission from parliament, which had assumed authority formerly belonging to the Crown. Yet this view did not imply that the colony was willing to let Parliament assert its authority within the colony or to interfere in its affairs. Thus far, according to the majority view, Parliament had showed that it wanted "to strengthen our liberties and not to overthrow them." But at the same time the colony made it clear that "if the parliament should hereafter be of a malignant spirit," it would "make use of salus populi to withstand any authority from" England aiming "to our hurt." Thus,

289

Massachusetts in the 1640s, as in the 1630s, still hoped to prevent the holy experience in the wilderness from being qualified or influenced by circumstances in England. It was still ready, as it had been in the 1630s, to resist English authority whenever a "malignant spirit" might endeavor to act against their unique religious experience in America.[68]

The Puritans' readiness to acknowledge Parliament's commission concerning the royalist ship was also attirbutable to the political consequences of the Civil War in the English colonies in America. For refusing to acquiesce to Parliament would encourage "those in Virgina and the West Indies to conform them in their rebellious course" against Parliament and would thereby "grieve all our godly friends in England, or any other of the parliament's friends." Consequently, Massachusetts decided to "suffer the captain" of the Parliamentary ship to "enjoy his prise." Obviously, the colonists had to come to a compromise between their denial of any authority outside Massachusetts to interfere in their affairs and their support of Parliament's cause in England. Yet, in order to keep their liberties, Bay Puritans constantly argued that "ours is perfecta respublica" and therefore "not subject to appeals, and consequently to no other power but among ourselves." At the same time, however, in order not to challenge Parliament's commission, they decided that "though our patent free us from appeals in case of judicature, yet not in point of state." If the colony had full liberty and authority by its charater to exercise the administration of justice within its jurisdiction, as a state or political corporation, it could consider directives from England such as Warwick's commission to seize royalist ships.[69]

Compromises, however, by their very nature, are made to avoid problems not to solve them, and the case of the Bristol ship was not over yet. Massachusetts merchants were naturally very angry to see their merchandise taken by the Parliamentary ship, and they contended for "a trial at law about it." This contention obviously raised a difficult dilemma for authorities in the colony, whether to comply with the merchants' interests or with Parliament's commission. The governor eventually persuaded the merchants "not to put" their case "to a jury" or "to use any force against the Parliament's authority."[70] But later in that summer of 1644, this compromise was put to a test, and the governor now showed that he was ready rather to meet the merchants' interests even if it meant armed confrontation with a Parliamentary ship.

Three months after the incident of the Bristol ship, a royalist ship from Dartmouth, England, came to Massachusetts. Two Parliamentary ships were then in Boston harbor. When they heard of the arrival of the royalist ship they went to seize it. At the same time, some Boston merchants demanded recompense for one of their ships that had been taken "by the king's party" in England. In this situation, the colony prohibited the captains of the Parliamentary ships from seizing the royalist ship, which they put under Massachusetts' "protection." When one of the Parliamentary captains ignored this order and indeed tried to seize the royalist ship, he was ordered to come ashore. When he again ignored the colony's order, "fire was given to a warning piece" from the the colony's the battery "which cut a rope in the head" of his ship, whereupon a sailor "ran down hastily to fire upon our battery," and battery returned the fire. Eventually, the colony seized the royalist ship, and "divers of the elders" pondered what to do with it. Finally, they decided to seize the ship as compensation "for our two ships which the king's party had taken from us." Thus did the Boston merchants get the right "to seize and use" the royalist ship.[71] As this case showed, notwithstanding its support of Parliament, Massachusetts was willing to oppose Parliament's commission to secure its own economic interests.

But the colonists soon learned that the policy of seizing ships in Massachusetts harbors worked rather to hurt the colony. In 1645, the seizure of another King's ship "occasioned much debate in the court," as many leaders argued that the colony's economic necessitites forced it to maintain free trade. As a result, the General Court drew up a bill "to give protection to all ships in our harbor, coming as friends." This proposed bill, some magistrates complained in alarm, "might put us upon a necessity of fight with some parliament ships, (which we were very unwilling to be engaged in), and so might weaken that

291

interest we had in the parliament."[72] Political obligation to Parliament seemed to clash with the need to protect the colony's economic interests. But the bill finally passed, and from that time on Parliamentary and royalist ships came to trade with the colony without further incidents.

VI "New England's Sence of Old Englands and Irelands Sorrowes"

In 1645 the churchs in the Puritan colonies in New England held "a day of generall Humiliation...in the behalf of Old Englands and Irelands Sad condition." On this occasion, the Rev. William Hooke again found it necessary to admonish against the separatist and isolationist tendencies among the members of his congregation in Taunton. In his sermon New Englands Sence of Old Englands and Irelands Sorrowes, Hooke addressed himself to the question, raised in his town, of "how are we concerened in the miseries of other men, so long as we are free?" "I say," preached Hooke, "it toucheth us." For the Protestant's cause in England and Ireland was a part of a cosmic struggle spoken of in Revelation, and New England had an indispensalbe part in this drama:

> There is at this time a great battle between Michael and the Dragon, and the Angels. The Beast and the Kings of earth, and their Armies have gathered themselves together to make war with the Lambe. All the Principalities, and Powers, and Rulers of the Darknesse of the World, and Spirituall wickednesses in High places are up in Armes this day, and there is scarce a Devill left in Hell.[73]

American Puritans were part of this apocalyptic battle. "I cannot but look upon the Churches in this Land this day, as upon so many severall Regiments, or bands of Souldiers lying in ambush here under the fearn and brushet of the Wilderness." Hooke did not advocate emigration back to England but, contending that at this moment "religion lies at stake, and therefore let us play the men," he demanded that New England Puritans show "the blood of Protestants." Furthermore, Hooke argued, because New England professed itself to be a society of covenanted churches, its duty was to ally itself with England and Scotland in the "Solemn League and Covenant." "What is a Politicke to a Religious Covenant?", asked Hooke, and he answered by arguing that a covenant obligation necessarily led to a political obligation. "The Lord will never have to say to England, or to us, If the Malignant party with their Cavaliers bee too strong for mee, then shall you help me; but we shall have need so to say to him." For

293

when godly people keep their covenant with God, "hee enters himselfe presently the generall of all their forces, leades their armies and fights their Battails." In this context, Hooke placed before his congregation the ultimate necessity of "a covenant of mutual assistance" between England and New England against their common enemy represented by "the malignant party with their Cavaliers."[74]

Hooke's sermon, which Parliament ordered printed in England, attempted to show that the Puritan presence in the wilderness should be seen in the context of the universal providential drama of salvation and redemption. Its specific occasion was a day of humiliation held in New England on behalf of England and Scotland, but circumstances in England in 1645 were again changing radically in ways that made Hooke's arguments of tenous character insofar as the Puritan experiment in New England was concerned. In June 1645 the Parliament's and King's armies clashed at Nasbey in one of the major and decisive battles of the Civil War. Parliament's army, in which the newly-formed New Model Army under the command of Fairfax and Cromwell had played a crucial role, defeated the King's army. Finally, after long years, Parliament had the advantage. One year later the King surrendered to the Scots' army, which turned him over to Parliament. The First Civil War was over, and Parliament, having defeated the king, was the sole authority and power in the kingdom.

VII   <u>Social and Political Agitation in Massachusetts</u>

Ever forced to redefine and reevaluate their relationship with England according to changing circumstances there, American Puritans once again had to adjust themselves to the profound change in England. Now, with the triumph of the Parliament in the First Civil War, on both sides of the ocean Puritans stood face to face with each other. As both sides discovered, there were many discordances between Puritan experience in old and New England. For events in England during the 1640s generated not only ecclesiastical change but social and political change as well. The struggle between the king and Parliament forced a redefinition of political obligations and reevaluation of political ends and aims as developments in England generated new theories concerning the nature and foundation of the English commonwealth. Far away, on the other side of the ocean, from their "refuge" and "shelter" in the wilderness, Bay Puritans looked on developments in England as a kind of Pandora's box. The struggle for religious reformation, they contended, gave rise to a host of plagues, including heresy and religious toleration. Yet the rise of Parliament and Puritanism in England gave hope to certain people in New England who, excluded from the churches and hence from political power, aspired to realize in the Puritan colonies the same liberties and rights now enjoyed by people in England. But because Massachusetts had always insisted that it had "an absolute government" within its jurisdiction, the only way to bring political and religious change to the colony was to appeal to Parliament to bring about those changes through its power and authority.[75]

By and large, then, the rise of Parliament and Puritanism to predominance in England during the 1640s rather complicated Massachusetts' relationship with England. During the 1640s, as in the past, the colony had the same old struggle with England, as it tried to keep its ecclesiastical and political independence in order to secure its unique holy experiment. But now, given the radical change of circumstances in England, the struggle was among the saints on both sides of

295

the ocean, and this would be no less bitter than had the colony's previous struggles with the crown.

Roger Williams was the first person who pointed out the way by which Parliament might secure the rights and liberties of the Englishmen in New England. When he returned to America in 1644 with his charter from the Earl of Warwick, the Massachusetts General Court ordered him to appear before it to answer "by what right you claime any such jurisdiction" over Providence. But Williams, secure now with his new charter, did not bother to appear and thus left Massachusetts to deal with his case directly with the English Parliament. Although authorities in Massachusetts directed the colony's commissioners in London to secure revocation of Williams' charter, they already knew that Parliament's decision was final. For Williams also brought with him a letter from the Commissioners for Plantations in which Parliament warned those Massachusetts Puritans who had been "exercised with the trials of a wilderness" to suffer Williams' Providence with "utmost endeavours" and "good affections."[76]

Williams lived outside Massachusetts, but what would happen to people within the colony who tried to follow his example by appealing to Parliament to secure their ecclesiastical and political rights in Massachusetts was soon revealed in two related cases. One involved William Vassal, an original assistant of the Massachusetts Bay colony whose name appeared on the royal charter of 1629. Living in 1646 in Scituate in Plymouth colony, Vassal petitioned the courts of Massachusetts and Plymouth to abolish "the distinctions which were maintained, both in civil and church estate." But, if that course "succeeded not," he warned in his petition, he intended to appeal "to the parliament...that we might be wholly governed by the laws of England." Thus, for the first time, a warning was issued to Massachusetts and Plymouth that unless the very foundations of the holy experience in the wilderness were changed, an appeal would be made to Parliament to regulate the ecclesiastical and political life of those colonies. In his petition to Parliament, already written but not yet sent, Vassal and others who "were not members of our churches" complained that, although they had been "freeborn subjects of England," they "were denied the liberty of subjects, both in church and commonwealth" in New England. Because only church members, or visible saints, could participate in Massachusetts government, Vassal and his followers charged that merely because "their consciences could not admit" them the "way of entrance" to the church and "church covenant" used in the colony, they had been "deprived of all power and interest in civil affairs and were subject to an arbitrary government and extra-judicial Proceeding."[77]

Vassal's petition gained many supporters in Plymouth and Massachusetts. In the same year, Dr. Robert Child, Samuel Maverick, and others, "in the name of themselves and many others in the country," presented a "petition to the same effect, much enlarged," to the court in Massachusetts. Their "Remonstrance and Petition" clearly shows the full implications of the Puritan reformation on social and political life in Massachusetts. The Remonstrance not only demanded a share in the colony's government, but also attacked the very roots of the Puritan theocracy in Massachusetts. The petitioners compalined that they could not discern in the "setled form of government" of Massachusetts that it had been established "according to the lawes of England." Seeing themselves as "freeborne subjects of the English nation," they advocated establishing in the colony "the fundamentall and wholesome lawes of our native country." Furthermore, Child and his followers claimed their rights to enjoy "civil liberty" in Massachusetts "as all freeborne enjoy in our native country." And viewing themselves "members of the church of England," they complained that in the colony they were "deteined from the seales of the covenant of free grace" because they could "not take these churches covenant," as was demanded in Massachusetts before one was admitted to a church. They pleaded, then, that along with civil liberty, the colony would give "liberty to the members of the Church of England" who until now had been excluded from the church in the colony's they demanded acceptance into the colony's "congregation" so that they too could enjoy the "liberties and ordinances" of Christ. Otherwise, they threatened to apply to

Parliament either to "provide able ministers for us" or, as a last resort, to "transport us to some other place."[78]

Confronted by the Child and Vassal petitions, Massachusetts in fact acceded to none of the petitioners' demands. To accept, on the one hand, the demand to abolish the close assocation between church and state, or, on the other hand, to acknowledge that Parliament had power to regulate the colony's affairs, meant sacrificing the very foundations of the holy experience in the wilderness. For in the roots of the Puritan theocracy in Massachusetts lay the essential correlation between the religious covenant and civil society. The two had not been identified as one by the Puritans, but their whole effort was to bring about the closest possible association between them. This was why one of the first laws the colony enacted was that only church members could participate in the colony's government. "That Form of Government in the Commonwealth which we plead for," declared John Davenport, "is that which the power of civil Administration is denied to unbelievers and committed to the Saints."[79] The covenant, thus, became not only the foundation of the churches in Massachusetts but also a necessary condition for any participation in the colony's government.

In practical terms, the demand to abolish the distinction between saints and non-saints and to nullify the condition that only church members could assume political office, as the Remonstrancers demanded, would permit ungoldy magistrates to rule over the saints. "The Danger of devolving" civil power "upon those that are not in Church," warned Davenport, was that it would disturb the peace of the church by placing power into the hands of those "worldly spirits" who "hate[d] the Saints and their communion...and being Satan instruments" were "resisting and fighting against Christ his Kingdome and Government in the Church."[80]

It had been exactly this "corruption" in England that the Puritans had tried to abolish in America, and they had emigrated to the wilderness convinced that only godly magistrates could maintain the true church. Godly ends required godly means, and thus the Puritans' expansion of the covenant into civil society

298

was intended to insure that only godly magistrates would rule the Christian commonwealth. In this context, obviously, any appeal to the Parliament to exercise its authority in the colony could lead to the same results; that is, ungodly magistrates in England would determine the affairs of the Puritan commonwealth in the wilderness.

In the past it has been argued that the Child Remonstrance was an attempt to establish Presbyterianism in Massachusetts at a time when congregationalists in the Bay colony were engaged in a struggle with Presbyterians in England concerning the issue of church government. Yet this argument is based on the assumption that Puritans on both sides of the ocean could not accommodate to each other's system of church government and that the struggle between Presbyterians and Congregationalists was, as one historian wrote, "a typical Reformation battle between absolutes; each claimed an exclusive divine authorization, and neither of them could see any possibility of tolerating the other."[81] However, according to Edward Winslow, who took an active part in the proceedings in Plymouth against Vassal and in Massachusetts against Child and his followers, this was not the main issue. In fact, Massachusetts was apparently willing to accept some sort of Presbyterianism. "I heard," wrote Winslow, that the Remonstancers "demand in Court the Presbyterian government, and [that] it was granted to them."[82] Presbyterians and Congregationalists could indeed accommodate each other in England and New England alike. The issue, then, with Child's petition, ran much deeper than the mere problem of church government. Indeed, the ultimate issue at stake was the essence of the Puritan theocracy as a whole and the covenant as the exclusive foundation for church and state. Child and his allies were attacking precisely what Massachusetts could not give up.

In "A Declaration of the General Court" held at Boston in 1646, the Court drew up a long and detailed answer to Child and his company. On the issue of civil liberty, the court compared many articles in the "Magna Charta" with the "Fundamentall" laws of Massachusetts in order to refute the charge that authorities governed the colony arbitrarily. But if it had not been hard to prove that in most cases the colony's laws differed little from those of England, the governance of the churches caused serious difficulties when compared with that of the Church of England. On "the church doore" all the differences became clear between the New England's way and England's. On the church issue, the court could not but admit that "many persons in the country are not admitted to the seals," but naturally blamed it on the evil consciences of those people and their lack of genuine religious conversion. "Those who are not church members," the court argued in its declaration, were "fraudulous in their conversation" as well as "notoriously corrupt in their opinions," or "grosly ignorant in the principles of religion." The churchs in Massachusetts, the court's declaration continued, "may not receive man blindfould" or such as "refuse to give account of their faith."[83]

In England men were born to the parish church, but in Massachusetts one had to first prove his conversion before the congregation, which then decided on his admission to covenant and church. In other words, in England a man's faith was a matter between him and the Lord, but in the Puritan colony the congregation stood in the middle, deciding if a man's faith justified his admission to the sacraments. Because the church was covenanted, the congregation had to have a role in one's admission to it. Thus, when the petitioners had urged abolition of the covenant as a necessary condition for memebership in the church, contrary to the custom in England, the court made it plain that the objection to the covenant was evidence of "something in their owne hearts, which they seeke to cover" and admonished the Remonstrancers for attacking the covenant in the colony.[84]

Furthermore, against the Remonstrancers' attacks on the covenant, the General Court in Massachusetts explained that Parliaments' actions were based too upon a covenant, namely the Solemn League and Covenant "lately imposed by the honourable houses of parliament" in 1643 in England. Thus, on both sides of the ocean "Covenant Politicks," to use Willaim Hooke's term, caused an overt discrepancy between the communion of saints and the terms of English nationality. In England, the Solemn League and Covenant was not only a political agreement but also a religious covenant "against the enemies of God" and an "encouragement to the Christian Churches groaning under or in danger of the yoke of Antichristian tyranny." Satan's presence had been within England, and so the whole nation was devided between Satan's people and God's people. Likewise in Massachusetts, declared the Remonstrancers, we "are not accounted so much as brethren" in the Puritan colony not being members of the churches there. "We account all our countrymen brethren by nation," replied the court in its answer, trying to answer the complaints that in Massachusetts religious principles divided Englishmen. However, when the petitioners compalined that they were "not publickly so called (especially in church assemblies)" brethren in the colony, the court had to admit that "for distinction shake" Massachusetts indeed "putt [a] difference between those that doe communicate together at the Lords table, and those who doe not."[85] Covenant politics, then, put sainthood over nationality, and the latter was indeed secondary to the communion of the saints. Here again were revealed the deeply religious premises the Puritans had carried with them into the wilderness.

By and large, then, acceptance of the Remonstrancers' complaints meant giving up the essential foundations of the Puritan holy experiment in Massachusetts. However, as long as the controversy stayed within the colony, the General Court could put its authors to trial and imprison them, as was indeed done eventually. Still, there was the problem of Child's intended appeal to Parliament. "Dr. Child prepares now in all haste to go to England," wrote Winthrop, in order to present a petition "to the parliament."[86] A confrontation with Parliament about the colony's liberties and rights was the last thing the colony wanted. Thus, in his Boston church, John Cotton warned his congregation that "if there be many amongst you my brethren, as 'tis reported there are, that have a petition to the high court of Parliament...let such know, the Lord will never suffer them to prosper in their subtile, malicious and desperate undertaking

301

against his people, who are as tender unto him as the apple of his eye." The colony's history, preached Cotton, provided evidence that any attempt against Massachusetts was doomed to fail. The Lord "brought his people hither, and preserved them from the rage of persecution," and He made Massachusetts "a hiding place for them." In the past, God had protected the colony from "forraigne plots of the late archbishop" William Laud. Now, Cotton promised, "there was no question to be made but Hee would preserve" the colony again "from the underminings of false brethren, and such as joyned with them."[87]

But Child was determined to appeal to England, and although the colony made every effort to stop him, he finally succeeded in smuggling to England the documents relating to his case. His brother in England, Major John Child, published them in 1647 in New Englands Jonas Cast Up at London, or, A Relation of the Proceedings of the Court at Boston in New England Against Divers and Godly Persons, for Petitioning for Government...According to the Lawes of England, and for Admittance of Themselves and Children to the Sacraments in Their Churches. This book recorded all the complaints Child and his followers had made the previous year, but added one more argument against Bay Puritans" namely, that they were Separatists. Pulpits in Massachusetts, wrote Child's brother, contained many "despitfull passages...against the Church of England...calling England Egypt and Babylon." With the controversy having been transferred to England, Massachusetts' agent there, Edward Winslow, attempted to refute Child's accusations in New Englands Salamander, Discovered by an Irreligious and Scornfull Pamphlet, called New England Joans Cast Up at London. Apologetically, Winslow admitted that not all Massachusetts laws were made in accordance with those of England, but they were at least, he argued, "as neere the Law of England as our condition will permit." On the other hand, Winslow declared that any intervention of Parliament in the colony's affairs would be "destructive to them that there live."[88]

VIII Massachusetts and the Long Parliament

The books of Child and Winslow brought an internal controversy of Massachusetts to public attention in England. Yet this was only a war of words that fell far short of what Child had really wanted or expected - to bring about political and religious changes in the colony. Child's failure brought to an end any serious attempt to generate a change from within Massachusetts. But in 1646 an act of Parliament not associated with Child's activities caused an alarm in Massachusetts and forced the Puritans to reassess their relationship with England. If Child had failed from within Massachusetts, there had always existed the posibility that Parliament, in order to satisfy the intersts of other English plantations in New England, would order Massachusetts to obey its authority. Such was the case with Parliament's patent to Samuel Gorton in 1646.

Gorton's religious radicalism had caused him to be driven out of the Bay colony in early 1640. Unable to live with the Antinomians and Williams' plantations in Rhode Island, he and his followers founded Shawomet. Like Williams before him, Gorton learned that the only way to save his plantation from Massachusetts and the United Colonies was to procure a charter from Parliament. Thus, he went to England where he secured a patent. In September 1646, Randell Holden, Gorton's close friend, landed in Massachusetts and presented Gorton's charter to Bay magistrates. What alarmed Massachusetts was that along with the charter Holden brought a letter from the Commissioners for Plantations ordering "the governor and assistants of...Massachusetts Bay" not only to acknowledge Gorton's jurisdiction in his plantation but also "to permit and suffer the said Samuel Gorton" with his company "to land at any port in New England...and from thence to pass, without any lets or molestation" within Massachusetts' "jurisdiction, to the said tract of land called Narrangansett." Again the whole framework of Massachusetts' relationship with England appeared to be shaken, for now for the first time Parliament was interfering with the internal politics of the colony. Some elders were so angry about the whole incident that they wanted to imprison Holden without delay, "but the great part, both of magistrates and elders, thought it better to give so much respect to the protection which the parliament had given" to Holden and "to suffer him pass quietly away."[89] For a moment then, the colony's resolution showed an attempt to obey Parliament's request, but the storm raised by this case over the colony's relationship with England soon appeared.

As was the case with that of Williams, Gorton's charter indicated that Parliament intended to protect those who had been persecuted by Massachusetts. Furthermore, Gorton's trip to England, as with that of Williams before him, was not only to procure a patent but also to conduct a crusade against Massachusetts by denouncing the colony's ecclesiastical and political ways. Thus Gorton published in 1646 in England his long and detailed description of the New England Way in <u>Simplicities Defence Against Seven Headed Policy</u>. Taking his title from Revelation 13:1, in which the Beast rose up out of the sea with seven heads, Gorton identified the "seven-headed church-government united in New England" with the Beast, or Satan, who fought with God's people.

> This story's strange, but altogether true: Old England Saints are banished out of New: Oh Monstrous Art, and cunning of the Devill, What hidden paths he goes, to spread his evil?[90]

Thus wrote one R.B. in his epistle to the reader in Gorton's book, and Gorton tried to convey this meaning to all who read his book. For according to his millennial expectations, Massachusetts' persecutions were a clear and irrefutable proof that the colony was aiding Satan's war against the saints.

The importance of Gorton's book lies in his attempt to unveil the close association between church and state in Massachusetts. "We know that the spirituality of your Churches, is the civility of your Commonwealth, and the civility of your Commonwealth is the spirituality of your Churches," he charged. This association, according to Gorton, was the root of the "seven-headed policy" of the Beast, or Massachusetts, and the colony's persecutions were evidence enough that Bay Puritans fought alongside Satan's camp against Christ and his soliders. By this way of reasoning, Gorton could argue that the Puritan exile into the wilderness had truned them into agents of the Beast instead of bringing about the Kingdom of God. "You know not," he denounced Massachusetts Puritans, "with all your libraries, [how to] give the interpretation" to God's word because "you have lost it in the wilderness." The Puritan exile thus became an aimless wandering in the wilderness during which the Puritans had turned their hearts from God to Satan. Thus, although for all saints the Lord's day was a time of joy, for Massachusetts "the day of the Lord" was "a day of darknesse and gloominesse."[91] Massachusetts, Gorton charged, had fallen in the wilderness into Satan's trap; its "errand" to raise the Kingdom of God had failed because the Puritans had turned to Satan and with him had begun to persecute God's people.

Gorton's controversy with Massachusetts on the colony's place in providential history became dangerous when Parliament's charter to Gorton showed, as had Williams' charter earlier, that Parliament was ready to protect certain "saints" in the wilderness against Massachusetts' Puritans. Although Edward Winslow went to England in 1646 in an attempt to secure revocation of Gorton's charter, and though he published there the colony's answer to Gorton, Hypocrisie Unmasked, Warwick and the Commissioners for Plantations did not revoke Gorton's charter.[92] Williams' charter of 1644 could be interpreted as a singular event but Gorton's charter revealed a consistent Parliamentary policy towards those banished by Massachusetts.

This policy was particularly threatening, in the eyes of Massachusetts Puritans, because the colony and Parliament had already been at odds on ecclesiastical policy. Thus Winthrop had to acknowledge that Gorton's patent signified Parliament's dissatisfaction with Massachusetts' ecclesiastical policy. "Gorton and two others of his company," wrote Winthrop, had been "favored by some of the commissioners" for Plantations "for private respects, and partly for their adhering to some of" Gorton's company's "corrupt tenets, and generally out of" the Commissioners' "dislike of us for our late law of banishing anabaptists." Gorton's charter, then, was evidence also that Parliament was angry with

305

Massachusetts' "rigorous proceeding" in ecclesiastical matters.[93] Thus, in the middle of the 1640s, Massachusetts' policies stood in contrast to those of Parliament, or at least to those of Parliament's Commissioners for Plantations. The contest between Puritans on the two sides of the ocean intensified strains and tensions between England and New England.

The reaction of Massachusetts to Gorton's charter should be understood in these terms. Parliament, as shown earlier, gave Gorton a charter, demanded that Massachusetts acknowledge it, and ordered the colony to give him free passage within its jurisdiction. This last demand raised a strom in Massachusetts, because for the first time the colony had to obey an order relating to its internal jurisdiction. In November 1646 the Massachusetts General Court began a long and profound self-searching debate on the colony's relationship with England. "It was propounded to consideration," reported Winthrop, "in what relation we stood to the state of England; whether our government was founded upon our charter, or not; if so, then what subjection we owed to that state." The magistrates and elders agreed that "the charter was the foundation of our government," wrote Winthrop, but they differed on the issue of whether the charter implied that the colony was "subordinate to the parliament" so that the Parliament "might countermand our orders and judgments."[94] The whole Puritan enterprise in the wilderness was now at stake and depended on the answer to this issue.

In the mid-1640s, then, Massachusetts had to face again the same issue about which it had fought with the Crown during the 1630s. The difference was that Massachusetts now had to deal not with the Crown but with the saints in England. During the 1630s Massachusetts was united in its defiance against the Crown's attempt to interfere in the colony's affairs, but how the saints' rule in England had divided Massachusetts Puritans over what the colony's relationship to England was and should be. Thus, some thought that the colony's charter made it "subordinate to the parliament" which "might countermand" the colony's authority and power within its jurisdiction. People of this persuasion not

306

surprisingly advised Massachusetts to "petition the parliament for enlargement" of the colony's powers and liberties. In other words, they adovcated seeking a redefinition of the colony's relationship with England through a new charter from Parliament to replace the old one given by the King.[95]

Against this approach, others believed that the charter gave the colony "absolute power of government" within its bounds "to make laws, to erect all sort of magistracy, to correct, punish, pardon, govern, and rule the people absolutely." This was indeed the traditional stand taken by Massachusetts from its beginnigns. On the basis of this stand, the colony up to that moment had denied the English any authority to interfere with the Puritan commonwealth in America. The definition of the word "absolute," then, is crucial to an understanding of Massachusetts' traditional attitude toward England. The word "absolute," according to those who held the traditional view, implied "a perfection of parts, so as we are thereby furnished with all parts of government" and "self sufficiency" - that the colony "should not need the help of any superior power...to complete our government." The colony, argued adherents of this view, "owed allegiance and subjection" to Parliament, but these related only to "the tenure of our land," to "protection," and to "advice and counsel, when in great occasions we should crave it." According to this view, then, allegiance and subjection to England did not conflict with the colony's claim of absolute government within its jurisdiction. Thus, Puritans could claim that, thought they owed subjection to England, "yet we might be still independent in respect of government." In the 1640s, then, as in the 1630s, Massachusetts repeatedly argued its right for the absolute independence of the colony's government. This interpretation, however, did not accord with the Crown's intentions in its original charter in 1629, in which it stated time and again that the Bay company's "laws and ordinances" should not be "contrary or repugnant to the laws and statutes of this our realm of England."[96]

In 1646, then, there were two views in Massachusetts concerning the foundation of the colony's relationship with England. The traditional view claimed that the colony had an absolute, independent and self-sufficient government within its jurisdiction. A competing view advocated reestablishing the colony's relationship with England on the basis of a new charter. In view of present circumstances in England, the arguments against seeking a new charter were grave ones. First, there was the issue of legitmacy, of whether Parliament could grant a charter without the Crown's royal assent. Furthermore, because of the colony's struggle with the Crown during the 1630s and the King's "displeasure" against Massachusetts, it was indeed doubtful whether the King would "give his royal assent" to any new charter for the colony. On the other hand, many feared that a charter from Parliament alone would prove even less satisfactory than the royal charer of 1629 because Parliament's charters "reserved a supreme power in all things."[97]

Not surprisingly, then, the argument that Massachusetts should seek a new charter from England lost out in the end, and Bay Puritans had to face the issue of Warwick's order concerning Gorton head-on, namely, the issue of "whether...we should acknowledge all that power they claime in our jurisdiction." First referrring the question to the elders, the court asked them for advice "concerning the question of our dependence upon" England. In their answer, the elders declared that in certain things the colony was indeed dependent upon England because

> 1. We have recieved the power of our government and other privileges derived from thence by our chater. 2. We owe allegiance and fidelity to that state. 3. Erecting such a government as the patent prescribes and subjecting ourselves to the laws here ordained by that government, we therein yield subjection to the state of England. 4. We owe unto that state the fifth part of gold... 5. We depend upon the state of England for protection and immunities of Englishmen.[98]

However, these instances of dependence, the elders argued, did not infringe upon the colony's absolute government within its jurisdiction. For "in point of government," they declared, the charter had granted to Massachusetts "full and ample power of choosing all officers that shall command and rule over us, of making all laws and rules of our obedience," as well as "a full and final

308

determination of all cases in the administration of justice," without "appeals or other ways of interrupting our proceedings" by authority outside the colony. On these terms, the elders advised that the colony could "give the Earl of Warwick" and the Commissioners for Plantation "such titles as the parliament hath given them" without accepting any subjection "to them in point of our government." The elders, clearly then, advised continuance of the traditional approach of acknowledging no interference within Massachusetts' jurisdiction by any outside authority. The elders knew, on the other hand, that this stand could lead to overt confrontation with England and Parliament, but they argued that "if the parliament should be less inclinable" to accept the colony's terms of its subjection to England, Massachusetts had to "wait upon providence for the preservation" of its "just liberties." Accordingly, they had advised calling the churches in the colony "to a solemn seeking of the Lord for the upholding of our state."[99]

So deep was the crisis concerning Warwick's order that many in Massachusetts recommended as a last resort to send John Winthrop to England in an attempt to save the colony's liberties and to establish again a good relationship with the Long Parliament. Although he had only three more years to live, the great leader of the Puritan emigration was willing now, as he had always been, to engage himself in the mission in order to rescue the Puritan commonwealth in Massachusetts. For Winthrop, as for many others in the colony, acknowledgment of Warwick's order would mean an end to his lifelong enterprise - the establishment of a Christian commonwealth in the wilderness. After all, Parliament had already shown that it intended to protect Williams, Gorton, and others in New England, and once Massachusetts acknowledged Parliament's authority within its jurisdiction, it could then be ordered to tolerate anabaptists or other heretical sects in the colony. From Massachusetts' point of view, then, its insistence upon having "absolute government" within its jurisdiction was uncompromising. Eventually Winthrop did not go to England, but his readiness to take upon himself such a task shows how seriously Bay Puritans viewed the danger to their experience.[100]

However, the legal, constitutional, and political controversies between Massachusetts and England during the 1640s were only part of the whole issue of the colony's relationship with England. Actually, little evidence exists to show how Puritans felt about England because Bay Puritans had always been cautious not to reveal in England the full implications of their holy experience in America. Yet there is some evidence to show that they were much more radical than they wanted people in England to know. When Child was put to trial in the winter of 1646, the court replied to his accusation that the government in Massachusetts was arbitrary in plain words: as "for the laws of England," Massachusetts, by its charter, was "not bound to them." Furthermore, when Child charged that the colony's laws were incompatible with its charter, the General Court replied that

> our allegiance binds us not to the laws of England any longer than while we live in England, for the laws of the parliament of England reach no further, nor do the kings' writs under the great seal go any further.[101]

This would be a revolutionary argument in the eighteenth century during the public debates in the colonies concerning their relationship to England. It was no less revolutionary in 1646, although it was heard only in Massachusetts and never declared in public by the colony. The fact that this revolutionary argument only came up in 1646 should not mislead us. "We claime" argued the Puritans, that "our government granted to us" by the charter was not a "commission, but a...free donation of absolute government." Moreover, they argued that though plantations were indeed "bodies corporate" they were "also above the rank of an ordinary corporation."[102]

Among the Romans, Greeks, and other nations, Winthrop wrote, colonies had "been esteemed other than towns, yea than many cities, for they have been the foundation of great commonwealth." This was the main thrust behind the Puritan emigration, to erect a great Christian commonwealth. In this context, the Puritans had always claimed that their colonial enterprise differed radically from

310

other English colonies of the time. "Other plantations have been undertaken at the charge of others in England, and the planters have their dependence upon the companies there, and those planters go and come chiefly for matter of profit," wrote Winthrop, "but we came to abide here, and to plant the gospel, and people in the country, and herein God hath marvellously blessed us."[103]

During the 1640s, as during the 1630s, the Puritans in the wilderness persistently opposed any attempt on the part of any English authority to force Massachusetts to conform to political and ecclesiastical policies in England, and the colony defied any attempt from England to interfere within its jurisdiction. At the same time, Massachusetts declined to accept invitiations from England which called the saints in the wilderness to come and assist in the English reformation. The pursuit of religious reformation, which initiated the whole Puritan migration, required some sort of political independence from any English authority. However, in the 1640s, Massachusetts faced in England not a hostile ruler, as had been the Crown during the 1630s, but rather the Puritan saints. Yet this encounter raised even more complexities in Massachusetts' relationship with England. For in England, because of its special circumsntaces, religious reformation led to radical social, political, and ecclesiastical developments, while in Massachusetts the pursuit of religious reformation led to the persecution of any view that stood in contrast to the premises of the covenant society. Consequently, any effort to realize in Massachusetts the same liberties and rights the Long Parliament had secured in England was sharply resisted by Massachusetts Puritans.

Yet in spite of the many differences between old and New England during the 1640s, Puritans on both sides of the ocean still had much in common. This was nowhere more clearly revealed than on the issue of order and authority or in the fight against heresy and toleration that Puritans on both sides of the ocean were engaged in during this decade. For, although Puritans in England and New England differed much on the issue of church government, orthodox Puritans on both sides of the Atlantic, as we will see in the following chapter, insisted that not only religious society but also civil society should be based upon covenant with God. They thereby acknowledged the decisive role of the state or the godly magistrate in religious matters, a role sectarians rejected strongly. In this fight for order and authority against heresy and the sects, Massachusetts Puritans formed a common front with the Puritans in England during the 1640s.

Notes

1. Anne Dudley Bradstreet, A Dialogue Between Old England and New Concerning Their Present Troubles, Anno 1642, in Old South Leaflets, pp. 159, 4 (172).

2. William Hooke, New Englands Teares for Old Englands Fears (London, 1641), p. 23. Hooke preached this sermon in New England in that year, and afterwards the Commons ordered to publish it in England.

3. Winthrop, History, II, p. 30.

4. John Cotton, An Exposition upon the Thirteenth Chapter of Revelation (London, 1656), p. 20.

5. Massachusetts General Court's reply to Robert Child's demands to rule the colony according to England's laws, given in his trial in 1646, in Winthrop, History, II, p. 35.

6. William Hooke, New Englands Sence of Old Englands and Irelands Sorrows (London, 1645), in The History of Taunton, by Samuel H. Emergy (Boston, 1853), I, p. 125.

7. William Laud, "The Diary of the Life of Archbishop Laud," in Works, III, p. 230.

8. Robert Baillie, Letters and Journals of Robert Baillie, ed. David Laing (Edinburgh, 1841), I, p. 23. On the need to expand the conceptual framework of "British History" and to include in the context of this title other "British" realms and culture, see J.G.A. Pocock, "The Limits and Division of British History: In Search of the Unknown Subject," AHR, 87 (1982).

9. Thomas Goodwin, A Glimpse of Sions Glory, or the Churches Beautie Specified (London, 1641), pp. 1, 2, 7. On the issue of the authorship of this sermon, see: Tai Liu, Discord in Zion: The Puritan Divines and the Puritan Revolution 1640-1660 (The Hague, 1973), p. 2; Peter Toon, Puritans, The Millennium and the Future of Israel, pp. 131-136; and John F. Wilson, "A Glimpse of Syons Glory," Church History, 31 (1962), pp. 66-73.

10. Winthrop, History, II, p. 25.

11. "John Tinker to John Winthrop" (Feb. 1639/40), in Winthrop Papers, IV, p. 205. On the economic recession and crisis in Massachusetts caused by the events in England during the 1640s, see: William B. Weeden, Economic and Social History of New England, 1620-1789 (Boston, 1890); Bernard Bailyn, The New England Merchants in the Seventeenth Century (New York, 1964); Richard S. Dunn, Puritans and Yankees, and Robert E. Wall, Jr., Massachusetts Bay: The Crucial Decade, 1640-1650 (New Haven, Conn., 1972).

12. William Hooke, New Englands Tears for Old Englands Feares (London, 1641).

13. Ibid., pp. 6-7, 9.

14. Ibid., pp. 6-7, 9.

15. Ibid., pp. 11, 14, 15. Hooke used Mark 3:25 - "And if a house be divided against itself, that house cannot stand."

16. Ibid., pp. 15, 17, 20, 22.

17. Ibid., pp. 16, 23.

18. Ibid., p. 23.

19. Rump, or an Exact Collection of the Choycest Poems and Songs Relating to Late Times...Anno 1639 to Anno 1661 (London, 1662), p. 95.

20. Winthrop, History, II, pp. 11, 37, 25. On the emigration from New England back to England, see: William L. Sachse, "The Migration of New Englanders to England, 1640-1660," AHR, 53 (1948), pp. 251-78, and "Harvard Men in England, 1642-1714," CSM, Publications 35 (1951), pp. 119-144.

21. Winthrop, History, II, pp. 35, 30. On the connections between Parliamentary leaders and the Puritan migration, see: Hexter, The Reign of King Pym.

22. Ibid., II, p. 30.

23. Ibid., II, pp. 30-31.

24. "John Endecott to John Winthrop" (Feb. 1640/41), Winthrop Papers, IV, pp. 314-315. 25. "John Endecott to John Winthrop," pp. 314-315; Winthrop, History, II, p. 31. Humfrey was already appointed at that time by Lord Say and Sele to be the governor of Providence. See: CSPC, I, p. 317.

26. MA. Records, II, p. 332; Winthrop, History II, pp. 37-38.

27. Winthrop, History, II, p. 50.

28. "The Root and Branch Petition" (Dec. 11, 1640), in The Constitutional Documents of the Puritan Revolution, 1625-1660, ed. S.R. Gardiner (Oxford, 1906), pp. 136-144; "The Triennial Act" (Feb. 15, 1641), in Gardiner, Constitutional Documents, pp. 144-155; "The Protestation" (May 3, 1641), in Gardiner, Constitutional Documents, pp. 155-156; "Bill on Church Reform" (July 3, 1641), in Gardiner, Constitutional Documents, pp. 167-176; "Resolutions of the House of commons on Ecclesiastical Innovations" (Sept. 1, 1641), in Gardiner, Constitutional Documents, pp. 197-198; "The Grand Remonstrance, with the Petition Accompanied It" (Dec. 1, 1641), in Gardiner, Constitutional Documents, p. 215.

29. Winthrop, History, II, p. 50.

30. The Commons' order of March 1642 appears in History, by Hutchinson, I, pp. 99-100.

31. Lord Say and Sele, "A Speech of the Right Honorable the Lord Viscount Say and Seale...in Parliament" (Feb. 1641/42), in Thomason Tracts, 259 E 200 (35), p. 5.

32. William Laud, "The Answer of...William Lord Archbishop of Canterbury to the Speech of the Lord Say and Seal, Touching the Liturgy," in Works, V, pt. 1, pp. 129, 141; Laud, Works, IV, pp. 21, 66-67, 291.

33. Lamont, Godly Rule, p. 78; C.V. Wedgwood, The King's Peace, 1637-1641 (London: Collins, 1955), p. 454; William Haller, Tracts on Liberty in the Puritan Revolution (New York, 1934), I, p. 1.

34. "The Grand Remonstrance," p. 229.

35. The invitation to the New England ministers appears in History, by Hutchinson, I, pp. 100-101.

36. Winthrop, History, II, p. 92; Hexter, The Reign or King Pym, pp. 160-164, 98n.

37. Winthrop, History, II, p. 92.

38. Ibid., II, p. 38; Sargent Bush, The Writings of Thomas Hooker, p. 97.

39. John Cotton, cited in The Career of John Cotton, by Ziff, p. 174. See also Ziff for the date of Cotton's sermons and their publication in England, pp. 261-268. John Cotton, An Exposition Upon the Thirteenth Chapter of the Revelation (London, 1656); John Cotton, The Powring Out of the Seven Vials, or an Exposition of the 16. Chapter of the Revelation, with an Application of it to Our Times (London, 1642).

40. Cotton, An Exposition Upon the Thirteenth Chapter of the Revelation, pp. 8, 9, 13, 17.

41. Ibid., pp. 90, 18, 20.

42. Ibid., p. 93.

43. Cotton, The Powring out of the Seven Vials, p. 16.

44. Cotton, An Exposition upon the Thirteenth Chapter of the Revelation, p. 241.

45. Perry Miller, Errand Into the Wilderness, p. 11.

46. "The Militia Ordinance" (March, 1642), in Gardiner, Constitutional Documents, p. 246; "The Nineteenth Proposition Sent by the Two Houses of Parliament to the King at York," in Gardiner, Constitutional Documents, pp. 249-254; Godfrey Davis, The Early Stuarts, 1603-1660 (Oxford, 1976).

47. Winthrop, History, II, pp. 103-104; Hubbard, General History of New England, p. 377; "Lord Say and Sele to John Winthrop" (1640), in Winthrop Papers, IV, pp. 263-267.

48. Winthrop, History, II, 104-105.

49. Ibid., pp. 104-105.

50. R.H. Tawney, Religion and the Rise of Capitalism, p. 277.

51. Sachse, "The Migration of New Englanders to England," pp. 260-261, 264, 275.

52. Winthrop, History, II, p. 118.

53. Mercurius Britanicus, in Thomas on Tracts, 232 E21 (8), pp. 476-477.

54. Winthrop, History, II, pp. 119, 121.

55. A Preter-Pluperfect, in Thomason Tracts, 239-E65 (1), pp. 12-16.

56. "The Solemn League and Covenant" (taken by the House of Commons in Sept. 25, 1643), in Gardiner, Constitutional Documents, p. 268.

57. James Kendall Hosmer, ed., Winthrop Journal, II, p. 99.

58. Winthrop, History, II, p. 121.

59. Winthrop, History, II, pp. 121-122.

60. CSPC, I, pp. 324-324; The True Informer, in Thomason Tracts, 240 E 75 (28), pp. 633-634; CSPC, I, p. 325.

61. Winthrop, History, II, p. 236.

62. Winthrop, History, II, pp. 191-192.

63. MA. Records, II, p. 69.

64. Winthrop, History, II, pp. 215-216.

65. Winthrop, History, II, pp. 222-223. Warwick's commission appears on page 223.

66. Ibid., II, p. 223.

67. Ibid., II, pp. 223-225.

68. Ibid., II, pp. 224-225.

69. Ibid., II, pp. 224-225.

70. Ibid., II, pp. 228-229.

71. Ibid., II, pp. 235-236, 238-239, 240.

72. Ibid., II, pp. 302-303.

73. William Hooke, New Englands Sence of Old Englands and Irelands Sorrowes (London, 1645), in The History of Taunton, by Samuel Hopkins, pp. 123, 125, 116, 117, 113-114.

74. Ibid., pp. 117, 113-114.

75. On the ideological and political developments in England during the 1640s and 1650s, see: William Haller, Liberty and Reformation on the Puritan Revolution (New York, 1955); Perez Zagorin, History of Political Thought in the English Revolution (London, 1965); J.W. Allen, English Political Though, 1603-1644 (London, 1938); Charles Webster, ed., The Intellectual Revolution of the Seventeenth Century (London, 1974); Christopher Hill, Intellectual Origins of the English Revolution (Oxford, 1965); Hill, Some Intellectual Consequences of the English Revolution (Madison, 1980); C.B. MacPherson, The Political Theory of Possessive Individualism: Hobbes to Lock (Oxford, 1962); John M. Wallace, Destiny His Choice: The Loyalism of Andrew Marvelle (London, 1968); J.G.A. Pocock, The Ancient Constitution and the Feudal Law (New York, 1967); Pocock, The Machiavellian Moment (Princeton, 1975); Pocock, ed., Three British Revolution, 1641, 1688, 1776 (Princeton, 1980). See also the series of articles by Quentin Skinner: "History and Ideology in the English Revolution," The Historical Journal. VII (1965); "Hobbes' Leviathan," The Historical Journal, VII (1964); "The Ideological Context of Hobbes' Political Thought," The Historical Journal IX (1966); "Conquest and Consent: Thomas Hobbes and the Engagement Controversy," in The Interregnum, ed. G.E. Aylmer.

76. MA. Records, III, pp. 48-49; Winthrop, History, II, 236-238.

77. Winthrop, History, II, pp. 319-320. A detailed discussion of Vassall's petition and its influence on Massachusetts can be found in Robert E. Wall, Massachusetts Bay: The Crucial Decade, 1640-1650 (New Haven, 1972).

78. Winthrop, History, II, pp. 319-321; Robert Child, et al., "A Remonstrance and Petition of Robert Child," in Collection, comp. Hutchinson, I, pp. 216-217, 221. See also George L. Kittredge, "Dr. Robert Child the Remonstrant," CSM, Publications, 21 (1920), pp. 1-146, and Philip E. Gura's excellent study A Glimpse of Sion's Glory.

79. John Davenport, A Discourse about Civil Government in a New Plantation whose design is religion, pp. 20, 23.

80. Ibid., pp. 20, 23.

81. Perry Miller, Orthodoxy in Massachusetts, pp. 268, 277.

82. Edward Winslow, New Englands Salamander (London, 1647), in MHSC, Ser. 3, II (1830), p. 112.

83. "A Declaration of the General Court Holden at Boston 4 (9) 1646, concerning a Remonstrance and Petition...by Doctor Child," in Collection, comp. Hutchinson, I, pp. 223, 241-242.

84. "A Declaration of the General Court...concerning a Remonstrance and Petition...by Doctor Child," p. 243.

85. Ibid., p. 243; "The Solemn League and Covenant" (1643), in Gardiner, Constitutional Documents, pp. 268, 271; "A Declaration of the General Court...concerning a Remonstrance and Petition...by Doctor Child," p. 245.

86. Winthrop, History, II, p. 356.

87. John Cotton, cited in New Englands Salamander, by Winslow, pp. 128-129.

88. Major John Child, New Englands Jonas Cast Up at London (London, 1647), in Tracts and Other Papers Relating Principally to the Origin, Settlement, and Progress of the Colonies in North America, ed. Peter Force, IV (1846), pp. 4, 23; Winslow, New Englands Salamander, pp. 110, 121, 123.

89. Winthrop, History, II, pp. 333-334. On Samuel Gorton, see: Philip F. Gura, "The Radical Ideology of Samuel Gorton: New Light on the Relation of English to American Puritanism," WMQ 36 (1979), and A Glimpse of Sion's Glory.

90. Samuel Gorton, Simplicities Defence Against Seven-Headed Policy (London, 1646), in Tracts and Other Papers, ed. Peter Force, IV, pp. 25, 29-30.

91. Ibid., pp. 25, 29-30.

92. Edward Winslow, Hypocrisie Unmasked (London, 1646). 93. Winthrop, History, II, pp. 332, 212.

94. Ibid., pp. 340-341.

95. Ibid., pp. 340-341.

96. Ibid., II, p. 341; "Massachusetts Colony Charter," in Collection, comp. Hutchinson, I, p. 13.

97. Winthrop, History, II, pp. 341-342.

98. Ibid., II, pp. 344-345.

99. Ibid., II, pp. 344-345.

100. Ibid., II, p. 346.

101. Ibid., II, pp. 365, 355, 366.

102. Ibid., II, pp. 355, 366.

103. Ibid., II, pp. 355, 366.

CHAPTER SIX:
RELIGIOUS TOLERATION AND ITS ENEMIES:
ORTHODOXY IN OLD AND NEW ENGLAND

[Toleration] was not so much an ideal, a positive end, that people wanted to establish for its own sake.... It was hardly even an "idea" for the most part - just a happening - the sort of thing that happens when no choice is left and there is no hope of further struggle being worth while.

-- Herbert Butterfield[1]

There is talke of an universal Toleration, I would talk what I could against it, did I know what more apt and reasonable Sacrifice England could offer to God...than an universal Toleration of all hellish Errors, or who they shall make an universal Reformation, but by making Christs Academy the Devils University, where any man may commence Heretique per saltum; where he that is filius Diabolicus, or simpliciter pessimus, may have his grace to goe to hell cum Publico Privilegio, and carry as many after him, as he can.

-- Nathaniel Ward, 1647[2]

It is a thing highly displeasing unto God, that his people should give toleration of any religion but that he hath established.

-- John Bastwick, 1646[3]

God did so wonderfully bless the labours of his unanimous faithful ministers that had it not been for the faction of the Prelatists on one side that drew men off, and the factions of the giddy and turbulent sectaries on the other side...England had been like in a quarter of an age to have become a land of saints and a pattern of holiness to all the world, and the unmatchable paradise of the earth. Never were such fair opportunities to sanctify a nation lost and trodden underfoot as have been in this land of late. Woe be to them that were the cause of it!

-- Richard Baxter[4]

319

It is common to view the Puritan experience in America during the first decades of Massachusetts Bay colony in terms of the Puritans' "Americanization" of their adjustment to the unique conditions of the New World and the beginning of their transformation "from Puritan to Yankee." Considerably less attention has been given to the relationship between their holy experiment in America and the Puritan movement in England, especially during the period of the Puritan Revolution. Particularly important in this regard is the orthodox Puritans' quest to preserve order and authority within the confines of the Christian commonwealth they were trying to establish in both old and New England during the 1640s. Since this search for order and authority was inextricably intertwined with the issues of religious liberty and toleration, this chapter seeks to explore some of the dimensions of the orthodox Puritans' struggle to maintain religious unity and conformtiy in both England and New England.

In 1642, in the midst of the political controversies between the Long Parliament and the Crown and on the eve of the English Civil War, Charles I noted that the Puritans' aim was to create "a new Utopia of religion and government into which they endeavour to transform this Kingdom."[5] But if in 1642 Puritans appeared to be united, in 1649, on the very day on which the king was beheaded, the royalist author of <u>Eikon Basilike</u> wrote thus on the Puritans:

> That the builders of Babel should from division fall to confusion is no wonder; but for those that pretend to build Jerusalem to divide their tongues and hands is but ill omen and sounds too like the fury of those zealots whose intestine bitterness and divisions were the greatest occasion of the last fatal destruction of that city.[6]

This assessment of the ill effects of the profound divisions among the Puritans was not too far from what even a Puritan divine like Richard Baxter felt. Writing for "the true information of posterity," Baxter lamented that

> God did so wonderfully bless the labour of his <u>unanimous faithful ministers</u> that had it not been for the faction of the Prelatists on one side that drew men off, and the factions of the giddy and turbulent sectaries on the other side...England had been like in a quarter of an age to have become a land of saints

and pattern of holiness to all the world, and the unmatchable paradise of the earth. Never were such fair opportunities to sanctify a nation lost and trodden underfoot as have been in this land of late. Woe be to them that were the cause of it![7]

Despite all their differences, the royalist and the Puritan divine both understood that something had gone wrong in England. By the late 1640s, Puritanism as a millennial movement aiming to create a new heaven and earth in England had failed to fulfill its own utopian aspirations.

In terms of millennialism and utopianism, the Puritan failure was indeed grounded upon the fact that the Puritan dream of order, the New Jerusalem, had been turned upside down. "Utopian thought," wrote George Kateb,

is dominated by a "a rage of order." A strong utopian impetus is to save the world from as much of its confusion and disorder as possible. Utopia is a dream of order, of quiet and calm. Its background is the nightmare of history.[8]

Millennial expectations are grounded essentially upon utopian visions, and utopian thought is an indispensable element in the pursuit of the millennium - the flight from disorder and the establishment of the heavenly city upon earth. This close association between utopian thought, with its essential impulse for order, and millennial expectations is important to an understanding of Puritan activities in England and New England between 1640 and 1660, or during the end of the Puritan Revolution. For during this time orthodox Puritans were engaged in a fierce battle against sects and heresies to preserve order and authority in the Christian commonwealth they sought to establishin both old and New England. This common struggle of orthodox Puritans on both sides of the ocean reveals, more than anything else, a need to reconsider Puritanism. Puritanism needs to be seen less as a revolutionary movement whose aim was to destroy existing established order and more as a conservative religious movement aiming to secure its own utopian vision of order and authoirty by enforcing unity and conformity in religious affairs, and by rejecting any plea for liberty of consicence and religious toleration.

I   Reformation, Revolution and Order

That events in England during the so-called Puritan Revolution could hardly be described in terms of order or authority is a well known fact. The great historian of the late nineteenth century, Samuel R. Gardiner, coined the term "the Puritan Revolution" and argued that "a Revolution" such as the Puritan revolution should be "an object of study...because it reveals more clearly than smaller changes the law of human progress." The historical development of a nation, according to Gardiner, stemmed from the struggle between "the conservatism of habit" and the goals of revolutionaries who "have bent themselves to sweep away the hindrances which bar the path of political progress."[9] From Gardiner on, the changes and developments England underwent in these years have been associated by historians with a struggle for "progress," "liberty," and "freedom"; and because the main forces in England at that time were the Puritans, the terms "Puritanism and Liberty" have been so closely associated that the whole period has come to be seen as "the revolution of the saints." In these terms, the radical impulse of the Puritans has seemed incompatible with the traditional system, and the saints have finally emerged, in Michael Walzer's words, as "the first of those self-disciplined agents" of revolution in the modern world whose "primary task was the destruction of traditional order."[10] The prime fault with this interpretation is that Puritans in England during that time hardly, if at all, thought of themselves in such terms. The Puritans rather, to use their own words, attacked "innovations' and tried to preserve the traditional order they thought Laud and others had changed by their policies. Moreover, no one during the seventeenth century described the events in England during the 1640s and 1650s as the "Puritan Revolution." Those who did use the term "revolution" implied something quite different from present usage of the term.

According to Vernon F. Snow in his important article, "The Concept of Revolution in Seventeenth-Century England," the "scientific usage" or astronomical concept of revolution as "the periodic return of a moving object (or

322

person) to the point of origins" had been the dominant concept during that time. In 1605, for example, the historian William Camden wrote, "all things runne round: and as the reason of the year; so men's manners have their revolution." And while some contemporaries in England described the events between 1640 and 1660 as a revolution, no one called them "the Puritan Revolution." Therefore, concluded Snow, in the late seventeenth century,

> the term revolution possessed divers political connotations. To all who used the word it denoted change, generally sudden, and to most it signified completed circular movement. To all the concept of revolution was compatible with cyclical (in contrast to the linear) interpretation of political history...which still dominated most political thought.[11]

Snow's distinction between two modes of historical interpretation, the cyclical and the linear, is important because it points directly to the fact that the Puritans carried on their revolution in the name of tradition and with the goal of preserving traditional society. Above all, this distinction showed that revolution in seventeenth-century England was associated with a return "to the point of origins" and was not congruent with the concept of "progress" that has dominated our modern, linear interpretation of history. The cyclical interpretation of time, it should be stressed, did not contradict millennial expectations, for in the millennium the whole circular movement of time and history was to come to its finale and the whole mystery of the history of salvation and redemption was to be solved.

Snow's finding that the prevailing interpretation of history in seventeenth-century England was cyclical points to two important conceptions or styles of historical consciousness. "It would be necessary to confront 'historical man' (modern man)," wrote Mircea Eliade in Cosmos and History, the Myth of the Eternal Return,

> who consciously and voluntarily creates history, with the man of traditional civilizations, who...had a negative attitude toward history. Whether he abolishes it periodically, whether he devaluates it by perpetually finding transhistorical models and archetypes for it, whether, finally, he gives it a metahistorical

meaning (cyclical theory, eschatological signification, and so on), the man of the traditional civilizations accorded the historical event no value in itself; in other words, he did not regard it as a special category of his own mode of existence.[12]

The essential difference between the cyclical conception and the linear notion of the "historical man" is that the former considers history as repetitive and regards its meaning as transcendental, while the latter conceives of history and time in terms of progress or development, so that the meaning history is immanent in time. In the former, the meaning of tradition is not as negative as it is in the modern view; tradition is rather the point of origins which time, in its circular movement, approaches.

As applied to the Puritan movement, the positive concept of tradition, the ends to which time and history lead, strongly suggests that the role of the revolutionary saints in England was less revolutionary and rather more traditional and that their actions were less "the politics of wreckers," as Walzer has argued, than those of traditionalists who, in their words, wanted to abolish "innovations."[13] The preservation of tradition and not the achievement of "progress" guided the Puritans and motivated their actions. Only in these terms can one explain the fact that the Puritans had no scheme of planned Revolution and were emphatically not ideologists of revolution. The Puritan aim was to reform the Church of England, not to abolish it, to restrain the king's prerogative powers, not to execute him, and if at the end the whole structure of the Church of England ceased to exist and the king was beheaded, these results had nothing to do with a revolutionary plan. They were merely the outcome of inner struggles within the Puritan movement, consequences considered as evil by the majority of Puritans in England.

Massachusetts's relationship with England, especially during the 1640s, should be considered in the light of the above discussion. Led by millennial expectations, the Puritan emigrants who came to America during the 1630s had no other place but the wilderness in which to prepare for the Kingdom of God by establishing visible churches and a godly society. However, the majority of

Puritans in England preferred to stay at home, and their millennial expectations were focused rather on reforming England and the Church of England. Thus, until the 1640s, millennial expectations led Puritans on both sides of the ocean to utilize very different social ecclesiastical means. While the majority of English Puritans associated the pursuit of the millennium with reforming the whole structure of the Church of England, the Puritan emigrants who established Massachusetts thought it essential to separate the saints from the ungodly, establish congregations of visible saints and were stymied in their efforts by the failure of godly magistrates in England to initiate reformation there. After events of the 1640s had radically changed the situation in England and Puritans had laid the foundation of a Christian commonwealth there, they found the main obstacle to their millennial and utopian visions in the spread of the sects and heresy. Thus, in spite of their ecclesiastical and theological differences, orthodox Puritans in England and New England were united during the 1640s in a fierce battle against the sectarians with their pleas for religious toleration and liberty of conscience. What follows will show that in their determination to preserve order and authority, orthodox Puritans in England and New England stood upon common ground. Orthodoxy existed on both sides of the Atlantic, not just in Massachusetts as a peculiar feature of American Puritanism.

II   Puritan Debates - Reformation, Separation and the Millennium

The relationship between Massachusetts and England during the 1640s has usually been described in the past in terms of crisis, as, in the face of developments in England, Massachusetts turned its back to the home country and strongly defended its orthodoxy against any new ideas that came out of England. However, if the theory of crisis suggests the abrupt destruction of a longstanding harmony between two partners, this was clearly not the case with Massachusetts Puritans and their brethren in England. We have already noted that the Puritans migration was a consequence of great controversy and debate in English Puritan circles, debates that became stronger as the foundations of the Puritan experiment in Massachusetts became clearer in England during the 1630s. The roots of Massachusetts' controversies with England are therefore traceable to the very moment at which some Puritans in England ceased to consider England as the place within which their millennial expectations would be fulfilled and began to regard New England as the location of the New Jerusalem.[14]

From its very beginnings, the holy experiment in the wilderness stimulated considerable debate among English Puritans. John White's The Planters Plea in 1630 provides the first clear evidence that the wilderness solution was not acceptable to many English Puritans mainly because most of them seemed to have viewed the Puritan migration as an explicit separation from the Church of England. Moreover, when English Puritans became aware of the exact nature of the Puritan commonwealth during the 1630s, they quickly rejected many of its components. Thus, from the early 1630s Massachusetts was engaged in fierce ideological controversies with English Puritans concerning the premises of religious reformation and the character of millennial expectations.

In 1636, one E.B. in England sent "Thirty-Six Questions" to Massachusetts Puritans concerning the colony's ecclesiastical way. Well acquainted with the colony's ecclesiastical polity, the author's many detailed questions concerned the constitution and validity of Congregationalism and the implications of such a system of church-government for a national church such a the Church of England. Thus, the author asked Bay Puritans "whether a solemne covenant be that which constituteth a church, and whether it be necessary to the essence and beeing of a church?" If so, the author wondered whether, according to the practice of the colony, "all true beleevers in a nation be bound to gather themselves together into distinct Congregations?" Consequently, he continued to inquire, should "any church...deny baptisme to the children of beleeving parents, only because their parents are not members, of their particular church?" And, concerning the relationship between church and state, the author questioned "whether any men may be admitted to office in the Commonwealth who are not members of the church."[15] One by one, then, the anonymous author called into question the entire ecclesiastical practice of the Puritans in the wilderness.

The "Thirty-Six Questions" proposed to the Bay Puritans in the early 1630s illustrate both how puzzled English Puritans were by the holy experiment in New England and how well aware they were of what was happening in the colony. Their main concern, no doubt, a concern probably shared by the majority of English Puritans, was their fearfulness of the implications of Congregationalism for the concept and entity of the Church of England as a national church. The majority of English Puritans had rejected Congregationalism in the 1630s and 1640s and had denounced any kind of religious reformation that threatened to undermine the existence and well-being of the national church of England. This was why English Puritans tended to identify Congregationalism with separation. In terms of order and authority, the mainstream of Puritanism in England had attempted to reform the Church of England as a national and traditional entity. Their politics were the politics of conservatism, in its proper meaning, and they therefore viewed with alarm both Congregationalism and Separation as radical movements threatening to abolish the Church of England by denouncing it as a false church.

Congregationalism indeed carried with it unbearable strains in relation to the concept and foundations of the Church of England as a national ecclesiastical

327

institution. This could be clearly seen in Richard Mather's answer to the "Thirty-Six Question," entitled "A Copy of an Answer of R.M. to the 36 Questions Proposed to Him by E.B." (1636). Mather's defense of Congregationalism vividly revealed how great was the discrepancy between Puritans on opposite sides of the ocean and, equally important, to what a great extent the whole Puritan migration to New England had been carried out by what Lamont termed "centrifugal millenarianism." Thus, Mather argued in his answer, the covenant was "necessary to the beeing of a visible church and of every member of the same" because "visible churches" were "distinct societyes." "And therefore," Mather continued, "it is that there is mention of the seven churches of Asia" in Revelation "as beeing distinct societyes." Constituted by a covenant the church was "compacted together in itselfe, and made a society distinct from other churches" through the very process of its members "agreeing, covenanting, or combining themselves together" to perform their duties "toward God and one toward another...for their holy edification in the Lord." This, claimed Mather, was what was "generally practised in New Engl[and]." However, if in Massachusetts the covenant was explicit, noted Mather, in England it was "implicite," though "obscure" in many churches because of the fact that many English churches contained "men mixed among themselves," that is, both profane and godly people. Congregationalism, in these terms, intended to purify the church by demanding that only visible saints constitute the visible church, a holy congregation in which the godly separated themselves from the vile.[16]

However, there was a special urgency for the saints to erect congregational or "visible churches," according to Mather, because God in the Apocalypse, as in other prophetic revelations, gave "special promises that he wilbee present in the midst among them, and walk in the midst of them." Therefore, contended Mather, "that beleevers ought to gather themselves into particular bodyes or churches" was "evident because Christ had ordeyned churches and given them speciall power and priviledges." In this process, the magistrate's role was crucial. By his authority, he could see that saints complied with God's word.

328

Through his power, he could facilitate the realization of the divine plan by permitting saints to gather themselves into visible churches. Thus, wrote Mather, if

> church-dutyes bee commanded and countenanced by authority in one place, and bee opposed and suppressed in another...it is the duty of all...to use their liberty by chusing to serve the Lord Jesus where they may do it with most purity and peace.

Here, again, can be seen the essential and crucial link between the Puritan migration and the pursuit of the millennium on the one hand, and the decisive role of the godly magistrate in the realization of the premises of reformation on the other. True reformation could only take place where "the magistrates do profess the gospel." Hence, the saints' duties were not only to gather themselves into visible churches, but also to look for a place in which "the Commandement or Countenance of magistrates is affoarded" and the Christian commonwealth would be ruled in accord with the pursuit of the millennium. Here was the main impetus behind the Puritan migration. Out of the pursuit of the millennium and an appreciation of the decisive role of the magistrate, the whole emigration came into being.[17]

In Massachusetts, the eschatological and millennial dimension was, however, largely associated with practical issues such as how to restrict admission into the church, as Mather's answers to the thirty-six questions revealed. Citing the passage in Revelation (11:1, 2), "and the angel stood, saying, Rise, and measure the temple of God.... But the court which is without the temple leave out, and measure it not," Mather wrote that the whole issue of the true church was grounded on "the temple and the court without the temple." For the temple is "the true church rightly constituted," that is a visible church, and "by the court is meant those that have some affinity with or relation to the church," so that they, belonging to the court, "were to bee left out, and not measured as beeing unfitt for temple work...and by appointment of Christ are not to bee taken in, but left out" of the church. Thus, concluded Mather, when christian churches are to bee framed according to the mind of christ, by the line and measure of his word, then the utter [outer] court (that is the common sort of christians) is not to be measured but to bee left out. (Rev. 11:1, 2)

This constitution of the church, according to Mather, was thus given from God. For when "the Angel" in Revelation "hath commanded to leave them out" and not to admit non-visible saints into the church, who, asked Mather, "then dare take them in ?"[18]

A visible church, as the New England Puritans defined it, was, according to Richard Mather, in accord with God's word as set down among other places in the prophecies of the Book of Revelation. Based on explicit covenant with God, each particular church could not be subordinated to any ecclesiastical jurisdiction. "True churches," wrote Mather,

> are distinct societyes, all of them of equall and independent spiritual power within themselves...and subject onely to the power and authority of Jesus...and therefore one true church hath no authority to impose their injunction and decrees upon another true church.

Thus, Mather, like Cotton, Hooker, and others in Massachusetts, had no use for the concept of a national church as an ecclesiastical institution ruling over particular congregations. "In the Old Testament the church of the Jewes was a national church," wrote Mather, "but in the New Test[ament] a nation or country is not spoken of as one church, but there is mention of many churches in one nation or one country."[19]

The significance of the "Thirty-Six Questions" and Mather's answer lies in the fact that both reveal the profound differences dividing Puritans in old and New England. These differences arose from the need to find means by which to reconcile the impulses of reformation with millennial expectations and eschatological visions. Reformation demanded purity and a godly life, but once they had combined it with millennial expectations and apocalyptic revelations, some Puritans believed that reforming the ecclesiastical order of England was not enough and that, with the millennium at hand, the saints had to act immediately to constitute visible churches in order to establish the Kingdom of God upon the earth. Mather's "answer" in particular illustrates how prophetic revelations had been interwoven with the ends of the Puritan emigration. From the point of view of English Puritans, however, the New England attempt to reconcile the demands of reformation with millennial expectations was unwarranted and unjustified, for the reconciliation was being made at the expense of the Church of England. Any attempt to fulfill the gospel of reformation at the cost of damaging the framework of the Church of England, contended the majority of English Puritans, led in the direction of separatism and the destruction, rather than the reform, of the Church of England. This was the view of the holy enterprise in the wilderness that many English Puritan ministers declared in a unique document they sent to Massachusetts in 1637.

It is well known that Massachusetts Puritans insistently denied that they were separatists, but it is less well known how English Puritans viewed them prior to 1640 and how they looked at the consequences of the Puritan migration from the point of view of the whole Puritan movement in England. This is the significance of the 1637 "Letter of Many Ministers in Old England, Requesting the Judgment of Their Revern Brethren in New England, concerning Nine Positions." "While we lived together in the same Kingdom," wrote the English Puritan ministers to Bay Puritans,

> we professed the same faith: joined in the same ordinances; laboured in the work of God, to gain souls unto his kingdom, and maintain the purity of worship against corruptions both on the right hand and on the left. But since your departure into New England, we hear, and partly believe, that divers have embraced certain opinions such as you dislike formerly, and we judge to be groundless and unwarrantable.

In particular, the English Puritan ministers protested that Bay Puritans considered their mode of ecclesiastical polity as "the only Church-way wherein the Lord is to be worshipped" and that they had left the English "Assemblies because of Stinted Liturgy." These and other "common tenets of New England," wrote the ministers, led Bay Puritans, "being turned aside themselves" and separated from the Church of England, to "labour to ensnare others; to the grief of the godly" people in England and "the scandal of religion." At the same time, not only separation, but also the ecclesiastical way in the colony, in which some people were refused admission to the church, wrote the English ministers, was made "to the disgrace of the gospel." The colony's exclusiveness concerning church membership was, they believed, based upon "weak and groundless imaginations" and "rash and inconsiderate zeal." All these practices and others, complained the English Puritan ministers, were evidence "that you have changed from that Truth which you did profess, and embrace for that Truth which, in former times upon sound grounds you did condemn as erroneous," namely separation. "Will you plead for Separation?" the English ministers boldly asked their brethren Puritans in America.[20]

But the ministers' letter was not only a list of complaints against ecclesiastical practices in the wilderness. Above all, it showed how fearfully English Puritans looked upon the religious enterprise in the wilderness and how threatening they found the Puritan migration to their own movement whose ultimate goal was to reform and conserve the Church of England, not to abolish or destroy it. "You know how oft it hath been objected, 'that Nonconformists in practice are Separatists in heart,'" the English Puritan ministers admonished their Massachusetts brethren, in reminding them of the longstanding effort in England to distinguish between non-conformity and Separation. This distinction had long been indispensable to the Puritan cause in England, and in this context the Puritan migration had failed to sustain the Puritan movement in England, which while advocating non-conformity to ecclesiastical innovations had always professed its loyalty to the concept of a national and inclusive Church of England. Under attack in England on the grounds that non-conformity would ineluctably lead to Separation, the Puritan ministers in England were especially resentful that the Massachusetts example seemed to lend credibility to the charges of their opponents, and they demanded an explanation from Bay Puritans concerning their stand:

> How shall your Brethren be able to stand up in defence of their
> innocency and the uprightness of their cause, when your example
> and opinion shall be cast in their dish? Must they leave you
> now, with whom they have held society? Or, will you plead for
> Separation which you have condemned as rash and inconsiderate.

Thus did the English Puritan ministers interpret the "sudden change" of Bay
Puritans from non-conformity to Separation and demanded from Massachusetts
the "strongest reasons that have swayed" Puritans there toward separation. "And
if we shall find them," wrote the ministers concerning the colony's reasons,
"upon due examination, to be such as carry weight, we shall be ready to give you
the right hand of fellowship: if otherwise, you shall receive our just and modest
animadversions, in what we conceive you have erred from the Truth."[21]

As the ministers' letter indicates, English Puritans in 1637 were willing to
distinguish themselves from Bay Puritans and their holy experiment in the
wilderness and to denounce the New England way as a heresy leading to
separatism. Only seven years had passed since the great migration had begun,
and now on opposite sides of the ocean, Puritans found themselves greatly at odds
concerning the principles and means of reformation. Theological differences,
however, were only part of this fierce controversy. Also at stake was the
existence of the Church of England as a national and traditional ecclesiastical
institution, which the majority of Puritans in England hoped both to reform and
to preserve, while the centrifugal millenarianism of the American Puritans had led
them to seek reformation outside the Church of England. Thus did English
Puritans who had always identified any pursuit of reformation outside the Church
of England with separation, come to denounce Bay Puritans as Separatists.

In 1639, "the Elders of the Churches of New England" answered the English
ministers' letter of 1637. "God hath set for us an open door of liberty," declared
Bay Puritans in their answer, yet they attempted to assure their English brethren
that "we might neither abuse our liberty in the Gospel, to run into any
groundless, unwarrantable, course, nor neglect the present opportunity to
administer, by the help of Christ, all the holy ordinances of God, according to the

pattern set before us in the scripture." However, what was missing here, obviously, was any mention at all of the Church of England as a model out of which to constitute the church in the wilderness, and this omission could only confirm the view held by English Puritans that the wilderness saints were trying to fulfill the premises of reformation outside the boundaries of the Church of England. Furthermore, the colonists candidly admitted that "in our native country...many of us took some things" in the Church of England "to be indifferent and lawful" but that, after emigrating to Massachusetts, "we have no cause to retain and practise" them in the wilderness. For "such things as man may tolerate when he cannot remove them, he cannot tolerate without sin when he may remove them." Consequently, continued Bay Puritans, many ecclesiastical customs they had practiced in the Church of England had to be abandoned "when we came to weight them in the balance of the sanctuary" in America.[22]

While admitting their ecclesiastical way to be different from practice in the Church of England, Bay Puritans insisted that theirs was not the way of "rigid Separation." It is significant, then, that the colonists did not try to refute the charge of separation as such, but only to distinguish their separation from the "rigid separatists" who explicitly separated themselves from the churches in England "as no Churches," "from the Ordinances" of the Church of England "as mere Antichristian," and, finally, from the saints in England "as no visible Christians." Their separation, argued Bay Puritans, was very different:

> We separate from corruptions which we conceive to be left in
> your Churches, and from such Ordinances administered therein
> as we fear are not of God but of men.

And in terms of the millennium, Massachusetts elders contended that their separation was necessary in order to raise the Kingdom of God on earth:

> Churches had still need to grow from apparent defects to purity,
> and from reformation to reformation, age after age, till the Lord
> have utterly abolished Antichrist 'with the breath of his mouth,'
> and 'the brightness of his coming' to the full and clear revelation
> of all His holy truth.[23]

The whole argument of Bay Puritans concerning separation depended, of course, on its acceptance in England, especially by the Puritans there. And on this point they utterly failed to persuade, as English Puritans refused to distinguish between "rigid" separation and that of the Puritans in Massachusetts. When the answer of the Massachusetts elders reached England in 1639, Puritan ministers there appointed John Ball, a Puritan divine, to reply. A non-conformist all his life, Ball had long been engaged in controversy with the separatists in many works, including a friendly Trial of the Grounds of Separation (1640) and an Answer to Two Treatise of Mr. John Can (1642), the leader of the Brownists in Holland. At the same time, his Treatise of Faith, originally published in 1632, was very popular in New England. However, in 1639 Ball analyzed the answer of the Massachusetts elders and concluded that Bay Puritans were indeed "rigid" separatists and not simply people separating themselves from corruptions as they had argued.[24]

Having read many of the writings that came from New England during the 1630s, Ball was thoroughly familiar with ecclesiastical practices in the colony and could thus point out precisely where and when "the Answer of the Elders of the Churches in New England" conflicted with actual practice in Massachusetts. "If we have not mistaken your judgement and practice both," wrote Ball to the Bay Puritans, "you have borne witness against" what "you call 'the rigide Separation.'" However, he continued,

> we have heard that you hold fellowship with professed 'rigid Separatists,' without any acknowledgement of their error, and receive them as members...in the privileges of the Church, though you profess you approve not their opinion nor practice; and if, in godly wisdom, you can see 'grounds' to join with them, we marvel you should be so timorous in this particular.

Ball scored a point here, for Bay Puritans indeed held fellowship with John Robinson's people at New Plymouth and accepted separatists and held communion with them in their churches, while at the same time excluding many members of the Church of England from their congregations. Moreover, Ball charged that the

335

exclusiveness of their ecclesiastical way explicitly separated Bay Puritans from the Church of England and the godly there. What reasons, he asked, did Massachusetts have "to exclude from the Sacrament true visible Believers, or, known recommended Christians formerly Members of 'visible' Churches among us" in England, and "their children, because they are not Members, as you speak, 'in Church Order'?" Above all, continued Ball, how could Puritans in the wilderness put "differences between Church-members of your societies and other visible believers walking in holiness, though not admitted Members of another society according to your 'Church Order,' as to receive the one, though Members of another society, unto the Seals, and to debar the other and their children?"[25]

From the point of view of English Puritans, Ball's detailed analysis of both the writings and practice of Massachusetts Puritans left little room for the latter to claim that they were non-separatists. For Ball showed clearly the essentially separatist thrust embodied in the premises of Congregationalism in the wilderness. Furthermore, Ball's "Reply" clearly showed that Puritans in England were less interested in the colonists' declarations than in those practices and actions in the wilderness that revealed over and over again separatist tendencies. the issue was not over terminology, over the meaning of the world "Separation," but rather over the implications of Congregationalism as a system of church-government. "The main ground of the former doubt and all others tending to Separation," wrote Ball in A Friendly Traill of the Grounds Tending to Separation in 1640,

> seemeth to be this; That the power of the keyes is primitively given to the community of the faithful, as the first receptacle. For they conceive that it pertinents to them to censure offenders, or else to separate from them. Then, likewise it will more probably be concluded, as they think, That that society which hath not the power of CHRIST keyes is not the true church of Christ.

Thus, according to the Puritan divine, Congregationalism as such meant separation because it assumed the keys to heaven to be in the possession of each particular congregation and not in the national church. Ball, therefore, like most English Puritans, denounced the whole concept of Congregationalism and never accepted the distinction Bay Puritans tries to make between their separation and "rigid Separation."[26]

Perry Miller's central thesis in <u>Orthodoxy in Massachusetts</u> was that two sorts of Congregationalism existed in England during the late sixteenth and early seventeenth centuries: on the one hand, "separatist congregationalism," and on the other, in his words, "non-separatist congregationalism," with the latter to be applied to the Puritan migration to Massachusetts. Clearly, Miller's distinction is exactly the one adopted and consistently adhered to by Bay Puritans, who were intent on distinguishing between their way and separation. According to Ball and English Puritans, however, this was not the issue at all. According to them, there were not two sorts of congregationalists. Rather congregationalism as such was necessarily identified with separation. This is the meaning of Ball's attacks on the separatists in Holland and America. By its very terms, he argued, Congregationalism as a system of church-government that provided each congregation with the power of the keys was separation from the Church of England. Consequently, Ball and the majority of English Puritans would have rejected Miller's distinction between two sorts of congregationalists just as thoroughly as they rejected Massachusetts' distinction among two types of separation. For most English Puritans Congregationalism was totally incompatible with the concept of the Church of England as a national church, which, as a national institution, held within itself the power of the keys, or the means for salvation.[27]

III <u>Puritan Rage for Order: "The Fast Sermons to Parliament"</u>

The denunciation of the holy experiment in Massachusetts by the English Puritans during the 1630s is crucial to an understanding of the relationship between Puritans on opposites of the ocean, not only during the 1630s, but especially during the 1640s. For it indicates that from its very beginnings, the New England way was unacceptable to the majority of Puritans in England. Furthermore, when English Puritans had the opportunity during the 1640s to design a godly Christian commonwealth for England, the ecclesiastical way of Massachusetts was emphatically not the model on which English Puritans sought to reform the Church of England. This was not surprising because, in the context of English Puritanism, the appropriate context within which to examine the holy experiment in the wilderness, the New England way did not offer any solution to the ultimate problem of how to reform the Church of England while at the same time preserving it as the national and ecclesiastical institution of the kingdom. Congregationalism, as Richard Mather's writings, for example, showed, was based upon centrifugal millenarianism and led ineluctably toward separation from the national Church of England. It was here, therefore, on the issue of a national ecclesiastical order and authority, that English Puritans came to identify Congregationalism with Separatism.

However, despite their bitter controversies, Puritans on both sides of the ocean came rather closer to each other during the 1640s because of the dramatic changes that occurred in England. In the past millennial expectations had led Puritans to emigrate from England to New England in order to bring about the advent of the Kingdom of God by establishing visible churches. But now with the fall of Laud and the whole ecclesiastical order in England in 1640, there was no longer any need to emigrate from England in pursuit of the millennium and radical religious groups could rather pursue the realization of their eschatological visions and millennial expectations in England. Thus, many sects or heresies, according to orthodox Puritans in old and New England, appeared upon the stage

338

of history in England during the 1640s. The rise of sects that explicitly separated themselves from the Church of England frightened orthodox Puritans on both sides of the Atlantic, who, despite their ecclesiastical differences, constituted a common front against the menace of the sects and waged a fierce war against sectarian pleas for religious toleration and liberty of conscience. Thus, when confronted by the rise of the sects, the most important issue for Puritans on both sides of the ocean was not their theological differences but the common struggle against any attempt to give room to heresy and sects within a Christian commonwealth, whether in England or New England.

In an age in which religion was the affair of the whole community and at a time when people believed that only one form of religion could be true, the demand and insistence upon an absolute unanimity in faith and practice and the assumption that some sovereign authority had to have coercive power to suppress heresy and defend the true faith was natural. Thus, in England and New England during the 1640s, orthodox Puritans looked to the godly magistrate to maintain uniformity within religious society and to sustain the Christian commonwealth against heresy and the multitude of evils arising out of sectarianism. This stand was the essence of Puritan orthodoxy. From its beginnings, Massachusetts had advocated the decisive role of the godly magistrate religious matters, while in England, with the fall of Laud in 1640, Puritans finally gained the opportunity to realize their premises of order and authority in church and state through the godly magistrates sitting in Parliament. In the 1640s, then, on both sides of the ocean Puritans were engaged in establishing the foundation of a Christian commonwealth, and in this enterprise they found themselves united in their battle against heresy. They found themselves allies because the sectarians, in order to make room for themselves in England during the 1640s, stressed the necessity of separating church and state and refused to admit that godly magistrates should have power in religious matters over men's consciences. They thereby challenged the very essence of Puritan orthodoxy. In this context of the holy struggle against the sects and heresy, Puritans on both sides of the ocean attempted, insofar as

339

they could, to overlook their internal differences and to constitute a united front whose main aim was to exclude sectarianism from the Christian commonwealth in old and New England. Before dealing with the Puritan struggle against religious toleration, however, it is first necessary to explore the Puritan "rage for order" in England during the early 1640s.

When Thomas Hobbes tried to explain in his book <u>Behemoth</u> the causes of the Civil War in England, he wrote that one of the causes was that people in England had been "so corrupted" by "ministers, as they call themselves, of Christ," who "in their sermons to the people" pretended "to have a right from God to govern every one his parish, and their assembly the whole nation."[28] Hobbes, no doubt, exaggerated the Puritan ministers' intentions. On the other hand, he captured in this passage the crucial importance of Puritan sermons during that time. For years the sermon served an essential role in the Puritan movement in England, and it was only natural that when the Long Parliament assembled in November 1640 it invited Puritan ministers to preach before both Houses of Parliament on many occasions. The "fast sermons to Parliament"[29] became a regular event during the 1640s, and many Puritan ministers used their sermons to reveal to the godly magistrates in the Parliament their expectations concerning the long-awaited reformation of the Church and Kingdom of England. At the same time, the "fast sermons to Parliament" also revealed the ways and means by which Puritan ministers hoped to achieve the true reformation in England. These sermons are also important for understanding of the contemporary issue of liberty and authority.

Parliament chose Cornelius Burges along with Stephen Marshall to preach the first sermons before it on November 17, 1640. Pleading for members of the House of Commons to adopt a "formall, solemne, entire engaging and binding" and "indissoluble Covenant" with God, Burges argued for the necessity of "setting up...a Faithfull, Judicious, and Zealous Magistracy." For without a powerful magistracy, he argued, "the Power of Godlinesse will soone degenerate into Formality, and Zeal into Lukewarmnesse." To maintain the covenant with God, preached Burges, the godly magistrate had to destroy "Popery, Arminianisme, Socinianisme, Prophanenesse, Apostacy and Atheisme." The meeting of the Long Parliament, declared Burges, in articulating what would become a central theme in sermons preached before Parliament in subsequent years, opened a "doore of hope" for the pursuit of the millennium. Thus, he reminded members of the Parliament,

> most of you are well seen in the history of the Church, and can soone point your finger to the time wherein Babylon began to besiege Hierusalem, and Antichrist began to pull his vizzard, in the Churches of Christ.[30]

Stephen Marshall, "that Genevah-Bull," as the poet John Cleveland described him, also asked the godly magistrates in the Parliament to destroy the many heresies in the kingdom, for "little...is to be expected in Christendome, till the Beast his Kingdom be ruined."[31]

A year later, in 1641, the godly magistrates in Parliament still had not turned to the reform of the church, and Marshall again admonished the Commons in his sermon A Peace-Offering to God for having neglected its duty to God: "as yet the Lord's Temple is not build, nor the Scepter of Christ throughly set up" in England. He Appealed to members of Parliament:

> Now that you have built your own house, and procure
> Civill Liberties, should you let Gods house lie
> waste, should you be (as many fear you are) lesse
> zealous in Gods cause, than in your own?[32]

In the same year Edmund Calamy told Parliament in his sermon, Englands Looking-Glass, that the great task before the godly magistrates "is about the ruine and repaire of Kingdoms" and demanded that Parliament redress "the sins of England," which "are the enemies of England." For, according to him, only "Repentance and Reformation repairs and upholds Kingdoms and Nations."[33] In May 1641, William Bridge similarly declared to Parliament in his Babylons Downfall that "the sword is now drawing whose anger shall not be pacified till Babylon be down and Sion rais'd." He accordingly demanded that the godly magistrates punish those who stood with Babylon's cause "according to their deserving."[34]

In 1641 Parliament had not yet addressed the issue of church reform, except in its orders "for the Abolishing of Superstition, and Innovation, in the Regulating of Church Affairs" and for "establishing of Preaching Lecturers."[35] Thus, when Burges preached again before Parliament in that year, he urged its members "to resume and pursue your first thoughts of setting up God and his Ordinances...by calling to your assistance a free Synode of Grave Ministers of this Nation."[36] A year later, 1642, Marshall reiterated this idea in his sermon Reformation and Desolation. He argued that in order to further the reformation of the church, Parliament had to call "a grave Synod of Divines" to inform its members' "consciences what is to be done" concerning the church's reformation.[37] Calamy in that year urged Parliament in his sermon Gods Free Mercy to England: "Do something to purge the land more and more of the innocent blood of the Martyrs" and to bring about "the reformation of Gods house."[38] And Thomas Goodwin argued in his sermon, Zerubbabels Encouragement to Finish the Temple in 1642, that it was Parliament's duty to "commend unto the people what is good and right." "Let no Church," he admonished, aiming at the gloomy conditions of the Church of England, "think it selfe perfect and needing nothing (as bragging Laodicea did)." Referring to the Book of Revelation, he called upon Parliament "to measure that temple, alter, worshippers anew, and to cast out that outward court that had defiled" the Church of England.[39]

These "Fast Sermons to Parliament" reveal that, in contrast to Massachusetts, where godly magistrates initiated and secured the reformation from the very beginnings of the Puritan migration, the situation in England was much more complex. The main concern of Pym and other Parliamentary leaders in the early 1640s was with the constitutional struggle with the king and, later, with the Civil War, and they had little time to take up the issue of church reformation. Thus, ministers in their sermons continued to urge the godly magistrates in Parliament to exercise their power on behalf of church reform. At the same time, the fast

342

sermons showed clearly that with the fall of Laud and the old ecclesiastical order in England, the affairs in the church had become unbearable to those who wanted, not to abolish the church, but to rid it of Popery, Arminianism, and heresy. Reformation and liberty went hand in hand with order and authority in the minds of the saints, whose conception of religious liberty was so limited as not to include within it the opinions and practices of other religious groups.

Puritan fears concerning the well being of the Church of England are easy to understand in the context of the time. In 1641 a small tract appeared in London called A Discovery of 29 Sects Here in London. The author explained that all of these sects "except the first," that is, the Protestants, were "most Divelish and Damnable." These sects, the author argued, threatened the very existence of the Church of England, and he therefore warned against the opinions and practices of "Puritans," "Papists," "Brownists," "Separatists," "Calvinists," and other less well known sects such as "Bacchanalians" and "Panonians."[40] The rise of sects in England terrified many. Thus, during the 1640s many tracts decried the sinful practices and beliefs of the members of these sects, and the authors warned again and again against these heresies.[41]

The specter of so many sects rising in the kingdom alarmed orthodox Puritan and provided the context for their sermons before Parliament in which they repeatedly admonished the civil magistrates to purge the land and reform the church. "God's work lies yet undone," complained Cornelius Burges to Parliament in 1641,

> Matters of religion lie a bleeding; all Government and Discipline of the Church is laid in her grave, and all putredinous vermine of bold Schismaticks and frantick Sectaries glory in her ashes, making her fall their own rising to mount out Pulpits, to offer strange fire, to expell the gravest, ablest, and most eminent Ministers in the Kingdom...out of the hearts of their people as a company of weak men, formalists, time-server, no Ministers of Christ, but Limbs of Antichrist, having no calling except from the Devill; and to forshake our Assemblies as Babylonists and Antichristian, so as in short time they will not leave us the face of a Church.

343

At present, noted Burges sadly, "no course is taken to suppress" the sectarians' "fury, and to reduce them to order." This task, he proclaimed to members of Parliament, would never be done "till You put your hand to the Cure." Consequently, Burges proposed that Parliament call "a free Synode of Grave Ministers" to assist it in "setting up God and his Ordinances" in England and thereby finally "put all men into a course of Order and uniformity in Gods way."[42]   But orthodox Puritans in England found that their search for ecclesiastical order and uniformity was indeed hard to accomplish because of the powerful presence of centrifugal millenarianism.

In May 1641 Parliament passed "The Protestation" in which its members "promise[d], vow[ed] and protest[ed] to maintain and defend...the true reformed Protestant religion expressed in the doctrine of the Church of England."[43] However, as Henry Burton argued in The Protestation Protested, in 1641, Parliament's "Protestation" was worth nothing in fact because popery could not be eliminated from the church, given the structure of the Church of England as a national church. Because the Church of England was a "National Church," declared Burton, it would be "very difficult, if not rather impossible, to constitute it so as is agreeable, in all points, to a true and visible Congregation of Christ."[44] Once a hero and martyr of the Puritans, whose ears had been cut off because of his attacks on popery during the 1630s, Burton now, in 1641, alarmed many orthodox Puritans by clearly advocating Congregationalism, which as we have seen, a majority of Puritans identified with separation. His bold attack on the "Protestation," which was clearly related to the eschatological visions and millennial expectations he set forth in his book The Sounding of the Two Last Trumpets in 1641,[45] caused many Puritans to immediately turn against him. John Geere, a Puritan divine, answered Burton in his Vindiciae Voti, or A Vindication of the True Sense of the Nationall Covenant and in Judahs Joy at the Oath, both published in 1641.[46] In these works, Geere sought to justify Parliament's "Protestation" and the necessity of keeping the Church of England as a national church. In the same year an anonymous author published A Survey of That

<u>Foolish, Seditious, Scandalous, Prophane Libell, The Protestation Protested</u> in angry response to Burton's denunciation of the Church of England as consisting of popery. He advised Burton to "go therefore with your conceit to <u>New-England</u> [and] there convert the Americans from Popery."[47] The author obviously sensed correctly that Burton would find the congregationalists in Massachusetts more congenial to his point of view. But the issue could not be resolved simply by dispatching Burton to America.

Burton's argument for congregationalism in <u>The Protestation Protested</u> seemed to many orthodox Puritans in England to promise nothing more than to open Pandora's box out of which all kind of heresy would escape. At a time when almost every day brought with it "a [further] discovery" of sects, those fears are completely understandable. In this context, one can appreciate the Puritans' total opposition to permitting the establishment of congregational or independent churches outside the Church of England. Thus, in 1641 Thomas Edwards published his <u>Reasons Against the Independent Government of Particular Congregations</u>, which he presented "in all humility to the honourable House of Commons." What moved Edwards to write this tract was the immediate danger he saw "in some petitions drawne, to be presented to the Honourable House of Commons, for a Toleration of some congregations, to enjoy Independent Government" outside the Church of England. On the same grounds, warned Edwards, "a Toleration may be demanded...for all rigid <u>Brownists</u> of the Kingdom, and for all the <u>Anabaptists, Familists</u>, and other Sectaries." Why should these Independent churches, he asked, be given toleration while they, like those in Massachusetts, would not, when in power, extend toleration to others?

> These independent men where they have power (as in New England) will not give toleration for any other Ecclesiastical Government or Churches but in their own way; they would not suffer men of other opinions in doctrines and government to live within the bounds of their patent, though at the furthest bounds, but have banished them.

345

The congregationalists in Massachusetts had indeed denounced toleration "for fear of disturbing the peace of their Church." Therefore he continued to refute the independents' plea for toleration in England on the basis of the very practice of Massachusetts Puritans, who refused to permit "any other form of government but one, seeing there is but one way of Church government laid down in the Word, and that unchangable, and therefore they cannot yeeld to it."[48] Identifying Independents in England with those in Massachusetts, Edwards thus argued that by their own arguments toleration should not be extended to them in England.

Edwards' identification of Independents in England with congregationalists in New England would of course have been rejected by both sides, as we will soon see. But Edwards pointed to a crucial problem involved with the issue of toleration: how could the Church of England tolerate other churches which did not tolerate it as a national church? If Congregationalists or Independents could not tolerate the Church of England, asked Edwards, why should the Church of England tolerate them? "I beleeve these present men," wrote Edwards on the Independents,

> who [are] here endeavouring a toleration for their Churches had they the power in their hands to settle a Government, we should have no Government tolerated, nor Church but the Independent way, and for this see The Protestation Protested, what he thinkes of our Church, and of whatever Government shall be established.[49]

IV Religious Toleration and Its Enemies

1. Puritans and Toleration

The rejection of religious toleration of the sects during the 1640s was what essentially linked orthodox Puritans in old and New England. Although Puritans on both sides of the ocean had profound differences among themselves over the issue of ecclesiastical polity, they stood on the same ground in their total opposition to toleration, while Bay Puritans and sectarians, despite their common impulse to erect visible churches, totally opposed each other on the issue of toleration. Massachusetts' controversies with English Puritans continued through the 1640s, but this struggle, in Lamont's words, was "over means, not over ends."[50] Most English Puritans in the 1640s, as in earlier decades, favored Presbyterianism - that is, a system of church government in which each particular church was governed by "a presbytery," or consistory of elders, which emanated from particular churches into classises and provincial and national synods. Presbyterianism, therefore, aspired to constitute a hierarchical ecclesiastical order in which religious uniformity and conformity could be maintained through ecclesiastical jurisdiction. They and the congregationalists of Massachusetts, along with the many Presbyterians who emigrated to the Puritan colony in America, struggled over this issue for many years, but they both shared a common understanding of the meaning of a Christian commonwealth and the role of the godly magistrate in ecclesiastical matters. Thus, when on each side of the ocean Puritans had tried to lay down the foundations for a Christian commonwealth, they found themselves engaged in the same fight against toleration of the sects or heresy.

The word "toleration" now implies something positive, almost virtuous. However, in the seventeenth century the word had a "pejorative meaning," connoting "a lax complacency toward evil" (Dictionary of History of Ideas), "the action sustaining of enduring; endurance (of evile, suffering, etc.) 1623" (The Shorter Oxford English Dictionary on Historical Principles). Thus, if "to tolerate" in our time means accepting the right of something to exist, in the seventeenth century it signified suffering the existence of something that was evil, something that should be condemned and eliminated. Therefore, as Herbert Butterfield has noted, toleration in the seventeenth century

> was not so much an ideal, a positive end, that people wanted to establish for its own sake; but, rather, a pis aller, a retreat to the next best thing, a last resort for those who often still hated one another but found it impossible to go on fighting any more. It was hardly even an "idea" for the most part - just a happening - the sort of thing that happens when no choice is left and there is no hope of further struggle being worth while.[51]

Butterfield's observation calls attention to the issue of religious toleration in its historical context. In the historiography of the English Civil Wars historians have given much attention to the issue of toleration, but most of them have treated this issue more in terms of its modern conception and less in the actual context of the times. Thus, many studies reveal a common argument concerning the development of toleration during the 1640s: namely, that during that decade in irreconcilable struggle between Independents and Presbyterians took place in which the former, being the minority, leaned toward general toleration.[52]

The correlation between Independency and the rise of toleration that is so common in English Puritan studies has had much influence on the historiography of early Massachusetts. According to this correlation, the Independents who advocated toleration in England were the "Dissenting Brethren," the congregationalist ministers who attended the Westminster Assembly of Divines. According to this view, while congregationalists in England, the "Dissenting Brethren," leaned toward general toleration, those in Massachusetts rejected this idea as a whole. Consequently, as wrote Perry Miller, the "Independents," or English congregationalists, "could...insure the cooperation of the sects" in the struggle for religious toleration in England "only by disowning New England." Thus "colonial support" for the progressive movement toward toleration in England "was an embarrassment." To Miller, the battle over toleration in England was the reason why Massachusetts "turned aside from the main currents

348

of English opinion." The "isolation of Massachusetts" had been completed when the colony, "by gathering her holy skirts closer about her heel," proceeded on "her unlovely way alone."[53] But it is not clear that English Independents, or, more precisely, the "Dissenting Brethren," really advocated toleration or even that the struggle between Presbyterians and Independents was actually an irreconcilable struggle. Nor is it clear that congregationalists in Massachusetts differed so greatly from their brethren in England. An accurate understanding of these issues is essential to determining whether Massachusetts really did become isolated from England and whether the "orthodoxy in Massachusetts" did indeed differ from the "main current" of though in England during the 1640s.

2. Puritan Independent Divines and the Issue of Toleration

To deal with the issue of the Independents in England, one needs to know the true meaning of the word in the early 1640s. "Till Mr. Ball wrote in favour of Liturgy, and against Canne, Allin, etc. and till Mr. Burton published his 'Protestation Protested,'" wrote Richard Baxter, "I never thought what Presbytery or Independency was, nor ever spoke with a man who seemed to know it."[54] Baxter's words have not only been confirmed, but as J.H. Hexter showed in his important study, "The Problem of the Presbyterian Independents," it was very hard to distinguish between Presbyterians and Independents during the 1640s. For this reason, Hexter warned historians not to attempt to correlate either religion and politics, or Independent ministers in the Westminster Assembly of Divines and Independents in the Long Parliament.[55] Moreover, the religious differences between the ministers who favored Presbyterianism and those who favored Independency do not seem to have been a matter of fundamental principle; thus, when congregationalist ministers came back from Massachusetts to England in that period, for example, some of them even embraced Presbyterianism in England.[56] The problem becomes even more complicated when one considers that contemporaries used the term "Independent" in more than one way.

In the early 1640s many contemporaries used the term "Independent" freely to describe those who adopted the principle of the free gathering of a congregation, or a church, and its independence in relation to any ecclesiastical order. For example the Antinomian William Walwyn grouped under the name "Independents" Anabaptists, Separatists, and other sects. Walwyn used the term as an inclusive name for many sects and included under it a wide range of sectarians who shared this particular ecclesiastical principle.[57] At the same time, however, the term "Independents" was applied to a special group, the Independent divines in the Westminster Assembly as well as to the congregationalists in Massachusetts. Yet the important fact about these latter two groups was that both consistently attempted to dissociate themselves and their "Independency" from the radical Independency of the various sects. Thus, the Independent divines denounced "the most to be abhorred maxim" the view that each "single and particulare society of men professing the name of Christ" should "arrogate unto themselves an exemption from giving account or being censurable by any other" churches.[58] In other words, it was far from the intention of the Independent divines to let every church be wholly independent from any kind of authority which would maintain unity and uniformity in ecclesiastical matters. Likewise, John Cotton lamented that under the name of Independency many sects were hidden: "The antipedobaptists, Antinimonians, Familists, yea, and the Seeker too, do all of them style themselves Independents." Thus, like the Independent divines in England, Cotton was not satisfied with the name Independency as it applied to Massachusetts' ecclesiastical way because this name "neither truly describeth us, nor faithfully distinguisheth us from many other."[59]

Why, one should ask, did Independent divines in England and congregationalists in Massachusetts resent being called Independents? Massachusetts Puritans, of course, rejected totally the idea of toleration and thus their attempt to dissociate themselves from the term is understandable. However, the question of why the Independent divines attempted to dissociate themselves from the very name and practice of Independency is somewhat more complicated, especially since historians have argued that it was this group that raised the issue of toleration in England during the 1640s. This problem can indeed be solved only by examining the Independents' activities in England in early 1640 to see whether, they indeed embraced and advocated toleration, and whether they differed as much as has been suggested in the past from their brethren in Massachusetts concerning the issue of the magistrate's power over religious matters. In order to avoid ambiguity in the following discussion, the term "Independents" will hereafter be used only to describe the Independent divines, or the group of Independent ministers who took part in the Westminster Assembly of Divines. All others who also advocated the principle of the independence of a particular church or congregation will be described as Sectarians, the people who belonged to the various sects that arose in England at that time.

The Independent divines who attended the Westminster Assembly of Divines in 1643 were ministers who had already advocated Congregationalism during the 1630s. However, in contrast to the ministers who came to New England in this decade these clergymen went to Holland. Apparently the point that most sharply divided Thomas Goodwin, Philip Nye, Sidrach Simpson, Jeremiah Borroughes and William bridge, from their brethern in America, was that their millennial expectations still centered on England. Contrary to Massachusetts Puritans, they thought that England still had a unique role to play in providential history. In any case, all of them came back to England following the meeting of the Long Parliament. The millennium was at hand, thought Thomas Goodwin, and thus he preached to his congregation in Holland before returning to England:

> It is the work of the day to cry down Babylon, that it may fall
> more and more; and it is the work of the day to give God no rest
> till he sets up Jerusalem as the praise of the whole world.

The New Jerusalem would be built, Goodwin believed, in England, and his goal could only be accomplished by the congregational way. "And (my brethren) if the Kingdome of Christ had bin kept in Congregations, in that way that we and some other Churches are in, it had bin impossible that Antichrist should have got

351

head."[60] However, in England at that moment the godly magistrate still had not chosen the appropriate ecclesiastical way by which to reform the kingdom. Thus, when Goodwin and other Independent ministers returned to England from the continent, they found themselves engaging in theological controversies with Presbyterians and Sectarians over how to construct the Kingdom of God on earth.

From the time they came back until the convening of the Westminster Assembly of Divines in 1643, the Independent divines' activities in England revealed that they strongly preferred to associate themselves with the Presbyterians rather than with the sects. In 1641, Philips Nye and Edmund Calamy, the prominent Presbyterian of London, concluded an agreement concerning the relationship between Independent and Presbyterian ministers in London. Both sides agreed that

> (for advancing of the publike cause of happy Reformation) neither side should Breach, Print, or dispute, or otherwise act against the other's way; and this to continue 'til both sides, in full meeting, did declare the contrary.[61]

This agreement, welcomed by members of Parliament, made it clear that both Presbyterians and Independents "decided to abandon religious controversy for the duration of the war."[62] Robert Baillie, who came from Scotland to aid the reformation in England, also gave evidence that in the face of the Civil War, orthodox Puritans needed to unite:

> We have to get determined to our mutual satisfaction, if we were rid of Bishop, and till then, we have agreed to speak of nothing or anything wherein we differ.[63]

The unity between Presbyterians and Independents continued in the following years in spite of the theological differences between them. Puritan unity was intended to reform the kingdom by ridding it of Papists and sectarian heresy. This was nowhere more clear than with the "Solemn League and Covenant" in 1643, by which England and Scotland formed a treaty for "the extirpation of Popery...superstition, heresy, schism, prophaneness, and whatsoever shall be found to be contrary to sound doctrine and the power of godliness."[64] The Scots were Presbyterians, but this fact did not hinder Philip Nye, one of the Independent divines, from playing a crucial role in forming the treaty with Scotland and subsequently justifying it in England. The aim of the "Solemn League and Covenant," explained Nye to Parliament, after the latter had affirmed the treaty in 1643, was 'swearing fealty and allegeance unto Christ the King of Kings: and a giving up of all these Kingdomes, which are his inheritance, to be subdued more to his Throne, and ruled more by his Scepter." And "the effect" of this treaty, he proclaimed, was "that the kingdoms of the world become the kingdomes of the Lord and his Christ, and he shall reigne for ever. Rev. 11."[65]

Thus, in spite of their ecclesiological controversies, Independents and Presbyterians attempted to secure the help of the Scots in the First Civil War. Moreover, Independent ministers in their "fast sermons to the Parliament" insisted, like Presbyterians, on Parliament's duty to reform the Church of England. Indeed, both Presbyterians and Independents favored the idea of the Westminster Assembly of Divines, in which ministers would advise the godly magistrates in Parliament on the ways and means to reform the national church. And both Independents and Presbyterians were united in their struggle against heresy and the sects. On December 28, 1643, both groups jointly published a pamphlet entitled Certain Considerations to Dis-swade Men from Further Gathering of Churches which was aimed at stopping the forming of independent churches of the sectarians.[66] The signatories of this declaration included the "five dissenting brethren" or the Independent divines, along with the leaders of the Presbyterians in the Westminster Assembly. The rationale behind this declaration stemmed from the fact that in November of that year, the Assembly of Divines decided "to launch a campaign against gathering congregations" and informed the House of Commons about "the liberty that many take in the city and other places in gathering churches" before Parliament and the Assembly had declared their opinions concerning ways and means to reform the Church of England.[67] What frightened the Divines in the Assembly was the rise of sects in the kingdom. For example, the London ministers, as one contemporary observed,

353

make all the pulpit in London...ring against Anabaptists, Brownists, etc., so loud that the divine echoes thereof might easily be heard beyond the River Tweed.[68]

The ministers turned to the Assembly in November, complaining about

the increase of Anabaptists, Antinomians and sectaries, the boldness of some in the city, and about it, in gathering separate congregations.[69]

And thus, in the following month, December 1643, Independents and Presbyterians in their joint declaration, Certain Considerations, argued that "our miseries [are] increased by the severall ways of Brethren...entering themselves into church-societies" and asked such brethren to amend their ways "until they see whether the Right Rule will not be commended to them in this orderly way" by the Assembly of Divines.[70]

So far we have seen that the Independent divines associated themselves with the Presbyterians and not with the sects concerning the issues of ecclesiastical order and authority. They were therefore much closer to the congregationalists in the Bay colony in their fight against heresy than to the sectarians and their plea for toleration. This is not surprising, because Puritans stood on the same ground not only against popery but also against the sects. "Our enemies," declared The Parliament Scout,

formerly in the Bishops days would root out Religion, and Liberties, and introduce Popery, and tyranny, they made the Common enemy the Puritan, the Puritan that always stood up in opposition to all innovations in Church and State.[71]

Once we understand Puritans in these terms, not as revolutionaries but rather as conservatives who aimed to preserve tradition, the differences between the Independents and Presbyterians, especially in the Westminster Assembly of Divines, appear in their proper context.

3. Independents and Presbyterians in the Westminster Assembly

After much delay, Parliament referred the issue of church reform to the Westminster Assembly in 1643 . This body consisted of 125 ministers, most of them Presbyterians, thirty laymen, and some Scottish observers. Less than ten ministers in the assembly are known to have been congregationalists or Independents. Yet, because fierce ecclesiological controversies, especially over the issue of church-government, broke out in the assembly between Presbyterians and Independents, it has become commonplace to view the relationship between these two groups as an uncompromising struggle and to assume that the Presbyterians constituted a united front against the Independents. But, as Lord Say and Sele noted, "the Presbyterians were not of one mind," and Robert Baillie, the observer from Scotland, could count only six English Presbyterians (among the total number of over one hundred Presbyterian divines in the assembly) who wholly supported the Scots' discipline. Moreover, there is much evidence that within the assembly Independents often joined Presbyterians against the Scots' proposals, as in the case of ordination; on the other hand, Independents and Scots united against Presbyterians on the issue of ruling elders.[72]

The relationship between Independents and Presbyterians in the Westminster Assembly was a subject of controversy between the royalist newspaper, The Spie, and Parliament's newspaper Mercurius Britannicus. The Spie, attempting to emphasize every difference among the divines, wrote that "there grew so kindly a debate in the Assembly between Master Nye and Master Henderson, that the Moderator could not possibly reduce them to any calmnesse."[73] The Mercurius Britannicus did not deny that there had been "a late heat in our Assembly, betwixt the Independents and Presbyterians," but these "holy Controversies," claimed the newspaper, were the result of the Puritans' attempt to "walk on so fast in the way of Reformation." Whatever the ecclesiological differences between Nye and Henderson, declared the newspaper, both stood on the same ground concerning "the Covenant," and the "light from Scotland, and other reformed Churches" in relation to the issue of Reformation.[74] Another newspaper, The Compleate Intelligencer, presented a picture of the fundamental similarities between Independents and Presbyterians, notwithstanding their ecclesiological differences. "Though the Presbitery" and the Independents "are ingaged upon very

355

inconsistent Principles, and incompatible fundamental, yet sure the Independents are as zealous against Idolatries and superstitions." The latter endeavored, continued the newspaper, "to assist with their godly zeale and labors, the defence of our Religion and State, against the Common Enemy."[75]

The actual stand of the Independent divines toward the Presbyterians can be seen clearly in an important document they issued in early 1644. The first Independent manifesto, An Apologetical Narration, was a joint publication of the "five dissenting brethren," Thomas Goodwin, Philip Nye, Sidrach Simpson, Jeremiah Burroughes and William Bridge. Constituting a minority in the Assembly of Divines, the Independents had appealed directly to Parliament,

> to unite the Protestant partie in this Kingdom, that agree in fundamentall truths against Popery and other Heresies, and to have that respect to tender consciences as might prevent oppression and inconveniences.

Historians have found in this sentence - the only one in all the apology - as a plea for toleration. Yet, the actual circumstances in which the apology was published suggested something very different. One of the clearest and most persistent claims which this tract makes is the need for unity among the "Protestant party." Time and again, the authors warn against "the danger of rending and dividing the godly Protestant party in this Kingdom, that were desirous of Reformation." There was, they argued, "an absolute necessity of their nearest union and conjunction" against the "common adversary." Moreover, the Independents complained that they "had enjoyed a long continued settlement which had rooted in the hearts of men" with the Presbyterians during earlier years and that the "unhappy differences" among these two groups had not prevented the Independents from coming into "strict engagement" with the Presbyterians for "common ends."[76]

Agreement between the Independents and Presbyterians (which had already worked well for over two years), and not toleration, was the prime consideration in the relationship between these two groups of divines in 1643-44. What, then, had changed in late 1643 and early 1644? The Apologetical Narration was published by the Independents at the very moment when the Assembly of divines began its campaign against the free gathering of churches by the sect in November 1643. This campaign in the Assembly and the city of London against the Sectarians created a peculiar situation for the Independents who leaned toward the principle of voluntary gathering of churches under which so many sects flourished. "Those that are called pure Independents," urged Richard Vines, a Presbyterian, had to show themselves clearly so that "pernicious opinions may not shelter under their name and wing."[77] Even more than Vines, the Independents wished to distinguish themselves from any association with the sects. To what extent Independency was associated at that time with the sectarians can be seen in contemporary pamphlets. According to W.K. Jordan

> thirty-four orthodox titles which attacked the growth of sectarianism were examined in the McAlpin Collection (Union Theological Seminary, New York, N.Y.) for the years 1641-1643. Of these, twenty-nine do not dissociate between Congregationalism and the more radical and eccentric sects which appeared in this period.[78]

The Apology of the Independents, then, should be seen as an attempt to clear Independency from any association with, not to mention responsibility for, the spread of the sects. Thus, the kind of Independency referred to in the expression "pure Independents" (Vine's words) should be distinguished from the Independency claimed by the sectarians. Philip Nye made this point clear when he argued

> that Independency of churches was asserted...in relation only to a superior Church-power properly spiritual, and as such claimed jure divino; and not in relation to that Ecclesiastical Power which is in or exercised from, the Civil Magistrate.[79]

4. Independents, Presbyterians, and Religious Toleration

By viewing the Apologetical Narration in its real historical context, then, we can explain why the word "toleration" never appeared in this tract: toleration was not the intention of the Independent divines. Rather, they hoped "to unite the

Protestant partie in this Kingdom, that agree in Fundamental truths against Popery and other Heresies."[80] If this is true, the differences between the congregationalists in New England and the Independents (congregationalists) in England did not exist in fact. This is evident not only in the activities of the Independents against heresy, activities in which as we have seen above, they sided with the Presbyterians. It can also be seen in the justifications given by the Independents, so similar to those of Massachusetts Puritans, for the coercive power of the civil magistrate. Nye, for example, maintained that

> though we affirm Church-Government is Independent, and immediately derived from Christ; yet we affirm also, that the Civil Magistrate is even therein (that is, in Ecclesiastical Matters) Supreme Governor civilly. And though nothing may be imposed on the Christian Churches against their Will, by any Spiritual Authority (for so only we intend) yet we affirm withall that the Civil Magistrate may impose on them spiritual Matters, by Civil Power, yea whether they like or dislike, if it be good in his eyes, that is if he judge it within his commission from God.[81]

This was exactly the stand of "orthodox" Puritans in the Bay colony. Moreover, in 1644 Thomas Goodwin and Philip Nye published in England John Cotton's The Keys of the Kingdom of Heaven in the hope that it would clarify their concept of Independency. "The substance of this" book, wrote Goodwin and Nye in their preface to Cotton's volume, agreed entirely with the ideas set forth in their Apology.[82] The Independents fully endorsed a book in which Cotton declared that the congregationalists "willingly acknowledge a power in the civil magistrate, to establish and reform religion, according to the word of God."[83] It is clear, then, that both Independency and Congregationalism, from their shared premise that the particular church was a self-sufficient entity, invested in the magistrate the crucial role of keeping and maintaining religious unity, order, and authority. Therefore, though far removed from each other, congregationalists in the Bay colony and Independents in England came by way of the same premises of church-government to the same conclusions concerning the crucial role of the godly magistrate in ecclesiastical affairs.

This congruency between English Independents and New England congregationalists concerning the decisive power of the civil magistrate in religious affairs has not gotten much attention from historians. That is why many have concluded that while the Puritans in Massachusetts opposed toleration, Independents in England, though holding exactly the same premises concerning church-government, led the way to toleration there during the Puritan Revolution. But English Independents and New England congregationalists sought to maintain religious society and Christian commonwealth by the same means - through the coercive power of the godly magistrate. That historians have overlooked this similarity concerning the magistrate's power over religious matters is not surprising, because many contemporaries used the name "Independents" or "Independency" as an inclusive term with which to describe the various sects and paid little attention to the "Independent Divines'" attempts to dissociate themselves and their "Independency" from the radical notion of the independence of the sectarians. Thus, John Selden in his Table Talk, said that

> both the Independent man and the presbiterian man doe equally exclude the Civill power...the Independent may as well plead they should not bee subject to temporal things, not come before a Constable, or a Justice of Peace.[84]

And Ephraim Pagitt wrote in Heresiography, which appeared in two editions in 1645 and was frequently reprinted until 1662, that the Independents

> take the power of gathering and erecting Churches both from the Magistrates and Ministers, placing it only in the hand of a few private Christians who are willing to make a Church Covenant.

He even claimed that the Independents in England and the Independents in New England "take into their Churches without scruple Anabaptists, Antinomians" and other sects.[85] Selden and Pagitt, undoubtedly, erred in their view of the Independent divines and the congregationalists in New England, but their descriptions showed clearly why Nye and Cotton, for example, always attempted to dissociate themselves from the "Independency" of the sectarians.

It was, then, a primary aim of the Independent divines to distinguish their principles of church-government from those of the sects. "We found," wrote the authors of the Apology, "our opinions and ways...environed about with a cloud of mistakes and misapprehensions," and they claimed, in relation to the Presbyterians, that "in all points of doctrine...our judgements have still concurred with the greatest part of our brethren, neither we know wherein we have dissented."[86] They were not alone in their belief that however great the ecclesiological differences between them and Presbyterians both should continue to seek union among themselves. The preface to the apology, by Charles Herle, one of the Presbyterian divines at the Assembly, thus announced that this

> Apologetical Narration of our Reverend and dear Brethren the learned authors of it, 'tis so full of preaceableness, modesty, and candour; and withall, at this time so seasonably needfull, as well toward the vindication of the Protestant party in generall, from the aspersion of Incommunicableness within itself, and incompatibleness with Magistracy.[87]

5. Independents, Sectarians and Toleration

So far at least, the Independents rather preferred to continue their union with the Presbyterians under the name of "the Protestant party." The Sectarians obviously were well aware of the Independents' intentions and this brings us to the issue of whether, at any time, the Independents sided with the sects against the Presbyterians. Historians who have accepted the view that toleration as an issue between Independents and Presbyterians have tended to consider the Independents as siding with the sects on that issue against the Presbyterians. But the Sectarians themselves repeatedly refute this view in their writings. William Walwyn, the Antinomian, for example, upon reading the Apology of the Independents, concluded that:

> Having heretofore met with an Apologetical Narration of Thomas Goodwin...I did with gladness of heart undertake the reading thereof, expecting therein to find such generall reasons for justification of themselves, to the world, as would have justified all Separation.... But finding contrary to that expectation that

their Apology therein for themselves and their Toleration was grounded rather upon a Remonstrance of the nearness between them and the Presbyterian, being one in Doctrine with them, and very little differing from them in Discipline, and how they had been tolerated by other Prebyster Churches, and indulged with greater priviledges, than the Separatists, how they differed from the Separatists, and had cautiously avoyded those roks and shelves against which the Separatists had split themselves, confirming by these words, the people disesteem of Separatists, suggesting by that phrase of theirs, as if there were amongst the Separatists some dangerous bypathes or opinions, which they warily found, though no mention be made what they are, which is the worst sort of calumny.[88]

Walwyn's observations in 1644 in The Compassionate Samaritane on the true meaning of the Independents' Apology, indicates that the supposed link between the Independents and the sects on the issue of toleration still remains to be proved. In another book The Power of Love, in which he attempted to clear the sect of the Family of Love, Walwyn attacked the Westminster Assembly of Divines, "our Divines (as they would have us call them)," and proclaimed,

I am not a preacher of the law, but of the gospell: nor you under the law, but under grace: the law was given by Moses, whose minister I am not: but grace and truth came by Jesus, whose minister I am.[89]

He then appealed to the Commons, asking whether the Divines, including the Independent divines, "obtained of you an Ordinance for suppression of all Anabaptists, Brownists, or Independent writing."[90]

What is most characteristic of the sectarian pamphlets of the time is their lack of distinction between the Independent and Presbyterian divines. From the sectarian perspective, all the divines in the Assembly appeared as oppressors of men's consciences concerning religious matters. John Goodwin, the Separatist, for example, warned the Assembly of Divines against "the danger of fighting against God" by trying to persecute different religious opinion and based his argument for general toleration on the following principle: "For any man, or men, to attempt the suppression of any Doctrine, way or practise that is from God, is to fight against God himself."[91] Walwyn, too, argued that any attempt on

361

the part of the Assembly to suppress God's people would fail: "I trust the present endeavours of our Divines in striving to raise themselves upon their Brethren's disgrace and ruine, will...prove vaine and fruitlesse."[92] Similarly, the separatist Henry Robinson attacked in Liberty of Conscience (1644) the whole idea of a national church:

> I know that much is said and done in many places in behalfe of uniformity, a National Church, and Covenant.... But wherefore such laboring in vaine.... Do we think that God's salvation is also National?[93]

Frightened by the attempts of Presbyterians and Independent divines to constitute a new oppressive ecclesiastical order in England, sectarians like John Goodwin, William Walwyn, and Henry Robinson, raised and defended the banner of religious toleration. In doing so, they clearly recognized that the Independent divines stood with the Presbyterians in rejecting any idea of toleration that would allow the sects a place in the future Puritan commonwealth in England.

The central issue in the controversy over religious toleration was whether magistrates had power over men's consciences. In this context, the Independent divines' stand favoring, like the Congregationalists in Massachusetts, the decisive and coercive role of the godly magistrate in religious matters stood in rigid contrast to the sectarians' plea for toleration. The latter attempted to refute the Presbyterians' and Independents' view of the godly magistrate's function in ecclesiastical matters and raised the concept or principle of liberty of conscience, which in turn required toleration as the only means of assuring its fulfillment. Thus, Henry Robinson argued that

> if Civil powers, or others, have authority in matters of Religion, then their commands and Laws in that respect, must be absolute, as in other, and ought equally to be obeyed, which would engage the whole Kingdom still to the Discipline of the Common-Prayer-Book, and government of Episcopacy...a Liberty of Conscience must be permitted to us to enjoy our own opinion in matters of Religion, or else there is necessity of being liable and subject against Conscience.[94]

362

The whole sectarian struggle in England on behalf of liberty of conscience was also directed against Massachusetts' stand concerning the magistrate's power over religious matters. Thus, Richard Overton, one of the members of the sect of Socinians (from Faustus Socinus, 1539-1604), upon reading Cotton's book The Keys of the Kingdom of Heaven, wrote in The Araignement of Mr. Persecution (1645) that

> The judgement of the Divines of New England are against the Toleration of any Church Government and way but one, they will not suffer Brownism, Anabaptism, &c. Mr. Cotton the greatest Divine in New England...is against Toleration and holds that men may be punished for their Conscience.[95]

Massachusetts, of course, as is well known, was against toleration. What is much less known is that the Independent divines in England were also against toleration. Yet, Roger Williams, who was in England from the summer of 1643 to the summer of 1644 attempting to secure a patent for his settlement in New England and who took an active part during his stay in England in support of the cause of toleration, knew better. He had no trouble in recognizing that English Independents stood on the same ground as the congregationalists in New England on the matter of toleration. Thus, he wrote in his The Bloudy Tenent of Persecution (1644),

> Under the wing of the Civill Magistrate doe three great factions shelter themselves...the Prelacy...the Presbyter...[and] that (so called) Independent.

The Independents, continued Williams, "cast down the Crowne of the Lord Jesus at the feet of the Civil Magistrate" exactly as did the orthodox Puritans in Massachusetts. Moreover, the Independents' aim in England, he declared, was to

> perswade the Mother Old England to imitate her Daughter New England's practice...to embrace themselves, both as the States and Peoples Bishops.

Williams recognized, then, the essential congruency between the Independents in England and the congregationalists in Massachusetts in relation to toleration, and

363

he denounced their view that God had commissioned magistrates to deal with religious matters. "Magistrates have received their power from the people," he argued, and their power was therefore "without respect to this or that religion." However, Williams found that Puritan England was not much different from the "orthodox in Massachusetts" when the Commons ordered his books Queries of Higher Consideration, Cottons Letter Lately Printed, Examined and Answered, and The Bloudy Tenent of Persecution to be burned in August 1644.[96]

As evidence provided by both sides indicates, there was no alliance between the Independent divines and the sectarians on the issue of toleration, because the essence of the issue of religious toleration at that time concerned the magistrate's power over conscience. The Independents, along with the Presbyterians, affirmed that power in magistrates, while the sectarians denied it. In this context, Massachusetts Puritans, with their strong defense of the magistrate's power in religious matters, were much closer to the Independents and Presbyterians than to the sects. Thus the Bay colony's "orthodoxy" was remarkably similar to the stand of the majority of English Puritans.

6. Orthodoxy in England

If the Independent divines indeed favored toleration, this opinion should appear in their sermons and writings. However, they consistently opposed this idea. When Burroughes preached before the House of Lords in November 1645, he set down the official stand of the Independent divines by saying: "There is a great outcry against toleration of all religions, & we are willing to join against such toleration."[97] Another Independent divine, Joseph Caryl, drew a similar battle line in his sermon The Arraignment of Unbelief as the Grand Cause of Our National Nonestablishment (1645). Directing his remarks against Overton's The Araignement of Mr. Persecution, Caryl declared that "we see this day…loose libertine Protestants mixt with Papist, against those who are close-covenanting, and close-walking Protestants." Those "close-covenanting" and "close-walking Protestants" were of course the Independents and Presbyterians, who, according to Caryl, fought both the Papists and the sectarians. And he concluded his sermon with an appeal to Parliament to take action to secure the purity of church and religion:

> As to bear all differences would make charity blinde, so not to bear some would make her more than lame. I know (Honourable Senatours) your wisdom will easily find and discerne the limit-stone, between liberty and libertinisme, between the humours of men, and their consciences.[98]

In the mid-1640s, Presbyterians and Independents were engaged in securing an accommodation of "tender consciences" that would permit Independents to operate within the Presbyterian establishment that the Assembly of Divines recommended to Parliament. But even in that period, the Independents' alleged alliance with the sects on the issue of toleration did not occur, and the Independents as Burroughes and Caryl's sermons revealed, continued their denunciation of toleration. The Ancient Bounds (1645), another Independent manifesto, clearly reflected the Independents' continuing position toward religious toleration and liberty of conscience, for it repeated the Independents' insistence on the magistrate's power over religious matters:

> We have committed to the magistrate the charge of the Second Table; viz., materially, that is, he is not to see God dishonoured by the manifest breach thereof, or any part thereof. But is that all? No, surely, He may enter the vault even of those abominations of the First Table, and ferret the devils and devil-worship out of [their] holes and dens.

This, of course, was also the official stand of Massachusetts Puritans. Moreover, idolatry, blasphemy, and profanation of the Lord's day, the Independents continued to argue in the same vein as did Bay Puritans, "ought not to be suffered by the Christian magistrate." Denying the doctrine of the Trinity, "where the Gospel has sounded, is not tolerable; or to deny the Resurrection, or a Judgment Day &c. I say, the Christian magistrate ought not to tolerate the teaching of such contradictions."[99] Clearly, because of their principles of church government, the Independents in England, like the congregationalists in Massachusetts, saw no other way to maintain and sustain religious society and Christian commonwealth except through the exertions of Christian magistrates. For this reason, the alliance between the Independents and sectarians, who totally opposed any role for the godly magistrate in religious matters, never occurred.

How close the principles of the Independents in England were to those of Massachusetts Puritans can be seen in relation to the issue of liberty of conscience, which the sectarians raised against the magistrate's coercive powers in religious affairs. As Thomas Shepard wrote from Massachusetts in 1645,

> toleration of all upon pretence of conscience I thank God my soule abhors it. The godly in former times never fought for the liberty of conscience by pleading for liberty for all.[100]

The Independents, likewise, were unwilling to accept any demand for religious liberty based on conscience:

> All vicious and scandalous practices, contrary to the light of nature or manifest good of society...deriving themselves not from conscience, but a malignant will and unconscienced spirit. Nor yet may all principles that derive themselves from conscience have the benefit of this plea of liberty, so as to save their owners.[101]

Given this stand concerning conscience, there is nowhere in the Independent divines' sermons and writings any plea for toleration. Preaching before the House of Commons in 1645, Thomas Goodwin maintained:

> If any man think I am pleading for liberty of all opinions, of what nature and how gross so ever, I humbly desire them to remember that I only plead for Saints, and I answer plainly, The Saints they need it not.[102]

Caryl in England Plus Ultra (1646) even appears to encourage the two Houses of Parliament to persecute rather than to tolerate:

> Whatsoever (I say) is an errour or heresy, let all the penalties which Christ hath charged upon it be executed to the utmost.... If Christ would not have had errour to be opposed, why hath he left us means both for the opposition and suppression of errour.[103]

The rigid insistence of the Independents, exactly as did Massachusetts Puritans, on the magistrate's role concerning religious matters, an insistence which so profoundly divided them from the sectarians, was nowhere more clearly expressed than in "The Whitehall Debates" of 1648-49. In those debates the Council of Officers of the Army discussed the question of "whether the civil magistrate had a power given to him from God [in matters of religion]?" Among the clergy invited to take part in the debates on this issue were Philip Nye, the Independent, and John Goodwin, the Separatist. Goodwin answered the question without hesitation: "God hath not invested any power in a civil magistrate in matters of religion." For Nye, on the other hand, as for the other Independent divines, the magistrate had an "edict from Heaven" to achieve the goals of a Christian commonwealth. On the basis of that edict, his power in religious matters was "lawfully exercised."[104]

"The Puritans of the left," observed A.S.P. Woodhouse, "discovered that you cannot effectually guarantee the liberty of the saints without guaranteeing the liberty of all men."[105] However, the Independent divines did not share this view. While the sectarians proclaimed liberty of conscience as one of the natural rights of man and therefore excluded from the magistrate's power, the Independent divines, exactly like the Presbyterian divines and the congregationalists in Massachusetts, insisted on such power for the magistrate and thereby separated themselves from the radical sects during the 1640s.

V   Orthodoxy in England and New England

This discussion of toleration and its enemies in old and New England provides us with a meaningful context to examine whether "orthodoxy in Massachusetts" was indeed isolated from the main currents of thought in England during the 1640s. The controversy about liberty of conscience and the magistrate's power over religious matters reveals, most importantly, that the Massachusetts Puritans' goal of constituting religious order and authority was in fact the very aim of the majority of orthodox Puritans in England. This is unsurprising, of course, because Puritanism on both sides of the ocean was a movement toward establishing an orderly Christian commonwealth in which religious unity would give countenance to the unity of the body politic. Therefore, Independents and Presbyterians in England, as well as congregationalists in America, whatever their differences   about church government, shared one important thing vis-a-vis the sectarians - all of them insisted over and over again upon the crucial role of the godly magistrate in sustaining ecclesiastical order and in maintaining a Christian commonwealth.

There was, however, an essential difference between England and Massachusetts that determined how far this vision of Puritan orthodoxy could be realized. The Puritan impulse for order and authority could be relatively easily fulfilled in America, simply because in Massachusetts the godly magistrate had assumed the role of defending the church and state against heresy from the very beginnings of the colony. In the context of the Puritan quest for order and unity, Massachusetts came to be the model of the Puritans' aspirations for a community in which religious unity and uniformity was intimately connected with political and social unity and vice versa. In England, on the other, it was much more difficult to realize the Puritan utopia of order, not because English Puritans embraced new views about the social and ecclesiastical order, but simply because the whole political, social, and ecclesiastical context in England was profoundly more complex - and conflictive - than was the case in America. Consequently, in England, in contrast to Massachusetts, the godly magistrates had to deal first with a civil war and a political settlement. Above all, they had to take into account political and social considerations that severely limited their ability to achieve those aims of Puritan orthodoxy that the Bay Puritan had attained so successfully.

The reasons why English Puritans were unable to realize their orthodox vision of order and authority are not hard to find. In the 1640s, argued Richard Baxter, two people stood against "the old cause" of Puritanism concerning the preservation of order and authority in England. Henry Vane, wrote Baxter, "had increased sectaries in the House," and Oliver Cromwell had recruited into the Parliamentary army as many "of the sectaries as he could get." For an orthodox Puritan like Baxter, as for other orthodox Puritans on both sides of the ocean, the fight against popery went hand in hand with the fight to extirpate heresy. "We took the true happiness of King and People, Church and State," Baxter wrote, "to be our end, and so we understood the Covenant," or the Solemn League and Covenant, "engaging both against Papists and Schismatical." This two-fold struggle was the essential policy of orthodox Puritans during the 1640s, who always urged that the battle against popery be joined with the suppression of heresy and the sects. But in the context of the First Civil War, a godly magistrate like Cromwell found it hard, if not impossible, to fight on two fronts, and he was unwilling to fight against the sects while the whole Protestant case in England was in such a terrible conflict with the King's army. Therefore, Baxter blamed Cromwell for having "headed the greatest party of the army with Anabaptists, Antinomians, Seekers or Separatists at best; and all this he tied together by the point of liberty of conscience, which was the common interest in which they did unite."[106] Baxter's words clearly reflected the fears of orthodox Puritans regarding the rise of the sects. However, in the political context in England, as the anonymous author of The Second Part of Vox Populi (1642), asked, "why should the Parliament quarrel with more enemies till they had first prevailed over the most potent (the Papists) against whom they were sure to have

369

these their coadjutors." Hence, it was unavoidable that "there hath been Brownists, Anabaptists, and Separatists amongst" the Parliamentary party.[107] However, the plea to give up suppression of the sects and to unite Parliament's forces and the Protestant Party against the main enemy, Popery, was always denied by orthodox Puritans.

The essential stand of orthodoxy was that only godly means should be used to achieve godly ends, and thus Independents and Presbyterians in England and Puritans in Massachusetts denied any association with the sects. They could not join with heresy to fight against Popery, lest sinful means lead to corrupt consequences. Orthodox Puritans in England and New England, therefore, thought it was their duty to fight Popery and heresy at the same time. Herein lay the profound differences between Vane and Cromwell on the one hand, and Baxter on the other. For Vane and Cromwell thought first and most of all to unite everyone against Popery. This was the central issue of the First Civil War. Because of the terrible difficulties of the Parliamentary army during the early years of the war, both men knew that in order to gain victory over Popery they had to recruit anyone who was willing to fight Popery, which the sectarians with their highly millennial expectations and strong enthusiasm had been more than willing to do. But not only reasons of expediency guided Vane and Cromwell; both men had been strong millennarians who wanted to establish a united front of all Protestants, within and outside England, against Popery or the Beast. Henry Vane, was already willing in 1637 to accommodate the Antinomians into the Puritan commonwealth in Massachusetts because "Christ commands us to do good unto all, but especially to them of the household of faith."[108] In his highly millennial views, Vane thought that all those who had been persecuted by popery were united in the same "household of faith." The orthodox Puritans on both sides of the ocean flatly denied this view: both Winthrop in Massachusetts and Baxter in England attacked Vane out of the orthodox desire of achieving total unity and conformity in church and state alike. Henry Vane, like Roger

Williams, thus had the opportunity to fight against orthodoxy in old and New England.

Oliver Cromwell's views were much the same as those of Vane concerning the ultimate stakes in the battle of Protestants of all persuasions and the unity of all those of "the household of faith" against popery. Thus he admonished orthodox Puritans in England,

> Those that were sound in the faith, how proper was it for them to labour for liberty, for a just liberty, that men should not be trampled upon their consciences! Had not they laboured, but lately, under the weight of persecutions? And was it fit for them to sit heavy upon others? Is it ingenuous to ask liberty and not to give it? What greater hypocrisy than for those who were oppressed by the Bishops to become the greatest oppressors themselves, so long as their yoke was removed.[109]

Cromwell, then, like Vane, had expanded the term godly people to include all those who were willing to fight popery or those who had suffered under it. Consequently, Colonel Cromwell recruited to his regiment of horse, as one contemporary wrote, those "who upon matter of conscience engaged in this quarrel" of the First Civil War against popery. Such actions, no doubt, raised the anger of orthodox Puritans in England, who accused Cromwell of having "a company of Brownists, Anabaptists, Factious, inferiour persons, &c."[110]

In Massachusetts, by contrast, the full and profound implications of Puritanism as a conservative movement was revealed. Herein lies the crucial importance of the history of early Massachusetts for the Puritan movement in England. For in New England, where Puritans were absolutely free from political and social considerations that people had to reckon with in England, the consequences of Puritanism as a religious and social movement appeared most fully. This was not because orthodox Puritans in England, like the Independents and Presbyterians, did not strive to establish orthodoxy in England but simply because godly magistrates in England, like Cromwell and Vane, found it impossible, as the orthodox Puritans demanded, to fight on two fronts - against popery and heresy. Given the political context in England, Parliament and the

371

Protestant party had first to win the war. Next to this main aim, the internal struggle within the Protestant party appeared to Cromwell and Vane to be secondary. Hence, out of reasons of expediency, godly magistrates in England sought to unite all Protestants against the common enemy of popery. For Cromwell, acceptance of the orthodox Puritan demand to fight against the sects in the name of the one true faith meant the possible defeat of the whole Protestant cause by the king. Thus, while orthodox Puritans argued that only the unity of the church would keep civil and public order, Cromwell and Vane argued, and made it the cornerstone of their policy, that civil and public order could be achieved only by upholding religious diversity. For to fight against heresy during the civil war would lead to the defeat of the whole Protestant party.

Yet if it was left mainly to Massachusetts to reveal the full and profound consequences of Puritan orthodoxy in church and state, this by no means implies that orthodoxy became a peculiar feature only to American Puritanism. Orthodoxy existed in England and advocated by the majority of Puritans there. Given the political context, however, orthodox Puritans, in spite of all their efforts in Parliament and the Westminster Assembly of Divines, had been unable to achieve their goal of order and authority, or their aim of constituting a Christian commonwealth as the Bay Puritans had succeeded in doing. The radical views of Cromwell, Vane and the sectarians, it should be stressed again, were not acceptable to the majority of Puritans. Orthodox Puritans still thought in terms of enforcing the one truth and establishing the one church. To abandon the concept of one truth and one church and to establish a pluralistic society, in which religious liberty would be given to almost all, was far from the intentions of the orthodox in old as well as in New England.

This is why the writings of orthodox Puritans in England so strongly resemble those of the congregationalists in Massachusetts. On both sides of the ocean, orthodoxy hoped to exclude all varieties of religious experience except the orthodox way in relation to faith. In England, Adam Stuart plainly stated that toleration was not given to men to decide upon; it was up to God, who never permitted it: "God in the Old Testament granted no toleration of divers religions, or disciplines; and the New Testament requireth no lesse union among Christian, than the Old among the Jews."[111] John Bastwick similarly argued that toleration was a sin against God: "It is a thing highly displeasing unto God, that his people should give toleration of any religion but that hee hath established."[112] To orthodox Puritans in England, as well as to those in America, religious liberty of the kind advocated by the sects entailed the ruin of church and state and giving the devil the upper hand in this world. For toleration, as Thomas Edward wrote in Cangraena in 1646, had "all errors in it, and all evils, and it is against the whole stream and current of Scripture...it overthrows all relationship, both political, ecclesiastical, and economical."[113]

On the other side of the ocean, in Massachusetts, orthodox Puritans clearly identified their cause with the struggle of orthodox Puritans in England against heresy, sectarians, and toleration. "The godly in former times," wrote Thomas Shepard,

> desired to kisse the flames and fill the prisons, and suffer to the utmost, as knowing that suffering for the truth, were more advantagious to the promoting of it than their own peace and safety with liberty for all errour.[114]

John Cotton, along with the orthodox in England, attacked in The Bloudy Tenent Washed (1647) Roger Williams' advocacy of liberty of conscience and the exclusion of the magistrates from religious matters. "The great Questions of this present time," wrote Cotton, were

> How farre Liberty of Conscience ought to be given to those that truly feare God? And how farre restrained to turbulent and pestilent persons, that not only raze the foundation of Godlinesse, but disturb the Civill Peace where they live?[115]

His answer to these questions we already know, but if some of England's orthodox Puritans remained confused regarding Cottons's views of toleration, they only needed to consult his The Way of Congregational Churches Cleared (1648). Writing as an answer to Robert Baillie's A Dissuasive from the Errors of the Time (1646), Cotton declared that as an orthodox Puritan he had much more in common with "Mr. Baylie's [Baillie's] zeal against [the] errors" of the "Anabaptists, Antinomians, Seekers," and "Prelates, Papists, Arminians, Socinians, Erastians," than with Williams' plea for liberty of conscience.[116]

In 1648, Thomas Hooker's A Survey of the Summe of Church-Discpline also appeared in London. This work was a vindication of the congregational way in Massachusetts. Relying exclusively on Thomas Brightman's Apocalypisis Apocalypseos in interpreting the history of the Church, Hooker argued that the time of the millennium was at hand, "when all the Kingdomes of the world are becoming the Lords and his Christ." Yet, he continued, in apocalyptic and eschatological terms, "the spiritual Kingdome of Christ, is most opposed by a generation of Enthusiasts; and Familists," who "under the pretence of free-grace, they destroy the grace of God in the power and operation of it, in the hearts and lives of men."[117] The quest for the millennium was essentially a quest for order and authority, and thus orthodox Puritans in Massachusetts, as well as in England, attacked sectarianism because it threatened to frustrate this quest.

The close association between "orthodoxy in Massachusetts" and orthodoxy in old England is nowhere revealed more clearly than in Nathaniel Ward's The Simple Cobler of Aggawam in America (1647). "One would have to search long," wrote Moses Coit Tyler on Ward's book,

> among the rubbish of books thrown forth to the public during those hot and teeming days, to find one more authentically representing the stir, the earnestness, the intolerance, the hope, and the wrath of the times than does this book.[118]

Ward was a pastor of the church of Ipswich, Massachusetts, the Indian "Aggawam" which appears on the book title. Frightened by the new views of toleration coming out of England and New England, Ward began to write this book in the early 1640s, taking the manuscript to England when he returned there in 1646. The orthodox Puritan from the new world found his ideas much in favor in England; his book was printed in 1647, and a year later, apparently because of his views against toleration, he was invited to preach before the Commons.

Ward's book was not peculiar to American orthodoxy, but was the product of an orthodox Puritan who opposed toleration in both Massachusetts and England. "The Truths of God are the Pillars of the world," wrote Ward, "whereon States and Churches may stand in quiet if they will." And he, like many other writers from the Bay colony, clearly intended to show that Massachusetts has no "Colluvies of wild Opinionists" who "swarmed into a remote wilderness to find elbow-roome" for their "phanatick Doctrines and practises." Therefore, he proclaimed boldly,

> I dare take upon me, to be the Herauld of New England so farre, as to proclaime to the world, in the name of our Colony, that all Familists, Antinomians, Anabaptists, and other Enthusiasts, shall have free liberty to keep away from us, and such as will come to be gone as fast as they can, the sooner the better.[119]

Although a minister himself, Ward was not interested in a debate; on the contrary, he regarded his view as the whole and only truth. His discourse is therefore not a theological one aimed at proving errors, but a rigid plea to the godly magistrates to destroy any deviation in ecclesiastical matters. It is the work of the devil, he wrote, "who would ask nothing else, but liberty to enfranchize all other religion." For "to authorise an untruth, by Toleration of State, is to build a Sconce against the walls of Heaven, to batter God out of his Chair." Thus, warned Ward, "if the State of England shall...willingly Tolerate" heresy, "the Church of that Kingdome will sooner become the Devills Dancing-Schoole, than Gods-Temple."[120]

Ward's anti-toleration stand was common indeed in Massachusetts during that time. Thomas Dudley, for example, wrote this verse:

> Let men of God in courts and churches watch
> O'er such as do a toleration hatch

And it was a common saying the colony that "Antichrist was coming in that backdoore by a general liberty of conscience."[121] Toleration, evidently, in the minds of those orthodox Puritans in old and New England was a policy that would destroy order. "That State that will give Liberty of Conscience in matters

375

of Religion," wrote Ward, "must give Liberty of Conscience and Conversation in their Morall Lawes." Consequently, he declared:

> There is talke of an universal Toleration, I would talk what I could against it, did In know what more apt and reasonable Sacrifice England could offer to God...than an universal toleration of all hellish Errors, or how they shall make a universal Reformation, but by making Christs Academy the Devils University, where any man may commence Heretique per saltum; where he that is filius Diabolicus, or simpliciter pessimus, may have his grace to go to hell cum Publico Privilegio, and carry as many after him, as he can.[122]

During the year of its publication, Ward's The Simple Cobler went through four editions, and in June 1648, he was invited to preach before the Commons. "Lament in a speciall manner," he admonished the Commons, "that your Townes, and Churches, are so belepered with errours and strange Opinions" which might bring "Gods wrath, and [put] the People spirits on fire."[123] For the Army, Ward's sermon was "worse than Edwards his Gangraena," for Ward's aim had been indeed to unite Independents and Presbyterians in England against heresy and toleration.[124] This had been, nonetheless, the official stand in Massachusetts as given in "The Cambridge Platform" in 1648. "The congregational Churches, or their way," declared the Bay Puritans, when "duely administrated, doe no less effectually extirpate the Antichristian Hierarchy, & all Blasphmies, Heresyes, and pernicious errours, than the other way of discipline doeth," namely, Presbyterianism.[125]

When confronted by the rise of sectarianism, orthodox Puritans in old and New England united against heresy and vehemently attacked the very notion of toleration and liberty of conscience. They stressed again and again the decisive role which godly magistrates should play in defending the church and sustaining the Christian commonwealth. Here, on the issue of the godly magistrate's role, lay the essential difference between old and New England. In England, because of the political context, those in power could not, for reasons of expediency, act on orthodox Puritan demands to suppress heresy. Their main concern had first been to destroy popery. For this reason, they accommodated the sects within Parliament's army. And this accommodation led Baxter to blame them for being the principal agents in the abandonment of the Puritan dream of New Jerusalem in England and for relinquishing aspirations for unity and conformity to sectarian demands for diversity of sects. However, religious toleration was not won as an idea because only a few advocated it as a matter of principle. When people in England turned to it, they did so only because it was the lesser of two evils. Not an end in itself, it was rather a means to achieve unity among rival religious groups faced with a common enemy. In Massachusetts, on the other hand, the godly magistrate was totally free from such considerations and obligations, and the colony could continue its policies of anti-toleration without hindrance. However, when Oliver Cromwell, the Lord Protector, enforced the policy of religious toleration in England during the 1650s, he indeed created a historical paradox in the relationship between Massachusetts and England. Cromwell's religious toleration became the basis of his policy towards the Puritan colony, and the great advocate of toleration in England, thus, unwittingly, upheld Massachusetts' right to maintain religious uniformity within its realm. The one who enforced the policy of toleration in England on orthodox Puritans there, by the very policy of toleration, allowed the Puritans in America to persecute other opinions and beliefs.

VI   The Essence of Puritan Orthodoxy

In sum, despite their ecclesiological differences, the Presbyterians and Independents in England, and the Congregationalists in New England, shared important and fundamental principles concerning the very nature of Christian society and the decisive role of the godly magistrate was to play in religious matters. Throughout the 1640s, therefore, these Puritan groups constituted a common and formidable orthodox front against the Sectarians' plea for religious liberty and toleration. They did so because orthodoxy, as the term suggests, signified principles of preserving religious unity and conformity within the confines of Christian commonwealth and civil and ecclesiastical harmony in maintaining the true church and the true faith within a godly Christian society. Originating in the Middle Ages, these principles also permeated the social and political thought of the Protestant Reformation of the sixteenth-century. Consequently, the ideal of orthodox Puritans in England, Presbyterians as well as Independents, was to achieve religious "uniformity based upon the will of a godly people and maintained with the support of a godly civil state."[126] Likewise, Massachusetts Bay Puritans adhered strongly to this ideal of Puritan orthodoxy by establishing in America "the principles of [religious] uniformity and of civil ecclesiastical cooperation.[127]

The premises of Puritan orthodoxy concerning the relationship between church and state should be seen above all in the context of the Protestant Reformation. More specifically, these premises go back to John Calvin who eliminated the distinction between the natural and supernatural within a theocratic universe ruled directly and immediately by God's divine providence. Hence, he revolutionized the theological and religious significance of the state in the drama of salvation. For according to Calvin, "Christ as the Head of His Church is also precisely the Lord of this world." The state thus "exists for the good of those who in this perishable world belong to Christ and his eternal kingdom."[128] It exercises an important role in providential history, or in the history of salvation, by helping the church's aims and goals in the world. Indeed, Calvin asserted that "the spiritual kingdom of Christ and civil government are things very different and remote from each other."[129] Yet he also emphasized their cooperation: "this civil government is designed, as along as we live in this world, to cherish and support the external worship of God, to preserve the pure doctrine of religion, [and] to defend the constitution of the church."[130] By seeking the spiritual welfare of its citizens, the political order was therefore not only responsible for promoting their religious life and the well-being of the church but also for protecting both from idolatry, blasphemy and sacrilege. This was, then as we saw earlier, the very essence of Puritan orthodoxy in old and New England. That is, this was nothing less than the view that the state had a crucial role to play within sacred, providential history by protecting the true church, preserving the true faith and extirpating heresy.

Ultimately, Puritan orthodoxy signified "the joining of Church and Commonwealth under the civil power" which entailed the magistrate's supremacy over and responsibility for the church.[131] It was because of these views that orthodox Puritans were never willing to relinquish their stand that the godly civil magistrate ought to have a decisive role in preserving religious order, authority, unity and conformity within the Christian commonwealth that they had been trying to establish in both England and New England. This is clearly born out in the official declarations of orthodox Puritans on both sides of the Atlantic ocean: The Westminster Confession of Faith of 1646 professing Presbyterian faith set forth by the Westminster Assembly of Divines; The Cambridge Platform of 1648 written by Massachusetts Bay Congregationalists; and The Savoy Declaration of 1658 which was a statement of Congregational principles and polity drawn up by the Independents in England. These official documents of orthodox Puritans show clearly and unmistakably that orthodoxy indeed existed in both England and New England.

The Westminster Confession of Faith was written by the Assembly of Divines that met at Westminster Abbey during the Puritan Revolution. It was adopted by

Presbyterians in England and Scotland and later became the dominant standard for Presbyterianism in the English-speaking work. The Westminster Confession defined clearly the role Presbyterians assigned to the godly civil magistrate in religious affairs and the part he ought to play in Christian society in order to maintain order and authority:

> The civil magistrate may not assume to himself the administration of the Word and Sacraments, or the power of the keys of the kingdom of heaven: yet he hath authority, and it is his duty to take order, that unity and peace be preserved in the Church, that the truth of God be kept pure and entire, that all blasphemies and heresies be suppressed, all corruptions and abuses in worship and discipline prevented or reformed, and all the ordinances of God duly settled, administered, and observed. For the better effecting whereof he hath power to call synods, to be present at them, and to provide that whatsoever is transacted in them be according to the mind of God.[132]

On the other side of the ocean, in Massachusetts, Congregationalists produced in 1648 The Cambridge Platform of Church Discipline which was a "publick confession of faith" in which, as with the Westminster Confession, the decisive role of the godly civil magistrate within Christian society was strongly asserted:

> It is the duty of the Magistrate, to take care of matters of religion, & to improve his civil authority for the observing of the duties commanded in the first, as well as for observing of the duties commanded in the second table. They are called Gods. The end of the Magistrates office, is not only the quiet & peaceable life of the subject, in matters of righteousness & honesty, but also in matters of godliness, yea of all godliness.

Therefore, like Puritans in England, the congregationalists in Massachusetts assigned the civil magistrate an important role in preserving unity and conformity in religious matters: "Idolatry, Blasphemy, Heresy, venting corrupt & pernicious opinions, that destroy the foundation, open contempt of the word preached, prophanation of the Lords day, disturbing the peaceable administration & exercise of the worship & holy things of God, & the like, are to be restrayned, & punished by civil authority."[133]

The Savoy Declaration, 1658, or "A Declaration of the Faith and Order Owned and practised in the Congregational Churches in England" as it was known in full, was drawn up by English Independents at a Conference held at the Chapel of the old Savoy Palace. In it, Independents pledged full adherence to the premises of Puritan orthodoxy as represented in The Westminster Confession and The Cambridge Platform. "God the supreme Lord and King of all the world," the section of The Savoy Declaration on the Civil Magistrate begins, "hath ordained civil Magistrates to be under him, over the people for his own glory and the publique good." Consequently, the crucial role which the godly Christian magistrate ought to play within a Christian commonwealth was derived from this divine appointment:

> The Magistrate is bound to incourage, promote, protect the professor and profession of the Gospel, and to manage and order civil administration in a due subserviency to the interest of Christ in the world, and to that end to take care that men of corrupt mindes and conversations do not licentiously publish and divulge Blasphemy and Errors in their own nature, subverting the faith, and inevitably destroying the souls of them that receive them.[134]

What is most evident in these official declarations of orthodox Puritans in old and New England is their overriding concern with preserving unity and conformity in religious matters within the confines of Christian commonwealth. For in an age in which religious affairs were so closely intermingled with the affairs of the whole society, it was only natural that the quest to maintain social and political order was deeply associated with the establishment of firm religious conformity. Accordingly, the official documents of orthodox Puritans reveal their unbroken commitment to order and authority within religious society through the power of the civil magistrate. Therefore, religious liberty and toleration were incompatible with reformation according to Scripture: "a toleration is against the nature of reformation, a reformation and a toleration are diametrically opposite; the commands of God given in his word for reformation, with the examples of reforming governors, civil and ecclesiastical, do not admit toleration.[135]

381

Though orthodox Puritan arguments against religious toleration are not appealing by today's standards, they were, nevertheless, much more representative of the seventeenth century than the pleas of a minority of Sectarians who advocated religious liberty. Therefore, throughout the 1640s, orthodox Puritans were engaged in a fierce battle to maintain religious unity and social order against the Sectarians' plea to exclude the state from any interference in religious matters and, consequently, to secure toleration for all religious persuasions. In their struggle against the Sectarians, orthodox Puritans in England could count upon a decisive majority in Parliament and upon their overwhelming majority among the nine thousand parish ministers.

In the context of the struggle against the Sectarians' search for religious toleration, one easily discerns an important dimension regarding the essential conservative character of the Puritan movement. Examination of orthodox Puritan attitudes toward religious toleration clearly indicates that, as a religious movement, Puritanism was indeed conservative. Its ultimate goals were preserving order and authority and maintaining the traditional unity between spiritual and social life and between church and state. "In order to understand Puritanism," wrote Perry Miller, "we must go...to an age when the unity of religion and politics was so axiomatic that very few men would even have grasped the idea that church and state could be distinct. For the Puritan mind it was not possible to segregate a man's spiritual life from his communal life."[136] This cherished traditional unity undoubtedly underlay the essentially conservative nature of Puritanism. For among orthodox Puritans, "practically everybody agreed that there could be but one true religion and that the church should be maintained by the state. The continuance of ordered society was as yet inconceivable without the Christian church, and the church was inconceivable except as a single comprehensive institution uniform in faith and worship."[137]

Notes

1. Herbert Butterfield, "Toleration in Modern Times," Journal of the History of Ideas, 38 (Oct-Dec, 1977), pp. 573-584.

2. Nathaniel Ward, The Simple Cobler of Aggawam in America (London, 1647), p. 10.

3. John Bastwick, The Utter Routing of the Whole Army of All Independents and Sectaries (London, 1646), p. 578.

4. Richard Baxter, The Autobiography of Richard Baxter, p. 84.

5. John Rushworth, Historical Collections, 8 vols (1659-1701), II, p. 727.

6. Philip Knachel, ed., Eikon Basilike: The Portraiture of His Sacred Majesty in His Solitude and Sufferings (Ithaca, 1966), p. 153.

7. Richard Baxter, The Autobiography of Richard Baxter, p. 84.

8. George Kateb cited in Utopia and the Ideal Society: A Study of English Utopian Writing, 1516-1700, by J.C. Davis (Cambridge, Cambridge University, 1981), p. 360. See also W.H. Greenleaf, Order, Empiricism and Politics: Two Traditions of English Political Thought, 1500-1700 (Westport, Conn., 1980).

9. Samuel R. Gardiner, The Constitutional Documents of the Puritan Revolution, 1625 1660, ix-x.

10. Michael Walzer, The Revolution of the Saints: A Study in the Origins of Radical Politics (Cambridge: Harvard, 1965), vii, p. 3. The story of the Puritan movement as inevitably correlated with "liberty," "freedom" and "progress," is well told in William Haller, Liberty and Reformation in the Puritan Revolution (New York, 1955); A.S.P. Woodhouse, Puritanism and Liberty: Being the Army Debates, 1647-49 (Chicago, 1951); and in many studies of Christopher Hill.

11. Vernon F. Snow, "The concept of Revolution in Seventeenth Century England," The Historical Journal, 2 (1962), pp. 267, 169, 172.

12. Mircea Eliade, Cosmos and History: The Myth of the Eternal Return (New York, 1965), p. 141.

13. Walzer, The Revolution of the Saints, p. 3.

14. The theory of crisis in Massachusetts' relationship with England, which eventually led to the isolation of the colony from the revolutionary developments in England during the 1640s, is most clearly seen in Miller, Orthodoxy in Massachusetts.

15. Richard Mather, "A Copy of an Answer of R.M. to 36 Questions Proposed to him by E.B.," in "A Letter of Richard Mather to a Cleric in Old England," by Richard Burg, WMQ 29 (Jan, 1972), p. 84. See also: Richard Mather, Church-Government and Church-Covenant Discussed (London, 1642).

16. Mather, "A Copy of an Answer," pp. 87-89.

17. Ibid., pp. 89,95, 89.

18. Ibid., pp. 92, 95.

19. Ibid., pp. 95, 89.

20. "A Letter of Many Ministers in Old England, Requesting the Judgment of Their Reverend Brethren in New England, Concerning Nine Positions...1637," in Historical Memorials, Relating to the Independents, or Congregationalists: from their rise to the Restoration of the Monarchy, by Benjamin Hanbury (London, 1841), II, pp. 18-19 (hereafter cited as Hanbury, Historical Memorials,).

21. Ibid., p. 19.

22. "The Answer of the Elders of the Churches of New England" appeared in England along with "A Letter of Many Ministers in Old England" of 1637 under the common title "A Letter of Many Ministers in Old England, requesting the judgment of their Reverend Brethren in New England, concerning Nine Positions: Written A.D. 1637. Together with their Answer thereto, returned anno 1639; and, the Reply made unto the said Answer, and sent over to them, anno 1640. Now published...upon the desire of many godly and faithful ministers, in and about the City of London, who love and seek the Truth" (1643), in Hanbury, Historical Memorials, II, pp. 22, 20.

23. Ibid., pp. 21, 22.

24. John Ball, A Friendly Traill of the Grounds Tending to Separation (London, 1640); Ball, An Answer to Two Treatises of Mr. John Can, Leader of the English Brownists in Amsterdam (London, 1642). Ball's "Reply" to the Bay Elders appears in Hanbury, Historical Memorials, II, p. 22.

25. Ball, in Hanbury, Historical Memorials, II, 26-28.

26. John Ball, A Friendly Triall of the Grounds Tending to Separation, p. 5.

27. Miller, Orthodoxy in Massachusetts, Chaps. III-IV.

28. Thomas Hobbes, Behemoth: or, The Epitome of The Civil Wars in England, in The English Works of Thomas Hobbes, ed. Sir William Molesworth (Scientia Aalen, 1962), VI, pp. 166-167. See also John F. Wilson, Pulpit in Parliament: Puritanism during the Church Civil Wars, 1640-1648 (Princeton, 1969).

29. H.R. Trevor-Roper, "The Fast Sermons to the Long Parliament," in Religion, the Reformation and Social Change (London, 1967), pp. 294-344; E.W. Kirby, "Sermons Before the Commons," AHR, 44 (April, 1939), pp. 528-548; John F. Wilson Pulpit in Parliament: Puritanism During the English Civil Wars, 1640-1648 (Princeton, 1969). On Puritan preaching in general, see: C.F. Richardson, English Preachers and Preachings, 1640-1670 (New York, 1928); John Brown, Puritan Preaching in England (New York, 1900); Babette M. Levy, Preaching in the First Half Century of New England History (Hartford, 1945).

30. Cornelius Burges, The First Sermon Preached to the Honourable House of Commons (London, 1641), "The Epistle," pp. 1, 43.

31. Stephen Marshall, A Sermon (London, 1641), p. 43. John Cleveland's description of Marshall appears in his poem "The Rebell Scot," in The Poems of John Cleveland, ed. Brian Morris (Oxford, 1967). p. 29.

32. Stephen Marshall, A Peace-Offering to God (London, 1641), p. 50.

33. Edmund Calamy, Englands Looking-Glass (London, 1642), "Preface".

34. William Bridge, Babylon's Downfall (London, 1641), cited in Kirby, "Sermons before the Commons," p. 535.

35. The Orders from the House of Commons for the Abolishing of Superstition and Innovation, in the Regulating of Church Affaires (London, 1641), in An Order Made by the House of Commons for the Establishing of Preaching Lecturers, Through the Kingdome of England and Wales (London, 1641), p. 63.

36. Burges, Another Sermon (London, 1641), p. 63.

37. Marshall, Reformation and Desolation (London, 1642), p. 52.

38. Edmund Calamy, Gods Free Mercy to England (London, 1642), pp. 49-50.

39. Thomas Goodwin, Zerubbabels Encouragement to Finish the Temple (London, 1642), pp. 51, 16.

40. A Discovery of 29 Sects Here in London (London, 1641); A Nest of Serpents Discovered (London, 1641).

41. See for example A Description of the Sect Called the Familie of Love, With Their Common Place of Residence (London, 1641); The Brownists Conventicle: or an Assembly of Brownists, Separatists, and Non-Conformists (London, 1641).

42. Burges, Another Sermon, pp. 60-61. An excellent discussion of the religious controversies in England during the 1640s can be found in William Haller, Tracts on Liberty in the Puritan Revolution, I, and Liberty and Reformation in the Puritan Revolution. For the history of the Church of England during that time, see: William A. Shaw, A History of the English Church During the Civil Wars and Under the Commonwealth 1640-1660, 2 vols. (London, 1900); John Stoughton, History of Religion in England: From the Opening of the Long Parliament to 1850 (London: 1901). For the events in the city of London in

early 1640s, see the excellent study of Valerie Pearl, London and the Outbreak of the Puritan Revolution (London, 1961).

43. "The Protestation" (May 3, 1641), in Constitutional Documents, ed. Gardiner, pp. 155-156.

44. Henry Burton, The Protestation Protested (London, 1641), not pag. 11.

45. Henry Burton, The Sounding of the two Last Trumpets, the Sixth and Seventh...of the Revelation, as Containing a Prophecie of These Last Times (London, 1641).

46. John Geere, Judahs Joy at the Oath (London, 1641), and Vindiciae Voti; or a Vindication of the True Sense of the National Covenant (London, 1641).

47. A Survay of that Foolish, Seditious, Scandalous, Prophane Libell, the Protestation Protested (London, 1641).

48. Thomas Edwards, Reasons Against the Independent Government of Particular Congregations (London, 1641), pp. 33, 32. On the issue of the independent and separatist congregations in England during the 1640s, see: Murray Tolmie, The Triumph of the Saints: The Separate Churches of London, 1619-1649 (Cambridge: Cambridge University, 1977); and Geoffrey Nuttall, Visible Saints: The Congregational Way, 1640-1660 (Oxford, 1957).

49. Ibid., p. 33. As a response to Edwards' book, Katherine Chidley published The Justification of the Independent Churches of Christ (London, 1641).

50. Lamont, Godly Rule, p. 30.

51. Herbert Butterfield, "Toleration in Early Modern Times," Journal of the History of Ideas, 38 (Oct-Dec., 1977), p. 573.

52. For the common pattern in the historiography of the Civil Wars to associate the Independents with toleration, see: Henry Kamen, The Rise of Toleration (New York, 1967), p. 170; Joseph Lecler, Toleration and Reformation, 2 vols. (New York, 1960), II, p. 456; W.K. Jordan, The Development of Religious Toleration in England, 4 vols. (Gloucester, 1965), III, pp. 51, 369-370; George Yule, The Independents in the English Civil War (Cambridge: Cambridge Univ., 1958), pp. 13, 45; A Tindal Hart, Clergy and Society, 1600-1800 (London, 1968), pp. 40-41; and William Haller, The Rise of Puritanism (New York, 1938), p. 174. I have considered the real stand of the Independent Divines toward the issue of religious toleration in my essay: "Religious Toleration and its Enemies: The Independent Divines and the Issue of Toleration During the English Civil War," Abion 21, No. 1 (Spring 1989), pp. 1-33.

53. Miller, Orthodoxy in Massachusetts, pp. 280-281.

54. Richard Baxter, The True History of Councils Enlarged (1682), cited in Hanbury, Historical Memorials, II, p. 69.

55. J.H. Hexter, "The Problem of the Presbyterian Independents," in Reappraisals in History (London, 1961), pp. 163-184. On the controversy that follows George Yule's attempt to find a correlation between religion and politics, or between "the Parliamentary

Independents party and religious Independency,"(The Independents in the English Civil War, p. 1), see: D. Underdown, "The Independents Reconsidered," The Journal of British Studies, 3 (1965), pp. 57-84. Yule's reply, "Independents and Revolutionaries," appeared in The Journal of British Studies, 7 (1968), pp. 11-32, and Underdown's answer in "The Independents Again," The Journal of British Studies, 8 (1968), pp. 83-93. See also on this issue, Stephen Foster, "The Presbyterian Independents Exorcized," Past and Present, 44 (August, 1969), pp. 52-77.

56.   Examples of ministers from Massachusetts who emigrated back to England and became Presbyterians appear in William L. Sachse, "The Migration of New Englanders to England, 1640-1660," AHR, 53, No. 2 (January, 1948), pp. 251-278.

57.   William Walwyn, A Help to the Right Understanding of a Discourse Concerning Independency (London, 1645), p. 6.

58.   Thomas Goodwin, Philip Nye, Sidrach Simpson, Jeremiah Borroughes and William Bridge, Apologetical Narration (London, 1644), p. 21.

59.   John Cotton, The Way of the Congregational Churches Cleared (London, 1648), in John Cotton on the Churches of New England, ed. Larzer Ziff, p. 187.

60.   Thomas Goodwin, A Glimpse of Sions Glory, pp. 2, 11.

61.   Tai Liu, Discord in Sion, p. 9.

62.   Lawrence Kaplan, "Presbyterians and Independents in 1643," English Historical Review, LXXXIV (April, 1969), pp. 247-248.

63.   Robert Baillie, A Dissuasive from the Errours of the Time (London, 1645), p. 130.

64.   "The Solemn League and Covenant," in Constitutional Documents, ed. Gardiner, pp. 268-269.

65.   Philip Nye, "An Exhortation Made to the Honourable House of Commons and Reverend Divines of the Assembly, by Mr. Nye before he read the Covenant," in Two Speeches Delivered...by Mr. Nye...by Mr. Alexander Henderson (London, 1643), p. 15.

66.   Certain Considerations to Diswade Men from Further Gathering of Churches in the Present Time (London, 1643).

67.   Tai Liu, Discord in Sion, pp. 39-41.

68.   Lawrence Kaplan, "Presbyterians and Independents," p. 254.

69.   William Haller, Tracts on Liberty in the Puritan Revolution, I, p. 36.

70.   S.W. Carruthers, The Everyday Work of the Westminster Assembly (Philadelphia, 1943), pp. 93-94. On the Westminster Assembly of Divines, see also: Alex F. Mitchell and John Struthers, eds., Minutes of the Sessions of the Westminster Assembly of Divines (Edinburgh, 1874); Robert Baillie, The Letters and Journals of Robert Baillie, ed. David Laing (Edinburgh, 1841); John Lightfoot, The Journal and the Proceedings of the Assembly of Divines, in The Whole Works of...John Lightfoot, ed. John Rogers Pitman (London, 1824), Vol. XII.

71.   The Parliament Scout: Communicating His Intelligence to the Kingdome (June 20-27, 1644).

72.   E.W. Kirby, "The English Presbyterians in the Westminster Assembly," Church History, 33 (1964), pp. 418-419, 423-424. On the relationship between the Independents and Presbyterians in the Assembly, see: Samuel C. Pearson, "The Reluctant Radicals: The Independents in the Westminster Assembly," Journal of Church and State, 11 (1969), pp. 473-485. For the list of people who were chosen for the Westminster Assembly of Divines, see: "The Name of the Orthodox Divines, presented by the Knights and Burgesses, as fit person to be consulted with by the Parliament touching the Reformation of Church Government and Liturgy," in A Catalogue of the Names of the Dukes, Marquesses, Earles and Lords, that have absent themselves from the Parliament (London, 1642).

73.   The Spie: Communicating Intelligence from Oxford (March 5-13, 1643/44), p. 51.

74.   Mercurius Britanicus: Communicating the Affaires of Great Britaine (March 11-18 1643/44), pp. 208-210.

75.   The Compleate Intellegencer and Resolves (Nov. 14, 1643), pp. 44-46.

76.   Thomas Goodwin, et al., Apologetical Narration, pp. 26, 25, 26.

77.   Tai Liu, Discord in Sion, p. 45.

78.   Jordan, The Development of Religious Toleration, III, p. 355.

79.   Philip Nye, The Lawfulnes of the Oath of Supremacy and Power of the King in Ecclesiastical Affairs (London, 1683), p. 42. Nye's view of the magistrate's power in religious matters can also be found in his The King's Authority in Dispensing with Ecclesiastical Law (London, 1687) and A Declaration of the Faith and Order Owned and Practised in the Congregational Churches in England (London, 1658). On Philip Nye, see: D. Nobbs, "Philip Nye on Church and State," Cambridge Historical Journal, 5-6 (1935-1940), pp. 41-59.

80.   Thomas Goodwin, et al., Apologetical Narration, p. 26.

81.   Nye, The Lawfulnes of the Oath of Supremacy..., p. 42.

82.   Thomas Goodwin and Philip Nye, "To the Reader," Preface to Cotton's The Keys of the Kingdom of Heaven, in John Cotton on the Churches of New England, ed. Ziff.

83.   Cotton, The Keys of the Kingdom, p. 154.

84.   John Selden, Table Talk of John Selden, ed. Sir Frederick Pollock (London, 1927), pp. 57-58.

85.   Ephraim Pagitt, Heresiography, or, A Description of the Heretickes and Sectaries of these Later Times (London, 1646), p. 86.

86.   Thomas Goodwin, et al., Apologetical Narration, pp, 23-24, 4, 29.

87.   Charles Herle's words appear in his "Preface" to the Apologetical Narration.

88.   Walwyn, The Compassionate Samaritane (London, 1644), pp. 1-3.

89.   Walwyn, The Power of Love (London, 1643), "To the Reader," p. 20.

90.   Walwyn, The Compassionate Samaritane, preface "To the Commons England."

91.   John Goodwin, Oeomaxia, or The Grand Imprudence of Men Running the Hazard of Fighting Against God, in Suppressing any Way, Doctrine, or Practice (London, 1644), p. 11.

92.   Walwyn, The Compassionate Samaritane, p. 172.

93.   John Robinson, Liberty of Conscience (London, 1643), p. 27. For an excellent study of the struggle for toleration during the 1640s, see Thomas Jackson, The Life of John Goodwin (London, 1822). On the radicalism of the sects in general, see: Geoffrey F. Nuttall, The Holy in the Puritan Faith and Experience (Oxford, 1946). See also: Joseph Fletcher, History of the Revival and Progress of Independency in England Since the Period of the Reformation (London, 1848).

94.   Robinson, Liberty of Conscience, p. 44.

95.   Richard Overton, The Araignement of Mr. Persecution (London, 1645), p. 19.

96.   Roger Williams, The Bloudy Tenent of Persecution, for Cause of Conscience in The Complete Writings of Roger Williams, ed. S.L. Caldwell, 7 vols. (New York, 1963), pp. 349-351, 355-356.

97.   Jeremiah Borroughes, A Sermon Preached Before the Right Honourable House of Peers (London, 1645), pp. 45, 48.

98.   Joseph Caryl, The Arraignment of Unbelief as the Grand Cause of Our National Non-Establishment (London, 1645), pp. 2, 47.

99.   The Ancient Bounds (London, 1645), in Puritanism and Liberty, ed. A.S.P. Woodhouse (London, 1938), pp. 250-251.

100.   Thomas Shepard, "Thomas Shepard to Hugh Peter, 1645," AHR, 4 (1898-1899), p. 106.

101.   The Ancient Bounds, p. 248.

102.   Thomas Goodwin, The Great Interest of States and Kingdomes (London, 1645), p. 53.

103.   Caryl, England Plus Ultra (London, 1646), pp. 24-25. For evident that Independent divines continued to associate themselves with the Presbyterians, see their sermons of the late 1640s. See, for example, Caryl, Joy Out-Joyed (London, 1646); Borroughes, A Sermon (London, 1646); William Bridge, The Saints Hiding-Place in the Time of Gods Anger (London, 1646), England Save with Notwithstanding (London, 1647), and Christ Coming (London, 1648).

104.   "The Whitehall Debates," in Puritanism and Liberty, ed. Woodhouse, pp. 126, 153, 160.

105. A.S.P. Woodhouse, Puritanism and Liberty, "Introduction," p. 81.

106. Richard Baxter, The Autobiography of Richard Baxter, pp. 47, 45, 49, 56.

107. The Second Part of Vox Populi (London, 1642), unpag. 3.

108. Henry Vane, "A Brief Answer to a Certain Declaration," 1637, The Hutchinson Papers, 2 vols. The Prince Society (New York, 1967), I, p. 96. The millenarianism of Henry Vane can be seen clearly in his writings, such as The Face of Time (London, 1662), A Letter of Sir Henry Vane to his Lady (London, 1662), A Healing Question (London, 1660), A Needful Corrective or Ballance in Popular Government (London, 1660), and Two Treatises (London, 1662). On the life and thought of Henry Vane, see: Margaret Judson, The Political Thought of Sir Henry Vane the Younger (Philadelphia, 1969), and James K. Hosmer, The Life of Henry Vane (Boston, 1888).

109. Oliver Cromwell, "Speech IV to his First Parliament," (Jan. 22, 1655), in The Letters and Speeches of Oliver Cromwell, ed. Thomas Carlyle (New York, 1904), III, p. 417.

110. Bulstrode Whitelock, Memorials of the English Affairs (Oxford, 1853), I, p. 209; Robert S. Paul, The Lord Protector: Religion and Politics in the Life of Oliver Cromwell (London, 1955), p. 65.

111. Adam Stuart, Some Observations and Annotations upon the Apologetical Narration (London, 1643), p. 62.

112. John Bastwick, The Utter Routing of the Whole Army of All the Independents and Sectaries (London, 1646), p. 578.

113. Thomas Edward, Gangraena, or A Catalogue and Discovery of Many of the Errors, Heresies, Blasphemies, and Pernicious Practices of the Sectaries of This Time (London, 1646), I, p. 58.

114. Thomas Shepard, "Thomas Shepard Letter to Hugh Peter, 1645," p. 106.

115. John Cotton, The Bloudy Tenent, Washed, And Made White in the Bloud of the Lamb (London, 1647). The quotation is from the title page of Cotton's work.

116. Cotton, The Way of Congregational Churches Cleared, pp. 176, 175.

117. Thomas Hooker, A Survey of the Summe of Church-Discipline (London, 1648), "The Preface." On Hooker's writings in the 1640s, see: Sargent Bush, Jr., "Thomas Hooker and the Westminster Assembly," WMQ, 29 (April, 1972). On the millennialism in the Bay colony during the 1640s and 1650s, see: J.R. Maclear, "New England and the Fifth Monarchy: The Quest for the Millennium in Early American Puritanism," WMQ, 32 (April 1975), pp. 223-260.

118. Moses Coit Tyler, A History of American Literature, 1607-1676 (New York, 1878), I, p. 230.

119. Nathaniel Ward (Theodor de la Guadr), The Simple Cobler of Aggawam in America (London, 1647), pp. 1, 3.

120. Ibid., pp. 4, 6, 9.

121. Thomas Dudley and Thomas Shepard are cited in History of American Literature, by M.C. Tyler, I, p. 108.

122. Ward, The Simple Cobler, pp. 1-3.

123. Nathaniel Ward, A Sermon Preached Before the Honourable House of Commons (London, 1648), pp. 25-26.

124. H.R. Trevor-Roper, "The Fast Sermons of the Long Parliament," in Religion, the Reformation, and Social Change (London, 1967), p. 326.

125. "The Cambridge Platform, 1648," in The Creeds and Platforms of Congregationalism, by Williston Walker, pp. 195, 202.

126. William Haller, The Rise of Puritanism (Philadelphia, 1972 [1938]), p. 173.

127. Perry Miller, Orthodoxy in Massachusetts, p. 72.

128. Wilhelm Niesel, The Theology of John Calvin (Philadelphia, 1956), p. 230.

129. John Calvin, Institutes of the Christian Religion, IV, 20, i.

130. Calvin, Institutes, IV, 20, ii.

131. Perry Miller, Orthodoxy in Massachusetts, p. 5.

132. "The Westminster Confession," 1646, in John H. Leith, ed., Creeds of the Churches: A Reader in Christian Doctrine from the Bible to the Present (Atlanta, 1977), p. 220.

133. "The Cambridge Platform, 1648," pp. 194-5, 236.

134. "The Savoy Declaration," 1658, in The Creeds and Platforms of Congregationalism, by Williston Walker (New York, 1893), p. 393.

135. Thomas Edwards, Antapologia: Or a Full Answer to the Apologetical Narration (London, 1644), p. 285.

136. Perry Miller and Thomas H. Johnson, eds., The Puritans: A Source of their Writings, 2 Vols. (New York, 1963), I, p. 181.

137. William Haller, The Rise of Puritanism, p. 6.

BIBLIOGRAPHY

BIBLIOGRAPHY

Abbott, Wilbur C. The Writings and Speeches of Oliver Cromwell, 3 Vols. Cambridge, 1937.

Adams, James Truslow. The Founding of New England. Boston, 1949 [1921].

Adamson, J.H. and Holland, H.F. Sir Harry Vane: His Life and Times. Boston, 1973.

Allen, David G. In English Ways: The Movement of Societies and the Transfer of English Local Law and Custom to Massachusetts Bay in the Seventeenth Century. Chapel Hill, 1981.

Allen, J.W. English Political Thought 1603-1660. London, 1638.

Ames, Williams. The Marrow of Sacred Divinity,. London, 1642.

_____. Conscience with the Power and Cases Thereof. London, 1641.

Andrews, Charles. The Colonial Period of American History, 3 Vols. New Haven, 1935-1943.

_____. Our Earlier Colonial Settlements. London, 1933.

_____. British Committees, Commissions, and Counciles of Trade and Plantation 1622-1675. Baltimore, 1908.

Arber, Edward, ed. The Story of the Pilgrim Fathers 1606-1623, As Told by Themselves, Their Friends, and Their Enemies. Boston, 1897.

Arieli, Yehoshua. Individualism and Nationalism in American Ideology. Baltimore, 1966.

Bacon, Francis. The Advancement of Learning, ed., A. Johnston. Oxford, 1974.

Bacon, Leonard. Genesis of the New England Churches. New York, 1874.

Baillie, Robert. The "Dissuasive from the Errors of the Time" Vindicated from the Exceptions of Mr. Cotton and Mr. Tombes. London, 1655.

Baillie, Robert. Letters and Journals of Robert Baillie, ed., David Laing Edinburgh, 1841.

_____. A Dissuasive from the Errours of the Time. London, 1845.

Bailyn, Bernard. The New England Merchants in the Seventeenth Century. Cambridge, 1955.

Baker, J. Wayne. Heinrich Bullinger and the Covenant. Athens, 1980.

Bale, John. Image of Both Churches, 1550, Selected Works of John Bale, ed., H. Christmas. Cambridge, 1849.

_____. John Bale's King Johan, ed., Barry B. Adams. San Marino, 1969.

Bale, John. Acts of the Privy Council of England, Colonial Series, 1613-1680.

Ball, Bryan W. A Great Expectation: Eschatological Thought in English Protestantism to 1660. Leiden, 1975.

Ball, John. An Answer to two Traetises of Mr. Iohn Can. Leader of the English Brownists in Amsterdam. London, 1642.

_____. Trial of the New Church-Way in New England and Old. London, 1644.

_____. Friendly Trial of the Grounds Tending to Separation. London, 1640.

Baltzer, Klaus. The Covenant Formulary. Philadelphia, 1971.

Banks, Charles E. The Planters of the Commonwealth. Boston, 1930.

Barkun, Michael. Disaster and the Millennium. New Haven, 1974.

Barnes, Harry E. A History of Historical Writing. New York, 1962 [1937].

Bastwick, John. Independency not God's Ordinance. London, 1645.

_____. The Utter Routing of the Whole Army of all the Independents and Sectaries. London, 1646.

Battis, Emery. Saints and Sectaries: Anne Hutchinson and the Antinomian Controversy in the Massachusetts Bay Colony. Chapel Hill, 1962.

Bauckham, Richard. Tudor Apocalypse: Sixteenth Century Apocalypticism, Millenarianism and the English Reformation, from John Bale to John Foxe and Thomas Brightman. Oxford, 1978.

Baxter, Richard. The Autobiography of Richard Baxter, eds. J. M. Lloyd Thomas and N. H. Keeble. London, 1974.

_____. A Holy Commonwealth, or Political Aphroisms Opening the True Principles of Government. 1659.

Beard, Thomas. The Theatre of Gods Judgments. London, 1612.

Bercovitch, Scavan. The Puritan Origins of the American Self. New Haven, 1975.

_____. The American Jeremiad. Wisconsin, 1978.

_____. ed. The American Puritan Imagination. Cambridge, 1974.

_____. ed. Typology and Early American Literature. University of Massachusetts Press, 1972.

Berlin, Isaiah. Historical Inevitability. London, 1955.

_____. Four Essay on Liberty. London, 1969.

Bernard, Richard. A Key of Knowledge for the Opening of the Secret Mysteries of St. Johns Mysticall Reuelation. 1617.

Bozeman, Theodore D. To Live Ancient Lives: The Primitivist Dimension in Puritanism. Chapel Hill, 1988.

Bradford, William. "Verses by Governor Bradford," Massachusetts Historical Society, Proceedings 11. Boston, 1869-1870.

_____. A Dialogue, or Third Conference between some Young Men born in New England, and some Ancient Men. Boston, 1870.

_____. The Collected Verse, ed. Michael G. Runyman. St. Paul, 1974.

_____. Of Plymouth Plantation, 1620-1647. ed. Samuel Eliot Morison. New York, 1967.

Bradstreet, Anne D. The Complete Works of Anne Bradstreet, ed. J. R. McElrate. Boston, 1981.

_____. "A Dialogue between Old England and New Concerning Their Present Troubles, Anno 1642," Old South Leaflets, no. 159.

Braunthal, Alfred. Salvation and the Perfect Society: The Eternal Quest. Amherst, 1979.

Breen, T. H. The Character of the Good Ruler: A Study of Puritan Political Ideas in New England, 1630-1730. New Haven, 1970.

_____. and S. Foster. "Moving to the New World: The Character of early Massachusetts immigration," WMQ, 30. April, 1973.

Breslow, Marvin A. A Mirror of England: English Puritan Views of Foreign Nations 1618-1640. Cambridge, 1970.

Bridenbaugh, Carl. Vexed and Troubled Englishmen, 1590-1642. New York, 1968.

Bridge, William. Babylon Downfall. London, 1641.

_____. England Save with a Notwithstanding. London, 1647.

_____. Christ Coming. London, 1648.

_____. The Saints Hiding-Place in the time of Gods Anger. London, 1646.

Brightman, Thomas. Apocalypsis Apocalypseos, or a Revelation of the Revelation. Leyden, 1616.

Brockunier, Samuel H. The Irrepressible Democrat: Roger Williams. New York, 1940.

Brown, Alexander. The Genesis of the United States, 3 Vols. Boston and New York, 1890.

Brown, Katherine B. "The Controversy Over the Franchise in Puritan Massachusetts, 1954 to 1974," WMQ, 33. April 1976.

Brown, J. Puritan Preaching in England. New York, 1900.

Bulkeley, Peter. The Gospel Covenant. London, 1651.

Burg, Richard. Richard Mather of Dorchester. Kentucky, 1976.

_____. "A Letter of Richard Mather to a Cleric in Old England," WMQ, 29. January, 1972.

_____. "The Cambridge Platform: A Reassertion of Ecclesiastical Authority," Church History, 43. December, 1974.

Burges, Cornelius. The First Sermon Preached to the Honorable House of Commons. London, 1640.

Burges, Cornelius. Another Sermon. London, 1641.

Burrage, Champlin. The Church Covenant Idea. Philadelphia, 1904.

_____. The Early English Dissenters, 2 Vols. Cambridge, 1912.

Burrell, S. A. "The covenant Idea as a Revolutionary Symbol: Scotland 1596-1637," Church History, 27. December, 1958.

Burridge, Kennelm. New Heaven, New Earth: A Study of Millenarian Activities. New York, 1969.

Burroughes, Jermiah. A Sermon. London, 1646.

_____. A Sermon Preached Before the...House of Peeres. London, 1645.

Burton, Henry. The Protestation Protested. London, 1641.

_____. The Sounding of the two last Trumpets. London, 1641.

Bush, Sargent. "Thomas Hooker and the Westminster Assembly," WMQ, 29. April, 1972.

_____. The Writings of Thomas Hooker: Spiritual Adventure in Two Worlds. Wisconsin, 1980.

Butterfield, Herbert. "Toleration in Early Modern Times," Journal of the History of Ideas, 38. October-December, 1977.

_____. The Origins of History. New York, 1981.

Calder, Isabel M. The New Haven Colony. New Haven, 1934.

_____. ed. Letters of John Davenport: Puritan Divine. New Haven, 1937.

_____. ed. Activities of the Puritan Faction of the Church of England 1625-1633. London, 1957.

Calamy, Edmund. Englands Looking-Glass. London, 1642.

_____. Gods Free Mercy to England. London, 1642.

Calvin, John. Institutes of the Christian Religion, Library of Christian Classics, 2 Vols. Philadelphia, 1960.

Capp, Bernard S. The Fifth Monarchy Men: A Study in Seventeenth-Century English Millenarianism. London, 1972.

Carroll, Peter N. Puritanism and the Wilderness: The Intellectual Significance of the New England Frontier, 1629-1700. New York, 1969.

Carruthers, S.W. Everyday Work of the Westminster Assembly. Philadelphia, 1943.

Caryl, Joseph. England Plus ultra. London, 1646.

Cassirer, Ernest. The Platonic Renaissance in England. Austin, 1953.

Charles, Amy M. A Life of George Herbert. Ithaca, 1977.

Chidley, Katherine. The Justification of the Independent Churches. London, 1641.

Child, John. New Englands Jonas Cast up at London. London, 1647.

Christianson, Paul. Reform and Babylon: English Apocalyptical Visions from the Reformation to the Eve of the Civil War. Toronto, 1978.

_____. "Reformers and the Church of England under Elizabeth and the Early Stuarts," Journal of Ecclesiastical History, 31. October, 1980.

Clap, Roger. Memoirs of Captain Roger Clap. Boston, 1844.

Clark, Peter. English Provincial Society from the Reformation to the Revolution: Religion, Politics and Society in Kent, 1500-1640. Sussex, 1977.

Cobbett, Thomas. A Just Vindication of the Covenant. London, 1648.

Cohen, Ronald D. "Church and State in Seventeenth Century Massachusetts: Another Look at the Antinomian Controversy," Journal of Church and State, 12. Autumn, 1970.

Cohn, Norman. The Pursuit of the Millennium. London, 1972 [1957].

_____. Europe's Inner Demons New York, 1975.

Cole, C. Robert and Moodny, Michael E. The Dissenting Tradition. Athens, 1975.

Collinson, Patrick. "Toward a Broader Understanding of the Early Dissenting Tradition," The Dissenting Tradition, eds. C. Robert Cole and Michael E. Moody. Athens, 1975.

400

_____. The Elizabethan Puritan Movement. Los Angeles, 1967.

Coolidge, John S. The Pauline Renaissance in England: Puritanism and he Bible. Oxford, 1970.

Cotton, John. A Brief Exposition with Practicall Observations upon the whole Book of Ecclesiastes. 1654.

_____. Gods Promise to His Plantation. 1634 [1630].

_____. The Keys of the Kingdom of Heaven, 1644.

_____. The Bloudy Tenent, Washed. London, 1647.

_____. The Powring of the Seven Vials, or an exposition of the 16. chapter of the Revelation, with an Application of it to our Times. London, 1642.

_____. An Exposition upon the Thirteenth Chapter of Revelation. London, 1656.

_____. The Way of the Congregational Churches Cleared. London, 1648.

Cromwell, Oliver. The Letters and Speeches of Oliver Cromwell, ed. Thomas Carlyle, 3 Vols. London, 1904.

Cross, Arthur L. The Anglican Episcopate and the American Colonies. New York, 1902.

Cross, Clair. The Royal Supremacy in the Elizabethan Church. London, 1969.

_____. Church and People 1450-1660: The Triumph of the Laity in the English Church. Trowbridge, 1976.

Curtis, Mark H. "The Alienated Intellectuals of Early Stuart England," Crisis in Europe 1560-1660, ed. Trevor Aston. London, 1965.

Cushman, Robert. "Reasons and Considerations Touching the Lawfulness of Removing out of England into the parts of America," in Edward Arber, ed., The Story of the Pilgrim Fathers. New York, 1969 [1897].

Danforth, Samuel. "A Brief Recognition of New Englands Errand into the Wilderness, 1670," The Wall and the Garden: Selected Massachusetts Election Sermons, 1670-1775, ed., W. Plumstead. Minneapolis, 1984.

_____. "The Saint's Anchor-Hold," The Puritans in America: A Narrative Anthology, eds. Alan Heimer and Andrew Delbanco. Cambridge, 1985.

Davenport, John. A Discourse About Civil Government in a New Plantation Whose Design is Religion. Cambridge, 1663.

Davidson, James W. The Logic of Millennial Thought: Eighteenth Century New England. New Haven, 1977.

Davis, J. C. Utopia and the Ideal Society: A Study of English Utopian Writing 1516-1700. Cambridge, 1981.

Davis, H. Worship and Theology in England from Cranmer to Hooker 1534-1603. Princeton, 1970.

Davis, Godfrey. The Early Stuarts 1603-1660. Oxford, 1976 [1959].

Dean, John Ward. A Memoir of Rev. Nathaniel Ward. Albany, 1868.

Deane, Charles. "The Forms in Issuing Letters Patents by the Crown of England," MHSP. 1869-1870.

Dickens, A.G. The German Reformation and Martin Luther. London, 1974.

_____. The Reformation in Historical Thought. Cambridge, MA 1985.

_____. The English Reformation. London, 1964.

Dudley, Thomas. "Letters to the Countess of Lincoln, March 1631," Tracts and Other Papers Relating Principally to the Origin, Settlement and Progress of the Colonies in North America, ed. Peter Force, 4 Vols. Washington, 1830-1840.

Dunn, Richard S. Puritans and Yankees: The Winthrop Dynasty of New England 1630-1717. Princeton, 1962.

Edward, Thomas. Gangraena, or, A Catalogue and Discovery of many of the Errors, Heresies, Blasphemies, and pernicious Practices of the Sectaries of this Time. London, 1646.

_____. Reasons against the Independent Government of Particular Congregations, 1641.

Eliade, Mircea. Cosmos and History: The Myth of the Eternal Return. New York, 1959.

Eliot, John. The Christian Commonwealth. London, 1661.

Elton, G. R. Reformation Europe, 1517-1559. London, 1963.

402

_____. ed. The Tudor Constitution: Documents and Commentary. Cambridge, 1960.

Emerson, Everett H. "Calvin and Covenant Theology," Church History, 35. June, 1956.

_____. English Puritanism from Hooper to John Milton. Durham, 1968.

_____ ed. Letters from New England: The Massachusetts Bay Colony 1629-1638. Amherst, 1976.

_____. Puritanism in America 1620-1750. Boston, 1977.

Emery, Samuel H. The Ministry of Taunton. Boston, 1853.

Erikson, Kai T. Wayward Puritans: A Study in the Sociology of Deviance. New York, 1966.

Erikson, Erik H. "Reflections on the American Identity," Childhood and Society. New York, 1965.

Everitt, Alan. The Community of Kent and the Great Rebellion 1640-1660. Leicester, 1966.

_____. "Nonconformatiy in Country Parishes," Land, Church and People, ed. Joan Thirsk. Reading, 1970.

Ferguson, Arthur B. Clio Unbound: Perceptions of Social and Cultural Past in Renaissance England. Durham, 1979.

Fierce, Richard. The Records of the First Church in Salem Massachusetts, 1629-1736. Salem, 1974.

Firth, Charles H. Oliver Cromwell and the Rule of the Puritans in England. London, 1947.

Firth, Katharine R. The Apocalyptic Tradition in Reformation Britain: 1530-1645. Oxford, 1979.

Foster, Stephen. Their Solitary Way: Puritan Social Ethic in the First Century of Settlement in New England. New Haven, 1971.

_____. "New England and the Challenge of Heresy, 1630 to 1660: The Puritan Crisis in Transatlantic Perspective," WMQ, 38. October, 1981.

_____. "The Presbyterian Independents Exorcized," Past and Present, 44. August 1969.

Foxe, John. Acts and Monuments, eds. G. Townsend and G.R. Cattley, 8 Vols. London, 1837-41.

_____. Actes and Mouments of these latter and perilous dayes. London, 1563.

Fussner, F. Smith. The Historical Revolution: English Historical Writing and Thought. London 1962.

Gardiner, Samuel R., ed. The Constitutional Documents of the Puritan Revolution. Oxford, 1905.

_____. History of the Civil War 1642-1649, 4 Vols. London, 1897-98.

_____. History of England from the Accession of James I to the Outbreak of the Civil War 1603-1642, 10 Vols. London, 1899.

Gay, Peter. A Loss of Mastery: Puritan Historians in Colonial America. Los Angeles, 1966.

Geere, John. Iudash Ioy at the Oath...for England example in embracing the Parliamentary Covenant. London, 1641.

_____. Vindiciae Voti, or a Vindication of the True Sense of the National Covenant. London, 1641.

George, Charles H. "Puritanism as History and Historiography," Past and Present, 41. December, 1968.

_____ and George, Katherine. The Protestant Mind of the English Reformation 1570-1640. Princeton, 1961.

Georges, Sir Ferdinando. Sir Ferdinando Georges and His Province of Maine, ed. James Phinney, 3 Vols. New York, 1967.

Gilpin, W. Clark. The Millenarian Piety of Roger Williams. Chicago, 1979.

Gilsdorf, Joy B. "The Puritan Apocalypse: New England Eschatology in the Seventeenth Century". Ph.D. diss., Yale University, 1964.

Goodwin, John. Oeomaxia; or The Grand Imprudence of men running the hazard of Fighting Against God, in suppressing any Way, Doctrine, or Practise. London, 1644.

Goodwin, Thomas. The Great Interest of state and Kingdomes. London, 1645.

————. A Glimpse of Syons Glory, or the Churches Beautie specified. London, 1641.

————. Zerubbabels Encovragement to Finish the Temple. London, 1642.

————. The Works of Thomas Goodwin, ed. J. C. Miller. Edinburgh, 1865.

————. A Reply of the Brethren to A.S. London, 1644.

————. et al. An Apologetical Narration. London, 1644.

Gorton, Samuel. Simplicities Defence against Seven-Headed Policy. London, 1646.

Greaves, Richard L. "The Origins of English Sabbatarian Thought," The Sixteenth Century Journal, 12. Fall, 1981.

Greene, Jack P. "An Uneasy Connection: An Analysis of the Preconditions of the American Revolution," Stephen G. Kurtz and James H. Hutson, eds., Essays on the American Revolution. Chapel Hill, 1973.

————, ed. Great Britain and the American Colonies 1606-1763. New York, 1970.

————. "Autonomy and Stability: New England and the British Colonial Experience in Early Modern America," Journal of Social History 7. 1974.

————. Pursuit of Happiness. Chapel Hill, 1988.

Greenleaf, W.H. Order, Empiricism and Politics: Two Traditions of English Political Thought 1500-1700. Oxford, 1964.

Greven, Philip J. The Protestant Temperament: Patterns of Child-Rearing, Religious Experience, and the Self in Early America. New York, 1977.

————. Four Generations: Population, Land and Family in Colonial Massachusetts. Ithaca, 1970.

Gura, Philip F. A Glimpse of Sion's Glory: Puritan Radicalism in New England. Middletown, 1984.

_____. "The Radical Ideology of Samuel Gorton: New Light on the relation of English to American Puritanism," WMQ, 36. 1979.

Hale, J.R. ed. The Evolution of British Historiography. London, 1967.

Hall, David D. The Faithful Shepherd: A History of the New England Ministry in the Seventeenth Century. New York, 1974.

_____ ed. The Antinomian Controversy, 1636-1638: A Documentary History. Middletown, 1968.

_____. "John Cotton's Letter to Samuel Skeleton," WMQ, 22. 1965.

Haller, William. "John Foxe and the Puritan Revolution," in Richard F. Jones, ed., The Seventeenth Century. Stanford, 1951.

_____. The Elect Nation: The Meaning and Relevance of Foxe's Book of Martyrs. New York, 1963.

_____. The Rise of Puritanism. Philadelphia, 1972.

_____. ed. Tracts on Liberty in the Puritan Revolution, 1638-1647, 3 Vols. New York, 1934.

_____. ed. The Leveller Tracts, 1647-1653. New York, 1944.

_____. Liberty and Reformation in the Puritan Revolution. New York, 1955.

Haller, William, Jr. The Puritan Frontier: Town-Planning in New England Colonial Development, 1630-1660. New York, 1951.

Hanbury, Benjamin. Historical Memorials, relating to the Independents, or Congregationalists, from their rise to the Restoration of the Monarchy, A.D. MDCLX, 3 Vols. London, 1841.

Hanson, Donald W. From Kingdom to Commonwealth: The Development of Civil Consciousness in English Political Thought. Cambridge, 1970.

Hart, Tindal. The Country Clergy. London, 1958.

_____. Clergy and Society 1600-1800. London, 1958.

Haskins, G. L. Law and Authority in Early Massachusetts. New York, 1960.

Hay, Denys. Annalists and Historians: Western Historiography from the Eight to the Eighteenth Centuries. London, 1977.

Headley, John M. Luther's View of Church History. New Haven, 1963.

Heimert, Alan. "Puritanism, the Wilderness, and the Frontier," New England Quarterly 26. 1953.

_____ and Delbanco, Andrew, eds. The Puritans in America: A Narrative Anthology. Cambridge, MA, 1985.

Hexter, J. H. The Reign of King Pym. Cambridge, MA, 1948.

_____. Reappraisals in History. London, 1962.

_____. Doing History. Bloomington, 1971.

Heyd, Michael. "The Reaction to Enthusiasm in the Seventeenth Century: Toward an Integrative Approach," Journal of Modern History, 53. June, 1981.

Heylin, Peter. Observations on the History of the Reign of King Charles. London, 1656.

_____. Cyprianus Anglicus, or the history of the life and death of.... William...Lord Archbishop of Canterbury. London, 1668.

Higginson, John. "Part of John Higginson's Letter, of Guilford, dated 25 of the 8th month, 1654, to his Brother the Rev'd Thomas Thatcher of Weymouth," Connecticut Historical Society, Collections, III. 1895.

_____. The Cause of God and His People in New England. Cambridge, MA, 1663.

Hill, Christopher. Antichrist in Seventeenth Century England. Oxford, 1971.

_____. The World Turned Upside Down: Radical Ideas During the English Revolution. New York, 1972.

_____. God's Englishman: Oliver Cromwell and the English Revolution. New York, 1970.

_____. Puritanism and Revolution. New York, 1967.

_____. Economic Problems of the Church from Archbishop Whitgift to the Long Parliament. Oxford, 1968.

_____. The Century of Revolution, 1603-1714. New York, 1966.

_____. Change and Continuity in Seventeenth Century England. Cambridge, 1975.

_____. Some Intellectual Conseqences of the English Revolution. Madison, 1980.

_____. Intellectual Origins of the English Revolution. Oxford, 1965.

Hiller, D.R. Covenant: The History of Biblical Idea. Baltimore, 1969.

Hoadly, Charles J. ed. Records of the Colony and Plantation of New Haven, from 1638 to 1649. Hartford, 1857.

_____. "Records of the Council for New England," American Antiquarian Society, Proceedings, 1867.

Hobbes, Thomas. Leviathan, or the Matter, Forme and Power of a Commonwealth Ecclesiastical and Civil. 1651.

Holden, William. Anti-Puritan Satires 1572-1642. New Haven, 1954.

Holifield, Brooks E. The Covenant Sealed: The Development of Puritan Sacramental Theology in Old and New England, 1570-1720. New Haven, 1974.

Hooke, William. New Englands Teares for Old Englands Fears. London, 1641.

_____. New Englands Sence of Old England and Irelands Sorrowes. London, 1645.

Hooker, Richard. The Laws of Ecclesiastical Polity, The Works of...Mr. Richard Hooker, ed. Isaac Walton. Oxford, 1850.

Hooker, Thomas. "The Danger of Desertion (1631)," Thomas Hooker: Writings in England and Holland, 1626-1633, eds., G.H. Williams, et al,. Cambridge, MA, 1975.

_____. A Survey of the Summe of Church Discipline. 1648.

Hosmer, James K. The Life of Young Henry Vane. Boston, 1888.

Hudson, Winthrop S. "Denominationalism as a Basis for Ecumencity: A Seventeenth-Century Conception," Church History, 24. 1955.

_____. "Protestant's Concept of Church and State," Church History, 35. June, 1966.

Huehns, Gertrude. Antinomianism in English History. London, 1951.

Hutchinson, Thomas. The History of the Colony and Province of Massachusetts Bay, ed. Lawrence S. Mayo, 3 Vols. Cambridge, 1936.

Hyde, A. G. George Herbert and His Times. New York, 1906.

Jackson, Thomas. The Life of John Goodwin. London, 1822.

Jantz, Harold S. The First Century of New England Verse. New York, 1962.

Johnson, Edward. Wonder-Working Providence of Sion Saviour in New England, 1628-1651, ed. J. Franklin Jameson. New York, 1910.

_____. ?. Good News from New England. London, 1648.

Jones, Mary J. A. Congregational Commonwealth: Connecticut 1636-1662. Middletown, 1968.

Jones, Rufus M. Mysticism and Democracy in the English Commonwealth. New York, 1932.

_____. Spiritual Reformers in the 16th & 17th Centuries. London, 1928.

_____. The Quakers in the American Colonies. London, 1911.

Jordan, Wilbur K. The Development of Religious Toleration in England, 4 Vols. Gloucester, 1965.

Judson, Margaret. The Political Thought of Sir Henry Vane the Younger. Philadelphia, 1969.

_____. The Crisis of the Constitution. New York, 1964.

Kamen, Henry. The Rise of Toleration. New York, 1962.

Kaplan, Lawrence. Politics and Religion during the English Revolution: The Scots and the Long Parliament, 1643-1645. New York, 1976.

_____. "Presbyterians and Independents in 1643," English Historical Review, 84. April, 1964.

Keayne, Robert. The Apology of Robert Keayne, ed. Barnard Bailyn. Gloucester, 1970.

Kelley, Donald R. The Beginning of Ideology. Cambridge, 1981.

_____. Foundations of Modern Historical Scholarship: Language, Law, and History in the French Renaissance. New York, 1970.

Kenyon, J. P. The Stuart Constitution: Documents and Commentary. Cambridge, 1966.

King, John N. English Reformation Literature: The Tudor Origins of Protestant Tradition. Princeton, 1982.

Kirby, E.W. "Sermons before the Commons," AHR, 44. April, 1939.

_____. "The English Presbyterians in the Westminster Assembly," Church History, 33. 1964.

Kishlansky, Mark A. The Rise of the New Model Army. Cambridge, 1979.

Kittredge, George L. Doctor Robert Child the Remonstrant. Cambridge, 1919.

Knappen, M. M. Two Elizabethan Puritan Diaries. Chicago, 1933.

_____. Tudor Puritanism: A Chapter in the History of Idealism. Chicago, 1965.

Knox, R. A. Enthusiasm: A Chapter in the History of Religion. Oxford, 1962.

Lamont, William. Godly Rule: Politics and Religion, 1603-1660. London, 1969.

_____. Richard Baxter and the Millennium: Protestant Imperialism and the English Revolution. London, 1970.

_____. Marginal Prynne, 1600-1669. London, 1963.

_____. "Puritanism in History and Historiography: Some Further Thoughts," Past and Present, 44. August, 1969.

_____. and Oldfield, S., eds. Politics, Religion and Literature in the Seventeenth Century. London, 1975.

Laslett, P. The World We Have Lost. London, 1965.

_____. Family Life and Illicit Love in Earlier Generations. Cambridge, 1977.

Laud, William. The Works of...William Laud. Oxford, 1850-1860.

Lauer, Paul E. Church and State in New England. Baltimore, 1892.

Lechford, Thomas. Plain Dealing or News from New England. London, 1642.

Lecler, Joseph. Toleration and Reformation, 2 Vols. New York, 1960.

Levy, Babette M. Preaching in the First Half Century of New England History. Hartford, 1945.

Levy, F. J. Tudor Historical Thought. San Marino, 1967.

Lightfoot, John. The Whole Works of...John Lightfoot, ed. J. R. Pitman. London, 1824.

Little, David. Religion, Order and Law: A Study in Pre-Revolutionary England. New York, 1969.

Liu, Tai. Discord in Zion: The Puritan Divines and the Puritan Revolution. The Hague, 1973.

_____. "Saints in Power: A Study of the Barebones Parliament". Ph.D. Thesis, University of Indiana, 1969.

Lockridge, K.A. A New England Town, The First Hundred Years: Dedham, Massachusetts, 1636-1725. New York, 1970.

Lowance, Mason I. The Language of Canaan: Metaphor and Symbol in New England from the Puritans to the Transcendentalits. Cambridge, MA 1980.

Lowenthal, David. The Past is a Foreign Country. New York, 1985.

Lowrie, Ernest B. The Shape of the Puritan Mind: The Thought of Samuel Willard. New Haven, 1974.

Lucas, Paul R. Valley of Discord: Church and Society Along the Connecticut River. Hanover, 1976.

Maclear, J. F. "New England and the Fifth Monarchy: the Quest for the Millennium in Early American Puritanism," WMQ, 32. April, 1975.

_____. "Anne Hutchinson and the Mortalist Heresy," NEQ, 54. March, 1981.

MacPherson, C. B. The Political Theory of Possessive Individualism: Hobbes to Locke. Oxford, 1962.

Mannheim, Karl. Ideology and Utopia. London, 1960.

Manning, Brian. Politics, Religion and the English Civil War. New York, 1973.

_____. The English People and the English Revolution. London, 1967.

411

Marchant, Ronald A. The Puritans and the Church Courts in the Diocese of York, 1560-1642. London, 1960.

Marshall, Stephen. The Song of Moses the Servant of God, and the Song of the Lambe. 1643.

_____. A Sermon. London, 1640.

_____. A Peace-Offering to God. London, 1641.

_____. Reformation and Desolation. London, 1642.

Mather, Cotton. Magnalia Christi Americana; or, the Ecclesiastical History of New England, 2 Vols. Hartford, 1820.

Mather, Richard. A Farewell-Exhortation to the Church and People of Dorchester in New England. Cambridge, MA, 1657.

Mayo, Lawrence S. John Endecott. Cambridge, 1936.

McGee, J. Sears. The Godly Man in Stuart England: Anglicans, Puritans, and the Two Tables, 1620-1670. New Haven, 1976.

McGiffert, Michael. "American Puritan Studies in the 1960s," WMQ, 27. January, 1970.

McLouglin, William G. New England Dissent, 1630-1833: The Baptists and the Separation of Church and State, 2 Vols. Cambridge, 1971.

Mede, Joseph. "The Apostasy of the Latter Times. (1641)," The Works of...Joseph Mede, ed. J. Worthington. 1664.

_____. "The Brief Meaning or Summary Exposition of the Apocalypse," The Works of...Joseph Mede, ed., John Worthington. London, 1672.

Middlekauff, Robert. The Mathers: Three Generations of Puritan Intellectuals. New York, 1968.

Miller, Perry. The New England Mind, the Seventeenth Century. New York, 1939.

_____. The New England Mind: From Colony to Province. Boston, 1968.

_____. Orthodoxy in Massachusetts. Gloucester, 1965 [1933].

_____. Rogers Williams: His Contribution to the American Tradition. Indianapolis, 1953.

_____. Errand into the Wilderness. Cambridge, 1976.

_____. and Johnson, Thomas, eds. The Puritans: A Sourcebook of their Writings, 2 Vols. New York, 1963.

Mitchell, A. P. ed. Minutes of the Sessions of the Westminster Assembly of Divines. Edinburgh, 1874.

Mitchell, William F. English Pulpit Oratory from Andrews to Tillotson. New York, 1962.

Moller, Jens G. "The Beginnings of Puritan Covenant Theology," Journal of Ecclesiastical History 14. April, 1963.

Morgan, Edmund S. ed. Puritan Political Ideas. Indianapolis, 1970.

_____. Visible Saints: The History of a Puritan Idea. Ithaca, 1975.

_____. Puritan Dilemma: The Story of John Winthrop. Boston, 1956.

_____. The Puritan Family. New York, 1966.

_____. Roger Williams: The Church and the State. New York, 1967.

Morison, Samuel A. Builders of the Bay Colony. Boston, 1964.

_____. Harvard in the Seventeenth Century, 2 Vols. Boston, 1936.

Morton, Nathaniel. New England Memorial. Boston, 1826.

Mosse, George L. The Holy Pretence: A Study in Christianity and Reason of State from William Perkins to John Winthrop. Oxford, 1957.

_____. "Puritan Political Thought and the 'Case of Conscience," Church History, 23. June 1954.

_____. "Puritanism and the Reason of State in Old and New England," WMQ. January, 1952.

Murdock, Kenneth B. Increase Mather: The Foremost American Puritan. New York, 1966.

_____. Handkerchiefs from Paul: Being a Pious and Consolatory Verses of Puritan Massachusetts. Cambridge, 1927.

_____. Literature and Theology in Colonial New England. Westport, 1970.

Nash, R. Wilderness and the American Mind. New Haven, 1973.

Neal, Daniel. The History of the Puritans, 2 Vols. New York, 1843.

413

New, John F. H. Anglican and Puritan: The Basis of Their Opposition.
Stanford, 1964.

Niebuhr, H. Richard. "The Protestant Movement and Democracy in the United
States," The Shaping of American Religion, eds., J. W. Smith and A. L. Jamison,
I. Princeton, 1961.

_____. The Kingdom of God in America. New York, 1937.

Newton, A. P. The Colonial Activities of the English Puritans. New Haven,
1914.

Nobbs, Douglas. "Philip Nye on Church and State," The Cambridge Historical
Journal, 5-6. 1935-1940.

_____. Theocracy and Toleration: A Study of the Disputes in Dutch Calvinism
from 1600 to 1650. Cambridge, 1938.

Norton, John. The Orthodox Evangelist, 1654.

_____. Abel Being Dead yet Speaketh, or the Life and Death of...Mr. John
Cotton, 1658. London, 1658.

Nozick, Robert. Anarchy, State and Utopia. Oxford, 1974.

Nuttall, Geoffrey F. Visible Saints, the Congregational Way, 1640-1660. Oxford,
1957.

_____. The Holy Spirit in Puritan Faith and Experience. Oxford, 1946.

_____. Richard Baxter. Edinburgh, 1965.

Nye, Philip. The King's Authority in Dispensing with Ecclesiastical Laws. London,
1688.

_____. A Declaration of the Faith and Order Owned and Practised in the
Congregational Churches in England. London, 1658.

Oliver, Peter. The Puritan Commonwealth. Boston, 1856.

Olsen, V. Norskov. John Foxe and the Elizabethan Church. Berkeley, 1973.

Osgood, Herbert L. The American Colonies in the Seventeenth Century, 2
Vols. New York, 1904.

Overton, Richard. The Arraignement of Mr. Persecution. London, 1645.

Pagitt, Ephraim. Heresiography, or, a Description of the Hereticks and Sectaries of those later times. London, 1646.

Parry, G. J. R. A Protestant Vision: William Harrison and the Reformation of Elizabethan England. Cambridge, 1987.

Paul, Robert S. The Lord Protector: Religion and Politics in the Life of Oliver Cromwell. London, 1955.

Pearl, Valeries. London and the Outbreak of the Puritan Revolution. London, 1964.

Pearson, Samuel C. "The Reluctant Radicals: The Independents at the Westminister Assembly," Journal of Church and State 11. 1969.

Pennington, D. and Thomas K., eds. Puritans and Revolutionaires. Oxford, 1979.

Perkins, William. A Godly and Learned Exposition or Commentary upon the three first Chapters of the Revelation, 1606.

_____. Lectures Upon the Three First chapters of the Revelation. 1604 [1595].

Pettit, Norman. The Heart Prepared: Grace and Conversion in Puritan Spiritual Life. New Haven, 1966.

Pocock, J. G. A. "Modes of Action and Their Pasts in Tudor and Stuart England," National Consciousness, History and Political Culture in Early Modern Europe, ed., Orest Ranum. Baltimore, 1975.

_____. "Time, History and Eschatology in the Thought of Thomas Hobbes," Politics, Language and Time. New York, 1973.

_____. "James Harrington and the Good Old Cause: Study of the Ideological Context of his Writings," Journal of British Studies 10. 1970.

_____. "The Limits and Divisions of British History: In Search of the Unknown Subject," AHR, 87. April, 1982.

_____. "Political Thought in the Cromwellian Interregnum," in G. A. Wood and P. S. O'Connor, eds., W. P. Morrell: A Tribute. Dunedin, 1973.

_____. Politics, Language and Time: Essays on Political Thought and History. London, 1972.

_____. Obligation and Authority in Two English Revolutions. Wellington, 1973.

_____. The Machiavellian Moment: Florentine Republican Thought and the Atlantic Republican Tradition. Princeton, 1975.

_____. The Ancient Constitution and the Feudal Law: A Study of English Historical Thought in the Seventeenth Century. Cambridge, 1957.

Popper, K. R. The Poverty of Historicism. London, 1960.

Powell, Summer C. Puritan Village: The Formulation of a New England Town. New York, 1965.

Prall, Stuard E. ed. The Puritan Revolution: A Documentary History. New York, 1968.

Prince, Thomas. Chronological History of New England. Boston, 1826.

Rabb, T. H. Enterprise and Empire: Merchant and Gentry Investments in the Expansion of England, 1575-1630. Cambridge, 1967.

Raleigh, Sir Walter. The History of the World. 1614, ed. C. A. Patrides. London, 1971.

Rathband, William. A Brief Narration of some Church-courses held, in Opinion and Practice, in the Churches lately erected in New England: Collected out of sundry of their own Printed Papers and Manuscripts, with other good intelligences. London, 1644.

Reeves, Marjorie. The Influence of Prophecy in the Later Middle Ages: A Study in Joachmism. Oxford, 1969.

_____. Joachim of Fiore and the Prophetic Future. New York, 1977.

Richardson, C. P. English Preachers and Preaching, 1640-1670. New York, 1928.

Richardson, R. C. Puritanism in North-West England: A Regional Study of the Diocese of Chester to 1642. Manchester, 1972.

Robinson, John. Liberty of Conscience, or the Sole means to obtaine Peace and Truth. London, 1643.

Rogers, Richard. Seven Treatises...called the practise of Christianitie, London 1605.

_____. "The Diary of Richard Rogers," Two Elizabethan Puritan Diaries, ed. M. M. Knappen. Chicago, 1933.

Rogers, Philip G. The Fifth Monarchy Men. London, 1966.

Rose-Troup, Frances. John White. New York, 1930.

_____. The Massachusetts Bay Company and Its Predecessors. Crafton Press, 1930.

Rosenmeier, Jesper. "The Teacher and the Witness: John Cotton and Roger Williams," WMQ, 25. July, 1968.

Rous, John. "Diary of John Rous," ed. M.A.E. Green, Camden Society, 1857.

Routley, Erik. English Religious Dissent. Cambridge,1960.

Russell, Conrad. Parliaments and English Politics, 1621-1629. Oxford, 1979.

_____. ed. The Origins of the English Civil War. New York, 1973.

_____. Russell, Conrad. "Arguments for Religious Unity in England, 1530-1650," Journal of Ecclesiastical History, 18. October, 1967.

_____. The Crisis of Parliament: English History, 1509-1660. London, 1971.

Rutman, D.B. Winthrop's Boston: Portrait of a Puritan Town, 1630-1649. Chapel-Hill, 1965.

_____. American Puritanism: Faith and Practice. Philadelphia, 1970.

Sabine, George H. A History of Political Thought. New York, 1961.

Sachse, William L. "The Migration of New Englanders to England: 1640-1660," AHR, 53. January, 1948.

Sadler, Richard. "Richard Sadler's Account of the Massachusetts Churches," NEQ, 42. Sept, 1969.

Saltonstall, Richard. The Saltonstall Papers, ed. Robert E. Moody. Boston, 1972.

Schaff, Philip, ed. The Creeds of Christendom, 3 Vols. New York, 1887.

Scholz, Robert F. "Clerical Consociation in Massachusetts Bay: Reassessing the New England Way and its Origins," WMQ, 29. July, 1972.

Seaver, Paul S. The Puritan Lectureship: The Politics of Religious Dissent, 1560-1662. Stanford, 1970.

Seelye, John. Prophetic Waters: The River in Early American Life and Literature. New York, 1977.

Seidman, Aaron B. "Church and Society in the Early Years of the Massachusetts Bay Colony," NEQ, 18. 1945.

Selden, John. Table Talk of John Selden, ed. Fredrick Pollock. London, 1927.

Shaw, William A. A History of the English Church during the Civil Wars and under the Commonwealth, 1640-1660, 2 Vols. London, 1900.

Shepard, Thomas. "The Autobiography," in God's Plot: The Paradox of Puritan Piety, being the Autobiography & Journal of Thomas Shepard, ed. Michael McGiffter. University of Massachusetts Press, 1972.

_____. "Thomas Shepard to Hugh Peter," AHR, 4. 1898-99.

_____. The Works of Thomas Shepard. Boston, 1853.

_____. and Allin, John. Defence of the Answer. London, 1648.

Shuffelton, Frank. Thomas Hooker, 1585-1647. Princeton, 1977.

Shurtleff, Nathaniel B. ed. The Records of the Governor and Company of the Massachusetts Bay in New England, 5 Vols. Boston, 1853-4.

Simpson, Alan. Puritanism in Old and New England. Chicago, 1961.

Skinner, Quentin. "Conquest and Consent: Thomas Hobbes and the Engagement Controversy," The Interregnum, ed. G.E. Aylmer. Hamden, 1972.

_____. "The Ideological Context of Hobbes's Political Thought," The Historical Journal, 9. 1966.

_____. "History and Ideology in the English Revolution," The Historical Journal, 7. 1965.

Skinner, Quentin. "Hobbes' Leviathan," The Historical Journal, 6. 1964.

Smith, John. Travels and Works of Captain John Smith, ed. E. Arber. Edinburgh, 1910.

Snow, Vernon F. "The Concept of Revolution in Seventeenth-Century England," The Historical Journal, 2. 1962.

Solt, Leo F. Saints in Arms: Puritanism and Democracy in Cromwell's Army. Stanford, 1959.

Spalding, James C. "Sermons Before the Parliament. 1640-1660) As a Public Puritan Diary," Church History. March, 1967.

Sprunger, Keith L. "William Ames and the Settlement of Massachusetts Bay," New England Quarterly, 39. 1966.

_____. "English and Dutch Sabbatarianism and the Development of Puritan Social Theology, 1600-1660," Church History 11. March, 1982.

_____. The Learned Doctor William Ames. Urbana, 1972.

Spufford, Margaret. Contrasting Communities: English Villagers in the Sixteenth and Seventeenth Centuries. Cambridge, 1974.

Starn, Randolph. "Historians and 'Crisis,'" Past and Present, 52. 1971.

Stearns, Raymond P. The Strenuous Puritan: Hugh Peter, 1598-1660. Urbana, 1954.

Steiner, Bruce E. "Dissension at Quinnipiac: The Authorship and Setting of a Discourse about Civil Government in a New Plantation Whose Design is Religion," WMQ, 38. March, 1981.

Steuart, Adam. Some Observations and Annotations upon the Apologetical Narration. London, 1644.

Stoeffler, F. Ernest. The Rise of Evangelical Pietism. Leiden, 1965.

Stoever, William K.B. A Faire and Easie Way to Heaven: Covenant Theology and Antinomianism in Early Massachusetts. Middletown, 1978.

_____. "Nature, Grace and John Cotton: The Theological Dimension in the New England Antinomian Controversy," Church History 44. March, 1975.

Stone, Lawrence. The Causes of the English Revolution. New York, 1972.

_____. "Social Mobility in England, 1500-1700," Past and Present, 33. April, 1966.

Stoughton, John. History of Religion in England: From the opening of the Long Parliament to 1850, 4 Vols. London, 1901.

Stout, Harry S. The New England Soul: Preaching and Religious Culture in Colonial New England. New York, 1986.

Sweet, Leonard I. "Millennialism in America: Recent Studies," Theological Studies, 60. Sept., 1979.

Tawney, R.H. Religion and the Rise of Capitalism. New York, 1954.

Thomas, Keith. Religion and the Decline of Magic. New York, 1971.

Thompson, James W. A History of Historical Writing, 2 Vols. New York, 1942.

Tichi, Cecelia. New World, New Earth. New Haven, 1979.

Tillian, Thomas. "Uppon the First Sight of New England, June 29, 1638," Seventeenth-Century American Poetry, ed. Harrison T. Meserole. New York, 1968.

Tolmie, Murray. The Triumph of the Saints: The Separate Churches London, 1616-1649. Cambridge, 1977.

Toon, Peter. ed. Puritans, the Millennium and the Future of Israel: Puritan Eschatology. Cambridge, 1970.

Trevor-Roper, Hugh R. The Crisis of the Seventeenth Century. New York, 1968.

_____. Religion, Reformation and Social Order. London, 1967.

_____. Archbishop Laud, 1573-1645. London, 1965.

Trinterud, Leonard J. "The Origins of Puritanism," Church History, 20. 1951.

Troeltsch, Ernest. The Social Teaching of the Christian Churches. 2 Vols. London, 1950.

Trumbull, J. Hammond, ed. The Public Records of the Colony of Connecticut, 10 Vols. Hartford, 1850-1890.

Tuveson, Ernest L. Millennium and Utopia: A Study in the Background of the Idea of Progress. New York, 1964.

_____. Redeemer Nation: The Idea of America's Millennial Role. Chicago, 1968.

420

Tyacke, Nicholas. "Puritanism, Arminianism and the Counter-Revolution," The Origins of the English Civil War. ed. Conrad Russell. New York, 1973.

Tyler, Moses Coit. A History of American Literature. New York, 1878.

Underdown, David. "The Independents Reconsidered," The Journal of British Studies, III. 1965.

_____. Pride's Purge: Politics in the Puritan Revolution. Oxford, 1971.

Underhill, John. News From America. London, 1638.

Vane, Henry. Two Treatises. London, 1662.

_____. The Face of Time. London, 1662.

_____. A Healing Question. London, 1660.

Voegelin, Eric. Order and History, I, Israel and Revelation. Baton Rouge, 1956.

Wall, Robert E. Massachusetts Bay: The Crucial Decade, 1640-1650. New Haven, 1972.

Wallace, John M. Destiny His Choice: The Loyalism of Andrew Marvell. London, 1968.

Walwyn, William. A Help to the right Understanding of A Discourse concerning Independency. London, 1645.

_____. The Power of Love. London, 1643.

_____. The Compassionate Samaritane. London, 1644.

Walzer, Michael. Exodus and Revolution. New York, 1985.

_____. "Puritanism as a Revolutionary Ideology," History and Theory, 3. 1963.

_____. The Revolution of the Saints: A Study in the Origins of Radical Politics. Cambridge, 1965.

Ward, Nathaniel. A Sermon preached before the...House of Commons. London, 1648.

_____. The Simple Colber of Aggawam in America. London, 1647.

Watkins, Owen C. The Puritan Experience: Studies in Spiritual Autobiography. New York, 1972.

Watts, Michael R. The Dissenters. Oxford, 1978.

Webster, Charles. The Great Instauration: Science, Medicine and Reform 1626-1660. London, 1975.

_____. ed. The Intellectual Revolution of the Seventeenth Century. London, 1974.

Wedgwood, Cicely V. The King's Peace, 1637-1641. London, 1966.

_____. The King's War, 1641-1647. London, 1966.

_____. The Trial of Charles I. London, 1967.

Weeden, William B. Economic and Social History of New England, 1620-1789. Boston, 1890.

Welde, Thomas. "A Letter of Master Wells from New England to Old England...1633," Massachusetts Colonial Society, Transactions, 13. 1910-1911.

_____. An Answer to W.R. his Narration of the Opinions and Practices of the Churches lately erected in New England; Vindicating those Godly and Orthodoxal Churches. London, 1644.

Wertebaker, T.J. The Puritan Oligarchy. New York, 1947.

White Jr., Lynn. "Christian Myth and Christian History," Journal of the History of Ideas 3. April, 1941.

White, John. The Planters Plea. London, 1630.

White, B.R. The English Separatist Tradition: From the Marian Martyrs to the Pilgrim Fathers. London, 1972.

Whitelock, Bulstrod. Memorial of the English Affairs. Oxford, 1853.

Wigglesworth, Michael. "God's Controversy with New England (1662)," Seventeenth-Century American Poetry, ed., H.T. Meserole. New York, 1968.

Willard, Samuel. A Complete Body of Divinity. 1726.

Williams, George H. Wilderness and Paradise in Christian Thought: The Biblical Experience of the Desert in the History of Christianity. New York, 1962.

_____. The Radical Reformation. Philadelphia, 1962.

_____. et al., eds. Thomas Hooker: Writings in England and Holland, 1626-1633. Cambridge, 1975.

Williams, Roger. The Complete Writings of Roger Williams, eds. Reuben A. Guild et al. New York, 1963.

Wilson, John F. Pulpit in Parliament: Puritanism during the English Civil Wars, 1640-1648.

Winslow, Edward. "The Reasons that Moved most of the Pilgrim Church to Migrate to American" The Story of the Pilgrim Fathers, ed., Edward Arber.

_____. Hypocrisie Unmasked. London, 1646.

_____. New Englands Salamander. London, 1647.

Winslow, Ola E. Meetinghouse Hill, 1630-1783. New York, 1952.

_____. Master Roger Williams. New York, 1957.

Winthrop, John. The History of New England from 1630 to 1649, ed. James Savage, 2 Vols. Boston, 1853.

_____. The Winthrop Papers, ed., Allyn Forbes, 5 Vols.. Boston, 1929-1947.

_____. A Short Story of the Rise, Reign, and Ruine of the Antinomians, Familists and Libertines. London, 1644.

Winthrop, R. C. Life and Letters of John Winthrop. Boston, 1869.

Woodhouse, A. S. P. Puritanism and Liberty. London, 1938.

Woolf, D.R. "Speech, Text, and Time: The Sense of Hearing and the Sense of the Past in Renaissance England," Albion 18. 1986.

Woolrych, Austin. "Oliver Cromwell and the Rule of the Saints," in R. H. Parry, ed., The English Civil War and After, 1642-1658. Berkeley and Los Angeles, 1970.

Wright, Louis B. Religion and Empire: The Alliance Between Piety and Commerce in English Expansion 1558-1625. Chapel Hill, 1943.

_____. The Cultural Life of the American Colonies, 1607-1673. New York, 1958.

Wright, John K. "Terrae Incognitae: The Place of the Imagination in Geography," in Human Nature in Geography. Cambridge, MA, 1966.

Young, Alexander, ed. Chronicles of the First Planters of the Colony of Massachusetts Bay, from 1623 to 1636. Boston, 1846.

Yule, George. The Independents in the English Civil War. Cambridge, 1958.

_____. "Independents and Revolutionaries," Journal of British Studies, 7. 1968.

Zagorin, Perez. History of Political Thought in the English Revolution. London, 1965.

Zakai, Avihu. "Epiphany at Matadi: Perry Miller's Orthodoxy in Massachusetts and the Meaning of American History," Reviews in American History 13. December, 1985.

_____. "The Ministers' View of Church and State in Early Massachusetts," Scripta Hierosolymitana, Vol. 32; Studies in American Civilization, E.M. Budick, et al., eds. Jerusalem, 1987.

_____. "The Millenial Quest in the New England Errand into the Wilderness," Religion, Ideology and Nationalism in Europe and America, Essays in Honor of Prof. Yehoshua Arieli, The Historical Society of Israel Jerusalem, 1986.

_____. "The Gospel of Reformation: The Origins of the Great Puritan Migration," The Journal of Ecclesiastical History, 37. October, 1986.

_____. "Theocracy in New England: The Nature and Meaning of the Holy Experiment in the Wilderness," The Journal of Religious History, 14. December, 1986.

_____. "Puritan Millennialism and Theocracy in Early Massachusetts," History of European Ideas, 8. 1987.

_____. "Reformation History, and Eschatology in English Protestantism," History and Theory, 26. October, 1987.

_____. "Religious Toleration and Its Enemies: The Independent Divines and the Issue of Toleration During the English Civil War," Albion, 21. Spring, 1989.

_____. "Thomas Brightman and English Apocalyptic Tradition," Menasseh Ben Israel and his World, Y. Kaplan, et al., eds. Leiden, 1989.

_____. "Orthodoxy in England and New England: Puritans and the Issue of Religious Toleration, 1640-1650," Proceeding of The American Philosophical Society, 135. September, 1991.

Ziff, Larzer. The Career of John Cotton. Princeton, 1962.

_____. ed. John Cotton on the Churches of New England. Cambridge, MA, 1968.

Zuckerman, Michael. "The Social Context of Democracy in Massachusetts," WMQ, 25. October, 1968.

INDEX

Adam 69, 372

Alienation 74, 167

Allin 42, 349

America 1-3, 5, 6, 8-12, 18, 22-24, 36, 40-43, 61, 63, 64, 78, 89, 90, 99, 102, 103, 117, 120, 122, 124, 127, 128, 131, 133, 136, 138, 139, 144, 148-150, 152, 154, 156, 158, 162, 163, 186, 189, 194, 199, 217, 219, 222, 230, 234, 235, 237, 238, 241, 244, 260, 264, 268, 270, 272, 277, 282, 284, 285, 287, 290, 296, 298, 307, 310, 320, 324, 332, 334, 337, 345, 347, 351, 368, 373, 374, 377, 378

Ames 19, 35-37, 127, 134, 135, 138, 146

Anabaptists 91, 127, 128, 305, 309, 345, 350, 354, 359, 361, 369-371, 374, 375

Antichrist 7, 12, 62-65, 67, 72, 74, 78-81, 84, 86, 88, 89, 94, 104, 107, 108, 119, 134, 136, 149, 166, 167, 181, 183-185, 195, 214, 217, 233, 241, 244, 274, 275, 276, 277, 334, 341, 343, 351, 375

Antinomians 43, 204-207, 210, 212, 232, 303, 354, 359, 369, 370, 374, 375

Apocalypse 3, 4, 7, 12, 59, 66, 69, 70, 72-74, 79, 80, 83-86, 89, 90, 93, 95, 98, 100, 103, 104, 106, 108, 137, 259, 274, 276, 277, 328

Apocalyptic tradition 5, 79, 82-84

Apostles 6, 90

Aristocracy 224, 226, 227

Augustine 72, 84, 87, 88, 106

Babylon 39, 75, 76, 78, 79, 84, 85, 108, 133, 136, 254, 255, 278, 302, 341, 342, 351

Bale 79, 83, 84

Baptists 237

Barebone's Parliament 237, 238

Baxter 31, 32, 38, 124, 238, 239, 320, 349, 369, 370, 377

Beast 10, 75, 92, 217, 242, 253, 254, 274-278, 293, 304, 305, 341, 370

Belial 50, 118, 150

Bible 26, 119, 208, 232

Book of Common Prayer 44, 127, 128, 131, 150, 153, 172, 254

Book of Sports 38, 44

Bradford 22, 124, 126, 130, 132, 156

Brightman 59, 79, 82-102, 105-107, 275, 276, 374

Brooke 219, 221, 222, 263, 272

Burgesses 191-193, 239

Calvin 65, 66, 189, 224, 226, 378, 379

Calvinism 66

Canaan 103

Catholics 159

Certain Proposals 219

Certain Queries 235, 236

Charles I 38, 63, 81, 98, 172-174, 235, 283, 284, 320

Christ 4-8, 11, 12, 15, 23, 38, 42, 44, 45, 59, 62, 63, 65-67, 69-78, 80, 84-95, 97, 98, 100, 101, 104-108, 117, 119, 130, 136, 138, 148, 181, 183-185, 191, 194, 195, 196, 202, 203, 205, 206, 210-214, 217, 230, 232, 234, 235, 236, 238, 239, 241, 243, 255, 269, 274-277, 285, 297, 298, 304, 328-330, 333, 336, 340, 341, 343, 344, 350, 351, 353, 358, 366, 370, 374, 378, 379, 381

Christian Commonwealth 1, 24, 37, 39, 43, 101, 108, 174, 184, 185, 188, 190-193, 195, 197, 207, 211, 220, 221, 223, 226-228, 233-236, 239, 255, 280, 299, 309, 310, 320, 321, 325, 329, 338-340, 347, 359, 365, 367, 368, 372, 376, 378, 379, 381

Christian Society 9, 24, 50, 220, 232, 378, 380
Church History 62, 80, 90
Church of England 10, 17-20, 32-35, 40, 43, 63, 64, 81-83, 89-91, 93, 94, 96-99, 117, 127, 128, 131, 133-140, 148, 152, 153, 159-162, 165, 170, 172, 200, 201, 218, 231, 267, 269, 271, 275-278, 283, 297, 300, 302, 324, 325, 326, 327, 331-339, 342-346, 353
Church-parliaments 236
Civil War 81, 99, 173, 228, 230, 256, 258, 259, 261, 279, 282, 283, 287, 288, 290, 294, 295, 320, 340, 342, 352, 353, 369-372
Clap 28, 36, 41, 141
Cobbet 21
Collier 236
Collinson 21, 27, 83
Conflagration 62, 69, 95
Congregationalism 6, 9, 10, 35, 100, 101, 198-201, 205, 207, 208, 212, 215-218, 228-230, 244, 273, 284, 326-328, 336-338, 344, 345, 351, 357, 358
Connecticut 132, 184, 196, 197, 226, 272, 284
Constantine the Great 85, 90
Cotton 10, 21, 34-36, 41, 44, 45, 48, 66, 99, 100, 102, 117, 123, 127, 129, 130, 132, 134, 136, 137-139, 146-149, 160, 181, 183, 188, 190, 200, 214, 217, 224, 225-231, 242, 253, 271, 273-278, 301, 302, 330, 350, 358, 359, 363, 373
Covenant 11, 16-24, 28, 30, 34-36, 86, 92, 96, 104, 119, 125-127, 136-138, 172, 187, 188, 190, 193-197, 199-201, 204-206, 210-212, 214, 221, 235, 237-239, 243, 254, 281, 283, 285, 293, 294, 297-301, 311, 312, 327, 328, 330, 340, 344, 352, 353, 355, 359, 362, 369
Cradock 27, 125, 157, 164

Creation 5, 8, 157, 164, 200-203, 236, 286
Cromwell 272, 285, 294, 369-372, 377
Culverwell 16
Daniel 64
Davenport 28, 42-44, 125, 160, 169, 181, 183, 188, 190-197, 211, 221, 272, 298
David 41, 216
Democracy 224, 226, 227
Devil 74, 79, 85, 104, 365, 373, 375
Dragon 7, 74, 88, 104-106, 254, 293
Ecclesiastical History 61-63, 69, 80
Eden 189
Edwards 345, 346, 376
Egypt 103, 253, 275, 302
Elect Nation 80, 83, 84, 93, 94, 255
Elizabethan Settlement of Religion 91
End of the World 65, 66
Endecott 27, 124-128, 130, 131, 141, 166, 167, 265-267
England 1-10, 15, 17-22, 24-30, 32-50, 59, 61-68, 77-84, 86, 87, 89-104, 107-109, 117-174, 181, 183, 184, 186-191, 194, 195, 197, 200, 201, 203, 206, 207, 215-219, 221, 222, 226-231, 233, 235-238, 240-242, 244, 253, 254-291, 293-312, 319-328, 330-353, 358, 359, 362-366, 368, 369, 370-382
English apocalyptic tradition 79, 82-84
English reformation 83, 97, 209, 311
Ephesus 70, 90
Errand into the Wilderness 1-3, 6, 7, 12, 65, 105, 107, 108, 146, 148, 241, 278
Eschatology 3, 6, 7, 12, 59, 61, 108
Exile 6, 253-255, 305
Exodus 1, 28, 147
Ezekiel 16, 64, 232
Fairfax 235, 294
Fiennes 219
Fifth Monarchists 237

Final Conflagration 62, 69
First Coming 62, 69
Foxe 59, 80, 81, 83, 84, 91, 93
France 91, 96, 284
Freemen 191-193, 219, 220, 222, 223
Fuller 132
Fundamental Orders 196
General Observations 61, 62, 68, 78, 90, 94, 96, 98-100, 102, 106, 143
Geneva 189, 224, 226
Germany 91, 96
Gog and Magog 76, 241
Goodwin 86, 254-256, 342, 351, 352, 356, 358, 360-362, 366, 367
Gott 23, 126
Great Puritan Migration 9, 15, 25, 32, 36, 48, 49, 133, 135
Greville 219
Haller 4, 19, 80, 271
Harrison 236
Hart 26
Hell 30, 73, 91, 92, 104, 254, 293, 319, 376
Herbert 15, 63, 64, 319, 348
Higginson 20, 21, 46, 48, 60, 100-102, 117, 120, 125, 126, 128, 132-134, 141, 142, 184
History 1-8, 12, 15, 18, 25, 36, 39, 40, 45, 46, 50, 51, 61-65, 68-80, 83-87, 89-94, 97-106, 109, 119, 124, 126, 165, 184, 217, 221, 227, 232, 237, 241, 242, 243, 254-257, 265, 266, 278, 284, 302, 305, 321, 323, 324, 339, 341, 347, 351, 371, 374, 378, 379
Hobbes 239, 240, 340
Holland 27, 36, 41, 43, 63, 122, 129, 130, 146, 160, 254, 255, 268, 271, 335, 337, 351
Hooker 27, 41, 43, 99, 100, 118, 130, 132, 146, 159-161, 184, 199, 204, 243, 271-273, 278, 330, 374
Huguenots 96

Independents 230, 237, 273, 346, 348-366, 368, 370, 371, 376, 378, 379, 381
Indians 99, 284
Isaiah 117, 120
Israel 18, 103, 167, 194
James I 38, 63, 98, 123, 131, 162
Jeremiah 351, 356
Jerusalem 60, 64, 71, 76, 77, 84, 88, 92, 93, 102, 104, 118-120, 148, 164, 209, 221, 255, 256, 257, 278, 320, 321, 326, 351, 377
Jews 373
John 10, 18-20, 22, 25, 27, 28, 33-35, 41, 42, 44, 59, 69, 70, 72, 76-83, 85, 99, 100, 102, 104, 117, 122-124, 127, 129, 131-134, 136, 138, 141, 142, 147, 149, 162-164, 166, 181, 183, 184, 188, 190, 200, 204, 206, 209, 211, 214, 217, 224, 233, 242, 253, 257, 262, 265, 272, 282, 298, 301, 302, 309, 319, 326, 335, 341, 344, 350, 358, 359, 361, 362, 367, 373, 378
Johnson 37, 38, 65, 78, 95, 100, 136, 146, 148, 181, 183, 185, 233, 234, 244
Jones 196
Kingdom of Christ 86, 91, 104, 130, 255, 379
Kingdom of God 4, 8, 12, 62, 65, 69, 72, 74, 77, 78, 84-86, 90, 98, 100, 108, 119, 185, 186, 214, 217, 221, 239-243, 255, 256, 305, 324, 331, 334, 338, 352
Kingdom of Heaven 10, 25, 199, 200, 229, 358, 363, 380
Laity 25-29, 151
Land of Promise 147
Last Judgment 62
Laud 41-43, 45, 61, 63, 154, 157-161, 169, 170, 172-174, 211, 231, 254, 263, 267, 269, 302, 322, 338, 339, 343

Law 23-25, 38, 132, 188, 206, 208, 210, 211, 220, 222, 223, 227, 238, 239, 290, 302, 305, 322, 361
Lockridge 22
Long Parliament 173, 174, 253, 255, 257, 262-264, 267, 269, 271, 303, 309, 311, 320, 340, 341, 349, 351
Lot 209
Luther 91
Magistrates 38, 39, 48, 129, 144, 145, 165, 167, 185, 191-195, 197, 199, 201-205, 207-213, 215, 216, 218, 220, 222, 223, 225, 228-234, 243, 264, 288, 289, 291, 298, 299, 303, 304, 306, 325, 329, 339-343, 353, 359, 362, 364, 366, 369, 371-373, 375, 376, 380, 381
Marian Exiles 80
Marshall 340-342
Mary 63, 80, 196
Massachusetts 1-4, 6-12, 19-21, 23, 25, 27, 28, 35, 36, 38, 39, 41-44, 47, 48, 50, 51, 61, 63, 78, 81, 90, 93, 96, 99, 101, 102, 108, 109, 117, 119, 120, 122, 124, 125-129, 131-134, 138, 139, 143-146, 148-151, 153-158, 160, 161, 162-166, 168-170, 172-174, 184, 185, 187-192, 196, 197, 200, 204, 205-212, 214, 215, 217-224, 226-234, 241-244, 253, 255-259, 262-273, 276-291, 295-312, 320, 324-326, 328-339, 342, 345, 346-351, 358, 359, 362-380
Massachusetts Bay Company 27, 43, 48, 122, 124, 125, 128, 131, 143, 155, 157
Mather, Cotton 66, 123
Mather, Increase 66
Mather, Richard 10, 41, 205, 328, 330, 338
Matthew 25, 27, 125
Maverick 28, 41, 141, 297
Mayflower Compact 22
Mede 103

Migration 1-10, 12, 15, 16, 22-25, 27, 29, 32, 34-37, 40, 43, 44, 48-50, 59, 61, 65-68, 81, 94, 95-97, 99, 101-103, 107, 108, 119, 120, 122-124, 129, 131, 133, 135, 138, 141, 146-151, 154, 155, 160, 161, 163, 172, 184, 185, 241, 242, 244, 260, 263, 269, 272, 275-278, 281, 282, 311, 326, 328, 329, 331-333, 337, 342
Militant Church 86, 107, 108
Millennialism 6, 8, 66, 321
Millennium 4-8, 12, 65-67, 72, 76-79, 82, 84-87, 89, 99, 100, 104, 184, 185, 214, 221, 237, 241, 242, 255, 321, 323, 325, 326, 329, 330, 334, 338, 341, 351, 374
Miller 1-5, 9, 21, 65-67, 126, 133, 208, 277, 278, 337, 348, 382
Milton 86
Monarchy 224, 226, 227
Morgan 187, 237
Moses 361, 374
Mount Sion 86, 244, 275
New England 108, 109, 122, 129, 141, 150, 162, 164, 170, 181, 183, New England cont. 235, 241, 242, 282, 319, 359, 368
New England Company 20, 27, 43, 48, 122, 124, 125, 143
New Haven 43, 169, 190-192, 196, 197, 211, 226, 272, 284
New Jerusalem 64, 71, 76, 77, 84, 88, 92, 93, 102, 104, 118-120, 164, 209, 221, 256, 257, 278, 321, 326, 351, 377
Non-conformists 103, 157
Norton 188
Pagan 15, 151
Papacy 79
Papists 92, 287, 343, 352, 365, 369, 374
Paradise 319, 321
Patmos 69, 70
Paul 71, 79, 164

Pergamum 161
Peter 32, 44, 103, 169, 190, 264-267
Philadelphia 70, 71, 89, 91-93, 95, 96, 101, 121
Pietistic Puritanism 17
Pilgrim Fathers 82
Pilgrims 22, 63, 122, 130
Plymouth 28, 36, 63, 122-124, 126-128, 132, 133, 136, 155, 156, 284, 296, 297, 299, 335
Pope 79, 166
Promised Land 103, 105, 160, 266
Prophecy 5, 66, 69, 71, 77, 79, 85, 87, 98, 225
Protestant historiography 5
Protestant Reformation 91, 378
Prudden 190
Puritan Commonwealth 11, 101, 167, 173, 174, 186-188, 196, 201, 207, 215, 222, 224, 226, 241, 264, 270, 299, 307, 309, 326, 362, 370
Puritan Migration 1-10, 12, 15, 16, 22-25, 27, 32, 35-37, 40, 43, 48-50, 59, 61, 65-68, 94, 96, 97, 101, 102, 107, 108, 119, 120, 122, 124, 133, 135, 138, 146, 147, 149-151, 154, 155, 160, 161, 163, 172, 184, 185, 241, 242, 244, 260, 269, 272, 275-278, 311, 326, 328, 329, 331, 332, 337, 342
Puritan Movement 1, 25, 26, 30, 49, 65, 67, 77, 81-83, 133, 209, 320, 324, 331, 332, 340, 371, 382
Puritan Revolution 1, 7, 8, 35, 39, 67, 81-83, 109, 209, 230, 231, 244, 320-323, 359, 379
Restoration 1, 4, 168, 223
Resurrection 273, 365
Revelation 3, 8, 10, 18, 59, 64, 66-74, 76-93, 96, 98, 101-103, 105, 107, 108, 119, 137, 138, 139, 161, 206, 239, 241, 257, 274-278, 293, 304, 328-330, 334, 342
Richardson 27

Rogers 16-21, 36, 44, 232
Roman Empire 85
Rome 79, 91, 94, 106, 117, 134, 136, 216, 242
Rose-Troup 20
Rotterdam 20
Sabbath 30, 31, 37
Sacred History 6
Salem 20, 23, 27, 102, 120, 124-129, 131, 132, 136-138, 141, 142, 145, 148, 166, 200, 264, 265
Salvation History 3, 7, 12, 61, 62, 78, 90, 184
Sanctuary 124, 184, 334
Sanhedrin 237
Sardis 63, 70, 71, 91
Say and Sele 188, 219, 221, 222, 224-228, 269, 272, 280, 285, 355
Scotland 1, 41, 91, 171, 172, 254, 257-259, 271, 276, 285, 293, 294, 352, 353, 355, 380
Second Coming 5, 62, 65-67, 69, 71, 84, 89, 90, 107, 108, 217, 241
Semi-separation 34
Separation 3, 4, 10, 34, 35, 61, 82, 97, 117, 128, 133-139, 148, 149, 152, 192, 199, 207, 208, 209, 215, 227, 269, 326, 327, 332-338, 344, 360
Separatists 117, 127-129, 132-136, 139, 149, 150, 152, 302, 331-337, 343, 350, 361, 369, 370
Serpent 74, 105
Shepard 19, 41, 42, 99, 366, 373
Smyrna 70, 90
Sodom 63, 95
Southcot 28
Spalding 18
Spufford 26, 32
Steiner 190
Stoeffler 17
Stoughton 167
Swan 33
Sweden 284
Tawney 81, 189, 224, 281

Temple 71, 73, 88, 105, 329, 341, 342, 375

Theocracy 3, 4, 8, 11, 12, 174, 181, 183, 186, 188-191, 194, 197, 199, 209-211, 218-221, 224-227, 229, 232, 233, 235, 236, 238-244, 269, 297-299

Theocratic Government 4, 11, 194, 197, 211, 235, 237, 239, 240

Theocratic Impulses 237

Theocratic Universe 3, 4, 11, 72, 73, 147, 227, 378

Thirty Years' War 1, 96

Thyatira 70, 71, 91, 118, 161

Tyndale 147

Vane 163, 209-212, 221, 369-372

Virginia 63, 131, 144, 163, 165, 263, 287

Virginia company 63, 131, 144

Visible Saints 8, 10, 11, 32, 34, 36, 37, 119, 126, 127, 134, 138, 187, 188, 195, 197, 199, 297, 325, 328, 330

Waldenses 91

Warham 28, 41, 141

Weld 41, 264-267

White 19, 20, 32, 35, 73, 75, 78, 123, 125, 132, 149, 150, 326

Whitehall Debates 236, 367

Wigglesworth 181, 183, 241

Wilderness 1-3, 5-8, 11, 12, 22, 41, 65, 78, 89, 90, 100-108, 122, 126, 129, 135, 139, 146, 148, 150-152, 155, 163, 181, 183-185, 187, 192, 195, 198-200, 210, 218, 219, 222, 227, 236, 238, 240-242, 244, 255, 256, 260, 264, 266, 269, 274, 276-278, 280-282, 286, 290, 293-296, 298, 299, 301, 305, 306, 309, 311, 324, 326, 327, 331-334, 336, 338, 375

Williams 41, 43, 79, 138, 139, 213-215, 284-286, 296, 303-305, 309, 363, 364, 371, 373, 374

Wilson 19, 21, 42, 59, 99, 104

Woman 71, 104-108, 277

Write 30, 70, 71, 92, 141, 162, 266, 345, 374

Ziff 190

Zion 104

DDS